DAVID MERRICK

THE ABOMINABLE SHOWMAN

the unauthorized biography

DAVID MERRICK

THE ABOMINABLE SHOWMAN

the unauthorized biography

HOWARD KISSEL

AN APPLAUSE ORIGINAL
DAVID MERRICK: THE ABOMINABLE SHOWMAN
the unauthorized biography

Library of Congress Cataloging-in-Publication Data
Kissel, Howard
    David Merrick, the abominable showman : the unauthorized biography
/ Howard Kissel
      p.   cm.
    "An Applause original."
    Includes bibliographical references and index.
    ISBN 1-55783-172-6 : $24.95
    1. Merrick, David, 1911-   . 2. Theatrical producers and
directors—United States—Biography.   I. Title.
    PN2287.M618K57 1993
792'.0232'092—dc20
[B]   93-21118
                                    CIP

British Library Cataloging-in-Publication Data
A catalogue record for this book is available from the British Library

APPLAUSE BOOKS

211 W. 71st Street
New York, NY 10023
Phone: (212) 595-4735
Fax: (212) 721-2856

406 Vale Road
Tonbridge KENT TN9 1XR
Phone: 0732 357755
Fax: 0732 770219

FIRST APPLAUSE PRINTING: 1993

"There's so much I must thank her for.
Where to start?
How am I to say
From the heart
What I owe?
To my critic, my partner,
The flavor of my life-
To my wife."
(Lyrics by Harold Rome from *Fanny*)

CONTENTS

ACKNOWLEDGMENTS

W HEN I ASKED Betty Comden if I could interview her about what it was like to work for David Merrick she said, "You mean while he's still alive?"

Though her response was more pointed than most, it reflected the fear that many people had when talking about the man who dominated Broadway for thirty years. Why, after all, during all that time, when he was a public figure not just in New York but across America, had there never been a biography? Clearly, the reason was fear. He sued at the drop of a hat. Moreover, if you were making your living on Broadway, what was the point of antagonizing him?

My task has been made simpler by the fact that, alas, fewer and fewer people are making their living on Broadway. At one point nothing could have been more terrifying to a writer or a performer than to hear his low voice utter the words: "You'll never work on a David Merrick show again." Though he continued to make that threat even as *Oh, Kay!* came to its ignominious conclusion, as late as 1991, the words carry considerably less weight today than they did only a decade ago.

To point these things out is not in any way to diminish the courage people have shown in recounting their experiences with him. Nor does it in any way diminish the profound gratitude I owe them. Many of the people I spoke to did so only "off the record." In the narrative I have tried to camouflage their contributions, but I would be an ingrate not to acknowledge my debt here. So, off and on the record, let me thank, in alphabetical order: Doris Cole Abraham, Richard Adler, Michael Alpert, Robert Anderson, Lisa Aronson, Emanuel Azenberg, Lauren Bacall, Martin Balma, Clive Barnes, Bill Becker, Louis Bellson, Stephen Bernard, Charles Blackwell, John Bloomgarden, Charles Bowden, Mark Bramble, Peter Brook, Donald Brooks, David Brown, Arthur Cantor, Marge Champion, Carol Channing, Martin Charnin, David Cleaver, Richard Coe, Alexander H. Cohen, Brian Colbath, Betty Comden, Eric Conklin, Alvin Cooperman, Tom Daly, Hal David, Alvin Deutsch, Frank DeVerna, Sanford Dody, Elizabeth Dribben, Fred Ebb, Max Eisen, Josh Ellis, Margo Feiden, Raoul Lionel Felder, Pete Feller, Sheila Ferrendelli, John Fiorillo, Kenneth Geist, Leonard Gersh, Madeleine Gilford, Charles Glenn, Peter Glenville, Fred Golden, Byron Goldman, Ulu Grosbard, Tammy Grimes, John Handy, Sheldon Harnick, Neil Hartley, William A. Henry III, Jerry Herman, William Herz, Norris Houghton, Bernard P. Jacobs, Cliff Jahr, Tom Jones, John Kander, Garson Kanin, Stanley Kauffman, Elizabeth Kaye, William S. Kenly, Jean Kerr, Jay Kingwill, Frank Langella, Ruben Lapin, Bob Larkin, Lionel Larner, Floria Lasky, Roger Lawson, Arthur Laurents, Irving "Swifty" Lazar, Robert Lewis, Samuel "Biff" Liff, Joshua and Nedda Logan, Dorothy Loudon, Charles Lowe, Cameron Mackintosh, Ken Mandelbaum, Judd Mathison, John Mazzola, Alma McCardle, Etan Merrick, Alec McCowen, Bob Merrill, Mort Mitosky, Helen Montagu, Ginger Montel, Rebecca Morehouse, Robert Morse, Fred Nathan, Charles Michael Nelson, Helen Nickerson, Brent Oldham, Jerry Orbach, Marta Orbach, Linda Otto, Rabbi Eli Pilchik, Warren Pincus, Don Pippin, David Powers, Michael Price, Lee Roy Reams, Jacqueline Rice, Claibe Richardson, Eleanor Schneider, Gerald S. Schoenfeld, Harold and Florence Rome, Susan Pilchik Rosenbaum, Milton Rosenstock, Maria St. Just, Harvey Sabinson, Vincent Sardi, Jr., Robert Schear, Harvey Schmidt,

Anne Kaufman Schneider, Sylvia Schwartz, Marian Seldes, Irene Selznick, Willard Shaffar, Aaron Shapiro, Carole Shelley, Thomas Z. Shepard, Michael Shurtleff, Stephen Silverman, Pat Hoag Simon, Dan Siretta, Lee Solters, Oliver Smith, Stephen Sondheim, Dennis Stanfill, The Honorable Martin Stecher, Frances Stein, Joseph Stein, Larry Steinfeld, Richard Stoddard, Peter Stone, Marvin "Bud" Stuhlbarg, Jule Styne, Sylvia Thea, Peter Travers, Jonathan Tunick, Robert Ullmann, Ted Van Bemel, Dona Vaughan, Benay Venuta, Robin Wagner, Sam Waterston, Jerome Weidman, The Honorable Frank Weissberg, Robert Whitehead, Billy Wilder, Charles Willard, Freddy Wittop and Eugene Wolsk.

I owe a special debt to Helen Nickerson, whose funds of knowledge and of generosity are both inexhaustible.

I have also been greatly aided by the solicitous staff of the Performing Arts Library at Lincoln Center.

This project would never have come about without the prompting, support and perseverance of my agent Arnold Goodman.

Among those who require special thanks are Sylvia Schwartz, who unlocked many doors of great significance; and Garson Kanin, who was not only generous with his memories but also allowed me to look through his meticulously kept archives.

I am very indebted to my colleagues at the New York Daily News—Pat Carroll, Eddie Fay, Mike Lipack, Fagy Rosenthal, and Carl Walker—for giving me access to photographs of Merrick over the years.

I cannot fully express my gratitude to Glenn Young, the publisher of Applause Books, who has treated this book with a care and intelligence I know are exceedingly rare in publishing today. It is an immeasurably stronger book than it was when it arrived at his doorstep. Its faults are mine. Many of its virtues are his.

Lastly, I must thank the "only true begetter" of this work, David Margulois. He, after all, created the character of David Merrick, and I only hope I have done it justice.

In the interests of "full disclosure," I feel I ought to mention my two encounters with him. We actually shook hands at the cast party of *Loot* when it moved to Broadway in 1986. Reviewers who had written favorably about it at Manhattan Theater Club were invited to the opening night party at the River Club. Even if it had not been so noisy, I think it would have been impossible to understand his thoroughly slurred speech.

In 1982, when John Osborne published the first part of his autobiography, a reporter at *Women's Wear Daily*, where I was the arts editor, interviewed him. He asked Osborne about Merrick, and Osborne replied he found Merrick a pleasure to work with since, unlike some other producers, "he didn't have any creative ideas." I edited the story and passed it on to the managing editor, Mort Sheinman, who thought it might be wise to alert Merrick to the quote and possibly get a response from him.

I read Merrick the quote. He chuckled and said, "Maybe he's right." An hour later a hand-delivered letter arrived from his lawyer threatening legal action if we published the quote that was "injurious to the reputation of Mr. Merrick."

What follows, I hope, will remind readers of that once unsurpassable reputation and of one of the great careers of the American theater.

CHAPTER ONE

Normally God does not concern Himself with the Broadway theater, but it is not surprising that on the one recent occasion when He came to its aid, it was a David Merrick musical.

Normally Merrick would not have needed God's help. By the summer of 1980 he had been producing plays and musicals on Broadway for over thirty years. He was not just a Broadway producer. In the minds of many people who worked in the theater as well as many who simply bought tickets, he was *the* Broadway producer, the man who summed up the mystique of the New York theater in its best years.

Some producers prefer to work quietly behind the scenes. Merrick, practically from the beginning of his career, tended to be part of the show. He had not changed his name from the ethnic, prosaic "Margulois" to the snappy "Merrick" (consciously rhyming it with the 18th Century actor David Garrick) for it simply to get lost in the shuffle. If his name eventually came to suggest power and magic, it was not an accident. He worked hard at it.

From the early Fifties through the late Sixties, David Merrick was a Broadway legend, as much for what he said as for the shows he produced. Some producers had as impressive a track record as he did, but they were, by choice, not public figures. Some others were indeed public figures, but not necessarily because of the high quality of what they produced. Only Merrick managed both with apparent ease.

In the Seventies his magic touch no longer seemed so certain. Judged by the talent he assembled to work on the musicals he produced during these years, several of them should have been surefire hits. One closed very quickly, another died out of town. It was true that for much of that decade Merrick was preoccupied with Hollywood—producing films, trying to take over an ailing studio—but he was still obsessed with the idea of success on the New York stage. In 1979 an associate of many years, passing through Los Angeles, stopped to see Merrick, who told him he was coming back East to produce a musical "to show them how it's done."

Now, in the summer of 1980, Merrick was presumably engaged in doing just that. But things were not going so well.

The show was *42nd Street,* a stage version of the 1933 Warner Brothers musical, an amalgam of cliches about show business and success, whose score contained such popular songs as "Lullaby of Broadway," "Dames," and, of course, the title number. It was intended to be a lighthearted, lavish musical.

Lavish, it certainly was. By the time *42nd Street* arrived in New York, after its tryout in Washington, D.C., it was already seriously over budget. What was supposed to cost $1.8 million already amounted to well over $2 million. (It would eventually reach $3 million.) The $370,000 budget for costumes had hit half a million. The dresses for a single number, "Dames," reportedly cost $52,000.

Merrick couldn't blame any underling for this state of affairs. The runaway budget was his own fault. It was his idea to have a 24-member chorus. It was his perfectionism that required the building of new sets and new parts of sets for the New York opening. "I think the musical public is fed up with those solemn ones and those tiny little ones with a half dozen people, skimpy sets and squeaky orchestras," he had told a friend.

If money could have insured the success of *42nd Street,*

Merrick had nothing to worry about. But Merrick knew better. His strongest guarantee of success was the man he had hired to direct and choreograph the show, Gower Champion. Over the previous nineteen years, Champion had worked on seven shows with Merrick. Among them, some of Merrick's most impressive and profitable hits, including the musical for which he was best known, *Hello, Dolly!*. It's true that, six years earlier, Champion had directed *Mack and Mabel*, a musical that had not won the hearts of the critics, and none of Merrick's expertise at publicity had been able to keep alive. But no one had been through so many battles with Merrick—against each other, against the world outside.

Merrick's relationship with Champion, through good times and bad, lasted longer than three of his four marriages. It was stormier but more durable. It was even thought by close associates that the two men, who were given to bad-mouthing each other, grudgingly admired one another.

However much confidence Merrick had in Champion, his natural wariness was intensified by an odd turn of events in Washington.

Champion had been adamant about casting a young woman named Wanda Richert in the leading role, as the chorus girl who gets her break on opening night and becomes a star. That Miss Richert was talented there was no question. That she was leading lady material was something else. The casting decision, Merrick felt, was unmistakably tied to the fact that, in the course of working on the show, Miss Richert had become Champion's mistress.

Having an affair with someone in the cast had been part of Champion's "work process" for the twenty years Merrick had known him. What angered Merrick this time was Champion's refusal to hire an understudy for Miss Richert. But after so many years of working with Merrick, Champion, too, was on the alert. He didn't want to give Merrick the impression that should he fire Miss Richert, a successor was already in place. And Merrick had already made it clear he did want to fire her. Champion stood his ground.

Merrick took matters into his own hands. He hired an understudy himself and forced Champion to introduce her to the cast. To make the situation all the more awkward, Champion had not had time to tell Miss Richert in advance.

Such tests of power were part of the game the two men had played for years. On *Hello, Dolly!* Champion had refused to continue directing unless Merrick was barred from the theater. Surprisingly, Merrick had complied. Score one for Champion.

What worried Merrick this time was an entirely different test of strength. Champion was sick. A virus, apparently. Serious enough that Champion had ordered the air conditioning turned off in the rehearsal hall of the Kennedy Center. This, in the heat of a Washington June. Still, Champion was leaping with his dancers as he had in the best of times, no small feat for a man of fifty-eight.

There were, however, nights during the Washington run when Champion was too sick to attend performances. This made Merrick uneasy. He sent for a director from New York who had a reputation as a "show doctor." Champion heard about it. This was a standard Merrick procedure: to bring someone from New York when a show was out of town as a kind of threat, a reminder that in a Merrick production only one man was irreplaceable.

But with Champion sick the standard technique seemed more than odd. Was it Merrick's nervousness that Champion might not be well enough to finish the job? Was it the usual malevolent desire to goad Champion into working harder despite his illness? Merrick-watchers could not say. Merrick's "cure," however, had the desired effect. Champion came back to work. The "doctor" was sent back to New York.

Once the show arrived in New York, however, hints of distress again began to appear.

Merrick had not placed his traditional full page ad in the *New York Times* announcing the opening date, an irregularity to which the *Times* itself called its readers' attention. Even odder for Merrick, the box office had not been opened. In fact it had been opened and then abruptly closed. No one ever accused Merrick of being uninterested in the activities of the box office. For him to close one so peremptorily seemed totally out of character.

The cast had arrived from Washington on July 28. Previews were scheduled to begin August 2 and the show was supposed to open August 10. On August 3, *42nd Street* was performed for delegates attending the Democratic National Convention. It was a disaster. The delegates, after partying and drinking all afternoon, were not in a mood to spend an evening in the theater. They were unusually rude and inattentive, a huge comedown from the enthusiastic audiences in Washington. Merrick ordered everyone back into rehearsal.

The box office opened Monday, August 4, and was closed by Merrick the next day. No one would say how many tickets had been sold, only that they would have to be recalled since they might be needed for the rescheduled opening night. The scenery, Merrick's press agent explained, looked frayed after the Washington run and needed to be redone. In fact, the reason was more serious. During the changes instituted in Washington, the scenery had gotten progressively heavier. Now it was too heavy for the grid of the Winter Garden Theater. It had to be totally redesigned and rebuilt.

Whatever the reason, tongues started wagging. Hadn't the Washington reviews been largely negative? They had. But they had not stopped *42nd Street* from setting a house record for the Kennedy Center. With no advance sale, the show eventually took in $1,150,000 during its five-week run. Whatever the Washington press had thought, the show had audience appeal. Besides, bad reviews had seldom deterred Merrick. Something else must be going on behind the scenes.

To stop idle gossip, Merrick issued a statement that appeared in the *New York Times* August 9. Next to a typically solemn photo of Merrick, in a two-column article about the postponement of the opening appeared this long quote from the producer: "The Great Man way up there has said that this show is very important for people all around the world to see in these gloomy times. He wants to be sure the show is ready, that it can be a memorable musical. He will give the word when He feels the show is ready.

"I am waiting for the courier to arrive. When he arrives and gives the word, I will place an ad for the show and promptly open it."

Far more than the public or the *Times*, Gower Champion was growing very impatient. He had made significant changes in the show in Washington. He had rehearsed the cast thoroughly on their arrival in New York. He needed to play the show for a New York audience. He, more than anyone, had reason to fear the tardiness of "the courier."

For Champion had something more serious and virulent than a simple virus. A rare blood disease, Waldenstein's macroglobulinemia, had attacked his system. His condition was deteriorating rapidly. In Washington he had been able to keep his condition a secret. The cast knew that one day his temperature hit 104. But he continued to work on the show, giving no indication that his illness was anything but the common virus and anemia he had claimed. A month earlier, in fact, he had announced his next project, on which he would start rehearsals in September. It was to be a musical version of James Michener's novel—whose title would ultimately take on great irony—*Sayonara.*

On the final night in Washington, when he could no longer doubt how quickly his body was succumbing to the disease, Champion told his secret to Merrick.

The knowledge that his director was dying of a rare form of leukemia did not make Merrick less difficult. But he did accede to Champion's desire to perform the show before a New York audience. On Tuesday, August 12, with no fanfare, Merrick sent 400 tickets—less than a third of the capacity of the Winter Garden Theater—to the TKTS booth in Duffy Square that sells remaining tickets for any show at half price. The 400 theatergoers who happened to buy them would be sitting toward the back of the orchestra section, surrounded by empty seats in front and on either side of them.

As it turned out, shortly after 8:00 even those 400 seats would be empty. A drama running concurrently with and, of course, not unrelated to the Gower Champion crisis, would explain the empty, now practically haunted house.

The final blessing a show received before its Broadway opening was a feature in the Sunday Arts & Leisure section of the *New York Times*. For a show *not* to receive the *Times* Sunday piece suggested it was insignificant. Merrick shows always did, and it was a rare Sunday piece that did anything but suggest the show in the spotlight that week had been created by some of Broadway's brightest talents scaling ever new heights.

This time, however, there was a hitch. The article was to be written by Cliff Jahr, a young reporter who was not on the *Times* staff. Why an outsider? The year before he had done a profile for *New York* magazine of another producer, Alexander H. Cohen, which could only be described as a "hatchet job." Did the *Times* have a similar fate in mind for Merrick?

Merrick had not forgotten that in 1966 the *Sunday Times* Magazine had commissioned a profile on him, which never ran. The magazine editor had claimed the piece was "not good enough," but the writer's agent had confirmed Merrick's own hunch that the piece was in fact "too favorable." Had the *Times now* put out a contract on Merrick? Merrick made every effort to obstruct the writer, even going so far as to tell his editor that Jahr had accosted him in front of his apartment building where he had offered not to write the piece for $50,000.

None of the courtesies normally extended to a *Times* reporter were given this one. Jahr was not allowed to attend a rehearsal. Everyone connected with the show was forbidden to talk to him.

With good reason. The run in Washington and the non-run in New York were marked by an insane acrimony that was, in fact, a Merrick trademark. He loved to set his creative team at each other's throats. He would phone them individually, generally at two in the morning, to complain, in his deep, solemn voice, of their colleagues' poor work.

In this case he had phoned Michael Stewart, whose relationship with him went back as far as that with Gower—and was much closer—to say, "Mike, I think that Gower is ruining the show." He then phoned Mark Bramble, Stewart's collaborator, to say that he didn't think Stewart was up to the demands of the show. The next morning all those who had received phone calls regarded each other with extreme wariness. They were unable to speak to each other. It left Merrick the only one able to speak to everybody, the only one with unmitigated power.

On *42nd Street* the effect of this tried and true procedure was to create an atmosphere of paranoia. The strained atmosphere was heightened when Merrick ordered that no one would be allowed into the theater without an identification card with the bearer's picture, his title, and the signature of David Merrick.

After an argument about the development of a character, Merrick had fired Stewart. It had more to do with chiseling away at his salary than any artistic question—if he could prove to the Dramatists Guild that Stewart had not attended rehearsals he could withhold part of Stewart's salary. Having been through this routine before, Stewart hired bodyguards to force his way into the theater.

Had any of these "developments" been reported in the *Times*, they might not have boosted ticket sales for *42nd Street*.

The reason for the unorthodox method of selling tickets to the August 12 preview—unannounced except at the Duffy Square booth—was to prevent Jahr from seeing the show at all. But the writer had sources in Merrick's office who tipped him off. He got into line at the half-price booth and duly bought a ticket.

When one of Merrick's staff spotted Jahr in the theater Merrick was livid. A security guard was dispatched to ask him to leave. He refused. A few minutes later a voice over the loudspeaker system announced that due to technical difficulties there would be no performance of *42nd Street*. The "400" were told their tickets would be honored at some future performance. The next day one of the disgruntled customers spotted Merrick at the stage door and demanded his money back. He got it.

When the *Times* reported on the cancelled preview of *42nd*

Street, the reporter commented, "Broadway, of course, has an inclination for the bizarre; *42nd Street* seems to have amazed even Broadway." The reporter went on to speculate that "the courier" could be expected soon, since the cost of salaries was thought to exceed $100,000 a week. Since the box office was not yet open, the Great Man's earthly partner had to pay this sum out of his own pocket.

The August 13 performance was also cancelled, but the cast performed a run-through of the show. When the curtain went up the performers saw the front row of the Winter Garden filled with stuffed cats, pandas and teddy bears. Champion had wanted an audience. Merrick provided one.

Two days later, on August 15, an ad appeared announcing *42nd Street* would open on Monday, August 25. The ad described the show as, "The All Singing All Dancing Extravaganza With a Cast of 54 (Some Younger)."

Early in the afternoon of the 25th, reviewers attending the opening received phone calls requesting them not to make the traditional scramble up the aisle as soon as the final curtain fell, but instead to remain in their seats through the curtain calls. It was an unprecedented request, but by this time nothing about *42nd Street* was conventional. Nevertheless it seemed especially odd to ask the reviewers to stay since this was the first show in some time to which none was admitted to previews. This time their rush up the aisle would be legitimate. There were deadlines to meet.

Well before the opening one of the TV stations had asked permission to shoot footage during the opening night performance. Several days earlier permission was denied. Now, suddenly, the afternoon of the opening, Fred Nathan, the press agent, called the TV station to say permission had been granted to shoot during the curtain calls. Another station, which had not even asked for permission, was notified a few hours before curtain that it too would be allowed to film the curtain call. After having deliberately avoided publicity, Merrick now seemed to be actively soliciting it.

It was conjectured that Merrick's unprecedented secretiveness stemmed from his experience producing the 1974 film version of *The Great Gatsby*, during which every move he made had received maximum press exposure. The result, Merrick thought, was too great a heightening of critical expectations. "When the movie bombed, David blamed all the ballyhoo," an associate suggested. "He said the critics were just dying to slam it. He thought it was better for *42nd Street* to sneak into town on tiny feet."

42nd Street had not exactly sneaked into town. Nor were its tap dancing feet unobtrusive. Nevertheless Merrick had achieved his objective. *42nd Street* had aroused enormous curiosity, and the critics, far from being led to expect too much, had no idea what to expect at all.

The first night of *42nd Street*, August 25, 1980, was probably the last grand opening night in Broadway history, the last occasion when old money and old glamour outshone the new.

Many of the opening nighters arriving at the Winter Garden amid the steady popping of flash bulbs were Merrick veterans. There was Ethel Merman, whose greatest show, *Gypsy*, Merrick had produced. There was Joshua Logan, the first of the established Broadway people to take Merrick seriously and one of the few with whom Merrick maintained a long, cordial relationship, with a minimum of game playing. There was Ruth Gordon, who, after a dazzling career as a Hollywood screenwriter, had made a triumphant return to the theater under Merrick's aegis in Thornton Wilder's *The Matchmaker*, which had, of course, inspired Merrick's longest running show, *Hello, Dolly!* There was Miss Gordon's husband, Garson Kanin, whom Merrick had hired to direct Barbra Streisand in her first and only starring Broadway role.

Among the other famous faces in the audience were those of Henry Kissinger, Neil Simon, Joseph Papp, Joan Fontaine, Anne Baxter and Bob Fosse, who was one of Champion's closest friends. Champion's second wife, Carla, was there. So were Greg and Blake Champion, his two sons by his first wife, Marge.

Champion himself could not be there. Knowledgeable theater-goers knew that he was in Memorial Sloan-Kettering Hospital with what the *Times* had reported was a virus. Some had heard rumors that Champion had checked himself out on Saturday afternoon to take a look at the final preview and give the cast his blessing but that immediately afterward he had checked himself back into the hospital.

Whatever clouds were cast over the proceedings by the absence of the director were dispelled as soon as the lights dimmed and the orchestra began the overture. Merrick had been true to his word. Instead of the antiseptic little preludes that often opened Broadway musicals, here was a full-blown overture that fairly erupted from the pit. The orchestra was full of brass, winds, and percussion. No fussy, genteel strings. It stepped forward brashly like some circus pitchman dressed in flashy duds describing in the most direct, most extravagant language the spectacle to follow.

The audience responded with a roar of approval. The applause became even more thunderous as soon as the curtain rose on a stage filled from one end to the other with people tap dancing.

Tap dancing had taken on an unexpectedly militant connotation during the Seventies. The traditional Broadway audience was beset by rock musicals on the one hand and pretension on the other. A producer who offered tap dancing early in the first act was signaling his audience that they were going to be entertained and didn't have to feel ashamed about it.

Normally the producer takes seats at the back of the orchestra section so he can survey both the spectacle on the stage and that in front of it. Sometimes, in order to accommodate backers, for whom a pair of opening night tickets may be the only tangible reward for their investment, the producer will forego seats and pace at the back of the theater.

On the opening night of *42nd Street* David Merrick did neither.

He did not have to worry about pacifying backers. Apart from himself, there was none. At one time there had been three—they had put up an aggregate of $180,000, less than ten per cent of the initial cost. After the Washington tryout Merrick bought them out. So the multimillion dollar gamble was all his.

The sound of forty-eight cleated shoes working at a frantic pace could not drown out the audience's wild applause. The laughter, the applause, the delighted gasps as Champion's stage wizardry unfolded were all genuine—not the phony, forced enthusiasm you sometimes hear on opening nights. The audience was a real audience, not a bunch of nervous backers. The show was a hit.

Merrick could hear everything without being seen and without being able to see. He sat on a folding chair under a box at the side of the theater, separated from the audience by a curtain hung from the box. Like The Great Man Himself on another auspicious occasion, he would not let his face be seen, but all his goodness, in the form of the opulent spectacle on the stage of the Winter Garden, passed before them.

As it happened there were things weighing on Merrick far more complicated than the conventional producer's worries about whether or not his show was a hit.

The knowledge that he had a real audience—the old guard of the theater community, all of the press, and that handful of people with whom he was genuinely intimate—made the task before him especially difficult.

For what Merrick and no more than six or seven other people in the Winter Garden knew was that Gower Champion was dead. Merrick had received a call from the hospital Sunday night to say that Gower had taken a turn for the worse. Early Monday morning the hospital called to say that he had not survived the night.

Merrick had gained the cooperation of the hospital and family to delay releasing the information until the curtain rose that night. He summoned the cast to the theater early in the morning and instructions were given for scenes to be rehearsed until the opening, to prevent their accidentally hearing the terrible news.

Merrick informs cast and audience that Gower Champion is dead.

When Merrick had announced the show's opening date ten days earlier Champion was in bad health but still working. On the 20th his condition had taken a severe turn for the worse. He began hemorrhaging. He was admitted to Sloan-Kettering's intensive care unit. The day before the opening he suffered kidney failure, and from that point there was no return. Every day Merrick had visited the hospital, as concerned about Champion's condition as he was about preventing the cast from learning about it.

On that score he had been successful. Who knows how—or if—they would have performed that night if they had known the truth?

Merrick himself had arrived at the Winter Garden at four in the afternoon. He spotted Mark Bramble on the stage and motioned him into a corner. He was bursting to tell someone the news. He fell onto Bramble sobbing, genuinely shattered by the loss. But he swore Bramble to secrecy and then went about the ritualized gestures of being a producer on opening night.

Amazingly, when the curtain rose, the secret was still a secret.

By the end of the intermission, however, the number of people who knew the secret had grown considerably. A *Daily News* reporter had arrived with what was then only a disquieting rumor. In a bad movie such news would travel from one shocked face to another, spreading like wildfire through the theater. Here the news progressed in faint spurts. Those who heard were chilled, but regarded what they heard as a kind of privileged communication—not for all ears.

By the time the curtain went up on the second act a significant part of the audience could no longer respond with innocent enthusiasm to the tap dancing extravaganza. The very dizziness of the show took on an almost gruesome quality—particularly during the title number, a melodramatic scenario at the climax of which the lover of the leading lady dies and she must go on dancing. The leading lady, of course, was Wanda Richert. She was not yet in a position to appreciate the irony. But for many of the people watching her the moment was nightmarish.

When the curtain finally came down the applause was fervent and long. The jubilant cast, without forcing the audience's hand, took ten curtain calls—a special treat in view of all the uncertainties of the preceding weeks.

The curtain rose for the eleventh time, and suddenly David Merrick appeared from the wings. The unsuspecting may have imagined he was taking the "star call," since, in everything written about the show prior to its opening, he had hogged the spotlight. None of the members of the cast, not even Champion, had had his name as closely associated with *42nd Street* as David Merrick had. Some members of the audience may have thought he was entitled to the final word. His appearance brought a huge new wave of applause.

"I'm sorry to have to report . . ." Merrick began. A roar went up from the house. Who would ever have expected false modesty from David Merrick? Clearly he was being ironic. But there was something odd about the way his arms were folded, the way one hand masked his mouth. "No, no," he shouted. "This is tragic.

You don't understand. Gower Champion died this morning."

Merrick had often presented to the world a mortician's aloofness and complacency. Tonight the self-assurance was not there. He looked distraught. No one could doubt he was shaken. The mortician had been touched by death.

As soon as he made his announcement, Merrick crossed the stage to embrace a horrified Wanda Richert. Was it genuinely a gesture of consolation? Was it a way of calling attention to her relationship with Champion? Was it a human gesture or a staged tableau for the TV cameras?

On both sides of the footlights people were as shocked by the way they learned the news as by the news itself. The show's leading man, Jerry Orbach, had the presence of mind to have the curtain brought down, so the actors' grief would not be on display. "Bring it in," he shouted to the stagehands in charge of the curtain, "Bring it in!"

The next day Merrick told the press he had decided during the intermission that he would make the announcement about Champion during the curtain calls. One close associate thought the decision reflected Merrick's well-seasoned appraisal of the critics' expressions. He had surmised they were not having a good time and thought this would counteract their reviews. Only weeks later did reports of the telephone calls to the TV stations appear in print, suggesting he had made his decision well before intermission. What he said the day afterward was, "When I stood in the wings during the show and watched those kids—happy faces, sensing Broadway success—I knew that shortly thereafter I would go out there and wipe all that out. But it would happen anyway."

Merrick's statement oddly echoes the mentality of *42nd Street*. When he mentions "those kids—happy faces, sensing Broadway success," then the melodramatic "I would go out there and wipe it all out," it is as if the two shows had merged in Merrick's mind—*42nd Street* itself and the larger drama of David Merrick Producing *42nd Street*. Merrick's identification with the show had popped up earlier. "I could have played that role 10 years ago," he had told Orbach, who played the tough, overwrought producer-director Julian Marsh. "And you're too *nice* to play it."

Niceness was not in danger of becoming a Merrick problem. In the months to come he would systematically antagonize the writers of *42nd Street* (by changing their billing from "Book By" to "Lead-Ins and Crossovers By"), its aged composer, his press agent, Broadway ticket brokers, group sales directors, the owners of the theater, even individual ticket buyers. The line to the box office was not allowed to wind through the theater lobby—it went directly onto the sidewalk, and no more than four people at a time could be inside the lobby; the rest had to stand outside—a kind of living advertisement for the show.

Merrick antagonized Champion's family, who had to fight to keep Champion's name on the marquee and posters. Merrick's name appeared in the papers constantly, to the point that Gerald Nachman, a columnist for the *Daily News* observed, "Either David Merrick is the city's wickedest man or its cleverest press agent. Everything he touches turns to ink."

On opening night, having created a sensation, Merrick became subdued.

For much of his career Merrick did not attend opening night parties. Often in the early years he could be spotted in some Times Square eatery, unnoticed among the bleary patrons, waiting for the early editions of the papers. Tonight, however, he was with the cast at the Waldorf Astoria, sitting at a table with Bob Fosse and Neil Simon, saying little, drinking wine. Like everyone else, Merrick was uncertain of the decorum of the occasion. Were they attending a celebration of a new life on Broadway or the wake for the life that had made it possible. What made it so difficult to react was, of course, that it was truly both.

"The people here don't really know how to deal with it," Simon told a reporter. "If you ever wrote a scene like this they'd say it was too melodramatic, too sentimental. Life is more absurd than we think."

Sometime after midnight Wanda Richert looked around the room and saw many dancers who, like herself, were alumni of *A Chorus Line*. She proposed that they do the final number of that show, "One," as a tribute to Champion. Within seconds a line formed, both men and women in evening dress. Even though it was the work of another choreographer, "One" was an appropriate way to pay tribute to a Broadway director. Its steps, like those of the countless numbers it parodies, are a magical blend of inanity and sharp precision. The keenness with which many of the dancers remembered those steps gave the moment a chilling quality, heightened by the intensity with which Richert threw herself into it. The effect was truly that of a *danse macabre*.

Around two o'clock Merrick took Richert and a few close friends to Elaine's, the Upper East side restaurant that looks like a quiet neighborhood place but which is always choked with celebrities. It was a way of prolonging the evening, a way to postpone facing what the evening meant, the end of one of Merrick's longest professional relationships.

Originally Merrick's reference to "the courier" and The Great Man had been a joke, a novel way of dealing with the problems of the moment. But in view of what had happened, who could not feel there was something uncanny at work? Merrick had presided over many memorable Broadway openings, but none like this. In thirteen hours he had left the realm of showmanship and entered that of myth.

A few months later Tammy Grimes, one of the stars of *42nd Street,* asked Merrick if he realized that what he had done that night was, in the eyes of many, tasteless. He said he did. But he also knew it would create interest in *42nd Street* on the part of millions who didn't particularly care or know much about the theater.

"I couldn't resist," he said.

42nd Street ran on Broadway for eight and a half years. During that time it played three separate theaters, the Winter Garden, the Majestic and the St. James. During that time Merrick married and divorced Karen Prunczik, one of the featured performers. He suffered a stroke that left him unable to speak clearly. If he had had a little more patience, a longtime associate noted, he might have relearned to speak, but he fired a succession of speech therapists who might have helped him.

For a time his mental condition was so unstable that his wife of very brief tenure had him committed to a rehabilitation center, from which he escaped in a wheelchair, taking refuge in a Korean noodle factory. At one point he was placed in legal conservatorship and had to engage lawyers to permit him to invest in the London production of *42nd Street,* which a judge had deemed inadvisable since, in the judge's words, "theater is too volatile and speculative."

Merrick had to fight even to keep *42nd Street* running, a point of pride, since he wanted to break his own record for the longest running show on Broadway. During its last year the show was not making a profit, and several of his associates wanted to close it.

After Merrick left for the opening of the Sydney production in December of 1987, the New York ads announced the show was in its last weeks. Merrick was livid when he returned. He devised a new publicity gimmick, announcing that *42nd Street* would raise its curtain fifteen minutes later than *The Phantom of the Opera,* across the street, in order to accommodate patrons who had been unable to secure *Phantom* tickets and still wanted to take in a show that night. The ad had a huge picture of the producer, his expression Svengali-like and imperious, with the slogan, "David Merrick is holding the curtain for YOU!"

By keeping *42nd Street* open, even during periods when it was only marginally profitable, he made it the second-longest running show on Broadway, still five years behind *A Chorus Line,* but longer than his own previous record-holder, *Hello, Dolly.*

During the eight and a half years *42nd Street* played, Broadway underwent enormous changes. For much of this century its greatest attractions had been musicals, which have been called America's most important contribution to world theater. But now the musicals that created the biggest stir were imports from London. In fact *42nd Street*'s final change of theater was necessitated by the arrival of the British blockbuster *The Phantom of the Opera*.

When *42nd Street* moved from the Majestic across the street to the St. James it had to be scaled down. The stage of the St. James was not as large as those of either the Majestic or the Winter Garden. The sets that were used were those designed for a bus and truck company. Some of the dazzling scenic effects that had delighted first nighters had been packed away long ago.

But the simplicity of the final production pointed up the difference between the American musical at its best and its British competitors. The American musical was built on an extraordinary pool of talent—that of the creators, the directors, the choreographers, and, most of all, the performers. The British shows tended to regard the performers as expendable. What mattered—and the enthusiasm of audiences confirmed this—was the grandness of the scenery. In a curious way the triumph of the British musicals was the ultimate triumph of a mentality the great British director Tyrone Guthrie had attributed to Merrick twenty-five years earlier.

"Each year David Merrick's ballyhoo grows more cynically, successfully and vulgarly sensational," Guthrie had written in 1964. "This is not a vulgar man: it is a man with a detached and Oriental sense of humour, whom it amuses to play the public as an angler plays a fish. Each year the public rises to a gaudier, more garish and more deadly bait. . . Without a policy, no theater can possibly create its *own* public; and unless it does so, it is compelled to surrender to the kind of policy which Mr. Merrick's management exemplifies: the pursuit of the smash hit at any cost."

Ironically the gaudy, garish, deadly bait Guthrie described was now on the hooks of his compatriots. Merrick's production looked positively innocent and wholesome by comparison. More poignantly, Merrick himself was now a humbled figure. At the final performance he sat on the aisle in the last row. Theatergoers who would have found him too intimidating to approach eight years earlier were now emboldened to thrust forward their programs for him to autograph, which, with no sense of graciousness or pleasure, he did.

If the opening night audience constituted one elite, the closing afternoon's constituted another. No invitation is required for the closing performance of a show. The "collectors" of closing performances tend to be people hopelessly in love with the theater, searching for memories to store away. Opening nighters are skeptical. Veteran closers bring a wealth of enthusiasm.

The curtain rose. It paused teasingly, about three feet from the floor, revealing the stage full of tapping feet. With little help from the sets, the excitement this afternoon had to be created by the talent, and the stage abounded in it. The entrance of some performers who had been with the show from the beginning was greeted by the connoisseurs with sustained applause. So were the now familiar numbers and lines. The largest ovation during the show came when Julian Marsh, now played by Jamie Ross, uttered the line about musical comedy being "the most glorious words in the English language." It was an effusion of nostalgia for a time when that seemed true.

Throughout the performance the man in the last row was weeping. There was talk about bringing back *42nd Street* in a few months with an all-black cast, a ploy Merrick had used twenty years earlier to keep *Hello, Dolly!* running. There were also rumors about new shows he might produce. But there seemed little doubt that *42nd Street* had been the culmination of the long and unparalleled career. For a man whose indomitable ego always demanded more, the realization that now there could only be less could not have been a happy one.

CHAPTER TWO

NOT JUST ANYONE could tell a reporter from the *New York Times* that the opening of a Broadway show depended on the arrival of a courier from On High. To do so with a straight face—and with the expectation of seeing it in print— was an acting exercise that had required a lifetime of preparation.

Long before he thought to become a producer, Merrick had become an actor on the stage of life. To be a producer, or even a lawyer, he had to give the impression of being something other than his true self.

What he was was a poor Jew. "Poor" and "Jew" were both epithets he shunned all his life. This aversion he shared with many of his generation, whose dreams of wealth and position were rooted in a desperate desire to put as much distance as possible between themselves and their origins.

An actor generally knows when he is acting and when he isn't. Even social climbers striving to conceal their actual identities have a sense of limits. Had he given himself limits, however, had he exercised caution, David Merrick would never have become a grand and commanding figure of Broadway legend.

Born November 27, 1911, David Lee was the youngest, by almost ten years, of the five children of Sam and Celia Margulois (pronounced Mar-gew-lis, with the emphasis on the first syllable).

David Margulois and his sister Sadye.

Even the name was a disadvantage, marking him as the son of Russian-Jewish immigrants. In the rigidly stratified Jewish community of St. Louis this was a strike against him, even among his fellow Jews. There were the wealthy German Jews, many of whom were heirs to great retailing fortunes. Many were descended from families who had settled in St. Louis in the mid-19th century and had successfully made their way into Society. And then there were their poor relations, the Jews who had come in floods at the turn of the century, the victims of great outbreaks of violent anti-semitism all over Eastern Europe.

The culture of Eastern European Jewry was essentially a culture of poverty. One of the maxims of the shtetl was, "If God lived here, His windows would be broken." In a culture where material things were difficult or impossible to obtain, religion was a solace and a bond. In the New World, however, poverty was not an inevitability. The cult of success often supplanted Judaism as the religion of the immigrants. Many Jews of David Margulois's generation placed a heavy value on success. They sought to create a huge financial gap between themselves and their origins.

Few, though, felt as great a need to disavow those origins as strongly as Margulois. Though few doubted he was Jewish, he would sometimes pretend he wasn't. He confessed to one of his wives—three weeks after they were married—that he was *half* Jewish, clearly a way of denying the totality of who he was.

His denial of his Jewishness even clouded his business acumen. The morning after *Fiddler on the Roof* opened, he was walking through the theater district with an associate, who pointed to a line of ticket buyers extending from the Imperial Theater, near Eighth Avenue, all the way to Broadway and around the corner. Merrick was unimpressed. "It's a Jewish show," he said. "No one will go."

The language of the immigrants was Yiddish. Here, too, David resolutely refused to identify with the tongue that—despite its riches—was branded as a language of the poor. In the world of the New York theater Yiddish was often a way to provide spice or seasoning to the conversation and was used by Jew and non-Jew alike.

Even with fellow Jews, Merrick studiously avoided it. It only seemed to emerge at extreme moments: he used the Yiddish word for ugly—"meeskite"—to describe a young auditioner named Barbra Streisand, to whom he took an immediate dislike; and in 1983, when he had a stroke and lost control, amid his babblings the word "gelt" (Yiddish for money) leapt pleadingly from his throat.

His parents' marriage had been arranged by a matchmaker in a shtetl, the tiny villages where Jews lived. Neither by economic nor by emotional criteria was the match a success. In the shtetl the strong sense of community and extended family could compensate for the imprecisions of the matchmaker's art. In the New World, however, where communal bonds were quick to dissolve, the weaknesses of the Margulois union were thrown into sharper relief.

Sam was a hapless provider, scrambling from one of his grocery stores to another to feed his family. Celia was mentally unstable. The amount of time Sam devoted to his business may have been a way to avoid having to deal with her emotional displays. In later years, Merrick would occasionally express sympathy for his mother. He seldom discussed his father, though he did have at least one happy memory. It was of a time when he brought home his report card, Sam looked at it and was surprised that the grades were good. David's older brother was supposed to be the bright one in the family, but Sam was pleased that the younger one was no slouch. "So you're not the sleepy one," he declared.

Did Sam erupted in the rages for which his son would become celebrated? Or was he, as some suspected, a dishrag, helpless in the face of Celia's emotional outbursts? Either way he left his son full of an anger almost too powerful to articulate.

David had an older brother, Benjamin, and three sisters, Sadye, Clara and Edda. Sadye was almost twenty years older than he was. By the time he was growing up they had all left home. There was no one to buffer him from the effects of his parents' vexatious relationship.

The drama of David's unhappy childhood was played out in the Jewish ghettoes of three Midwestern cities—Terre Haute, Chicago, and St. Louis. He reserved his bitterest hatred for St. Louis. Years later he refused to fly TWA because their flights passed over or through St. Louis. In 1984, when he was given the key to the city, he feigned illness and sent his wife to accept it.

Merrick once compared his childhood to "growing up on the set of *Who's Afraid of Virginia Woolf?*" The remark was intended to amuse, but, consciously or not, it may say a lot about his parents' marriage and the atmosphere of his early years. In Edward Albee's play, marriage is seen as a perpetual battleground. There is no physical violence, only a steady stream of verbal assaults. The chief weapon each partner wields in this ongoing struggle for supremacy is the tongue, a corrosive that rips through any veneer. The tongue was, throughout his career, Merrick's own weapon of choice, and it may have been during his unhappy childhood that he saw firsthand how destructive it could be.

When he was seven his parents were divorced. One of his sisters remembered that they all had to appear in court. When the judge asked David to speak, he could only stand and bite his nails. There would not be many days of judgment when David would be rendered speechless.

Whatever relief the boy felt at having his father out of the house was cut short by Sam's astounding decision to remarry Celia, an offer she inexplicably accepted. Fortunately their second attempt at marriage was of short duration. Sam abandoned Celia and David. The bewildered boy also attempted to abandon his disturbed mother. He ran away. He lacked the resources to go it alone, however, and was forced to return to the unsettling, painful place he knew as "home."

The struggle to deny his origins was one of the few things he had in common with his older brother Benjamin. Benjamin, too, later in life, tried to pass himself off as a non-Jew. Even as a young man Benjamin had deliberately estranged himself from his family. It was an all too common occurrence for the children of immigrants to be embarrassed by their parents. Benjamin was deeply ashamed of his mother's pronounced Yiddish accent. He had nothing to do with David and Celia, who were living in a poor neighborhood in Chicago in the shadow of the noisy, sooty El trains while Benjamin was in medical school in St. Louis. An excellent student, and at the top of his class, Benjamin must have known how proud his mother would have been to see him graduate, but he did not invite her to his graduation.

Celia found out about it and dragged little David on the bus from Chicago to St. Louis to attend. They found places at the ceremony, and when Benjamin came down the aisle he saw them. "What are you doing here?" he hissed out of the side of his mouth. The proud mother was bewildered, the younger brother humiliated.

Interestingly, Ben pursued his medical studies and became a psychiatrist. He eventually moved to Los Angeles where he had minimal contact with his family.

Shortly afterward the family committed Celia to a state mental institution. Now that she was institutionalized, David lacked even the place where "when you have to go there, they have to take you in." He found himself being shunted between the apartments of his married sisters. In one of them, he said, he "played second fiddle to the dog."

One of the harshest memories of his Dickensian childhood was of overhearing one of his older sisters on the telephone. Either she did not realize the boy was listening or she was too worn down to care: "I had him for six months in the spring— now it's your turn" she said.

In the midst of this bleak cycle of indifference and rejection, there was one odd ray of hope—Uncle Maurice, Etta's husband. Maurice Bloch was infatuated with the theater. He and Etta had a large family, which he managed to support. But all his spare time was devoted to directing the amateur productions of the St. Louis Young Men's Hebrew Association.

Commencement, St. Louis Central High School, 1930: David Margulois, Sylvia Thea, Millie Basden and Eli Pilchick

If, as Moss Hart has written, the theater is the refuge of the unhappy child, the world Uncle Maurice introduced him to was a welcome retreat from the harshness of the boy's everyday life. In the theater you could assume any identity you wanted to, an enticing proposition for a child whose early years had left him with no security, no clear sense of himself.

Shortly before he entered high school he asked his oldest sister, Sadye, if he could live with her and her husband, Samuel J. Margulis (no relation), a hat salesman with a mildly sarcastic manner. They agreed. They lived in University Heights, a comfortable, middle class suburb near the prestigious Washington University.

Sadye and Sam had no children of their own. They treated David with a concern and care he had never known. Sadye offered him his first understanding of what a normal home was like. He had his own room, which he kept meticulously clean. Sadye encouraged him to invite his friends to dinner. She never knew how many to expect, but she was a gracious hostess. The friends remembered her as a kindly, solicitous woman. Often, especially on Jewish holidays, the Margulises were either hosts or guests of the Stuhlbarg family. Their son, Marvin, nicknamed "Bud," remembered David as a shy, lonely boy whose favorite topic of conversation was the theater.

David was enrolled in nearby Central High School. On September 29, 1927, less than a week after the school year began, a tornado ripped through St. Louis. Central, then a 75-year-old brick building, was torn apart. Five girls were killed and sixteen other children injured. That day, by chance, David had played hookey. He had gone to a movie. He was safe inside the movie theater when the tornado had devastated his school. Show business had saved him.

The tornado had other consequences. The Central building had to be renovated and rebuilt, which took several months. In the meantime the students had to go to Yeatman High School, which was outside the St. Louis Jewish community's "pale of settlement." For the first time some of the Central students were coming in contact with anti-semitism. David encountered a world to which he felt he could not belong.

He was a creditable student, graduating seventh in his class. Apart from standard courses, he took one in Sales-Advertising. That his grade point average was so high and that he was able to participate in extracurricular activities seems remarkable in view of the fact that he also had to hold down part-time jobs. He sold crystal sets and components at Barney's Radio Store. He hawked soda in the bleachers of Forbes Field, the ballpark near Yeatman. One summer he was a caddy at an exclusive WASP country club. With help from Sadye's husband he worked in a shoe store. Later, with Benjamin's help, he got a desk job at the City Hospital.

As early as high school his fellow students noted a theatricality in his behavior. As one put it, "There was no naturalness about him—he was putting himself on stage even then."

Despite all his determined extracurricular activity the impression he made on people was one of great loneliness. Something about the tall young man with the mustache suggested an out-sider, someone who did not fit in. To some he seemed forlorn. To others he seemed arrogant and superior. Many years afterward one of his classmates remembered that he was a good tennis play-er. He took no part in social activities, and later on friends could not remember him showing any of the conventional interest that young men have in girls. He taunted the athletes who had pretty girlfriends that later they would be envious of the women who would be attracted to him. To do so, he must now devote himself to succeeding in his studies and making money.

He made few friends. The closest was a boy very like himself, Eli Pilchik, who was born in Poland in 1913 and grew up in a shtetl whose streets were traversed by various armies. The soldiers were generally able to take time out from pillaging the surround-ing countryside to brutalize the local Jews. The little boy remem-bered seeing a soldier hack off a rabbi's beard with a knife. Pilchik and his mother came to the United States after the war. His father, who had arrived beforehand, had adopted American ways, and the strains between mother and father were too great to maintain the pretense of a marriage. The parents separated. The boy stayed with his mother. Disturbed by his firsthand memories of the horrors of war and by his parents' discord, Pilchik was as lonely as Margulois, whose experience of battle was merely domestic. The two became inseparable.

Another friend, Reuben Lapin, was half a year ahead of the other two in school. He immediately sensed Margulois's competi-tiveness. They belonged to a Jewish fraternity called "the Ramblers." Once, at a meeting given over to formal debate, Margulois lost to Lapin and spent the whole trip home on the streetcar trying to persuade Lapin that he had won unfairly, that he had relied on rhetoric and demagoguery rather than sound argument.

Lapin was president of the class that graduated in January of 1930. He was certain that when David ran for president of the class that graduated that June he did it for no other reason than to show that he could achieve anything that Lapin did.

Margulois won the presidency campaigning on an anti-fraternity platform. His victory was a surprise since he was perceived as standoffish and even condescending, though some sensed his air of superiority was "a reaction to—maybe a denial of—what his background actually was." In any case he had "none of the easy camaraderie that was normal with the other kids. He was very, very guarded about who he was and from where he came." His eagerness to compete, to win, apparently triumphed over his natural discomfort with others.

It was in high school that he adopted the uniform that he wore for the rest of his life—a pinstripe suit. Pinstripes were not uncommon among high school students then, but for David they held special meaning. They were the uniform of the middle class or upper class businessman, many notches above the shirt-sleeve practicality of, say, a grocery store owner.

(There was also a practical reason for a heavy, three-piece suit. For someone who, all his life, suffered from low blood pressure, it was a way of keeping warm. But the same effect could have been achieved by wearing sweaters. The pinstripe signified more than mere practicality.)

If his grasp of "issues" won him the class presidency, his quiet intelligence won him election as one of the four commencement speakers. The others were Pilchik and two young women, Millie Basden and Sylvia Thea.

The four speakers wrote and presented their own speeches. At one of the rehearsals Margulois took it upon himself to criticize the others' delivery. The class adviser drew him aside and told him this was none of his business. From then on he simply sat quietly and observed, though he managed to convey to the others the feeling that somehow he had *allowed* them to be part of the proceedings.

This sneering sense of superiority, which never left him, was in those years balanced by abundant evidence of his weakness and insecurity. Once, to tease him, a few of the Ramblers threw him into a swimming pool. Even in water that only came up to his waist David floundered helplessly. One of his friends "rescued" him, but they all thought it odd that he lacked the basic common sense to right himself in the shallow end of a pool.

On another occasion the Ramblers went camping in a state forest near St. Louis. They settled in, building a little campfire on which they set an aluminum coffee pot. A few of the boys began tossing a football back and forth. One accidentally dropped a match on the grass. It burned in a little circle before he stomped it out. This began an adolescent sort of competition. Another boy dropped a match onto the dry autumn grass. He waited until it created a larger circle, which he too stomped out.

The fires grew bigger and finally one got out of control. The boys became frightened. Someone was dispatched to a nearby ranger station to get help. The boys began using their jackets to put out the raging fire. Except one. Margulois took the coffee pot—which did not belong to him—and ran toward home.

CHAPTER THREE

HAD THE FIRE SPREAD into the nearby forest, it might have been catastrophic. Fortunately it crackled its way into a little hollow, out of range of the wind, where the boys were able to put it out before the forest rangers arrived.

The boy running toward home carrying an aluminum coffee pot could not have known the episode would end harmlessly. He had too many ambitions to be caught with a bunch of fraternity boys—Jewish fraternity boys at that—who had started a forest fire.

His ambitions were of two sorts. There were the common yearnings of a poor boy who wanted money, who had aspirations to college and eventually law school. There were also yearnings of another sort. The seeds Uncle Maurice had planted were bearing fruit. David longed to go into show business.

Though he acted in plays throughout high school and college, he did not want to be an actor. For a while he thought he might become a writer. In a number of profiles of Merrick you come across the fact that he and another St. Louis boy entered a playwriting contest in 1930. He placed second. The other boy, whose name was Thomas Lanier Williams, later Tennessee, did not place at all. This vignette does not pop up in profiles of Williams. (To his credit, after recounting the anecdote, Merrick once observed, "It only proved that the judges knew nothing about playwriting.)

Nor was it really as a writer that he wanted to make his mark in the theater. He wanted to be a producer. His idol, he confided to his friend Eli Pilchik, was Florenz Ziegfeld, the legendary showman whose musical revues were the last word in lavishness and glamour.

The hunger for money and the desire to enter show business were not such disparate ambitions. Ziegfeld's spectacles, with their long-legged beauties in extravagant costumes, were a form of alchemy. They took the base element of money—by itself abstract—and turned it into something tangible: fleshly allure and fairy tale splendor. Ziegfeld's entertainments would pass out of fashion by the time the young Margulois was ready to follow in his idol's footsteps, although, of course, the Ziegfeld esthetic made a splendid comeback in *42nd Street.*

For the time being creating fantasies like Ziegfeld's was out of the question. As David Margulois entered Washington University, a prestigious liberal arts school, in the fall of 1930, he could only worry about one thing—earning money. He continued to live with Sadye and Sam but they could not pay for his college education. Though his high school grades had been good, they had not won him a scholarship.

David's boundless industry managed to support him through the first two and a half years at Washington; but ultimately work and study took their toll and he was forced to drop out in the middle of his junior year because of severe ill health. By the time he was thirty he had developed an ulcer, and this may have been an early warning of things to come.

When he returned to school it was at the less expensive St. Louis University, a Catholic school. After receiving his undergraduate degree there, he continued on at its law school. He received a Bachelor of Law degree in 1937.

Later in life, he would reward associates with little glimpses of his early life, not to encourage intimacy, but to let them measure the great distance he had traveled. To some he would confide the unhappiness of the time when he would be shunted from one sister to another. To some he would confide the odd jobs that he had done, almost with incredulity, as if it were extraordinary that a man of his eminence could once have sold men's suits at Famous-Barr, the St. Louis department store, or that he could have sold dining room table covers door to door.

There was another way to make a little money—the dog race track in East St. Louis, the frowzy little town across the Mississippi that had once been the goal of slaves trying to reach freedom and was, in 1917, the site of bloody race riots.

Even as a teenager he was preoccupied with "systems." When he went to the races he claimed it was not "for the fun of it." Although the races and their raffish clientele had a theatrical aura, there was a limited amount of gratification to be had in watching dogs chase a mechanical rabbit around a track. To prove one of his theories about gambling, he limited his betting carefully.

His bets were never wild or imprudent. He would always bet on the favorite to "show," which meant he would win if the dog came in first, second or third. This meant he would never win spectacularly, but he would always win *something*. He would never go home with less than he had come with.

Such modest gambling remained his style for years. It took him a long time to see that he had to raise the stakes considerably if he wanted to follow in the footsteps of Flo Ziegfeld. The prospect of always having to scramble for money—like his father—was not attractive. He decided to become a lawyer, a logical decision for someone who had already shown an agile, sharp tongue. The law was a way for someone who had known only powerlessness to achieve power.

Throughout his schooling he retained an interest in theater, which drew from the boy a poetic side that over the years he kept muffled. In a play he did during his senior year in high school, David played the role of a poet who sought but did not win the hand of a multimillionaire's daughter.

As an undergraduate he took one class in theater. He got a C.

The teacher, W.G.B. Carson, remembered him more than thirty years later not so much for his theatrical skills as for his pencil mustache.

At St. Louis University he watched rehearsals of the Playhouse Group, where he eventually won a part. He was cast as Tubal, Shylock's friend, in a production of *The Merchant of Venice*. The director, a cast member recalled, "was acutely sensitive to the delicacy of having a Jewish student in the most unsavory role in a Catholic school production of the play. None of us had met Dave yet, and before he came in the director explained to us at least five times that we weren't to confuse casting with personality." When Margulois finally appeared, they found him "quiet, unassuming and nice."

He continued to make a respectable impression when he attended law school. People were beginning to notice that he had a chip on his shoulder, "a touch of the persecuted about him." While he was in the top third of his class, a classmate later suggested he might have done better had he had any genuine interest in the law. But the law was merely a means to an end. He would spend the rest of his life manipulating it to his own purposes.

During the summer Margulois and Pilchik hawked ice cream and soda at the St. Louis Municipal Opera, or "The Muni," as it's still called, a huge, open-air summer theater in Forest Park, where there were lavish productions of musical hits from New York— shows by Sigmund Romberg or the Gershwins, even a scaled-down version of the Jerome Kern-Oscar Hammerstein II *Show Boat*.

In 1939 a writer for Theater Arts magazine declared, "St. Louis will never become an American Salzburg, for the entertainment it offers is not Mozart or Beethoven; but as a center for that truly popular American theatrical form, the musical show, it is outstanding," a fascinating observation in view of the impact the young ice cream vendor would later have on American musical theater.

The young Margulois could not help but be impressed by how

potent a draw the Muni's productions of musicals were. In the Muni parking lot you could see, on any given night, license plates from half the states in the Union.

Apart from the productions he saw at the Muni, the young man had plenty of opportunities to see high quality entertainment in St. Louis. It was common for the stars of New York hit shows to tour at the end of the Broadway run. Among the stars young Margulois saw was George M. Cohan, who appeared in O'Neill's *Ah, Wilderness!* at the American Theater in downtown St. Louis. There was also live entertainment before the featured films began at the Loew's downtown. Al Jolson appeared there. So did a local girl named Ginger Rogers.

His friends noticed very quickly that the one subject that made Margulois perk up was the mention of money. One described his mind admiringly as a calculator.

He may have been facetious when he first conceived the idea of marrying a wealthy girl. Such a girl, after all, might easily have nothing to do with the tall, shy law student who had been born on the wrong side of the tracks. Margulois did not lack charm or intelligence, but in the precarious world of the Depression it would have to be a very remarkable young woman who would overlook his material drawbacks, who would ignore the fear that her suitor might be interested in her for material reasons.

In the summer of 1934, a young woman Pilchik was dating asked if he knew someone who might come on a double date with her friend Leonore Beck. Pilchik naturally suggested his friend David. The two couples went to Forest Park and sat in the cheaper seats of the Muni, where only a few summers before, the boys had worked the aisles together.

Pilchik later said he would bear "a scar of guilt" for having introduced them, but Leonore, years later, confided to a friend that she had, in fact, first met Margulois when she was 16, in 1928; the fact that David waited ten years to marry her was proof that he loved her as much as she loved him. Marvin Stulhbarg, whose family had been close to the Margulises, conjectured that they might have met at the YMHA, since Leonore's love of theater was as great as David's.

Pilchik could not recall that Margulois had ever shown any particular interest in girls. He had never socialized or dated the way other young men did. Perhaps the reason was that he was already secretly devoted to this young woman who had shown an interest in him—and who had so much to offer him.

Leonore, a strawberry blonde, was the only child of a successful St. Louis cooperage firm owner, a lucrative business in a city with several large breweries. His widow Blanche and their daughter lived in the well-heeled suburb of University City. They lived in a house that must have appeared to Margulois as a mansion, on Linden Street, one of the most beautiful streets in St. Louis, facing Forest Park.

Like David, she was shy. Also like him, she had been a Jewish student at a Catholic school, Fontbonne College. If he had experienced anti-semitism of the mild, veiled American variety, she had experienced the more virulent European variety. In the late Twenties she and her mother had traveled in Europe, where, in a Germany not yet conquered by National Socialism, they had been called "damned Jews."

Beyond that she and David had little in common. She fit in perfectly with what a classmate later described as David's "regular day-dream of marrying a rich girl so that he wouldn't have to practice law." Another recalled that "Dave made no bones about the fact that he was intending to marry the Beck girl for her money. I don't think he had too much regard for her as a woman." And another remembered Leonore's docility. She "gave in to everything Dave suggested."

The course of true love in University City, as elsewhere, did not run smooth. Blanche Beck detested her daughter's suitor.

A sick and lonely woman, dependent on the companionship of her daughter, she might have had reservations about any man who would threaten to take Leonore away from her. But her skepticism toward Margulois went even further. He was, of course, a social inferior. Though Czech by origin, Mrs. Beck had the hauteur, Pilchik remembered, of a "German-Jewish dowager." This may have been why Leonore was initially reluctant to bring her suitor home. By 1934 he was already in law school and thus more presentable.

But he didn't get far. He was not allowed to come into the house to pick her up for a date. He sat in the car outside and honked the horn until she came out.

As if his being poor weren't enough, he had also made clear his interest in the theater. In this sense he did not mislead the Becks. Whatever financial advantages might accrue from his legal education might be lost if he planned to involve himself in the uncertain world of show business.

Most important, Blanche's maternal intuition may simply have told her Margulois's motives were largely mercenary.

None of these things mattered to Leonore. She was willing to go to great lengths to please David. He took her to law school balls at the smart Chase Hotel in downtown St. Louis. They went to parties given by Uncle Maurice at the YMHA's Little Theater, where, in 1936, David appeared in Clifford Odets' *Awake and Sing.*

Their behavior, like David's clothes, was reserved and conservative. What gave him a little dash was that he wore his hair slicked back.

Had her health been better, Mrs. Beck might have been a more formidable adversary. Her illness was Margulois's staunchest ally. Surgery on a brain tumor weakened her substantially. But Mrs. Beck was not without resources. She alerted her family to her suspicions about Leonore's boyfriend.

Time and her faltering condition were on his side, but Margulois realized he needed to hedge his bet. If he did not take action, she might be able to wear down Leonore's resolve. In a heartless calculation, he persuaded Leonore to file a petition with the St. Louis County Court to have her mother declared *non compos mentis* and seek appointment of a court guardian.

In June, 1937, shortly after his graduation from law school, before it became necessary for him and Leonore to take what would have appeared a self-interested legal action, Mrs. Beck died.

She left an estate totalling $157,863.87, all to Leonore. The money was largely in U.S. Treasury Bonds, which, after payment of various debts, came to $116,319.66. In 1937, this was a fortune.

On January 16, 1938, Leonore became Mrs. David Margulois. For him it was the first of a series of exceedingly small weddings. None of his marriages ever seems to have struck him as a cause for general public celebration. This one was a private ceremony performed on the pulpit of the United Hebrew Congregation, a Reform synagogue on the edge of Forest Park. Apart from a close friend of Leonore's, Bernice Safarian, the only guests were Sadye, Sam and Eli Pilchik. Leonore's family refused to attend. They shared Blanche's mistrust of and distaste for the groom.

The bridal couple left on their honeymoon trip to Mexico in a Packard convertible. When they returned, David set his well-schooled tongue to practical use. He applied himself with particular rigor to supervising the myriad details concerning Leonore's inheritance. Throughout his career, when money was at stake he went after it with tenacity and imagination, seizing any little detail that might prove fruitful.

All the preliminary motions in regard to the estate had been handled by an attorney named Brainer W. La Tourette. After the sum due to Leonore had been secured, Margulois questioned La Tourette's $5,000 fee. In the sort of determined wrangling that characterized all his professional negotiations, David petitioned the court for repayment of the fee. He lost. La Tourette kept his $5,000.

Having pursued this tack unsuccessfully he tried another. He petitioned the court to have the principle of his wife's trust turned over to her in its entirety. As originally drawn up, the will gave Leonore the interest, but her lawyer-husband resourcefully demonstrated that the terms of the will entitled her to receive the entire amount at once. The court agreed.

While these legal motions were making their painstaking way through the courts, Margulois tried on the life of idle leisure. It was not a life that suited him. At one point he and Leonore drove out to California, where he thought he might find work in the movies. His efforts were fruitless.

Despite their comfortable financial situation, they were living the life of newlyweds struggling to find their identity. Leonore was extremely supportive of her husband as his attempts to be a breadwinner failed.

She in turn was trying to be a housewife. Her mother had not prepared her for this role, and her culinary skills were limited. Once, when they lived in Hollywood, Leonore cooked fish for the first time. It looked beautiful, but when her husband took his first bite he intoned, "This is not cooked." She realized she had only cooked one side.

During these years Pilchik was in Cincinnati studying to become a Reform rabbi. It was a decision that struck his friend as "a sign of insanity."

"David had no use for religion at all, no sense of faith," Pilchik recalled. "When I told him I was going into the seminary, he thought I had lost my mind." Margulois had tried to persuade his friend to become a lawyer, suggesting they might share a legal partnership. Pilchik, however, had no inclination toward the law.

When Pilchik came back to St. Louis between terms he became increasingly aware of David's moodiness. The financial stability of his marriage allowed his personal instability to come to the fore. Margulois was prone to fits of anger. He and Pilchik might be driving around and arguing. Margulois would pound the steering wheel in rage. Pilchik was struck by how contemptuous his friend had become of other people, how he took pleasure in deriding and "dropping" them. Only one thing mattered to him—success. And he would let no one stand in his way.

In the spring of 1939 David went to Cincinnati to see his friend ordained as a rabbi. During his visit Pilchik received a blow. He had hoped the Reform movement would send him to

Sydney, Australia, so he could help make Australia a haven for the beleaguered Jews of Germany. His superiors, however, decided the Sydney pulpit needed a more seasoned occupant.

Margulois "pounced" on this setback to urge him to leave the rabbinate, which he had barely entered. He proposed another partnership. "Let's go into the theater together," he urged Pilchik.

Pilchik shared his friend's love of theater. He was still unmarried, and at least for the coming summer he had no obligations. He decided to accompany the Marguloises to New York. There Pilchik had "connections." He knew Nathan Pearlman, an assistant rabbi at the wealthy Temple Emanuel on Fifth Avenue. One of the members of Emanuel, Pearlman told Pilchik, was a man named Bela Blau, who ran a summer theater called Deertrees in Harrison, Maine. The Marguloises and Pilchik spent the summer of 1939 there.

Blau was an excellent mentor for a young man intent on becoming a producer. Hungarian by birth, brought up in London, Blau came to New York at the age of ten. His early training was in economics, which he taught at City College during the Twenties. He became interested in applying up-to-date theories of economic efficiency and fund raising to Broadway.

One of his principles was the importance of raising enough money to have a reserve fund to help plays through their difficult early stages, until they found their audience, an idea Merrick later adopted.

Backstage at Deertrees Margulois and Pilchik had a jack-of-all-trades apprenticeship in the nuts and bolts of the theater, helping to build scenery, running errands, watching rehearsals. That summer Margulois also had an opportunity to make his first theatrical investment. A show was trying out in Connecticut. Margulois wanted to take a look.

Pilchik dissuaded his friend from investing in the play, a nostalgic look at 19th century New York. The plot hinged on whether the stern, somewhat priggish father of an upper-middle class household should, well into middle age, be baptized.

The Lunts had turned down the starring roles because Alfred

couldn't imagine worrying about this issue eight times a week. So perhaps the considerably less savvy Pilchik could be excused for dissuading his friend from putting money in it. The play, based on Clarence Day's memoirs, was called *Life With Father*. It was a huge success and is still the longest-running non-musical in Broadway history. Merrick never forgave Pilchik.

Still, the summer with Blau gave him a basic education in the theater. If the Deertrees company reflected Blau's thinking, it may have exerted a personal draw for Margulois as well. After a brief stay in Hollywood in 1937, Blau told a reporter, "Everything out there has to be done on such a lavish scale that the family atmosphere of a Broadway production is lost."

The theater, then, still had the feeling of a family. That may have enhanced its appeal for the lonely young lawyer from St. Louis. Many years later he would be accused of having destroyed the family feeling of Broadway. But this may have been inevitable. What he had known as family was not quite like Clarence Day's.

Without any prospects for work in the theater, they returned to St. Louis in the fall. Pilchik found a job through Abram Sachar, a professor of history at the University of Illinois. Sachar had founded the first Hillel, an organization for Jewish students, at Illinois. He gave Pilchik the assignment of establishing a Hillel chapter in College Park, Maryland.

Margulois, disappointed that the summer in Maine had not infected his friend with his own passion for the theater, resumed his legal gambits on behalf of Leonore's inheritance. The litigation was finally wound up May 13, 1940.

Margulois had now tasted a world larger than St. Louis, the site of so many humiliating memories. In St. Louis, no matter how far he might propel himself as a lawyer, his humble origins would always be known and hold him back. He persuaded Leonore that if he had any future in the theater, they had to move to New York, where, after all, he had already made some contacts and where possibilities were boundless.

The distance her family kept between themselves and the newlyweds may have facilitated Leonore's decision. She consented to his wishes. Shortly after David had secured the principle of her estate, they moved to New York, confident that, with her money and his tongue, a new, more exciting life awaited them.

CHAPTER FOUR

TWO THINGS ARE ABSOLUTE CERTAINTIES: the speed of light, and the imminent death of the New York theater.

"The era of sterling drama and talented actors is in the past, perhaps never to return," the author of a guide to New York declared in 1868, when, by our standards, it had not even begun. Brooks Atkinson declared Broadway moribund in 1952 (when Tennessee Williams, Arthur Miller and William Inge were in mid-career). Stark Young had pronounced it mortally ill in 1932 (when O'Neill was in full stride and the Group Theater was beginning).

In the spring of 1940, when the young couple from St. Louis was settling in New York, the respected magazine Theatre Arts declared the current season a disaster. There was no clearer evidence of the dire straits Broadway had reached during the 1939-1940 season than the fact that one day that winter only twenty-two of its theaters were open. Why, even in the West End of London, a city at war, there were forty-five theaters open.

Theater Arts asked a number of eminent theater people what this ominous number signified.

For Clare Boothe, who had not yet added Luce to her name, the problem was lack of interest in quality. "At present," the author of *The Women* wrote, "it is almost impossible to put on any show which does not seem in advance to be a 'sure thing' to a producer."

Several respondents blamed the greed of the unions. One noted that "if one wardrobe trunk is moved into the theater, two men are called for a minimum of two hours, to do one minute's work." He also cited the fact that if a theater actor travels, the producer must buy him a railroad ticket and put him in a sleeper if he rides after ten p.m. If the same actor works in vaudeville, the producer can put him on a bus or anything else that moved.

Some traced the problem to the avarice of the theater owners, who demanded as much as forty per cent of the weekly take. One saw the heavy rate of failure as the result of the "unjustified panning of the critics."

Lynn Fontanne cited the dearth of worthwhile plays. She and her husband Alfred Lunt had read hundreds of new plays in the last few years, the vast majority of which "had neither writing nor story to commend them. They were so bad you couldn't chain your thoughts to them, no matter how hard you tried."

John Shubert, whose family owned many of the Broadway theaters, noted the competition of radio and films. No one yet suspected the threat of the little box with moving images that had caused so much excitement the previous summer at the New York World's Fair.

The producer Herman Shumlin urged everyone to calm down. A staunch leftist, he refused to blame the unions. As far as he could see, production costs had not gotten out of hand in the fifteen years he had worked in the theater. Shumlin pointed out the naivete of imagining the theater could be financially resilient in the midst of an economic disaster that afflicted the entire country.

In a clearheaded assessment, the designer Boris Aronson saw that the ills of the theater were "the children or stepchildren of one very prolific parent. [The theater] has been built up as a gambling institution rather than a sound business. In a word, the theater is a sweepstake. It is impossible to name another enterprise, outside of professional gambling, in which the investor has only one chance to succeed. In many cases he stakes everything on one production. If the production is not immediately successful there is no second chance.

"Normal progress, based on training, experience and accomplishment, is impossible under this system," Aronson wrote. "It victimizes both the beginner and the established theater people. The latter are in constant danger of being dropped from the heights suddenly; the former have little chance to gain experience. To sum up: Immediate success means too much in the present. Failure teaches too little."

Years later Merrick would be accused of having turned the Broadway theater into a crapshoot with unreasonably high odds. The theater seems already to have been in that state before David Merrick had set foot in it.

The season that occasioned so much handwringing among the professionals might not have seemed so catastrophic to the average theatergoer. The despair seems extremely difficult to reconcile with hindsight. After all, this was the season that offered Howard Lindsay and Russel Crouse's *Life With Father*, William Saroyan's *The Time of Your Life*, Paul Osborne's *Morning's At Seven* and Kaufman and Hart's *The Man Who Came to Dinner*. Paul Muni had created a sensation in Maxwell Anderson's *Key Largo*, as had Paul Robeson in a play with music about the mythical figure John Henry. Franchot Tone had starred in Ernest Hemingway's *The Fifth Column*, directed by Lee Strasberg. The range of offerings was wide, from an adaptation of Dostoyevsky's *The Possessed* to the ineffable *Yokel Boy*, featuring Buddy Ebsen, Judy Canova and Phil Silvers.

There had been short-lived vehicles for Ethel Barrymore and Helen Hayes. Burgess Meredith and Ingrid Bergman had appeared in a revival of Ferencz Molnar's *Liliom*, Barry Fitzgerald and Sara Allgood in a revival of Sean O'Casey's *Juno and the Paycock*. Maurice Evans performed the title roles in *Hamlet* and *Richard II*. You could still see Katherine Hepburn, Joseph Cotten and Van Heflin in *The Philadelphia Story*, held over from the previous season. On a sad note, John Barrymore parodied his own unfortunate career in *My Dear Children*, directed by Otto Preminger. As the season came to a close the Lunts, who had presented their version of *The Taming of the Shrew* that spring, appeared in Robert Sherwood's play about the war in Europe, *There Shall Be No Night* with Sidney Greenstreet and Montgomery Clift. There was a London import, *Romeo and Juliet*, starring Laurence Olivier, Vivien Leigh and Dame May Whitty.

Musicals played a smaller role on Broadway than they did even a few years later, but, all things considered, the situation was far from grim. The topical 1937 Harold Rome revue about the garment center, *Pins and Needles*, was still running, as was Olson and Johnson's *Hellzapoppin'*. Both had been updated. Cole Porter's *Du Barry Was a Lady*, starring Ethel Merman and Bert Lahr, opened this season. So did a new show by Jerome Kern and Oscar Hammerstein II, *Very Warm for May*, which featured Eve Arden, costumes by Vincente Minnelli and a song called "All The Things You Are". There was a musical version of *A Midsummer Night's Dream* called *Swinging the Dream,* with a cast that included Louis Armstrong, Dorothy Dandridge, Butterfly McQueen, Dorothy McGuire and Ruth Ford. It also featured the Benny Goodman Sextet, among whose members were Lionel Hampton and Fletcher Henderson.

There were two Rodgers and Hart shows. One, *Too Many Girls,* ran for most of the season. It introduced the song, "I Didn't Know What Time It Was," and featured Eddie Bracken, Van Johnson, Richard Kollmar and a young Cuban performer, Desi Arnaz, singing "She Could Shake the Maracas."

There were several revues whose casts now seem astonishing. *Walk With Music*, for example, had Kitty Carlisle, Mitzi Green, Frances Williams and Stepin Fetchit. *Keep Off the Grass* had Jimmy Durante, Ray Bolger, Jane Frohman, Ilka Chase, Larry Adler, Jack (sic) Gleason, Emmett Kelly and Jose Limon. The choreography was by Balanchine and one of the dancers was the young Jerry Robbins. *The Streets of Paris*, held over from the previous season, featured the burlesque star Bobby Clark, Abbott and Costello, Carmen Miranda and the dance team of Gower and Jeanne (the former being the young Gower Champion.) That season Robbins also appeared in *The Straw Hat Review*, imported from Temament, a resort in Bushkill, Pennsylvania, with Imogene Coca, Danny Kaye and Alfred Drake.

If the theater community was disturbed about its health, its fears seemed unwarranted to a sophisticated English visitor. Cecil Beaton wrote in 1939, "The theater is more alive than in any other capital today. . . On the legitimate stage in London there are no more long runs. In New York a play can still draw after four years, and the list of attractions is enormous, for the New Yorker goes to the theater more often than the Londoner."

As to the quality of what he saw, Beaton was similarly enthusiastic: "In all New York the tempo is quick. In the theater it is breathless. The actors have a natural wit and begin their careers early without the hindrance of a dramatic school training, accompanied as it is by clipped accent, exaggerated vowel sounds and other essays in gentility. These actors are not, as in London, trying to be, above all, gentlemen and ladies."

Boris Aronson, who had been so eloquent on the problems of the theater when writing in Theatre Arts, was blunter when he spoke to friends in private. "In the theater, we're either under the control of the poets or the delicatessen owners," he had said in his gruff Russian accent. "Right now, we got the delicatessen owners."

Though no one ever accused Merrick of being a poet, it would be unfair simply to place him in a league with the delicatessen owners. It was to his advantage to court the delicatessen owners, because they held the power and the money, but from the very beginning, he was not averse to the claims of the poets.

In the spring of 1940, although the United States was avowedly isolationist, everyone sensed that war clouds were gathering. This European front was not a matter of concern to Merrick. Because of his ulcers he was exempt from the draft. He was preparing his own offensive.

He had changed his name legally. Years later he joked that if his new career in New York had not worked out, whatever failures he committed would be attributed to David Merrick and he could resume his identity as David Margulois back in St. Louis. But the new name was the first step toward a new identity, an audition for a new life.

Like other theatrical aspirants, he may have hoped to take New York by storm. But the siege lasted many years, an unusual number considering his later reputation for drive and ruthlessness. It would be ten years before the aspiring producer would have his name above a title he was proud to take credit for, fourteen years before he would produce a musical that would give him the respect of the theater community.

In part the long wait to achieve his objective was due to the war being waged within, between the cautious, insecure Margulois, conscious of being an outsider, and the gradually emerging Merrick, who was learning that, depending on how you went about it, in the theater you could be what you wanted; and you could take what you wanted.

On their arrival from St. Louis, the Merricks took a suite in the Windsor, a residential hotel on 58th Street a block below Central Park, a very comfortable address for someone who was unemployed. The apartment was so small a rudimentary kitchen had to be made out of a hall closet. Perhaps to expunge the memory of Blanche, David had forced Leonore to sell most of her mother's furniture and china before they left St. Louis. Yet the valuable antiques and rugs that were left enjoyed proud places in their new home.

On one of his visits to New York earlier that year, David made his way to the office of the producer Herman Shumlin, to whom he had been given an introduction by Rabbi Pearlman, who had earlier sent Margulois and Pilchik to Deertrees.

Shumlin's office was in the Selwyn Building at 229 West 42nd Street. The address was significant. Though it had once been an important hub of theater activity, few theater producers maintained offices on 42nd Street any more because it was, in the view of many, growing tawdry. What tawdry meant in 1940 was not the presence of drugs or pornography but a proliferation of stands selling hot dogs and orange juice. In the Twenties the theaters along 42nd Street had still been "legit." By the late Thirties most had been converted to movie theaters or burlesque houses.

The office Merrick entered was spartan. Other Broadway producers decorated their quarters lavishly to advertise their taste or simply their success. Not Shumlin. Dramatic display, he felt, was for the stage, not for the place where he did business. It was a no-nonsense style Merrick would later emulate.

Merrick had come as an "angel." He wanted to put money in a new play. The work in which he invested $5,000—approximately 20 percent of the entire capitalization—was about a professor of English fretful that his wife has fallen in love with her former boyfriend, an ex-football player, now a successful businessman. The professor becomes convinced he must challenge his rival not on intellectual grounds but physical ones. He is also embattled at work. He has announced that he will read his senior English class the famous final letter Vanzetti wrote before his electrocution. The university trustees are convinced he is a Communist.

This is hardly the sort of play people would later associate with Merrick. What made its commercial prospects greater than its plot suggests is that it was co-written by James Thurber. The play was called *The Male Animal,* and among its virtues was that it had a young actress named Gene Tierney in a small role.

The Male Animal was a hit. Merrick received $20,000 on his investment. He was turning Leonore's money into his own. More importantly, he now had entree into the office of Herman Shumlin.

By the time he produced *The Male Animal,* in the fall of 1940, Shumlin was one of the most prestigious producers on Broadway. He had been born in a Colorado town too small to have an office in which to record his birth. He was the son of Russian emigrants attempting to homestead. They failed and moved back East to Newark. Young Herman dropped out of high school and, at fifteen, found a job in a Newark hardware manufacturing plant. When he expressed concern about the safety of the workers, his boss called him a socialist and fired him.

Shumlin drifted into show business, where he held a variety of jobs. He began producing in the late Twenties and scored his first hit in 1930 with *The Last Mile*, a prison drama that brought stardom to Spencer Tracy. Shumlin achieved his greatest eminence producing and directing *The Children's Hour* and *The Little Foxes*, both of which were written by a young woman who had worked for him as a script reader, Lillian Hellman.

Despite the seriousness of the plays he produced, despite his ardent left wing politics and despite his charmless office, Shumlin was something of a dandy. Well before Otto Preminger or Yul Brynner, he began to shave his head on a daily basis. In 1941 he made the best-dressed list, along with Henry Ford II, Walter Pidgeon and Winthrop Rockefeller.

The disparity between his sartorial bravura and his otherwise Puritanical mien was typical of a man of the theater. Success in more staid businesses used to carry certain social obligations— an avoidance in dress or behavior of anything that seemed unbusinesslike. Success in the theater carried no such prohibitions. Success in the theater was a veritable license for self-transformation.

Becoming a Broadway producer was the ideal way for the young man from St. Louis to trade the mental torment and helplessness that constituted the legacy of being a Margulois for something better. Even in high school he had begun to develop a carapace—the pinstripe suits, the theatrical manner—to conceal the disturbed child who had survived the battlefield of his parents' marriage, the "displaced person" who had been shunted from sister to sister until Sadye and Sam gave him his first real home.

In these early years in New York a battle was going on inside him. The contrasts were not quite as stark as in Aronson's formulation—the poets on one side, the delicatessen owners on the other—but he was aware that there were two approaches to theater, the one he acquired from Uncle Maurice, who had urged him to read Shaw, Chekhov and Ibsen, and the more practical one that he saw all around him in his adopted city.

Soon after his arrival he took a job—without pay—with the producing firm of Abbott & Dunning. George Abbott and Philip Dunning had written *Broadway*, an enormous hit in 1926, and their production office was one of the most successful firms on Broadway for many years. Merrick read scripts for them in hopes of finding something he himself could produce. He found nothing.

Merrick continued to hope he might find a property that would enable him to see his name on a marquee above a title, but the lucky break was not the only way to become a producer. There was another possibility—to learn the business from the bottom up.

He made his way back down 42nd Street to Shumlin's office, where he took a job as an office assistant. In contemporary terms, Merrick's job might be described as a "go-fer," someone to run errands, to lighten the burdens of others, to write press releases, to handle "house seats" (preferred locations reserved for friends of the management).

During the years Merrick worked for him, Shumlin produced and directed two plays by Lillian Hellmann, *Watch on the Rhine* and *The Searching Wind*, as well as Emlyn Williams' *The Corn Is Green*, starring Ethel Barrymore.

For Merrick, it was the first step in what was a standard theater apprenticeship. From office assistant you would work your way up to stage manager, who supervises all backstage operations; then company manager, who deals with the financial and union concerns; and finally general manager, who oversees everything. Along the way you learned about all the details of the business.

Not all the things there were to learn would have been on the "formal curriculum." There was, for example, "ice." The term came from politics. It stood for Incidental Campaign Expenses, a catch-all term campaign managers used to increase their fees. In the theater it referred to the money paid under the counter to obtain house seats for hit shows. In addition to using "ice" to supplement the relatively modest salaries they earned, box office personnel had another device, "stiffing the ticket." If business was marginal, they might dissuade people from buying tickets simply by claiming there were none to be had. This way the show would close, and the theater would become available for a show that might be a hit and reestablish the possibility of "ice."

Kickbacks were also common. General managers and stage managers were given large sums by set builders to be tipped off as to what the lowest bid was on a contract. By bidding slightly lower, they could win it, (though the sets might actually be built for considerably less).

Such financial advantages were not offered to those on the bottom rungs. These were the perks of seniority. Whether or not they were available, Merrick did not really require such enticements to remain with Shumlin. He had, after all, left his home town and left the potentially lucrative practice of law to take a job as an office boy. Admittedly he had a wealthy wife at home, but he was clearly in it for the long haul.

Moreover, his awareness of all these devious practices impressed on him that the job of the producer was never-ending. In addition to everything else, you had to be a policeman. You either had to have lieutenants you could trust implicitly or you had to instill such fear in all your subordinates that the possibility of cheating you was unthinkable. No wonder producing was more likely to attract delicatessen owners than poets.

Because the hours were flexible, Merrick spent a lot of time further along 42nd Street, at the theater collection of the New York Public Library, immersing himself in the lore of the theater.

Leonore, who read scripts for David, still looking for something he could produce, devoted herself to being a good Jewish housewife. Her cooking skills had improved greatly since California. Sometimes their dinner guest was a fellow refugee from St. Louis, Tennessee Williams, none of whose plays had yet been produced and whose financial resources were meager.

Some nights, instead of coming home, Merrick would amble

up to 44th Street, to the culinary and social hub of the theater community, Sardi's.

Sardi's bustled at all times of day and night. It was ideally located, across the street from the Shubert Theater, where the busiest New York theatrical management was located. The Shubert Organization consisted essentially of Lee Shubert, who sat in a circular office, where he received petitioners. They described the plays they wanted to produce as succinctly and persuasively as possible, an early instance of the "pitching" that now goes on in TV and movies. If Shubert liked the project, he would put up half the money and rent them a Shubert theater.

Sardi's was a home away from home. When the Tony Awards were instituted, in 1947, the senior Vincent Sardi was given a special Tony, in part for having allowed actors to use his rest rooms while they were "making calls" on producers. It was also a center for theatrical intelligence gathering. Even the coat-check girl, Renee Carroll, was esteemed for her script reading acumen by both aspiring playwrights and producers. Her familiarity with new scripts also made her a valuable contact for actors, who wanted to know what parts might soon be available. She had enough confidence in her taste and ability to make shrewd investments herself.

You were never sure whom you might see at Sardi's. Actors, writers, producers, of course. But, also a Wall Street financier who loved to invest in the theater, like Brock Pemberton. Or Eleanor Roosevelt. Or the philanthropist Mary Lasker.

Dress was not carefully regulated, but Mr. Sardi insisted that men wear jackets and ties, so that Mrs. Roosevelt or Mrs. Lasker would feel comfortable. If you were an impoverished actor, Renee would supply an appropriate jacket and tie. And Mama and Papa Sardi would feed you on the cuff until a career materialized.

Performers would come to Sardi's to unwind after the show. Since curtain time was then 8:30, the shows broke around 11:30, and the actors began arriving closer to midnight. Dress was more casual. In such an atmosphere a man in a pinstripe suit was more likely to stand out. The conductor Milton Rosenstock, who was a regular in the bar of Sardi's, found himself staring at a man in black pinstripes sitting, evening after evening, looking forlorn "way in a corner at the bar."

One evening Rosenstock went over to chat with him and was surprised that so glum and withdrawn a figure was in show business. Merrick told him he was a manager.

"Are you enjoying it?" Rosenstock asked him.

"I'm studying show business," Merrick answered.

"Studying?" Rosenstock repeated.

"I go to the library every day and read reviews."

Rosenstock asked him why. "To get an understanding of critics' taste, the public's taste," Merrick replied. And then he said something that impressed Rosenstock: "It's good to keep in touch with the past."

Not all of his research was about matters of taste. He was also very eager to understand the theater as a business. He would spend a week amassing figures in the library, then show them to Shumlin, pointing out what plays had been most successful over a period of twenty years and in what category.

"If this is so," he asked Shumlin, "Why produce serious plays?" He had outlined Shumlin's career. "Look, you've had a good average of successes," he said. "But if you average them out, you've made only one tenth a year what some other producer has made putting on comedies and musicals."

Merrick, Shumlin later observed, had "a genuine passion for theater, a genuine artistic and esthetic feeling for it. But he has been able to say, 'I don't want that to rule my life.'"

Shumlin's overall memory of Merrick in those years was as "a very sensitive person . . . In those days he spoke very little; when he had something to say it was very much to the point." Shumlin continued to be aware that "there is going on in him a considerable set of emotional conflicts involving his ego. I think David was in very great control of himself in that period—he *visibly* controlled himself —and his quietness was part of that deliberate control."

Shumlin saw the turmoil beneath the placid, businesslike pinstripe suit. He sensed that it took effort for Merrick to maintain a composed surface.

Even if he gave Shumlin and Rosenstock the impression that he was sensitive and thoughtful, even if he gave others who met him in the early Forties the impression of being quiet, deferential and a very good listener, there were other sides to him. One was the opportunist, quick to turn things to his own advantage. One of his colleagues in the Shumlin office, who nurtured a lifelong resentment of Merrick, discovered this fairly early.

Shortly after Merrick arrived in the Shumlin office, Kermit Bloomgarden tried to befriend him. Bloomgarden was seven years older than the new employee. Like Merrick, he was the son of extremely poor Jews. His father had opened the first matzoh factory in Brooklyn, which burned down a month before Passover. (It was, alas, not insured.) Kermit had worked as an accountant and a business manager for several theatrical institutions including the Group Theater.

Like Merrick, Bloomgarden had aspirations to produce; he had already mounted one unsuccessful production. The Shumlin office was flexible. As long as you did your job, you were free to work on your own productions. If they succeeded, your desk would be taken over by another aspirant. If they failed, your desk was still yours.

Despite this flexibility, the Shumlin office had more than its share of tension. Shumlin had a reputation for being a difficult boss. Soon after Merrick began working there Bloomgarden invited him to lunch and warned his new colleague about the boss's idiosyncrasies. Shumlin was not a very communicative person. It was easy to make him angry, hard to predict his moods. Bloomgarden offered the wisdom of several years' experience to the neophyte.

To curry favor, Merrick immediately reported Bloomgarden's observations on his volatile temperament back to Shumlin. Shumlin "thanked" Bloomgarden for "orienting" the new employee. Bloomgarden never forgot Merrick's treachery.

If his early childhood taught him the efficacy of a sharp,

wounding tongue, it can be said that his apprenticeship with Shumlin "bettered the instruction." Shumlin made extremely practical use of his apparently fiery temper. Years later, in a letter to Jo Mielziner, who was then designing a Shumlin production, Merrick wrote, "This is about the time things must be getting tough with Herman. For you, I mean. If screaming and yelling will get him a success, then I'm for him screaming and yelling, but not at you, of course." Merrick would develop his own reputation for screaming and yelling, but he had been taught by a master of the art.

Among his other colleagues was Arthur Beckhard, whom he met in Los Angeles, where Beckhard ran "little theaters" in L.A. and Santa Barbara. Now remembered as a somewhat disreputable Broadway "character," Beckhard lived in a frowzy hotel on West 44th St., romanced would-be actresses, and became a model for Max Bialystok, the seedy, scheming producer Zero Mostel played in Mel Brooks' 1968 satire on show business, *The Producers*.

But when Beckhard arrived on Broadway in the early Thirties, after a brief, prestigious career as a concert manager, he was considered a Bright Young Man, full of promise for the theater. A round, roly-poly man with an infectious, high-pitched giggle, he was known for his sense of humor and his immense charm. He was described as "owlish, seemingly benign, with a soup-strainer black moustache and puckish ways." Merrick and Beckhard—similarly puckish and mustached—must have made an interesting pair.

In 1932 Beckhard had produced a play by an unknown writer, Rose Franken, called *Another Country*, which was enthusiastically received by the critics. The good will generated by this venture served him well for some time. He had a knack for innovation, for unconventional means of financing and for finding new talent. (Among the young people he hired were Henry Fonda and Joshua Logan.)

By 1934, however, despite his genuine theatrical acumen, Beckhard had produced a string of flops and decided to take a screenwriting job with MGM. But he floundered in Hollywood.

By the early Forties he was back in New York, working at a desk in Shumlin's office, his early achievements all but forgotten, a useful object lesson for the young Merrick.

Beckhard and Merrick used to go to the races at Jamaica and Belmont Park together. Merrick had a tendency not to get caught up in the excitement of sporting events. He once asked to be taken to Madison Square Garden for a championship hockey game. As a frenzied crowd raved around him he sat stoically with his coat and homburg on his lap. He was once taken to a similarly frenetic World Series game by a friend. They sat in a box with an excellent view of an extremely close game. The crowd around them was wild with excitement. It was clear from Merrick's distracted air that he would rather be back in his office. Or perhaps he was busy calculating the odds.

Whatever pleasure he took in watching horses run around in circles, he did see them as a way to test a theory. He was known among his friends, Leonore later recalled, as "The Professor," because he had analyzed the odds so carefully.

He had advanced somewhat from the system he had used in East St. Louis, where he only bet on the favorites to "show." As Beckhard recalled, Merrick "had a system that worked. He didn't enjoy watching the horses and he wasn't really a gambler. He'd evolved a system of betting only on certain very low odds. If you bet $200 roughly 10 times a week, you could make $75 a week.

"He was proving his system to me, and under it you could only bet one, two or at the most three races. So you'd sit there and die of boredom all day long because Dave wouldn't let you ruin the system."

Such systems were extremely important to Merrick. To be a producer you had to know how to gamble. Selecting shows was a gamble. Budgeting them was an even greater gamble. Casting them, choosing a director was a way of improving your odds. When *42nd Street* was trying out in Washington, Jerry Orbach came across Merrick backstage and invited him to a poker game in his room. Merrick gestured toward the wings and said, "This is my poker game."

In his apprenticeship in the Shumlin office, his visits to the Public Library, even at the racetrack, Merrick had proved himself an adept and thoughtful student. Now he desperately needed a chance to show what he had learned.

CHAPTER FIVE

ONLY A YEAR AFTER he had arrived in New York Merrick thought he could hitch his star to that of Orson Welles.

Welles, who had been a *wunderkind* on Broadway in the late Thirties, had gone to Hollywood, where he had created a furor with the as-yet-unreleased *Citizen Kane*. On February 5, 1941, Welles made his return to New York known by taking a young actress named Dolores Del Rio to the opening of Philip Barry's *Liberty Jones*. (The play was an allegory in which Liberty, dying on a couch of Luxury, is attended by Drs. Education, Letters, Divinity and Law, who can do nothing for her.)

The morning after the opening, Bill Herz, who had worked with Welles in the Mercury Theater, showed him a dramatization of *Native Son*, Richard Wright's novel about a bright, young Black who commits an ugly, gratuitous murder. The book created a sensation with its unflinching, unstereotyped treatment of its Black characters.

Welles loved the play. The very next day he went to Harlem to begin rehearsing with Canada Lee, who would play the lead. Lee, a former jockey, violinist and prizefighter, had played Banquo in Welles' Mercury Theater production of *Macbeth*.

Merrick realized *Native Son* would make a perfect entree into the Broadway theater. He hadn't had to find the play, and he certainly wouldn't have had the usual producer's concerns of finding the proper director or the proper star.

More important, producing was not just about making money. Lawyers made money. It was about projecting an aura, a mystique. If you just wanted to make money, there were plenty of comedies around that you could produce, but they wouldn't alter the perception people had of you as a schlep from St. Louis. *Native Son*, directed by Orson Welles, would change that image forever.

He immediately phoned Herz. He told him he knew about Welles' enthusiasm for the play. He told Herz he would be willing to finance it—singlehandedly. Could he meet with John Houseman, Welles's second-in-command? Herz arranged the meeting.

Houseman found himself astonished at Merrick's audacity. He sensed that Merrick was new to New York, new to the business, but Merrick gave the impression that he had untold sums to invest. He offered to put up the entire amount required for *Native Son*—$40,000—on the condition that the billing read:

David Merrick Presents

The Orson Welles Production of

Native Son.

Some artists might have accepted such a condition in order to get the money. Houseman knew Welles well enough to tell Merrick that it was out of the question.

The play opened at the St. James Theater March 24, 1941, to admiring reviews. The next day there was a line at the box office. By chance Herz ran into Merrick later that day at Sardi's. Merrick had seen the line and was crestfallen.

"I made a mistake, didn't I?" he asked Herz.

As it happened, he hadn't. Herz had already spoken to the box office manager. The only seats selling were those in the second balcony, which went for 55 cents, not the orchestra seats, which commanded $3.30.

In 1942, a year after *Native Son*, while he was still a Shumlin employee, Merrick was the associate producer of *The Willow and I*, an early play by John Patrick, who would go on to write *Teahouse of the August Moon* and *The Hasty Heart*. The play, produced by Donald Blackwell and Raymond Curtis, starred Martha Scott, Cora Witherspoon and Gregory Peck. The show opened December 10, 1942, and closed January 2, 1943. Merrick had raised some of the money from friends back in St. Louis. When the show closed he sent the wife of one of his hometown investors one of Martha Scott's costumes as a souvenir of the failed enterprise.

If these years were frustrating, the goal of being able to call himself a producer always lying outside his reach, they were nevertheless years in which he was building a foundation, learning his trade, meeting people. In 1942, for example, he began to build a professional relationship with his sometime dinner guest, Tennessee Williams.

In the summer of 1942 Williams, who had yet to be produced on Broadway, showed Merrick a play called *Stairs to the Roof*. Williams wrote to his friend and sometime collaborator Donald Windham, "David Merrick, the Shumlin man, has written me twice and we are sure of a very sympathetic reading there. He is awfully sweet and said some lovely things about *Stairs to the Roof*, which he said would not make any money during these times." (Merrick's judgment was astute. The only production the play ever received during the author's lifetime was at the Pasadena Playhouse, where it played for two weeks in the spring of 1947.)

In 1943 Merrick acted as company manager for a play Arthur Beckhard produced called *And Be My Love*, which starred Walter Hampden. One of the characters in the play was a dog. The Merricks owned a Scottish terrier, which landed the role. Leonore walked the dog to and from the theater every night.

The stage manager, who met her at the stage door every night, was Bill Becker, who became Leonore's lifelong friend. At the time he was struck by her bright blonde hair. It was not the natural color. She had dyed it—clearly to please David. During these years that were filled mainly with frustration for him, she was his staunchest ally.

In 1944 Merrick produced his first play, with Beckhard, *Bright Boy*, by Lt. John Boruff, USNR, an actor with whom the Merricks became very close. On the one hand *Bright Boy* was full of the standard high jinks people expected in plays set on the campus of a boys' prep school. (Carleton Carpenter played a cutup named Shake, short for Shakespeare.) On the other hand, several critics noted that the play was clearly a parable about fascism. Its title character steals money from the other boys only to lend it back to them in what appears—to them—as a noble gesture. He does other boys' homework—out of his contempt for them.

At the end of the play his roommate, a generous, honest soul, toward whom The Bright Boy is especially contemptuous, delivered The Message. One of the reviewers satirized the play's theme as "that we should cure these potential Hitlers while they are young by outsmarting them with the one weapon against which they have no defense—that of understanding and sympathetic pity." Another reviewer noted that when this homily was delivered, "a giggle of incredulity ran through the audience. If the play hadn't been so nice up till then the giggles would have been guffaws."

An attempt was made to build an advertising campaign for the play. One critic complained that the ads quoted him out of context, probably an early instance of Merrick's creative stretch for publicity. It didn't matter. The play closed after 16 performances.

Bright Boy may have taught Merrick that Message Plays were an unwise investment of time and money. *Jeb*, which Shumlin produced, brought the message home even more directly, for, unlike *Bright Boy*, *Jeb* was a play of quality whose Message was timely.

Jeb was by Robert Ardrey, a playwright and screenwriter who later wrote anthropological books, such as *The Territorial Imperative*. *Jeb* was about a Black veteran who returns from World War II minus one leg but with "what for him is a treasure, the ability to run an adding machine, only to discover in his town down South that the adding machine is a white man's job."

The play starred Ossie Davis, Ruby Dee, and the child Reri Grist. It got excellent reviews but closed in a week.

It was not simply a case of the public not being ready for such a play. Part of the problem was that earlier that season there had been a similar play, *Deep Are the Roots*. One critic considered Ardrey's play far the superior of the two, but its timing was unfortunate. *Deep Are the Roots*, the first successful play Bloomgarden produced on leaving Shumlin's office, ran for 477 performances, probably attracting the theatergoers who might have gone to *Jeb*.

The failure of Ardrey's play unnerved Shumlin, who produced nothing at all for several seasons. It may also have reinforced for Merrick, who had been the business manager on *Jeb*, the implications of his question to Shumlin: Why produce serious plays?

In 1946 Merrick solidified his relationship with the two men who remained his most loyal backers for the next two decades, Max Brown and Byron Goldman. Brown, a frustrated playwright who had studied with the famous George Pierce Baker at Harvard, had produced and directed in New York in the late Twenties before devoting himself to the family business, essential oils. Brown sold huge quantities of spearmint, for example, to the Wrigley Company. Brown's family and the headquarters of the business were in Indiana, but in order to maintain his ties to the theater he had his office in the Sardi building.

When Brown first met Merrick he thought the young man did not have long to live. The pain from Merrick's ulcers was so severe Brown thought he was already on his last legs.

Among Brown's friends was Byron Goldman, whose family was related to two multi-million dollar enterprises, one the financial firm of Goldman-Sachs, the other the GGG Clothing Company, a manufacturer of high quality men's suits. From an early age Goldman was smitten with the theater.

Goldman's office was in the GGG Building on 14th Street. In those days the work week was six days, though executives would leave early on Saturday afternoon. On one such Saturday

Goldman went up to visit Brown in his office on West 44th Street. Brown excused himself for a minute, and Goldman waited alone in his office. Suddenly he became aware that on the other side of the frosted glass door, which was ajar, were bulging eyes and a walrus mustache.

"Hello? Hello?" the owner of these features asked, in a nervous, high-pitched voice. When Goldman answered, the eyes and mustache, apparently thrown by the unfamiliar voice, disappeared. A moment later Brown returned, and Goldman recounted the strange incident.

"Oh, that must have been David Merrick," Brown told him.

Soon afterward Brown introduced Goldman to Merrick. A friendship and collaboration began. The three were all stagestruck. Nothing could have given any of them greater pleasure than to find someone with whom to discuss the subject that excited them the most, the theater. Brown and Goldman made it clear to Merrick they would be eager to invest in his productions.

Brown was also impressed with Merrick's idealism. One of Merrick's favorite topics was "ice." Merrick would inveigh against it, declaring that when he became a producer he would have nothing to do with it.

Brown and Goldman saw Merrick at his most charming, his most persuasive. He felt at ease in their company. He was able to relax, to loosen the conscious control over himself that, Shumlin had correctly noted, expressed itself in shyness and silence.

Only once, Goldman recalled long afterward, did Merrick lose control. Merrick and Leonore were having dinner with Brown and his wife and Goldman. In the midst of an otherwise engaging conversation Goldman was shocked to hear Merrick use the word "fuck." In the late Forties it had not yet become an everyday word; in a mixed gathering like this it seemed particularly jarring. The breach in social etiquette reflected, perhaps, the strain Merrick was under and the limits to his ability to repress the anger stored up so many years before.

Yet most people who met him during these years still saw him as shy and retiring. The set designer Oliver Smith, who was one of the founders of American Ballet Theater and who produced plays during the Forties, remembered interviewing Merrick for the position of company manager for a production of Jean Giraudoux's *Ondine*. (Ultimately the production was postponed, and the Giraudoux play did not reach Broadway until 1952.) He knew that Merrick had an excellent reputation as a business manager but was surprised to find him "a shy, reticent man. I was impressed by his knowledge, but he was so self-effacing."

Harold Rome remembered an unobtrusive man representing Shumlin at an early audition of *Wish You Were Here*. Rome, who later had a long association with Merrick, never forgot the remark he made on this occasion. As far as Merrick was concerned, the show was not "classy" enough.

"Classy" was a category that meant a lot to him. It may have been his way of translating Uncle Maurice's esthetic notions of theater into the rougher terms of West 44th St. When Merrick finally left Shumlin's employ, in 1949, it was to co-produce, with another Shumlin employee, Julia Clayburgh, an adaptation of a Rumer Godden novel, *A Candle For St. Jude*. The project was never completed.

Merrick could not justify his own office yet. So he took a room in Max Brown's office in the Sardi building. It wasn't until 1950 that he produced the first show for which he wanted to take credit, *Clutterbuck*.

Clutterbuck, by a genial English comedy writer, Benn Levy, had been a hit during the 1946-47 London season. Levy, a member of the House of Commons, had also written *Springtime for Henry*, which had been a success on both sides of the Atlantic. *Clutterbuck* was old-fashioned when it was new, and although Levy's style of writing did not change, he remained a beloved and respected figure for some time to come. As late as 1959 Laurence Olivier directed one of his plays, *The Tumbler*, in New York, starring Charlton Heston and Rosemary Harris.

Clutterbuck took place aboard a ship cruising the Caribbean. Among the passengers are two longtime girlfriends, each of whom had premarital flings with a man memorably named

Clutterbuck. They have married, respectively, a novelist and a "stuffed shirt" planter, both of whom had affairs with a girl named Melissa. Naturally Clutterbuck and Melissa are also onboard. This was standard West End fare, and though the eminent London critic Harold Hobson might complain that "Clutterbuck doesn't say anything," this was less of a drawback in 1946 than it would be a decade later.

The rights to *Clutterbuck* were secured by a young Denver producer, Irving Jacobs, who, in addition to running the oldest summer theater in the U.S., owned Mammoth Gardens, the Denver equivalent of Madison Square Garden. Jacobs was a pioneer distributor of foreign films.

Not only was *he* classy, but so were the people in his circle. One of his close friends from Denver was Mary Chase, the author of the Pulitzer Prize winning *Harvey*. She invested in *Clutterbuck*. So did the mayor of Denver. Jacobs himself invested $1,000. His co-producer, Merrick, invested $5,000 in the $50,000 production.

Norris Houghton, a gentle soul who would soon co-found one of the most important institutions in New York theater history, the Phoenix Theater, directed *Clutterbuck*. He did not think of Merrick as the producer. He saw him as "shy, rather subdued, but missing not a trick. He sat in the back row and listened to what was happening. I thought he was involved in the legal end of things."

Houghton was correct. Merrick was indeed involved in the legal end of things. It was he who negotiated the artists' contracts, and he demonstrated particular toughness in haggling over the financial terms of Houghton's own contract.

Merrick's chief contribution to *Clutterbuck*, however, was as a promoter. If you happened to be sitting in the lobby of the Waldorf, the Plaza or some other posh hotel during the 1949-50 theater season, you might have heard the bellboy paging a Mr. Clutterbuck in the manner of the popular commercial of the day, "Call for Philip Morris!" You might have noticed that this odd-sounding name also happened to be the title of a Broadway play. Struck by the coincidence, you might have decided to see it. The paging of the nonexistent Mr. Clutterbuck was arranged by Merrick as an unconventional way of bringing his play to people's attention.

More important was an advertising campaign in the *New York Times*. Merrick took small ads above the daily directory listing the basic information about every Broadway show. At first these small ads contained quotes from critics, all of which contained the word sex.

The show had opened December 6, 1949. By February the ads took on a quality entirely their own, coining words: "It's SMARTL!" "Don't be a PRUDL! See . . . Clutterbuck." "It's FOOZLY GOOZLY!"

Around the same time a drawing of Clutterbuck began to appear in the ads, a weasel-like figure wearing a baseball cap backward and with a cigarette in his mouth. Invariably a woman kneels at his feet, crawls toward him or somehow registers awe at his prowess.

Four days a week, doggerel accompanied these drawings. The doggerel was Merrick's. His verse made no pretension to cleverness or wit. The important thing was that it was almost always different. So, however silly it may be, the casual reader of the *Times* might find himself looking at the entertainment ads to see what was happening with Clutterbuck the way he might a favorite cartoon character.

The verse itself admits to being vulgar and childish:

> He's the guy who prowls the decks
> So darned attractive to the other sex,
> CLUTTERBUCK!

> Even without a zither . . .
> He had all the girls in a dither.
> CLUTTERBUCK!

> No matter how stuffy or rigid,
>   With him no gal stays frigid.
>   CLUTTERBUCK!

> We Make No Claim That He's a Saint.
>   As a Matter of Fact We Insist He Ain't.
>   CLUTTERBUCK!

> The Kind of Gal He Likes to Escort
>   Is the Kind of Gal Who'll Be a Good Sport.

> When Moody or in a State of Vex
>   He Calmed Himself with the Weaker Sex.

As the show approached the end of its run, the sexual explicitness of the ads became more desperate. Clutterbuck's cigarette now appeared in a holder, which made it twice as long. Lest the symbolic significance of the cigarette not be entirely clear, the angle at which it jutted forward clarified matters.

Elsewhere in the newspaper were headlines about McCarthyism, the trials of Alger Hiss and Owen Lattimore, frequent labor unrest, the fear of nuclear war, a growing concern about civil rights and increasing instances of disturbing juvenile delinquency. *Clutterbuck*, of course, was supposed to be a relief from these concerns, but one ad declared, "It's RUMORED There'll Be McCarthy Investigations/ Into Clutterbuck's 'Special' Relations." It was an early case of Merrick using whatever was handy to publicize his show.

Despite lukewarm notices, *Clutterbuck* ran for 218 performances. It was considered significant enough to be selected as one of the ten "Best Plays" for an annual volume under that name. Among its companions in the 1949-50 volume were T.S. Eliot's *The Cocktail Party*, Carson McCullers' *The Member of the Wedding*, Jean Giraudoux's *The Enchanted* and William Inge's *Come Back, Little Sheba*.

It was a start.

In 1947 Merrick's childhood friend Eli Pilchik secured a pulpit with a reform congregation in Newark, New Jersey. Pilchik had served in the army during the war (Merrick had ridiculed him for enlisting), had lived in Tulsa just afterward and was now living just across the river. He found that his friend had hardened. All that mattered to him was success.

When Pilchik's first child was born, Merrick reiterated that he wanted no children. They would be a burden and hinder his career. (Pilchik's daughter Susan recalled, as a child, seeing Merrick and Leonore on their infrequent visits to Newark. The sight of Merrick, with his eccentric mustache and his formal pinstripe suit lounging on their sofa made an oddly sinister impression on her.)

At one point Pilchik received a telegram from Merrick informing him that his mother, Celia Margulois, had died and asking if Pilchik would go to St. Louis for the funeral. Pilchik flew out immediately, assuming his friend would want consolation.

His friend never showed up.

Several times during the late Forties Reuben Lapin and his wife visited New York. The first time, just after the war, he asked his former fellow Rambler to find them a reasonable hotel. Merrick would not tell him the name of the hotel he had found. Instead he asked him to bring their bags to the Windsor. When the Lapins arrived they discovered that their "hotel" in New York would be their friends' small, but comfortably furnished apartment.

When they returned to New York a few years later the Lapins were too embarrassed to ask the Merricks again for help. They found their own hotel. But during their visit, Lapin called his old friend, who asked him to come to his office in the Sardi building, from where they would go to lunch.

When Lapin arrived, he heard a familiar voice on the other side of a beaded glass door. He knew it was the voice of his high school friend, but the tone shocked him. Merrick was screaming into the phone. As he listened to the conversation he grew more and more uncomfortable. It was clear that Merrick was berating the man on the other end of the phone for no other reason than to show his power. He seemed to be doing it for the sheer pleasure of venting his rage on someone.

It chilled Lapin. Although his business as a naval architect brought Lapin back to New York many times over the years, he never again looked up Merrick. The Merrick he had heard on the other side of the door was not the friend of his youth. Whatever his shortcomings, David Margulois had been a vulnerable, even pathetic human being. David Merrick was somebody else.

Had he known his friend's misgivings, Merrick might have been delighted. The changes he sought were being achieved.

DAVID MERRICK and JOSHUA LOGAN

present

EZIO PINZA   WALTER SLEZAK

A NEW MUSICAL PLAY

"FANNY"

Musical Play by
S. N. BEHRMAN and JOSHUA LOGAN
(Based on the trilogy of MARCEL PAGNOL)

Music and Lyrics by
HAROLD ROME

Directed by
JOSHUA LOGAN

Scenery and Lighting by
JO MIELZINER

Costumes by
ALVIN COLT

Dances by
HELEN TAMIRIS

Musical Direction
LEHMAN ENGEL

Orchestral Arrangements
PHILIP J. LANG

Musical Continuity
TRUDE RITTMAN

with

FLORENCE HENDERSON · WILLIAM TABBERT

Scene Photos by ZINN ARTHUR
Caricatures by GERALD PRICE
Edited by DICK WEAVER

CHAPTER SIX

O N FEBRUARY 2, 1950, the ad for *Clutterbuck* showed a young woman crawling longingly toward the title character, who sat casually, confidently in a chair. The copy read, "Casanova Couldn't Hold a Candle to . . . CLUTTERBUCK!"

A mere two columns away was an ad the same size. It had the photo of a venerable French film star and the sort of charming, old-fashioned lettering you might find on the canopy of a provincial French bistro. The ad was for a trio of classic French films from the Thirties that were being shown at the Thalia, a tiny revival house on the Upper West Side.

Assuming that he had the usual pride of an author, Merrick, checking on his own creation that day, must have seen the ad for the Marcel Pagnol trilogy about a young woman named Fanny.

Whether he had seen these films as a young man in St. Louis and the ad triggered a happy memory, or whether he was enticed to see them for the first time by their proximity to his own work, *Fanny* came into David Merrick's life and occupied a dominant position for the next five years.

Merrick had now been in New York for ten years. He had developed a reputation as an excellent businessman and a clever huckster. But people still saw him as shy, diffident, even self-effacing. Several people who met him in the Fifties said the melancholy-looking Merrick reminded them of the photograph of Proust on the Modern Library edition of *Remembrance of Things Past.*

In all this time he had only produced one play that he was willing to list on his official biography, *Clutterbuck.* Although *Clutterbuck* had enjoyed a respectable run—one clearly attributable to his own efforts as a promoter—it was not a play that would build a dignified reputation in the field. Writers, young or established, were not going to turn first to the producer of *Clutterbuck* to mount their plays. Nine years had passed since he had offered to put up all the money for *Native Son* simply in exchange for his name above Orson Welles'. Would Welles' response have been any different now? Probably not.

Three years had passed since he left Shumlin's office. He had not had the kind of immediate success Bloomgarden did when *he* left Shumlin. Bloomgarden had produced *Deep are the Roots* and established himself at once as a producer of plays of social significance. Only two years later he had been entrusted with *Death of a Salesman.* With *Clutterbuck* Merrick had only demonstrated his success at getting the maximum mileage out of a piece of amiable fluff. For a man so concerned with proving himself, it was certainly not enough. If no one would bring him the right kind of material, he would have to come up with his own.

Michael Korda once observed that one of the attractions of Hollywood was its intellectual egalitarianism—the man who had the idea for a movie about a gorilla on top of the Empire State Building was the equal of the man who decided to film *War and Peace.* If anything, the former was a superior producer, since the determining factor was, of course, the grosses.

In the theater, "moguls" were made by musicals. If you had the idea, you took precedence over the writer. When you produced a *play,* you were, in effect, the writer's servant. When you produced a musical, the writers were yours. Like a Hollywood studio, you could regard the "talent" as expendable. It was not their vision that mattered. It was yours.

The trick was to find the right material. *Fanny,* the work of the internationally renowned French writer and filmmaker Marcel Pagnol, was, for Merrick, an audacious choice, if only because Pagnol's writing was so tenaciously rooted in the soil of his native Provence. Most of the big Broadway musicals of the Forties were intensely, unabashedly American. By contrast, Pagnol's *Fanny* trilogy was extremely worldly, set on the resolutely un-American docks of Marseilles. Fanny, the daughter of a fishmonger, is quite unlike the coquettish, winsome, virginal heroines of the American musicals. Hers is the story of an unwed mother.

She is deeply in love with the handsome Marius, the son of Cesar, a waterfront barkeeper. Marius loves Fanny, but after a night of lovemaking that leaves her pregnant, he runs away to his first love, the sea. Fanny's mother, Honorine, arranges for her to marry Panisse, a successful merchant, an older, childless widower who is delighted at the prospect of gaining both a wife and an heir. Long afterward, Marius returns. Their son is growing up, and Marius wants him to know who his actual father is. Cesar teaches him that paternity goes beyond planting a seed.

Throughout the three films many poignant moments center on fatherhood—what it means to be a father and how difficult it is to be a true father, how desperately men want to be good fathers. This motif may have been what attracted Merrick to this complex and deep work of art. His own father had failed miserably at the task of fatherhood. So, years later, would Merrick himself. His own attitude toward children was well known: they would be an impediment to his career. At this early stage, when Merrick still wanted desperately to prove himself as a producer, it seems telling that the work he chose to show his mettle was a drama about paternity.

When Merrick decided he wanted to bring the *Fanny* trilogy to Broadway, he was not dealing with a young writer eager for New York success. Pagnol, born in a suburb of Marseilles in 1905, was elected to the Academie Française in 1947, the youngest person and the first filmmaker to be so honored. In France, members of the Academy are referred to as "the Immortals." This was not a man likely to be won over by conventional American business ploys.

The first task Merrick faced was simply acquiring the rights to *Fanny*. He besieged Pagnol with letters, telegrams and telephone calls, none of which was answered.

Finally Merrick decided to plant himself in front of Pagnol's door in Monte Carlo. Instead of writing for an appointment, he simply flew over and rang the bell. Fortuitously, Pagnol answered the door himself. The tall, smooth-faced, suave Provencal was confronted with a formally dressed American whose eyes stared with formidable intensity and whose voice had a funereal ardor. Merrick immediately launched into his pitch. Pagnol was amused that anyone would go to as much trouble as Merrick had and invited him in.

American musicals have seldom appealed to the French, but Pagnol was hardly a typical Frenchman. The son of a teacher, he himself became an English teacher at seventeen. His facility was so great that he was able to teach Chaucer in the original Middle English. He sought and won a position in Paris at the prestigious Lycee Condorcet, mainly as a way of supporting himself in the capital while he pursued his theatrical career.

He was surprisingly appreciative of American popular art. He translated both *Hamlet* and *A Midsummer Night's Dream* into French, and, in the preface to the latter, he declared that the only director who could really bring it to the screen was Walt Disney, whom he considered "a great poetic genius."

In addition to understanding popular entertainment, Pagnol was, like Merrick, a shrewd businessman. Early in the Thirties, as he supervised the transference of his *Fanny* trilogy to the screen, he saw how important it was to control every part of the process. By the time he came to direct the last part of the trilogy, *Cesar*, he owned his own studio, his own labs and his own distribution companies.

Pagnol's financial success was ended by World War II. During the war a sympathetic German overseer, a former theater director, told him the only way he could avoid making propaganda films for the Nazis would be to declare himself ill. To prove he could not make films any more, he had to sell his film empire. When the war was over, he had nothing, which may have increased his receptivity to Merrick's cajoling. Merrick later estimated he traveled about 25,000 miles in three trips to secure the rights to the material. The task was further complicated by the necessity of securing rights to some of the material from Pagnol's illegitimate children.

Securing the rights was only the beginning. Making these three French films into one American musical was like having an uncut stone potentially worth a fortune. Only the right gem cutter could realize its value. To entrust it to anyone other than a master was to risk losing everything.

Merrick had a literal translation made of the three plays. He first approached Albert Hackett and Frances Goodrich to adapt them into a musical. Shumlin had produced and directed one of their plays, *The Great Big Doorstep*, starring Dorothy Gish and Louis Calhern, while Merrick worked for him. Later Bloomgarden would produce their adaptation of *The Diary of Anne Frank*.

The Hacketts wanted to set *Fanny* in New England. Merrick sensed that this was not right for the material. He paid them for the work they had done and started over. The script adaptation, he realized, was important, but what really mattered was the score. What would make *Fanny* a successful musical would be a great score. The powerful emotions in the story needed to be translated into soaring melodies. Considering the richness of the story, was it presumptuous to approach the most successful practitioners of musical theater, Richard Rodgers and Oscar Hammerstein?

To reach them, he had to have an intercessor. The most logical choice was Joshua Logan, the director who had given the team the idea for *South Pacific*. As he had with Pagnol, Merrick besieged Logan relentlessly. He phoned. He relayed messages through friends. His name, however, meant nothing to Logan.

Someone had to arrange an introduction. One possibility was

Arthur Beckhardt, who had been one of Logan's first employers during the Depression. Unfortunately, he had not treated Logan well, overworking him and constantly borrowing money he never repaid. Beckhardt was not likely to be an ingratiating ambassador.

Another possibility was the scenic designer Jo Mielziner, whom Merrick had also met during the Shumlin years. In January of 1952 Merrick had a meeting with him and gave him the literal translations. Mielziner responded with great enthusiasm, expressing an eagerness "to make more of a contribution than the conventional designer's approach." Merrick told him how much he wanted Logan to be a part of the project.

Mielziner wrote Logan a letter, enclosing the scripts, which he admitted were a "bad" literal translation, but adding that "they give a great deal of the charm and warmth of the characters." Merrick, he writes Logan, was frank that he wanted Mielziner as the designer and also wanted Mielziner to suggest the material as "a future directorial assignment for you [Logan]."

Mielziner, too, thought the material should be Americanized. His suggestion was relocating the story to either New Orleans or Tampico, both of which "have the Latin and Southern warmth." Merrick said nothing. Mielziner's creative ideas were secondary to his ability to reach Logan.

Logan agreed to meet with Merrick. Like Pagnol, he was won over by Merrick's boundless enthusiasm for the material. He agreed with Merrick that if Rodgers and Hammerstein—who, in 1952, had two blockbusters on Broadway, *South Pacific* and *The King and I*—were to write *Fanny*, it would undoubtedly be a hit.

When Logan approached his former collaborators, they balked. They refused to have as insignificant a figure as Merrick as their producer. Merrick had a lot to gain by being associated with them. They could gain nothing by joining forces with the producer of *Clutterbuck*.

Logan explained to the imperious pair that Merrick had already gone to great lengths to secure the rights to the material. Surely they must understand he would not accede to having his producer's credit usurped by them.

Rodgers and Hammerstein were very particular about billing. Logan, who wrote significant chunks of *South Pacific*, had had to fight with them to have his authorship credited. He had to fight even harder and much longer to receive any royalties as an author. He did not receive any such royalties until years after both Rodgers and Hammerstein were dead.

Logan came back to Merrick with the unhappy news that while the pair wanted very much to work on the material, they did not want to work with him. Perhaps because he still nurtured regrets about *Native Son*, Merrick remained surprisingly deferential. Although the project had already cost him a great deal of time and money, he did not blow up when Rodgers and Hammerstein insisted their billing must be above the title: "Rodgers and Hammerstein Present *Fanny*." He told Logan to tell them he would accept that formula if, just below the title, he could have, "In Association with David Merrick."

Logan relayed the offer. They refused. Rodgers, who generally acted as spokesman for the pair, went further. He said he did not want to be associated in any way with "that schmuck."

It was an insult Merrick never forgot. According to the Merrick Apocrypha whenever he spotted Rodgers in a nightclub with an orchestra he slipped the bandleader several hundred dollars *not* to play any Rodgers tunes. It may have happened once or twice; but then again, it may not have happened at all, since Merrick hated nightclubs. He hated smoke. He hated being recognized. Like Proust, he didn't like being jostled.

The inability to bring the three men together left Logan in a quandary. He had fallen in love with *Fanny*. He certainly knew that to work on the show with Rodgers and Hammerstein offered a greater likelihood for success than to work on it with the co-producer of *Clutterbuck*. And yet he felt a certain sympathy for Merrick, in addition, no doubt, to a lingering wariness about working with Rodgers and Hammerstein. Without the sympathy on the one hand or the wariness on the other, he might simply have proposed to Merrick that the others buy the rights from him. But Logan could not make up his mind.

In a letter from Paris dated September 12, 1952, Merrick wrote Mielziner that Pagnol had granted him a lengthy extension on the contract, "which puts me in the clear so far as the Broadway pirates go." But, Merrick continues, "Josh continues to baffle me. He's excited enough about the project but he still wants to go back to R&H—He seems to be afraid without them. He'll have to decide soon."

Merrick himself made one last attempt to woo Rodgers. He had introduced Logan to Pagnol in Monte Carlo, and the two men got along famously. Merrick wrote to Rodgers describing the meeting: "We were saying how magnificent it could be if you and Mr. Hammerstein were to write it and how sad that the negotiations ended so quickly." Merrick suggests that perhaps their respective lawyers were at fault. His tone is humble when he writes, "I know that I haven't had good results when I have allowed an attorney to negotiate with writers or other creative people. I think the eventual working relationship on the kind of deal we were trying to arrange is much too personal to be concluded by anyone other than the principals."

If only Rodgers would consent to a meeting, Merrick felt he could persuade Rodgers to work on the project. As it was, Logan's inability to reach a decision left Merrick back at square one. From an early point he had seen Logan as vital to the project. Merrick had in fact given Mielziner one per cent of his own royalties for having effected the introduction to Logan, a gesture of generosity unparalleled in his later career.

But during the period when Logan was waffling, Merrick could not remain inactive. He had to make other contingency arrangements. He got in touch with Burton Lane, the composer of *Finian's Rainbow*. Lane was eager to do *Fanny*. There was, however, a problem. He was under contract for a three-picture deal at MGM with Alan Jay Lerner.

Merrick couldn't wait. If Lane could disengage himself, *Fanny* was his. Lane was so thrilled with the prospect that he spent a weekend making frantic phone calls to the Coast. By

Monday morning he was disengaged from Metro and available for Merrick.

He phoned Merrick to give him the good news.

"David, I'm free," he announced jubilantly.

There was silence on the other end of the phone.

"David, are you there?" Lane asked.

Merrick had unhappy news. The very weekend Lane had wriggled out of his $250,000 contract with MGM, Logan had decided to stick with Merrick. But he insisted he could not work with a composer he had never worked with before and demanded Merrick hire Harold Rome, with whom he was working on *Wish You Were Here*.

Logan's decision to remain with Merrick may have stemmed from his own squabbles with Rodgers and Hammerstein (with whom, in fact, he never again collaborated.) Perhaps he felt that if he co-produced *Fanny* with Merrick, at least he would be the senior partner. Years later both sides agreed it was a pity Merrick and the songwriters could not come to terms. Hammerstein later told Logan he regretted they had not written *Fanny*. Merrick told friends he wouldn't have had to promote it so feverishly if they had written it.

Logan had three projects he had to finish before he could commit himself wholly to *Fanny*. One was in its final stages, *Wish You Were Here*, a musical about Jews summering in the Catskills. Another was a comedy by the veteran Broadway writer Norman Krasna called *Kind Sir*. The third was a new play by William Inge called *Picnic*.

Logan invited Merrick to come along on the pre-Broadway tour of *Kind Sir*, a comedy about an affair between a suave diplomat and an actress, played by Charles Boyer and Mary Martin. (The material was later fashioned into the film *Indiscreet*, which starred Cary Grant and Ingrid Bergman.)

Perhaps because he recognized how slight the material was, Logan, who both produced and directed *Kind Sir*, had decided to begin the pre-Broadway tour not in any of the traditional cities

(Boston, New Haven or Philadelphia), but rather in New Orleans, where no modern play had ever begun its pre-Broadway life. The sheer novelty of the event might generate publicity to offset any disconcerting reviews.

There was another reason Logan may have wanted to begin the tour in New Orleans. He had grown up in the nearby town of Mansfield. Though he had achieved extraordinary fame and recognition in New York, he may have wanted to have his celebrity validated near the site of childhood insecurities and unhappiness that had been as traumatic as Merrick's.

The opening night, September 26, 1953, was a great success. The local critics were aware that the play had problems, but they were gentlemanly in their assessment of it. For the audience, the evening was one of great glamour.

Merrick had contributed to the festivity of the opening with great sensitivity. He had sent Logan a gift he knew would touch him deeply. The Logans collected automatons, mechanical dolls of an exotic nature that were built in France around the turn of the century. (One of the dolls in their collection, a grinning blackamoor in a fez who performed the shell game, had been given to them by Coco Chanel.) In New Orleans Merrick found one that smoked a hookah. It was a perfect way to seal their growing friendship.

The excitement of the opening of *Kind Sir*, however, was overshadowed by an event that took place a few days later. Logan had worked on the show during a period of intense personal strain and exhaustion. On opening night he did not have the look of triumph the occasion warranted. He looked distraught, profoundly so. A few days later he suffered a severe nervous breakdown. He was taken from his hotel in a straitjacket.

Among those watching the heartbreaking scene was Merrick. In late September, New Orleans is still extremely hot. Everyone else was sweating profusely. Merrick, in his dark suit and homburg, didn't have a drop of sweat on him, but his face betrayed extreme horror. "It was as if he saw his life going out in a straitjacket," Richard Halliday, Mary Martin's husband, recalled.

Merrick, who, at an early age, had seen his mother taken to a sanitarium, had every reason to be horrified. He had spent the last three years working on what would be his first musical, the first Broadway show that could really demonstrate his ability as a producer. And now the man who was his co-producer, who would write and direct the show, was being taken to an asylum.

In view of his later reputation for ruthlessness, it seems remarkable that, faced with this crisis, Merrick exhibited great patience, loyalty and understanding. He decided to wait for Logan to recover.

It may have been less personal attachment than strategic importance. When Merrick met him, Logan was at the zenith of his career, his name invariably coupled with that of Elia Kazan as the two most innovative forces in the American theater. Logan offered him an entree into the inner circles of the theater that no amount of industriousness or shrewdness could give.

Fortunately, Logan's stay in the New Orleans hospital after his breakdown was relatively short. By early 1954 he was able to begin directing *Picnic*.

It was on the pre-Broadway tour of *Picnic* that Logan saw that Merrick's theatrical acumen went beyond merely financial or entrepreneurial. Inge's play was about the effect of a virile, uninhibited young man on the population of a severely repressed Midwestern town. It was receiving bad notices on its tryout and Logan could not figure out why.

Merrick came to see the show and blamed its failure on the leading man, Ralph Meeker. He realized that the women in the audience found him very attractive, but the men regarded him warily. "Every time he comes on stage I bristle," he told Logan. "He has so much bragadoccio. He's so loathsome."

Logan realized Merrick had put his finger on why the audience resented the character, which Meeker, he felt, was playing very ably. Logan wrote a short scene, with Inge's approval, in which another character said of the young man that he boasts a lot but has done most of the things he boasts about. It was a way of telling the audience to be patient, Logan felt, and not to judge the young man too quickly. The inclusion of the scene changed subsequent audiences' response to the character, and to the play—favorably.

Although the two men began to trust each other, the relationship was not without its tensions. In addition to being part of the "royalty" of the New York theater, the Logans were socially very prominent. To be invited to the Logans' parties in River House, a grand apartment building overlooking the East River, meant a great deal. To know that glamorous parties were being given and that David and Leonore Merrick were not invited wounded Merrick bitterly. "I'm good enough to work with him, but not good enough for their parties," he complained.

Merrick was still an outsider. All in all, however, he had no qualms about sharing his producer's credit for *Fanny* with one of the most respected figures in the American theater.

Merrick had learned on *Clutterbuck* the necessity of having first class talent. With Logan as his co-producer he was able to assemble a team of writers and a cast of the first rank.

Logan invited S.N. Behrman to collaborate with him on the adaptation of the screenplays. Behrman, a writer whose refinement and wit almost seem more English than American, had written several plays for the Lunts. If he seemed more at home in the high style of drawing room comedy or on the pages of *The New Yorker* than he did in "show business," he nevertheless confessed, "I have always loved musical comedies and revues; they are the last stand of glamour in a bedeviled world."

For the score Logan wanted Harold Rome, with whom he had worked on *Wish You Were Here*. Rome, who had studied architecture at Yale, had turned to songwriting during the Depression. The first song he sold was to Gypsy Rose Lee in 1935. Two years later he wrote material for a revue to be performed by members of the International Ladies Garment Workers' Union. *Pins and Needles* was intended as a weekend show in which the ILGWU Players would entertain their fellow garment workers. The critics, however, were so enthusiastic about the revue that it became a hot ticket. Limousines lined up outside the Labor Theater (formerly the Princess) on West 39th Street. Inside, celebrities and fashionplates sat side by side with the ILGWU rank and file as they heard the chorus chant, "Sing me a song of social significance!"

In 1946 Rome wrote *Call Me Mister*, a musical revue about soldiers returning from World War II. Then in 1952 came *Wish You Were Here*, which produced two hit songs, the title number and "Where Did the Night Go?" The score may not have been "classy" enough when Merrick heard it auditioned a few years earlier, but its commercial success made Rome, in Merrick's eyes, a desirable commodity.

The cast was equally impressive. The towering Metropolitan Opera bass Ezio Pinza played Cesar, the father of the wayward Marius. Walter Slezak played Panisse, the man who marries Fanny to legitimize her child. For the title role Merrick and Logan had originally wanted Mary Martin, who did not feel it was suitable for her. Eventually the role went to the vivacious Florence Henderson, who had understudied Martin in *South Pacific*.

With some help from the playwright and "doctor" Paul Osborn, Behrman and Logan achieved a remarkably economical retelling of Pagnol's trilogy. Even more remarkable was Rome's score, a work of great emotional power.

Rome himself felt the reason the material spoke so deeply to both him and Logan is that at heart it was about parenthood. Unable to have children of their own, both the Logans and the Romes had adopted children. This may account for the deep poignancy in the musical's frequent assertions that true fatherhood comes from love and care, not simply physical paternity.

For Merrick, *Fanny* was really his first major encounter with "the artistic process." With *Clutterbuck*, he had produced an already proven play. Here he watched the show grow from a seedling into a flower. If the years with Shumlin were years in which he was consciously keeping his temper under control, the months in which *Fanny* was written and rehearsed were an even more severe trial of his self-control.

There was, for example, Pinza. Possessed of a huge voice and an arresting stage presence, Pinza had been a leading bass all over the world for several decades. He was, however, musically illiterate. The sixty operatic roles he knew he had learned by rote. For *Fanny* he had to have his music six months in advance. At one point Rome came to him with a new song he thought would add a lot to the show. He played it for Pinza, who said, "My boy, it's a great song. But we open in four weeks," apparently not enough time for him to master it.

Moreover, Pinza hated change (So much so that he when he watched baseball games on TV he became angry when the manager substituted players.) He threatened to quit the show when, after it opened to mixed reviews, Logan made some changes in the opening scene that did not involve him at all. He withdrew his threat when, listening in the wings, he sensed the audience's quicker involvement in the story.

Because Pinza had such great stage presence, his co-star, Walter Slezak feared he would be overshadowed. During rehearsals he was unfailingly polite to Pinza. Afterward he would confide his fears to Logan.

Logan, of course, was used to dealing with such problems and kept both men working together agreeably, but he was himself haunted by insecurity. At one rehearsal he apologized to the cast for having directed them the previous day without really understanding what he was doing. He charmed the cast with this confession of inadequacy, but not his co-producer.

On a similar occasion during the Boston tryout, when Logan was begging their indulgence for his indecisiveness, Merrick stalked out of the theater. Standing in the alley near the stage door, he turned, quite literally, purple with rage. "I'm paying Joshua Logan a Joshua Logan salary," he fumed, "but what I've got in there is Norrie Houghton."

In a few years such explosions would not take place out of ear range. They would be done in full view of the cast and creators, chilling everyone. But Merrick had not yet learned how effective his tantrums might be. Sometimes he was not even aware that he had thrown them. As it happened, Florence Rome, the composer's wife, had heard his explosion about Logan at the stage door. When she mentioned it to him the next day, he said he could not remember shouting it.

Merrick launched a national drive to publicize *Fanny*, an unprecedented campaign at a time when advertising for Broadway shows was generally limited to New York newspapers, as if the theater were primarily a local amusement. Merrick, with the wisdom peculiar to provincials, knew better. Ads appeared in *Time, Good Housekeeping, Harper's Bazaar, Vogue* and *Better Homes and Gardens*. He also spent an unheard of $4,400 to place ads in Sunday papers in Atlanta, Baltimore, Chicago, Cincinnati, Detroit, Houston, Memphis, Minneapolis and even St. Louis. He placed ads in the *Paris Herald-Tribune* on the principle that the bulk of transatlantic passengers still traveled by boat and passed through New York on their way home. The one musical they were likely to know about before they docked was *Fanny*. These were the fruits of the research he had conducted while he worked for Shumlin.

The show opened at the Majestic Theater on November 4, 1954, to lukewarm reviews. Nevertheless business was excellent, doubtless because of the presence of Pinza and Slezak. The first week after the opening the box office cleared $66,000. The figure, regarded as high for a week's take, was bolstered by the fact that the top price for *Fanny* was an unprecedented $7.50, which had contributed to the hefty advance sale of $950,000.

Merrick considered the ticket price rise necessary for two reasons, both to insure a speedy return for his investors and to make certain there was enough money for promotion. He achieved both aims. The sixty-five backers who had contributed to the show's $300,000 capitalization were repaid in seventeen weeks. As for promotion, Merrick was relentless.

Fanny featured a belly dancer named Nejla Ates. Although she appeared onstage for barely a minute she achieved great stardom in the publicity. One morning at dawn a papier-mache statue of her was erected in Central Park. The police and the tabloids were notified simultaneously. Both groups arrived around the same time, so the papers all carried photographs of the police removing the offending statue, a way of bringing *Fanny* to the attention of those who did not read theater reviews.

A photograph of Ates was erected outside the Majestic. At 11'8" this was the tallest photographic blow-up on West 44th Street, and police were concerned about the flow of traffic as motorists slowed down to ogle it.

Until 1960 there was a waterfall as part of a billboard in Times Square across from the Astor Hotel. Shortly after *Fanny* opened Merrick rented a room on the fifth floor of the Astor from which to project a slide with a *Fanny* ad on the water, which would act as a natural, iridescent screen. Merrick and an associate carried suitcases with the parts for the large projector into the room. They made the mistake of inquiring whether the hotel's wiring would be adequate for the high-powered projector. Their inquiry raised suspicions. Their scheme was uncovered and they were ejected from the hotel.

During the summer of 1955 Merrick's press agents asked the U.S. Weather Bureau if the next hurricane, which was supposed to be called Flora, could be renamed Fanny. They were informed that names for hurricanes are established the previous February at a meeting of weather bureaus from all over the U.S. and Canada. Merrick was invited to their next meeting. The item appeared in newspapers across the country.

In the summer of 1956, journalists attending the wedding of Grace Kelly to Prince Ranier reported skywriting over Monaco urging them to see *Fanny*.

Merrick employed three press agents (at a total of $600 a week) to devise such stunts, which extended the show's run. He himself handled the negotiations that maximized the show's weekly profits. No detail was too small to escape his attention.

He wrangled with Slezak over the relatively minor matter of a dresser's salary. Slezak's contract stipulated that Merrick supply him with a dresser. But the contract did not specify the dresser's salary. The standard rate was $75 a week. Merrick would only pay $60. "I just couldn't understand it," Slezak complained. "He was quibbling about $15 a week on a show that was budgeted to earn $19,400 a month in profits."

When he negotiated for the Majestic Theater he took advantage of the fact that two independent theaters, the 46th Street and the Mark Hellinger, were available in order to extract unusually advantageous terms from the Shubert Organization. At capacity the show could gross a weekly $65,900. In a normal contract, everything over $46,000 would be shared on a percentage basis with the theater owner. In the contract Merrick won from the Shuberts, everything over that sum would accrue to Logan and himself.

He had also inserted a clause in very fine print in the contract with the Shuberts. It concerned the breakoff point of low weekly grosses for several weeks running, when the Shuberts had the right to evict *Fanny* to make room for a more lucrative tenant. In the small print Merrick specified a much smaller figure than what was standard.

When the normal breakoff point was reached, the Shuberts phoned him about posting the customary closing notice. Feigning surprise, Merrick said the breakoff point had not yet been reached. That can't be, the Shuberts' lawyer insisted. Why, Merrick countered, he had the contract right here. As he suspected, they had signed it without reading it carefully. After that the Shuberts treated contracts with Merrick more seriously.

When, despite mediocre reviews, *Fanny* became a hot ticket, Merrick initiated what would be a career-long assault on ticket brokers. He announced they would not get any tickets for *Fanny* for the first two months of the run, theoretically in order to give the public first chance at seats. As it happened, there was a huge advance and many theater parties, which meant he was not dependent on brokers. He told them that there were between 150-200 seats at the back of the orchestra that were available. Despite the fact that these were not prime locations, one of the brokers asked Merrick for permission to buy them so he could at least offer his customers something before January 15. Merrick offered similar terms to other brokers.

To beat Slezak on the trivial matter of a dresser's salary was hardly a significant conquest. But to have so quickly established control over the ticket brokers was a major victory. On a later show a public announcement that no tickets would be offered to brokers was followed by a private meeting with brokers, in which he told them he would indeed supply them with tickets, but at an exorbitant fee, almost double the box office price. It seems likely that this practice of gouging brokers began with *Fanny*. All this shrewdness from the man who had earlier protested with horror at the idea of "ice."

Another Merrick practice that began with *Fanny* was sending the backers hazy, imprecise statements of the grosses. The backers complained that instead of detailed weekly breakdowns, including the box office grosses, they received a general financial statement.

A week after an article appeared in *Variety* outlining the backers' grievances, Merrick took out an advertisement in the form of a Western Union telegram. It read:

Knowing of your Melancholy Preoccupation with box-office grosses, and since you have been guessing the *Fanny* grosses erroneously of late, here is the way you can determine *Fanny* grosses for last week and henceforth. Whenever the average high temperature for the preceding week is 63 degrees or less, the gross for *Fanny* is $63,000. Thereafter the gross recedes in inverse ratio to the rise in the average high temperature for the week. For example, if the average high temperature is 64 degrees then our gross is $62,000, and if the average high temperature for the week is 75 degrees then our gross is $51,000. This will make it easy for you and if any change in the trend occurs I will keep you informed. Your obedient servant

David Merrick

Whether composing press releases, *Clutterbuck* doggerel, or idiosyncratic advertisements, part of Merrick's identity as a producer would be bound up with his eccentric authorial voice. Merrick was an author, of sorts. His most notable creation was David Merrick, and in this letter, his voice—comic, condescending, cynical, almost contemptuous—emerges robust and fearless.

When *Fanny* had been running more than a year, Elliot Norton of the *Boston Globe*, came to take a second look. He described it as a much better show than it had been on opening night. He had only one complaint, the actress who had replaced Florence Henderson in the title role. He described her as "a pretty brunette, with a baby voice which is effective at only one point. When she sings the delightful 'Be Kind To Your Parents,' she relaxes for a moment from a stiff kind of ingenue pose and does herself proud. She should be able to sing with that same kind of clarity and ease during the rest of the evening, shouldn't she?"

The actress may have been guilty of everything Norton said, but her position with the show was secure. She was Merrick's girlfriend. She had been in the road company and been brought back to take over the lead when Henderson left. This made the relationship easier for Merrick, who had frequently followed her out of town.

Such relationships were also traditionally part of the role of the Broadway producer. His marriage to Leonore had begun to sour sometime before. Well before *Fanny*, she confided to the Pilchiks that she required surgery but that Merrick would not hear of it. He was abusive of the doctor who had recommended it. He considered it a waste of money, though, until *Fanny*, most of their money was still really hers. However he behaved toward her, her money and her unbounded loyalty was his. Presumably to help him save money, she even helped sew costumes for *Fanny*.

During the run of *Fanny* an exasperated press agent, trying to locate Merrick, had the temerity to call him at home. When Leonore answered, she told him Merrick was not there.

"If you find him, let me know," she added.

S.N. Behrman had described Merrick as "a mouse trying to be

a rat." But then Behrman had not had daily contact with him. Those who did would have considered this a grave underestimation of his character.

CHAPTER SEVEN

L EONORE WAS SEEING LESS AND LESS of her husband. When he left in the morning, she would ask him what he would like for dinner. No particular reply.

"Roast beef?" she would ask.

"Fine," he'd say.

She would ask when she might expect him, and he might say, "7:30." She would have dinner ready, but she would not see him until 11:30 or even later.

By the mid-Fifties the Merricks had separated. As his career gained momentum he began to distance himself from old friends. The Pilchiks now seldom saw the Merricks.

But Leonore only expanded her own circle of friends, all of whom became closer to her when Merrick left. Her friends persuaded Leonore to restore her hair to its natural strawberry blonde. She began to sell real estate, both in New York and Connecticut. Her natural vivacity, which had been overshadowed by his strange and formidable personality, now came into its own.

Curiously, the separation improved Merrick's attitude toward her. Around the end of the decade Leonore had a hysterectomy. This time there was no question from Merrick about the necessity of the surgery. He made it possible for her to have the best care, even arranging a limousine to take her to and from the hospital.

Making the occasional magnanimous gesture was easier than the day to day business of being a husband. The idea of Home, after all, held little appeal for him. Nothing he had experienced of Home as a child had given him any feeling it was something worth building for himself. He was a man, a close associate observed, whose "ideal style of life would have been to have a hotel room and bring girlfriends in."

He did not need a home in the way many men did, as a place to relax or to recharge his batteries. His batteries were perpetually charged, with phenomenal energy. Sleeping seemed to be an insignificant part of his schedule. He had meetings from breakfast on. He always carried his passport with him. If, for example, he happened to overhear at lunch that a play of interest had opened in London, he took a taxi from the restaurant directly to the airport. Once, having liked a book he read on the plane—*The Rievers* by William Faulkner—he took a cab from the airport directly to Random House to secure the rights. (By the early Sixties he estimated he spent an average of $80,000 a year on options. Often these projects never materialized, but they invariably brought him publicity. So it was money well spent.)

Leonore Merrick (second from right) at the Plaza in 1957, with (l to r) Wilson Lehr, May Freedman, wife of agent Harold Freedman, and Bill Becker.

During the great years, when he routinely produced six or seven shows a season, he was often on the road, observing a show trying out in Boston, another in Philadelphia, flying to Los Angeles or Chicago, London or Paris, to scout material he might bring in.

By contrast, Home was a reminder of all the years of waiting for something to happen. Years of being deferential to people who had kept him waiting, like Logan. Or people who had treated him shabbily, like Rodgers.

At home he was, in effect, still Margulois. Outside he was being accepted more and more as David Merrick. Increasingly he came to see that his real home was the theater, where he could be the man he set out to be.

The show that established Merrick as a producer of "classy" material was an English production of an American play. It was a revival of a play that Herman Shumlin had produced during the 1938-1939 season, Thornton Wilder's *The Merchant of Yonkers*, which had been a flop.

Shumlin's production opened in December of 1938, the same year Wilder won a Pulitzer Prize for *Our Town*.

The Merchant of Yonkers was an adaptation of a play by the 19th century Viennese comic writer and performer Johann Nestroy, who had himself adapted it from an 18th century English comedy, John Oxenford's *A Day Well Spent*. Wilder transposed the farcical events of a day in 19th century Vienna to the 1890s in New York. He made one significant addition, the role of a scheming, aggressive woman named Dolly Gallagher Levi. It was written for Ruth Gordon.

The tiny, peppery Gordon is probably best remembered for her screen performances in *Rosemary's Baby* and *Harold and Maude*. But she had a distinguished career on Broadway before she became an actress and writer in Hollywood. With her husband Garson Kanin, the author of *Born Yesterday*, she wrote screenplays for such films as *Adam's Rib* and *Pat and Mike*.

From her 1915 debut at the age of nineteen as one of the Lost

Boys in Maude Adams' revival of *Peter Pan*, Gordon's work invariably aroused admiration, even from her fellow actresses. When Gordon played Nora in Wilder's adaptation of *A Doll's House*, Lynn Fontanne stopped the applause after her own performance in Giraudoux's *Amphitryon '38* to urge her audience to see Gordon do Ibsen. When Gordon scored an enormous success in London as Mrs. Pinchwife in Wycherly's *The Country Wife*, it was Helen Hayes, who, along with Gilbert Miller, produced and backed a New York production of the play.

Though Gordon loved the role of Dolly Gallagher Levi, she was disturbed that *The Merchant of Yonkers* was going to be directed by Max Reinhart, a distinguished refugee from Hitler's Germany whose English was minimal. She did not like the idea that she could not communicate with her director except through an interpreter. She and Wilder quarreled and, with regrets, she turned the role down.

The role of Dolly Levi, which Wilder had tailored to Gordon, went instead to Jane Cowl. Though Cowl's skills were formidable, many attributed the failure of the play to her heavy-handed approach, which, added to Reinhardt's equally heavy-handed Middle European style, weighed down the very American farce Wilder had written. The play, which opened December 28, 1938, closed after thiry-nine performances.

Fourteen years later, in 1952, the great English director Tyrone Guthrie, who had directed Gordon in her London triumph as Mrs. Pinchwife, was in New York to direct *Carmen* at the Metropolitan Opera. He had rented a house near the Kanins' in Turtle Bay. After dinner one night, they came up with a project in which he could again direct her: *The Merchant of Yonkers*.

To give it a chance to evolve outside the commercial arena, Guthrie scheduled it for the 1954 Edinburgh Festival, where he was the artistic director. He also arranged with his old friend and colleague, the British producer Hugh "Binkie" Beaumont, for a London run.

Wilder's modest revisions resulted in a retitled play *The Matchmaker*. First in Edinburgh and then in London, it was a wild success. The young critic Kenneth Tynan caught a glimpse of its future when he wrote that it "has the impact of a musical comedy from which the music has been discarded as superfluous."

One night during the spring of 1955, Beaumont, an elegant man who was admired for his ability to handle the delicate egos of actors and especially actresses, knocked on Gordon's dressing room door after the performance. He brought in Merrick, whom Kanin vaguely remembered as a personable young man who used to work for Herman Shumlin.

When Merrick entered the dressing room the first impression he gave was of enormous shyness. He could not help being deferential to Gordon, who had been a transatlantic star while he was still struggling to get through law school. He bit his nails as he professed his love for the play and her performance. He was eager to bring it to New York.

Without missing a beat, Gordon thanked him and said she had only one condition. He must bring over the whole company and Guthrie's production. Apart from the difficulties such an arrangement would create with Actors' Equity in New York, it would make the undertaking unusually expensive.

Merrick questioned the need for importing the whole cast. "David, I know more about the theater than you do," she told him. "If you change one thing, it affects the whole balance of a production. We've been playing it for a year. If you start replacing people, it will be a different show."

Merrick took respectful leave of the dressing room but over the next few weeks he would reappear at the Haymarket, with increasing frequency, to bargain with her. Each time he would agree to a few more actors. During this tentative courtship, Brooks Atkinson visited London to do his annual survey of the season. He gave *The Matchmaker* a rave review.

This tipped the balance, and Merrick finally acceded to Gordon's original demand. As a co-production of Merrick and the Theater Guild (which held the rights to the original play), *The Matchmaker* was announced for the 1955-56 Broadway season. Merrick already saw it as a potential musical. An early report said that when *The Matchmaker* arrived in New York it would have a few songs by Harold Rome, which, of course, it did not.

Actors' Equity did raise the problems Merrick had anticipated. A higher percentage of the company, they demanded, had to be American. For now, Merrick had to respect their wishes, just as he had had to yield to Gordon's. But he was taking the measure of everyone he dealt with. How firm were they about these demands? How far could you push them?

In order to mollify both Gordon and Equity, Merrick was able to hire understudies and other backstage personnel to achieve the necessary percentage of Americans in the company. Some of the British actors had to be sent home. One such casualty was the young English actor Alec McCowen, who was replaced in Philadelphia by the young American Robert Morse.

Years later, during the eternal run of *Hello, Dolly!* McCowen was seated next to Merrick in the Oak Room of the Plaza. Merrick leaned over to him and said, "You've been doing great things since *The Matchmaker*."

Alluding to *Dolly*, McCowen said, "You're still doing it."

"Touche," Merrick said. It was one of the few times an actor bettered him in banter. But, as Merrick observed later in their conversation, "Actors never forgive me for having employed them."

It was in the course of bringing *The Matchmaker* to Broadway that Merrick solidified his relationship with the agent Harold Freedman. Freedman's clients included Thornton Wilder, Jean Kerr, Paul Osborn, Arthur Laurents, John Osborne, Philip Barry, Clifford Odets, Robert Sherwood, Jerome Lawrence and Robert E. Lee, and Mary Chase.

When Freedman died, in 1966, Jean Kerr said, "He made the theater seem an occupation for gentlemen," and S.N. Behrman eulogized, "There's a kind of vulgar aura about the word 'agent,' and it's a pity, especially so far as Harold Freedman was concerned. He was a man of exquisite sensibility, a man who had a passion to get the very best work out of his writers." Norris Houghton remembered him as "a very dour, grumpy-looking kind of man. But when you got to know him he was all charm."

A Scottish Jew, he was also apparently a man of secrecy, a model perhaps for Merrick himself, who loved to surround his simplest actions with a conspiratorial aura. Among Freedman's achievements for Merrick would be the sale of *Hello, Dolly!* to the movies for $2 million, an extraordinary figure in 1964.

Merrick had reason to be grateful to him, and Freedman had much reason to be grateful to Merrick, which may explain why, in his living room, at the very center of a grand piano whose top was bedecked with autographed photos, presided the photo of David Merrick.

Merrick was learning that, with some effort, you could get the upper hand on the unions; you could cow ticket brokers and backers. The one thing beyond anyone's absolute control was the audience. *The Matchmaker* tried out in Philadelphia and Boston before its New York opening. Everyone was baffled by the fact that the very same staging and timing that had drawn huge laughs in London drew many fewer in Philadelphia. Part of the problem was simply that the theater was much larger than the Haymarket. But both Merrick and Wilder were disturbed by the audience's impassive response to what seemed a surefire entertainment. "This is not the show I bought in London," Merrick said ominously to Gordon.

Tyrone Guthrie was, in his own way, as rigorous a tyrant as Merrick. At 6'4", Guthrie conveyed authority simply by his presence, which was commanding and firm, but kindly. Merrick communicated his extreme unease to the whole company, including the normally gentle Wilder. Guthrie recalled, "He and Merrick fell upon me as if I were a fraudulent dog-breeder who had sold them a mongrel with a forged pedigree. Undignified scenes in hotel rooms kept coming to the boil and were only averted by the extreme tact and good sense of Garson Kanin who, an old friend both of Thornton and myself, could act as a sort of umpire and impose order and restraint on us two foolish, excited, elderly gentlemen."

By the time *The Matchmaker* reached Boston, it had begun to find a rhythm American audiences responded to. Everything seemed to be working well. All the laughs that could be counted on in London were back in place. But the first few performances in New York reduced the company again to despair. They were benefit performances, for which patrons had paid as much as $50 for a $6.90 ticket. If they were there for the sake of charity, they showed none to the performers. They chatted openly during the performance.

At the end of these ordeals, however, came opening night, December 5, 1955—the first time the cast played to a New York audience that genuinely wanted to see the play. Their relief was immense, their performances exhilarating.

The reviews were enthusiastic. Louis Kronenberger, who remembered *The Merchant of Yonkers*, wrote "*The Matchmaker* now worked amazingly well—careened where it once only clattered, and where it once sputtered, here exploded sky-high." It was a happy vindication for Wilder. Walter Kerr, in the *Herald-Tribune*, said that in his adaptation of Nestroy's comedy, Wilder "has actually been busy taking a veritable inventory of the comic spirit, itemizing all the dives into cupboards, all the absurd uprushings of love, and even all the picture-postcard settings that have ever done duty in the cause of merriment . . . Director Tyrone Guthrie has leaped into the fray with the enthusiasm of a child tearing open birthday presents."

John Chapman in the *Daily News*, called it "a long, lunatic ballet which has had no peer since the early Marx Brothers movies. With sound—words written by Thornton Wilder and spoken, growled, squealed and roared by a wonderful company—it is ten times funnier."

With such reviews Merrick's savvy promotional machinations were unnecessary. This, of course, did not deter him. The promotions, after all, were *his* creative contribution. He had a man in a chimpanzee outfit driving around midtown in a Rolls Royce on which there was a sign, "I'm Driving My Master to see *The Matchmaker.*"

Here, at last, was the unmitigated success he had so long sought. Even this triumph, curiously, did not ease his feelings of insecurity. Shortly after *The Matchmaker* opened he appeared on a radio talk show with Robert Whitehead, a former actor who began producing in 1947 with a celebrated revival of *Medea* starring Judith Anderson. Whitehead had produced Carson McCullers' *The Member of the Wedding* the same season Merrick produced *Clutterbuck.*

Whitehead was on the show to talk about his production of Marlowe's *Tamburlane the Great,* also directed by Guthrie. But he expressed his unabashed admiration for *The Matchmaker* on the air. Merrick, instead of responding with gratitude, became flustered and uneasy. Whitehead attributed Merrick's surprising lack of graciousness to his essentially suspicious nature. It was inconceivable to him that a colleague might praise or, as in this case, assist him unless there were some hidden agenda.

CHAPTER EIGHT

I N JULY OF 1956, when both *Fanny* and *The Matchmaker* were going strong, a story on the front page of the *New York Times* announced a campaign to finance the construction of a new cultural center on the Upper West Side of Manhattan. The site—Lincoln Square, at 64th and Broadway—was a slum, but in a few years, the article promised, it would boast a new home for the Metropolitan Opera and a concert hall that would house the New York Philharmonic when Carnegie Hall would be torn down, only a few years hence. There would also be a theater.

At the end of the long story, the reporter, Ross Parmenter, one of the *Times*'s music critics, waxed eloquent. "The men behind the project," he wrote, feel "that the creation of the center will show other countries that the United States is not, as some think, a Caliban, or savage, among nations. It will show that the United States is so concerned about culture that it has created an outstanding center for it."

The men behind the project were not upstarts like Merrick. They included John D. Rockefeller III, who would head an Exploratory Committee to raise funds for the center. Nevertheless the mind-set of even such established figures reflected a general American sense of being, by comparison to Europeans, cultural parvenus.

Lincoln Center was one of the numerous arts centers all across the country that began to take shape during the Fifties. From the perspective of several decades later, it seems clear that, for the most part, these arts centers were a greater boon to local contractors than they were to "the arts." At the time, of course, they were seen as harbingers of a new cultural dawn.

These edifices appeared on the scene just as Merrick was getting his first taste of success. Planned and financed by municipalities, these arts centers were often seen as a way of revitalizing decaying downtown areas. It was as if cities were discovering what Merrick had seen, that nothing transforms your image as radically as association with the arts.

What was not immediately apparent was that these arts centers would define a new approach to financing the arts. They would be run by corporate boards, not by plucky entrepreneurs. It would be harder to launch the kind of career Merrick had once these institutions were entrenched. They would be more concerned with prestige than profit. They were essentially faceless, as unadorned and unembellished as their bland granite and marble facades.

They reinforced the communal ego, not the individual one. They would have been of no use to the young Margulois.

Had Merrick been interested merely in financial success, he might have been content to import a *Matchmaker* from London every few seasons and produce a new musical every other year. Conventional success, however, was not what he was after. To be a success was not the same as to be a presence, a force.

For a child whose sense of identity had been so fragile, so battered, there was something reassuring about looking from his office window across 44th Street to the marquee of the Majestic Theater. There, above the names of Ezio Pinza and Walter Slezak, was the name of David Merrick, the same size as that of the veteran producer-director Joshua Logan. Around the corner on 45th Street, David Merrick's name stood alone atop those of Thornton Wilder and Ruth Gordon.

Throughout his career Merrick made a great production over

window cards, posters about two feet high that stood in the windows of ticket brokers, bookstores, barber shops, drug stores, supermarkets, etc. It was a form of free advertising. Merrick said he did it to bolster the egos of his actors, who would be thrilled to find their names all over the city. But it was also a way of bolstering his own.

He would drive advertising people crazy over this relatively minor form of promotion. They could submit a dozen different designs for window cards before he might approve one. (He would, of course, refuse to pay for all the others.) One might be rejected because the lettering was not right, another because the shade of red was wrong, yet another because of the proportions of the drawing.

It was, of course, not really a matter of the lettering, the color or the drawing. Each window card was the equivalent of the letters SPQR on the paving stones of Rome, the manifestation of an imperial presence and thus something that required precision and infinite care.

Multiple manifestations at frequent intervals were necessary to keep the Merrick legend alive. One or two shows a season could not have given him the *presence* he needed on Broadway and in the city at large.

Admittedly a huge output had its practical advantages as well. It gave him a bargaining ploy. If he had all the sets for his shows built in one shop, he expected that shop to give him a deal on the cost. If he had one agency handle all his ads, he would ask that agency to make some concessions. There was another bookkeeping advantage when it came to advertising. If you took a high number of lines, the newspaper would give you a break on the cost. Merrick would bill the individual productions the standard rate. The newspaper billed Merrick a somewhat lower rate. Merrick saw no reason why he should not pocket the difference.

He had also discovered an advantageous clause in standard Equity contracts. One actor could only understudy three roles. The contract did not, however, stipulate how many shows these roles might be in. If Merrick happened to have three plays next door to one another on West 45th Street, why might one actor not serve as understudy for them all?

Another reason to bring in so many shows a season was to secure theaters. He might book a highbrow British drama into a theater for a limited run as a way of reserving the space for a potentially smash musical due to come in a few months later.

Yet another reason for the sheer number of shows he would produce in any season was his fear of failure. If one of the shows were a flop, he could persuade himself that it did not matter, since three more potential hits were on their way in.

His ability to mount five or six shows a season (in one season, eight) was a way of proving his prowess to a world that had begun by not taking him very seriously. To his credit, the volume, at least in the early years, was never attained at the expense of quality.

The name David Merrick on a marquee or a window card was an assurance of taste, of class.

What enabled him to be so productive and to maintain such high standards was a first-class staff. In the early years this meant two men in particular, Jack Schlissel and Neil Hartley.

Schlissel, a graduate of CCNY, had begun his career as a book-keeper with the firm of Pinto, Winokur and Pagano, which handled the accounts of many Broadway firms. He had been a company manager for Bloomgarden, a general manager for George Abbott and Robert Fryer on their musical *A Tree Grows in Brooklyn,* and had been business manager for the Pittsburgh Civic Light Opera.

He began his association with Merrick as company manager of *Fanny.* It was around this time that Merrick left Max Brown's quarters in the Sardi building to take his own next door in the St. James Theater Building. Schlissel's title was changed to general manager, but, without any further aggrandizement of title, his importance to Merrick increased steadily. He negotiated most of the contracts, including the talent and the deals for the rental of the theaters. He handled Merrick's dealings with the unions and supervised ticket sales, both at the box office and through the mail. He made the deals with the brokers and the theater party agents.

Even Merrick admitted Schlissel put in a fourteen-hour day six days a week, as strenuous a schedule as Merrick himself kept. In 1959 there was an "in" joke in Paddy Chayefsky's play *The Tenth Man*. Chayefsky named one of his characters Schlissel. At the beginning of the play one of the characters invites him to go to the cemetery to look at his prospective grave. "Why not, what else have I got to do?" Schlissel answers, a joke to anyone who knew how busy Schlissel was.

Short and muscular, Schlissel gave the impression he was a tough Seventh Avenue garment manufacturer. His zestful, earthy manner made him very popular with the ladies who brokered theater parties, and who enjoyed flirting with him. Schlissel was a good conversationalist, on subjects as diverse as baseball and grand opera.

Merrick, however, had not hired him for his conversational skills. Schlissel was Merrick's hatchet man, the man who had to do the dirty work, and he could play his role with relish. Merrick's propmaster, Leo Herbert, once gave him a prop axe with stage blood and hair on it, which he displayed proudly in his office.

Even Schlissel was wary of Merrick. Schlissel's assistant, Jay Kingwill, had once reported to Merrick that one of the shows was sold out for the week. Schlissel was upset. "Never give Merrick the right figures," he said. "If we're wrong he'll be annoyed, and I don't want him to be annoyed."

Those who liked Schlissel said he was never malicious on his own initiative, that he simply treated people the way Merrick wanted them treated.

Others thought he took pleasure in an unpleasant job. A young man who thought he was a steady part of the Merrick office had been a stage manager on a musical that was closing. As he supervised the load-out of the set the young man was asked by Schlissel, "How does it feel to be out of work?"

"Well, this show is closing, but I'll be back in the office Monday morning," he said.

"No, you won't," Schlissel informed him, casually. "You're fired."

On one of her tours of *Hello, Dolly!*, Carol Channing was informed by Schlissel that she would not have a budget for her own sound man, someone she considered indispensable in view of the huge amphitheaters with poor acoustics in which she would be performing. She had no choice, she decided, but to spend $200 per week of her own salary to hire the sound man she wanted.

"When Mr. Merrick found out about it, he was very apologetic," Channing recalled. "He took me to lunch and gave me a gift certificate for $20,000 at Bergdorf's." It was the amount she had dispensed in the course of the tour. Apart from a way of apologizing for "Schlissel's tightfistedness," Channing conceded, the lunch was a pretext to offer her a role in another Merrick project, a play called *Four on a Garden*. Whether Merrick would have made the gesture if he didn't need her again is a question hardly worth asking.

In most cases Schlissel knew instinctively what Merrick wanted. Merrick and Schlissel were a well-drilled team. Merrick could be particularly frightening on the phone. He would raise an argument with some hapless artist to a fever pitch, then slam down the phone. A minute later the artist's phone would ring. It would be Schlissel, there to pick up the pieces. Sometimes the ploy would have been orchestrated in advance. Other times, if you happened to be in Merrick's outer office, you would see him rushing out of his own office and into Schlissel's to bark orders on what to do.

On one such occasion, after Merrick had slammed down the phone, Schlissel handled his assignment with some humor. When the writer Bob Merrill heard Merrick slam down the phone, he was dazed. Barely a minute later his phone rang. Merrill answered it warily. It was Schlissel, who said, in Yiddish, "Du vaisst deh mishigoss (you understand the craziness)."

Though Schlissel was invariably the "bad" cop, Merrick might play either role. But the office also had someone who was always allowed to play the "good" cop. That was Neil Hartley, who had the title director of production. There would be times when a show was out of town and Merrick would throw a tantrum, threatening to close it Saturday night. He would storm out and leave the creative staff terrified and bewildered. Once they got over their initial shock and had begun to find solutions to their problems, they always knew where to find Neil Hartley. And they knew that Hartley always knew where to find Merrick.

A Virginian by birth, extremely handsome, firm and authoritative in a gentlemanly way, Hartley commanded an affection neither Merrick nor Schlissel could. When he came onto the scene, people recalled, it was like the arrival of royalty. Merrick and Schlissel stirred up the waters. Hartley calmed them.

Hartley became especially useful as Merrick imported more and more shows from London. After his service in the navy, Hartley had lived in London. He understood the British and he projected the kind of class the British associated with the theater, a class they did not often find in New York. Hartley was also a first rate man of the theater. Once, when *Stop the World—I Want to Get Off* was on tour, it got dreadful reviews in Milwaukee. Hartley flew out and totally redirected it. When it opened a week later in Chicago, it got raves.

Another important addition to Merrick's team was his attorney, William Fitelson, a glowering bulldog of a man whose belligerence matched and sometimes exceeded his client's. Even Fitelson, however, was a man passionately in love with the theater. In 1946 he had started a production company and hired one of the founders of the Group Theater, Lee Strasberg, to scout scripts for him.

Over the years many—but by no means all—of the men who worked for Merrick were homosexual. This was not by chance. It was the result of calculation on Merrick's part. He had analyzed the matter. As he told the writer Jerome Weidman, "The theater 'wakes up' at six in the evening. If you're dealing with straight people, they're thinking about going home and having dinner with their families. All the troubles in the theater start at 7:00 and continue until the curtain comes down. The only people who can lead this kind of life are people who don't have to worry about families. Homosexuals have no other place to go."

"It's as if he instinctively knew they were the kind of people he could work with," Weidman observed, "the kind of people he could dominate."

Merrick did manage to inspire absolute loyalty from his employees. Before Emanuel Azenberg came to work in the Merrick office as a company manager, he would occasionally drive to work with his neighbor, Jack Schlissel. One morning, when they arrived on 44th Street, they saw a line forming at the box office of a theater where a rival's show had opened to good reviews the night before.

"Isn't that wonderful?" Azenberg asked Schlissel rhetorically.

"That's why you're not working for us," Schlissel told him. Schlissel mirrored his boss's belief that it was not enough for him to succeed. Others must fail. Merrick employees were expected to be on call at all hours of night or day. He did not sleep much. Why should they? (Azenberg once had to wait at a Detroit airport at 3 a.m. for a prop plane bearing a briefcase his boss had inadvertently left in Cleveland.)

The only reason people who worked in the Merrick office had Sunday off was that the elevator in the St. James Building did not work that day. On the other six days it was manned until 11:30 p.m., when the workday was obliged to end.

That the welfare of the Merrick office must take precedence over everything was thoroughly ingrained even in the mind of Sylvia Schwartz, who came to work the switchboard in 1959 and remained until 1972. When her husband died she was very touched that Merrick came to the funeral. When she turned around to see who else had come she was stunned to see the key personnel from all the Merrick box offices. For a second her grief was upstaged by the concern of a perfect Merrick employee:

"Thank God it's not a Wednesday."

From his earliest years in New York, when, late in the evening, he was more likely to be at the bar of Sardi's than his apartment in the Windsor, Merrick himself had never felt more at home any place than he did in the environs of the theater.

The mid-Fifties, when Merrick's career began to take wing, was an unusually propitious moment for someone who would build his reputation both as an importer of foreign plays and as a creator of musicals. Broadway had always been a bazaar that offered a great variety of merchandise—plays, revues, musicals, burlesque, vaudeville. Until the Fifties the goods on display had a provincial quality. The onset of the Cold War might have been expected to intensify the American-ness of what was offered. In fact, it was the opposite. Broadway had never been more cosmopolitan.

The 1955-56 season, to which *The Matchmaker* added so much luster, was representative. Though Wilder's play was vintage Americana, it had been refurbished by an English director. There were conventional American comedies like *No Time for Sergeants*, starring Andy Griffith, *The Desk Set*, with Shirley Booth, *The Great Sebastians*, a vehicle for the Lunts, and an adaptation of Eudora Welty's novel *The Ponder Heart*.

There were serious American plays like Arthur Miller's *A View From the Bridge*, Michael Gazzo's *A Hatful of Rain*, with the young Ben Gazzara and Shelley Winters, and Paddy Chayefsky's *Middle of the Night*, which starred Edward G. Robinson and featured the young Gena Rowlands and Anne Jackson.

It was a great season for musicals: *My Fair Lady* and *The Most Happy Fella* opened within a six week period that also included a vehicle for Sammy Davis Jr., *Mr. Wonderful*. No doubt to Merrick's satisfaction, Rodgers and Hammerstein had the biggest flop of their careers that season, *Pipe Dream*.

There were English plays, such as Enid Bagnold's *The Chalk Garden*, and a revival of Noel Coward's *Fallen Angels* that starred Nancy Walker. Joyce Grenfell appeared in a one-woman show. There were also two distinguished French plays, Jean Anouilh's *The Lark* (adapted by Lillian Hellman) and Jean Giraudoux's

Tiger at the Gates (translated by the British poet Christopher Fry). The Comedie Francaise itself visited New York for two weeks.

Orson Welles, who had broken his leg in one of the final rehearsals for *King Lear*, played the title role in a wheelchair at the City Center, where, the same season, Tallulah Bankhead played Blanche du Bois in *A Streetcar Named Desire*. Earl Hyman played Mister Johnson in an adaptation of Joyce Cary's novel. Also that season New York got its first taste of the theater of Samuel Beckett, when *Waiting for Godot* made a brief and controversial appearance in a production best remembered for the performance of Bert Lahr.

It was in these years that Tyrone Guthrie declared that the greatest experimental theater in the world was Broadway, since revivals were, especially by comparison to London, few. Most of what was produced was new, and often—as in the work of Tennessee Williams—quite daring.

Starting in the early Sixties, experimentalism took on more radical, more explicitly political connotations and found other havens. The word "Broadway" ceased to be a noun denoting a street or an industry. Increasingly it became an epithet. In the years when Merrick was steadily conquering it, however, "Broadway" was undeniably a word connoting prestige. Its lights may have seemed garish, but it conferred distinction on those who toiled in their glare.

CHAPTER NINE

I N THE FALL OF 1957 Merrick opened three shows in a little over a month. It was a pattern he would repeat over the years to confirm his prodigious presence. If he had spaced the openings over a period of several months, whether or not they were successful, it would not have had the same impact. It would not have given the impression of an extraordinary prolific genius.

The first of the three was a play Merrick had seen in 1956, when he was in London for the opening of *Fanny*. He had been urged to see the work of a young writer at the Royal Court Theater. Located in the fashionable borough of Chelsea, for many years the Royal Court had done revivals of classics. Now, a group called the English Stage Company, under the leadership of George Devine, had leased the theater and was embarking on a program of new plays. In its first such season the Royal Court had presented a remarkable debut play by a 27-year-old actor, John Osborne, *Look Back In Anger*.

Osborne's play depicted a group of disaffected young people railing against the hollowness and stodginess of postwar Britain. Even its ostensible lack of action set it apart from the predictable, well-made plays of the West End. What most set it apart, however, was the abrasive voice of its leading character, Jimmy Porter, the first of a generation of "angry young men" that enlivened British writing for the next decade. *Look Back In Anger* was

Merrick at his desk, 1960.

unmistakably the work of a major new force in London theater.

Was it too parochial for American tastes? Could an American audience identify with disaffected working class British youth? Broadway audiences had always been snobbishly responsive to English drawing room comedies, but *Look Back In Anger*, though it had sharp humor, was a far cry from the congenial *Clutterbuck*. It seemed a huge risk for New York.

Nevertheless Merrick found the play getting under his skin. When he went back to New York he found himself discussing it with friends and backers Brown and Goldman. He gave a script to Goldman, who agreed that the highly original play should come to New York.

So did a man named Ed Kook, who ran an innovative lighting business from an office near Brown's in the Sardi building. Kook, who at one point established a foundation to help young playwrights, told Merrick that if he was so taken with the play, he must produce it in New York. (Many years later, in one of Merrick's rare testimonials, he acknowledged how important Kook's voice was in deciding to take the risk.)

It was hardly a simple matter. Merrick had eventually seen why Ruth Gordon made him import the entire cast of *The Matchmaker*. How much more essential would it be to import an English cast in a play that caught so intimately the specific mood of England in its current malaise.

Fortunately it was a cast of six, as opposed to the sixteen in the Wilder play. They were, however, all unknowns. Newcomers even in London, what kind of draw would they have in New York? And what were his chances of convincing Equity that these unknown actors were essential to the play's success in New York?

Nevertheless, Merrick decided he would fight for the British cast. In the case of *The Matchmaker*, he had felt his way with Equity. He now knew enough to sense that the belligerence that served him so well in other areas of negotiation would be effective with the actors' union. "I'm a lawyer, and I know more about your rules and contracts than you do," he informed an Equity official. His tactics worked. The entire cast was allowed to come to New York.

The role of Jimmy Porter was taken by Kenneth Haigh, who was supposed to come to New York in a musical called *Cranks* in the spring of 1957. Had he done so, he could not have appeared in *Anger* in the fall, since Equity demanded there be six months between an "alien's" appearances. Because he recognized the importance of Jimmy Porter to his career, Haigh withdrew from *Cranks.* (He was replaced by a young performer named Anthony Newley.)

Among the other young actors were Mary Ure and Alan Bates. They were directed by an equally young director, who, like Osborne, was a former president of the Oxford University Dramatic Society. Tony Richardson would also direct most of Osborne's subsequent plays in London and New York before receiving international acclaim in 1963 for his film *Tom Jones.*

In retrospect, the collection of talent seems amazing, but there was no way of knowing in 1957 that it would succeed. Merrick was so concerned that the play might fail that he decided to open it in New York without an out-of-town tryout, to minimize the losses on his $40,000 investment. He also made a shrewd observation during rehearsals. The actors were speaking in authentic lower class accents that might not be easy for American audiences to understand. He hired a vocal coach to help them modify their accents.

Merrick gave *Look Back In Anger* all the benefits of his promotional imagination. The advertising featured a steamy drawing that really does not reflect the play at all. It showed a nude woman and man in a passionate embrace on the floor. Though most of the New York newspapers accepted the ad, the *Times* refused to run it, even when assured no such scene took place in the play.

The strident, accusatory tone of the play was much less threatening to Americans than it had been to the British. New York embraced Osborne quite readily. Some of the reviews noted the play's longueurs, but almost all recognized Osborne as a writer of importance.

Apparently not *all* the audiences were able to take Osborne's play in their stride. A few weeks after the New York opening, there was a disturbing moment in the first act. A young woman, shocked by Jimmy Porter's cynicism, went up to the stage and hit him with her umbrella. By chance some members of the press were in the audience, and the story made news not just in New York but in newspapers across the country.

So did the revelation, a few days later, that the woman who struck Kenneth Haigh was not an irate customer but an actress. Merrick had paid her $250 to create a little bit of news about his play. (He also paid $3,000 to a man named Jim Moran, a publicist with a knack for extravagant ideas like this one.) Merrick had taken almost no one into his confidence. Even the journalists in the audience were there on some other pretext, so when the incident occurred virtually everyone believed it was genuine. Someone who had breakfast with Merrick the morning after the incident was, in hindsight, impressed with his acting ability, that is, with the sincerity of his denials that the incident was a stunt.

Apart from introducing New York to a significant writer, producing *Look Back In Anger* solidified Merrick's relationship with the Royal Court, which was quickly becoming one of the most important theatrical institutions in London. It was a relationship that lasted healthily for about a dozen years, the most productive of Merrick's career, guaranteeing the Royal Court welcome American revenues, guaranteeing Merrick a reliable source of plays that would reinforce his image as a purveyor of "classy" merchandise.

On October 10, just ten days after *Look Back In Anger* opened, Merrick introduced another British import, Peter Ustinov's *Romanoff and Juliet*. Ustinov was also a young writer but hardly an iconoclastic one. His play was a Cold War parody of Shakespeare, set in the capital of some mythical European country where the embassies of the U.S. and the Soviet Union face each other across the main square. The ambassadors' children are the ideologically star-crossed lovers. Ustinov himself played the role of an updated Friar Lawrence, solving the problems of the young couple with greater efficiency, charm and success than his counterpart in Shakespeare.

Merrick had learned that fine tuning was required to calibrate the rhythms of a comedy to American audiences, especially since Ustinov was both author and star of *Romanoff.* To direct the Broadway production, Merrick hired one of the most distinguished figures in the American theater, George S. Kaufman, who had once been the theater editor of the New York Times. He was also the collaborator of Moss Hart on such beloved comedies as *You Can't Take It With You*, which had won the Pulitzer Prize, and *The Man Who Came to Dinner*. Kaufman was also a respected director and play "doctor."

By the time Merrick hired him to direct the Ustinov play he was also a very sick man. Over the past few years he had suffered a series of strokes. Serious illness had kept him from working for two years, and even his last assignment, directing the Cole Porter musical *Silk Stockings*, had ended unhappily. He had been fired in a cruel manner by the producers, Feuer and Martin, whom he characterized as "Jed Harris rolled into two."

Kaufman, however, loved working, and Merrick persuaded him to come out of retirement to help Ustinov acclimate an American cast to his comic rhythms. Kaufman told Merrick he might not be able to finish the job. Merrick told him, "I'll take that chance."

However much his return to the theater may have helped Kaufman's spirits, it was clear that he was not contributing his usual polish to the show. He could only spend three or four hours a day at rehearsal. Ustinov remembered him "sit[ting] around listlessly . . . like a deck chair that could never be folded up correctly." Ustinov respected Kaufman but felt he was adding nothing to *Romanoff and Juliet*.

Ustinov found Merrick obdurate. He seemed to be more protective of Kaufman than of the show. In Boston Ustinov begged Merrick to fire him, "I will close the show if you want me to," Merrick told him, "but I will not fire George S. Kaufman."

In these early years Merrick was very conscious of the keen sense of aristocracy in the theater. By behaving so paternally toward Kaufman, Merrick was advancing his own right to a be part of that aristocracy. He had first glimpsed its existence as he had grown closer to Joshua Logan. In later years it would have given him a confirmation of his own power to fire so legendary a figure. At this point it was more important to preserve the link to tradition than to sever it.

It has been suggested that Merrick hired a "doctor" to watch the show and give notes to the actors privately. That would have been unlikely, since one of the actresses in the show, Natalie Schaeffer, was an old, close friend of Kaufman's and would have reported back to him. While Ustinov himself took a stronger hand in bringing the show to Broadway, the actors felt his primary concern was securing his own laughs rather than theirs.

Nevertheless the reviews were strong enough to give Merrick his second hit in ten days. This guaranteed the show a healthy run in New York and, according to the contract, several months in which Ustinov would tour across America.

The part Ustinov played in *Romanoff and Juliet* was a strenuous one. Ustinov had created the role for himself, but it was stated in the contract that there would be a sixteen-week period during the road tour when he could not play it because he would be making the film *Spartacus*. Merrick had technically "leased" the play from Ustinov. Working on the assumption that no one could play the role as well as the author, Merrick had arranged that the rights would revert to Ustinov for those sixteen weeks.

Well, in fact, there was one actor who could have played it. Merrick himself had thought of him—Bert Lahr. He had offered Lahr a chance to do it in New York, but he had fumbled the negotiations, and Lahr had declined.

Charles Bowden, a producer and director who knew both Ustinov and Lahr, realized how unfortunate it would be to disband the company for sixteen weeks. During that time many would get new jobs. When it was time to resume the tour it would probably be with a new cast who would require extensive rehearsal to bring the comedy back to peak running form. He also saw an opportunity to produce a lucrative sixteen-week engagement. He called Lahr and asked if he would do the part in Chicago during the sixteen weeks Ustinov could not. Lahr was enthusiastic.

Ustinov called Merrick to inform him of the good news. Moments later, stunned, he called Bowden to say Merrick was in "a wild fury" that someone else had been able to persuade Lahr to do a role Merrick hadn't. Apart from the personal affront Merrick was doubtless angry that he would be deprived of sixteen weeks' profits.

Bowden did not hear from Merrick personally, but shortly thereafter Schlissel called to remind Bowden that there was some paperwork that needed to be formalized and signed, since Bowden would be using the physical production that belonged to Merrick. The lawyers were working on it, Schlissel told him, and the papers would be ready the week between Christmas and New Year's.

Every day that week Schlissel would call to say the papers were not yet ready. Finally he told Bowden and his partner, Richard Barr, who would later be known as the discoverer and producer of Edward Albee, that the papers should be ready some time the afternoon of December 31. He suggested Bowden and Barr come to Merrick's office around 6:00 that evening.

When Bowden and Barr arrived they were shown into a tiny room with one chair and a radiator without its cover. The radiator was going full blast. The room was stifling. One hour went by. Two. Three. From time to time Schlissel would open the door to say that the lawyers had still not finished. Nothing about his cheerful, unapologetic manner suggested there was anything odd about keeping two businessmen waiting an unconscionably long time on New Year's Eve.

It was after 9:00. No sounds issued from the surrounding offices. Barr became livid. "He's going to leave us here," he told Bowden. "He's going to humiliate us."

Bowden knew that Barr was right, that Merrick was probably

trying to maneuver them into a position where some verbal altercation might provide a pretext not to sign the contracts. Bowden looked at Barr and told him, "If it *kills* you, when that door opens, you put on your biggest smile."

Barr understood Bowden's point. When Schlissel finally ushered them into Merrick's office, they saw a gleeful smile on Merrick's face. The two men, managing to feign holiday cheer, shouted "Happy New Year!" to him. Their message had the best possible effect.

"David got quite green," Bowden recalled. "He looked at us with hatred and loathing. He signed the contracts with such hatred that the pen tore through the paper."

Barr and Bowden managed to maintain their air of high spirits. "I think he was in a kind of catatonic fit," Bowden recalled. "As we left we wished him Happy New Year again, and I added, 'I think we're going to have a very happy sixteen weeks.' He never said a word." Making people wait for hours (though not necessarily on New Year's Eve) was routine. So was making them wait for months to be paid. Sometimes you had to be creative to win. Pete Feller, who over the years built sets for Merrick's shows, once refused to let the work out of his shop until he received a bank check. After years of fighting with Schlissel over bills, he took a new tack. He stopped sending bills altogether. After a while Schlissel would become nervous, call him and ask, "Don't we owe you money?" Feller would give an amount and it would be paid the next day.

Doing business with Merrick was itself a kind of theater. Invariably those who succeeded with him were those who saw how calculated his theatrics were, those who understood Schlissel's remark, "Du vaisst deh mishigoss."

The third of the shows that Merrick presented that fall was *Jamaica*, which opened October 31, 1957, three weeks after *Romanoff and Juliet.*

When Fred Saidy, E.Y. "Yip" Harburg and Harold Arlen auditioned the show for Merrick and a few friends the year before, it was an intimate piece, clearly the kin of *Finian's Rainbow*, which Harburg and Saidy had written with Burton Lane in 1947. Saidy and Harburg happened to be excellent performers of their own material, so good in fact that sometimes they couldn't resist laughing at their own jokes.

The whole room, in fact, was full of gaiety. With one exception. Merrick faced the auditioners with fierce black eyes, his arms folded across his chest, not moving a facial muscle throughout their performance, while everyone around him laughed uncontrollably.

Noting Merrick's stony silence, Saidy went over to him when the audition was over and kidded, "David, you gusher you . . ."

Merrick said nothing.

Jamaica, he realized, would be a real gamble. It differed from the other musicals Merrick would produce in the Fifties in two significant ways. It was not based on material that had already been successful in some other form. Perhaps more importantly, it was not based on one of Merrick's own ideas.

Jamaica was completely original. It was about a good-hearted Jamaican fisherman whose girlfriend, Savanna, has fallen in love with another island, one called Manhattan. She had seen alluring images of it on a television set. The TV was seen as a contemporary serpent, disturbing the innocence and peace of this Caribbean Adam and Eve. Harburg and Saidy had written a charming, funny little musical.

Whatever Merrick's estimation of the material, he knew he was dealing with some of the most talented men on Broadway. Arlen alone had been responsible for an astonishing number of popular songs over the last few decades. By producing *Jamaica*, he was linking his name with quality, as he had with Logan and Kaufman.

Jamaica was originally written as a vehicle for an engaging young singer-actor who specialized in calypso music, then enjoying a great vogue in America. His name was Harry Belafonte. Between the time the show was conceived and the time it was ready to go into rehearsal, he became an international star. He had personal engagements booked until well into 1958. To wait for him would have delayed the Broadway opening of *Jamaica* for a year.

Sidney Poitier, who had just begun to make a splash as a serious actor, was viewed as a replacement for Belafonte, but he confessed kiddingly to Harburg that he was "probably the only black man who can't sing or dance." Harburg and Arlen asked him to sing "My Country, 'Tis of Thee," convinced they could discover a range in which they could write comfortably for him. By the time he had attempted a few bars, they realized that his own assessment of his musical talent was correct. The role eventually went to screen star Ricardo Montalban, a matinee idol but hardly a Broadway star.

The supporting cast was distinguished. It included Adelaide Hall, Ossie Davis, Erik Rhodes, Josephine Premice and, as lead male dancer, Alvin Ailey. But ten days before rehearsals were to begin, there was still not a name big enough to carry the show.

Perhaps they could find a star for the role of Savanna. A few years before, Arlen had offered Lena Horne a role in *House of Flowers*, which she had, reluctantly, turned down. He and Harburg went to see Horne, who was performing at the Waldorf-Astoria. Harburg said the material would be good for Horne at this point in her career because it would show her as the earthy, warm creature she really was, rather than as a sophisticated, glamorous star, a role that had begun to tire her.

She did not know that the show had originally been conceived from the point of view of the character to be played by Belafonte. When she heard the score she realized there was very little for her. She also sensed that Savanna was the villain of the piece and that even Savanna's wisecracking friend, a smaller part, had funnier lines. Arlen and Harburg assured her they would write material especially for her.

Horne's initial judgment was correct. Savanna, the role she played, was not really attractive. The plot lent itself to satire but not to the kind of ballads she knew how to sing. Once the show went into rehearsal, however, and once it became clear the songs being written for her were really not right, she did not feel confident enough to exercise the star's prerogative to complain.

The production, constantly being revised, quickly began to mushroom out of control. Its ironic folk quality—what had attracted everyone to it in the first place—was an early casualty. Horne, in her insecurity, was uncomfortable about appearing on Broadway as a poor little native girl. She insisted on turbans designed by Lilly Dache.

From time to time attempts were made to reclaim the original intentions of the show. One of the key roles, that of a wily old village grandmother, should have been played by someone with a sense of earthy charm. Instead it was played by Adelaide Hall, who had appeared in the original *Blackbirds* revues of the Twenties, a singer of sophisticated poise and elegance.

In Philadelphia, Harburg pointed out to Merrick that the class Hall brought to the stage would confuse the audience. The role required someone who projected less sophistication. He suggested an actress whose work he admired, Claudia McNeill, who would make her mark on Broadway a few years later in *Raisin in the Sun*. Merrick seemed to think it was a good idea. He told Harburg's assistant, Madeleine Gilford, "OK. I'll have her contract in my office tomorrow. You go back to New York and bring her back for rehearsal tomorrow."

Gilford phoned McNeill and told her to meet her in Merrick's office on 44th Street the following morning. She took the train back to New York and met McNeill at the office in the St. James building at the appointed time. They were both disconcerted when they found no one had any idea why they were there. Not only was there no contract. No one was even aware that McNeill had been hired.

Humiliated and disgusted, Gilford went back to Philadelphia alone. Merrick was nowhere in the theater. No one seemed to know where he was. Eventually she waited for him outside his hotel room. When he finally emerged she confronted him: Why had he sent her on a wild goose chase to New York? He said nothing. He ignored her and walked toward the elevator. As he pressed the button, he turned to her and said, "You didn't think I meant that, did you?"

McNeill was, in fact, lucky. A steady stream of black performers had arrived in Philadelphia without the sponsorship of Harburg or even an agent. They had been recommended for small parts. They arrived with signed contracts—signed by themselves but by no one in the Merrick office. If they were not right for the parts, they would be sent back to New York without even train fare.

By the time the show opened in Philadelphia, *Jamaica* was extremely confusing. At one point, Harburg, exhausted from fighting with Merrick over changes, had to be hospitalized. He had reached a point where he felt he could no longer do anything to salvage the show. Merrick sent for Joseph Stein, who had written comedy for radio and for the theater (including some sketches for Carol Channing in a celebrated revue of the late Forties, *Lend An Ear*). He had recently enjoyed a great success with his book for a musical about the Amish, *Plain and Fancy*. Merrick wanted him to "doctor" the book for *Jamaica*.

On subsequent shows bringing in "doctors" was the kind of intrigue that delighted Merrick. He took pleasure in watching the writers squirm as they saw their potential replacements arrive. In this case, however, there was no such pleasure. Stein's arrival was greeted with relief. Stein himself had never been called in as a "doctor" before. He was extremely nervous when he arrived at the theater in Philadelphia. The first person he met was Harburg, who was standing with a packed suitcase.

"Are you Stein?" he asked.

Stein said he was.

"Thank God," Harburg said. He put on his hat and walked out.

Stein was ushered into a room where Arlen was lying on a cot. He too asked if the newcomer was Stein. Informed he was, Arlen also thanked God, got up and left.

Stein joined Lehman Engel, who had been sent to replace the

musical director. The pair watched a runthrough of *Jamaica*.

"Do you understand what this is about?" Stein asked Engel. Engel said no. Neither could figure out even as basic a matter as who was supposed to be in love with whom. The most expedient way of solving the book's myriad problems, they decided, was to pare it to a minimum, so the audience would know just enough to get it from song to song.

That had been Merrick's own prescription for the show: "Flush the book down the toilet" and focus on the songs.

Every musical has its own chemistry, and eventually Merrick became a master chemist, knowing the right ingredients and how to mix them. *Jamaica*, even more than *Fanny*, was still an apprentice work. The catalyst in this case was the star. Robert Lewis, the veteran director who had guided such hits as *Brigadoon* and *Teahouse of the August Moon* to Broadway, was impressed at how little temperament Horne displayed. On opening night in Philadelphia one of her costumes was not ready. Instead of throwing a tantrum, which, he felt, would have been her right, she pinned it up herself.

As the show moved toward Broadway, the company, having sensed her insecurities, rallied around her. On opening night in New York she opened her dressing room door to find a huge bouquet of flowers with a card: "Savanna, we love you, The Crew."

Something even more bracing happened once the opening performance began. When the curtain went up Horne was hidden in a tiny hut, waiting to make her entrance. Out of town, when she made her entrance the applause was polite, as if the audience wanted her to prove herself before they demonstrated any more enthusiasm. On opening night in New York the audience consisted of the same people who had been attending her openings in posh nightclubs for years. When she stepped out of her hut they gave her a two minute ovation. The applause inspired her to give the performance Lewis had so far been unable to coax out of her.

The impression she made was powerful. *Life* magazine said she shone "like a tigress in the night, purring and preening and pouncing into the spotlight and hurling herself into eight first-rate songs." The other reviewers did not share *Life's* enthusiasm for the score, but they were all enthusiastic about Horne. What they wrote almost didn't matter. *Jamaica* was a financial success before it opened. Its $1.5 million advance was then the largest in Broadway history. The show had been capitalized at $300,000.

Merrick had been so gloomy about about the prospects for *Jamaica* that he had not even bothered to plan an opening night party. Horne herself made all the arrangements.

Had the reviews been as negative as he expected, it is entirely possible that he might not have come to the party at all. As it was, he waited until the early editions of the papers appeared, and, buoyed by the positive reviews, he made a beaming entrance, moving from table to table, greeting everyone in his best *grand seigneur* manner. No one would suspect he was not the host of the party. No one would suspect he had not even been invited.

When he reached the actual hostess he kissed her cheek and said, "Well, I always said you were a money runner." In fact, during the entire rehearsal and tryout period, he had never said anything that made her feel secure. He had never visited her in her dressing room, never spoken to her directly. He had always sent Schlissel. It suggested an insecurity in the presence of someone he knew was more powerful than he was. Success was what he needed to surmount that insecurity. Opening night he knew he had it.

At the party Merrick projected bonhomie and a sense of victory. What he really felt was relief. He found Joe Stein and confided to him that he felt as if he had been on a sled racing downhill toward a giant oak tree. At the last minute, through no agency of his own, the sled had swung away and avoided hitting the tree.

Jamaica had a healthy year and a half run. Its artistic merits were slight, but the show was historic for other reasons. It was the first Broadway show to provide employment for black stagehands. It was Merrick himself who informed Local One, the stagehands' union, that he would refuse to open *Jamaica* and that he would make a public case of the job discrimination issue unless the backstage crew included five black hands.

Merrick's detractors would later claim that he had only made this demand because Lena Horne had prodded him to, but this was not so. Horne was not involved in the burgeoning civil rights movement until a decade later, when her son Teddy became actively concerned. Shortly before *Jamaica* she had been blacklisted in the infamous Red Channels for no other reason than having been friendly with Paul Robeson. In the Fifties, that association was enough. Having cleared herself, she was not prepared to land herself in trouble again, (though, in fact, both Harburg and Saidy, the creators of *Jamaica*, were also blacklisted.)

There had been rumblings about the need to integrate Broadway for some time. The stagehands union had in fact adopted a non-discrimination policy when the AFL and CIO had merged a few years earlier, but until *Jamaica*, black stagehands had worked only on Off-Broadway productions.

Merrick's demand may have been a way of assuaging his guilt for his shabby treatment of the performers who had paid their own way down to Philadelphia only to be rejected for chorus roles. Or was it a manifestation of genuine liberalism? Or did it stem from his desire to see how far he could pressure one of Broadway's tougher unions? Was it all of these things? Whatever his reasons, Merrick won. Local One complied with his demand.

The stage manager for *Jamaica* was also black. Charles Blackwell first met Merrick when he was a dancer in *Fanny*. He found it odd that, during a break in rehearsal, Merrick sidled up to him and, as if uttering news that must be kept in confidence, outlined his advertising plans for the musical. He had found out that Blackwell had worked in advertising before becoming a dancer and wanted Blackwell's counsel on what were then unusual advertising plans. Blackwell thought his ideas were sound.

Blackwell was one of the select few of any race toward whom Merrick always displayed paternal affection. Once, while he was stage managing *Jamaica*, Blackwell saw that a cast member was drunk. Instead of sending him home and docking his pay, he had someone hide him in the basement and sent the understudy on. The next morning he was summoned to Merrick's office. "I hope you noticed all the people you passed on your way in," Merrick said. "They're all lining up to kiss my ass. Nothing you do is *not* reported to me." Someone else might have been sacked. Blackwell was warned.

For Merrick, confrontation was as important as the actual production of the shows. As far as some were concerned, the actual production of the shows was simply the pretext that gave him the opportunity to confront—and conquer—a series of adversaries. On *Jamaica* he was still honing these skills.

One morning, during the tryout in Philadelphia, Judd Mathison, Robert Lewis's assistant, went to have breakfast in a deli near the theater. When he entered the restaurant, Merrick came toward him and began shouting all sorts of questions he was evidently too afraid to ask Lewis. "When is Bobby going to do X? Why hasn't Bobby done Y?" Mathison was stunned, but when he tried to answer him, he found Merrick unwilling to look him in the eye. The two did a bizarre dance. Every time Mathison tried to stand face to face with him, Merrick tried to step behind him.

It was ostensibly a meaningless confrontation, since Merrick seemed more interested in venting his fury than actually solving problems or learning answers. But that was precisely what he wanted, a chance to display his power. With time he would be able to stage such encounters without any awkwardness.

When Merrick had announced he would bring *Look Back In Anger* to Broadway, the pundits thought he was taking a foolish risk. The writer was unknown. So was the cast. This was the sort of play, the "experts" opined, to be produced Off-Broadway. Before the show opened Merrick himself wondered if the experts weren't right. "We have an advance sale of $3.60," he joked. In fact it was about $3,000, but for a $40,000 investment, the difference between the two sums was negligible.

In the spring of 1957, before *Look Back In Anger* had opened in New York, a new Osborne play had been produced in London. It had been panned by all the London critics but Harold Hobson and Kenneth Tynan. Despite this reception the new play had an advantage *Look Back In Anger* did not—a star named Laurence Olivier.

The play had been written for him, though the circumstances of the "commission" were awkward. Olivier had gone to see *Look Back In Anger* and not enjoyed it very much. Although he made no public pronouncements, his opinion became quickly known, publicized and attacked. Among his opponents were his own children, whose argument he later summarized: "It's all very well for you: you can make a Shakespeare film every few years, go to Stratford-on-Avon and have a London season in Shakespeare every time you feel like it, but when someone comes along who really understands us, then you will have nothing to do with him."

Olivier conceded he had been unfair to Osborne. He said he had seen and admired Osborne as an actor, before his plays began to be produced. He went to see *Look Back In Anger* again, this time in the company of Arthur Miller. He found himself enthralled, arranged to meet Osborne and asked him if he would be interested in writing a play for him. Osborne went to work immediately and sent him the first act of a play called *The Entertainer*. Olivier bought it.

Even those London critics who hated *The Entertainer* considered Olivier's performance one of the most remarkable of his career. Unlike *Look Back In Anger*, which attracted few American bidders, there was fierce competition to secure the rights to bring *The Entertainer* to Broadway.

The likeliest contender was a former Detroit real estate man named Roger Stevens, who had a longstanding relationship with Olivier. Over the years Merrick tended to condescend to most of his fellow producers, but he had a particularly contemptuous attitude toward Stevens, perhaps because the gentle, patrician Stevens embodied the qualities he most envied. Merrick once told a reporter that he loved to make offers for London shows of no quality, knowing that Stevens would then try to outbid him. He would raise the bidding to a level quite ridiculous in view of the weak commercial potential of the project, then bow out, leaving Stevens the unlucky victor.

In addition to Stevens and Merrick, the suitors for *The Entertainer* included Merrick's one-time partner, the Theater Guild, as well as a team consisting of the actor Martin Gabel and his partner Henry Margolies. Representatives of Olivier and Osborne had talks with all these suitors throughout the spring and summer, but Merrick clinched the deal on a quick trip to London between the Boston closing of *Jamaica* and its Broadway opening the following week. Olivier informed Stevens that he had given the rights to Merrick "as I was told you were no longer interested." It is not hard to guess who had conveyed this news to Olivier.

Certainly Merrick had an edge with Osborne since virtually every major Broadway producer had turned down *Look Back In Anger*. He, on the other hand, had not only produced it but was now beginning to see a profit, proof of his managerial prowess.

At first Merrick's victory seemed short-lived. The deal to bring over *The Entertainer* hinged on his finding a suitable theater for a limited run, since Olivier was already committed to a film version of *Macbeth* in the late spring. One of the few available theaters was managed by Stevens, who was part of a group called the Producers' Theater, which both produced plays and owned theaters. Stevens was willing to lease Merrick the Helen Hayes, a suitably large theater that used to stand on 46th Street. Stevens offered the theater to Merrick, but he was determined to exact some retribution from him. Merrick would have to pay the prevailing London rental, 40% of the gross, rather than the standard New York rental of 30%.

A 33% rent increase would have tempered Merrick's victory considerably. For a while he considered taking the Belasco, a Shubert theater east of Broadway, isolated from the "walk-in trade" that exists on blocks where theaters are clustered together.

Because the ultimate theater remained uncertain and because it would have to be a limited run, Merrick feared he might have to finance the $50,000 project himself, since backers were fearful they might not see their investment repaid. Or so he informed *Variety*. Merrick's pose seems disingenuous. By now Osborne was clearly a marketable playwright. And since this would be Olivier's first Broadway appearance in seven years, the venture was hardly that risky. Merrick may have given the impression that no one wanted to invest so that he could maximize his own profits. (As it happened, he did allow Byron Goldman to help him finance it.)

The problem of a theater, however, was genuinely crucial. Until a theater was booked it was not even possible to determine the box-office scale. Briefly there was talk of moving *The Entertainer* into the Plymouth, where *Romanoff and Juliet* was playing, but it seemed foolish to interrupt the momentum already built on that show.

Merrick initiated some serious talks with the Shuberts, who owned all the theaters in which he already had shows. They now had very good reason to treat him well. *Jamaica* was doing record-breaking business at the Imperial. *Romanoff and Juliet* was selling out, and *Look Back In Anger* had done so well at the Lyceum, another east-of-Broadway theater, that the Shuberts had moved it to the Golden, west of Broadway. With three Merrick shows so profitable, it seemed fair and shrewd to make room for a fourth.

So, on January 15, 1958, less than a month before *The Entertainer* was scheduled to open, the Shuberts decided to take a show that was slated for the Royale, which is between the Plymouth and the Golden on West 45th Street, and put it in the Belasco, the house Merrick considered undesirable for *The Entertainer*. The play shunted to the Belasco was *The Day the Money Stopped*, which was by Maxwell Anderson and New Yorker writer Brendan Gill, based on the latter's novel.

To add insult to injury, one of the producers of *The Day the Money Stopped* was Roger Stevens. Although the play had an interesting cast (Richard Basehart, Kevin McCarthy and Mildred Natwick), it closed after four performances.

Lest there be any problem about repaying the investment (principally to Merrick himself), the prices for *The Entertainer* were scaled close to a level generally reserved for musicals. The top price for both *Look Back In Anger* and *Romanoff and Juliet* was $5.75. The top for *Jamaica* was $8.35 and for *The Entertainer* $7.50. (The play calls for a few musicians, who play in the music hall sequences; the number of musicians was less than the number the musicians' union required even for non-musical plays—had it been greater, that fact and the presence of a star might have justified charging the same price as a musical.)

Even during its pre-Broadway run, *The Entertainer* began to win big. It set a record for a non-musical show at the 49-year-old Shubert Theater in Boston, grossing over $56,000 in a single week. (The all-time house record had been set only a few months earlier by *Jamaica*, which grossed $56,655.)

The Entertainer was Merrick's seventh Broadway venture since *Clutterbuck*. So far there had been no losers. At the end of the 1957-58 season the New York Drama Critics' Circle named *Look Back In Anger* the Best Foreign Play. In only a few years Merrick would be mounting constant feuds with its members, but now the validation of the critics, while it might mean less than the validation at the four box offices, gave him a new prestige among his peers.

At the beginning of 1958 Merrick had established a beachhead on West 45th Street. Of the seven theaters that then stood on 45th between Broadway and Eighth Avenue, three had David Merrick productions. The addition of *The Entertainer* made a powerful visual demonstration of his achievement, of his rise to power. The four theaters clustered at the end of the block were nicknamed the "Merrick Parkway." It was a little corner of Broadway Merrick hoped would be forever his.

CHAPTER TEN

S OME DAYS YOU COULD see David Merrick lunching at
Sardi's, where the headwaiter, an Englishman, Martin
Balma, called him "Sir David." Other days you could see
him strolling down 44th Street toward a sandwich shop on
Eighth Avenue whose owner, a New York "character" of the Old
School, took particular delight in ribbing him.

"What did you fuck up today, Mr. Merrick?" the counterman
greeted him. "You should be working here and I should take over
your job," he boomed as he prepared Merrick's sandwich.
Merrick took no umbrage. In fact he seemed to take pleasure in
these indirect tributes to his success.

By the fall of 1958 that success had been extraordinary. Seven
shows. Seven financial successes. Four, the imports from London,
were accounted artistically successful as well.

For a while it seemed he could achieve a balance between his
desire to be seen as "classy" and his desire to succeed. In the next
few years the eagerness to be perceived as a purveyor of high class
merchandise began yielding fewer tangible returns. Financial success, on the other hand, gave him ever-increasing freedom.

In the fall of 1958 he experienced his first failures, though even
these were honorable defeats. One was an Osborne play, *Epitaph
for George Dillon*, which Osborne had written even before *Look*

Back In Anger, in collaboration with Toronto-born Anthony Creighton, a fellow actor.

The title character is a precursor of Jimmy Porter, but since it was the third Osborne play to reach New York, the trademark "anger," though often sharp and stimulating, had come to seem a bit shopworn.

The reviews were respectful, but business was weak, and even Merrick's aggressive salesmanship was unable to change matters. He would have closed the show except for the intervention of no less a personage than Marlene Dietrich. He had taken her to dinner at Sardi's one night to discuss an upcoming project, a musical version of a film in which she had starred in 1939, *Destry Rides Again*. She used the dinner to plead with him to keep *George Dillon* open until it could find an audience.

He took an ad in the *Times* with the unprecedented headline: YOUR MONEY BACK!

A letter to the public signed by Merrick and his co-producer, Josh Logan, read: "'Epitaph for George Dillon' is a play we believe in. People from the press, from the theater [an asterisk referred the reader to a list that included Noel Coward, Marlene Dietrich, Ruth Gordon, Moss Hart, Garson Kanin, Joseph Mankiewicz and Tennessee Williams] and from all walks of life have told us how spellbinding and thoroughly entertaining they've found this new play. We are so confident that you, too, will find this an exciting evening in the theater that if we are mistaken, we will refund your money at the end of the performance."

It didn't work. Merrick and Logan reluctantly posted their epitaph for *George Dillon* after twenty-three performances. They were originally going to close it after fifteen performances. Warner LeRoy had offered to put the play into a 299-seat theater he owned at First Avenue and 64th Street (later the site of his popular restaurant Maxwell's Plum), but the move was contingent on union cooperation; a concession by the stagehands union allowing Broadway sets to be moved to an Off-Broadway theater, and another by Actors' Equity to permit a similar move by

English actors. Merrick tried to accelerate the move, but at a certain point it seemed more prudent simply to close the show.

Shortly after *George Dillon* closed, two other producers, Norman Twain and Bernard Miller, announced they would reopen it at lower prices at the 54th Street Theater. Since this was a Broadway house, it simplified matters with the unions. Eileen Herlie and Robert Stephens, who played the two key roles in the initial production, also appeared in the second. From a $5.75 top at the Golden, there would now be a $3.60 top at the considerably larger (though remotely located) 54th Street Theater.

Twain and Miller announced their production with an ad that read, "CLOSED BY MISTAKE!" When he saw the ad, Merrick was "apoplectic." He had reason to be angry over an ad that implied he had been guilty of misjudgment. Merrick and Logan had made the second production feasible by donating the original scenery. The play lasted longer "uptown," but not long enough. The second production closed after forty-eight performances.

Another classy flop that fall was *Maria Golovin*, an opera by Gian-Carlo Menotti. The work was commissioned by NBC, which had its own opera company. In 1949 a similar commission had resulted in *Amahl and the Night Visitors*. Several commissions followed, none as successful as *Amahl*.

Maria Golovin was to have its premiere at the American pavilion at the Brussels World's Fair in August of 1958. All spring NBC courted Merrick, trying to get a commitment from him to produce *Maria Golovin* on Broadway after its Brussels engagement and before its network telecast. Though several Menotti operas had played Broadway, none had been financially successful. So Merrick was understandably reluctant to make a commitment.

NBC arranged for him to be invited to the premiere in Brussels, where he was treated like an honored guest, accorded the same deference as Gen. David Sarnoff, the head of NBC, and Elizabeth, Queen of the Belgians. He was now hobnobbing not just with the aristocracy of the theater, but with the genuine aristocracy. After seeing *Maria Golovin*, he agreed to produce the show on Broadway.

For many of his productions Merrick had placed the first ad offering tickets in the *Saturday Review*. This time *SR* subscribers were not only given first crack at the tickets; they were also given a 10% discount. The response was not encouraging, despite the fact that nowhere in the ad was *Maria Golovin* referred to as an opera. It was labeled Menotti's new "musical drama."

There was some justification for this chicanery. When Howard Taubman, then the chief music critic of the *New York Times*, reviewed it in Brussels, he said of Menotti, "The theater is in his blood, and his latest work, *Maria Golovin*, pulses with theatricalism." He particularly praised its libretto.

Merrick and his co-producers, NBC and Byron Goldman, insisted the opening at the Martin Beck be covered by theater critics, in order to further impress the public that this was theater, not opera. Five of the seven critics were favorable, but it was not enough to sway the public. After four performances *Maria Golovin* closed.

Though he considered the opera "second-rate Menotti," Walter Kerr found its failure dismaying: " . . . it is depressing to realize that there is—literally—no place in which work of this kind can be performed often enough, or long enough at a time, for its special contribution to be felt and soaked up. An audience large enough to fill the Martin Beck every night in the week could not be found, and that is understandable for a work in progress. Get rid of the expensive scenery and go to a smaller Broadway house? The house must be large enough to support a decent orchestra. Go Off-Broadway altogether? Once more we are in danger of losing the very scale, the sheer size and sound, that are most provocative about the effort."

Both *George Dillon* and *Maria Golovin* were the sort of ventures that might find a more congenial home in the cultural centers like the one planned for 64th and Broadway.

Although failure was never something Merrick took in stride, it was easier to accept these two flops, not simply because he knew they added to his luster as a serious producer, but also because he had had a healthy commercial show only a few weeks before. It was an adaptation of a novel about the conflict between East and West called *The World of Suzie Wong*. The adaptation was by Paul Osborne, the author of *On Borrowed Time* and *Mornings at Seven*, who had helped doctor *Fanny*.

By the time *Suzie Wong* opened, on October 14, 1958, it had a $750,000 advance. However almost none of the critics liked it. Unlike some plays, which never transcend their bad reviews, *Suzie Wong* led a charmed life. In the course of her travels across the country both before and after her Broadway engagement, she never won the admiration of the press.

It didn't matter. Something about the subject—the affair of an Asian hooker with the proverbial heart of gold and an English artist working in Hong Kong—captured the imagination of the public. In the wake of the confusing "military action" in Korea, this play—set in an Orient that posed no mysteries, no threats, an Orient that existed only to satisfy Western fantasies—struck a responsive chord.

By chance the opening of *Suzie Wong*, on October 14, coincided with the premiere, the next morning, of a new television show, *Open End*, produced by and starring a former theater producer named David Susskind.

It was Susskind's idea to inaugurate his own program by sharing with his audience the excitement of a Broadway opening, especially that moment when, after months of preparation and anxiety, the cast and members of the creative team find out how they've fared with the critics.

The fact that *Suzie Wong* was directed by the revered Joshua Logan and produced by the hottest producer on Broadway made it seem an ideal choice to kick off *Open End*.

As far as Susskind himself was concerned, *The World of Suzie Wong* was a winner. He began this segment of the program with his own enthusiastic review of the play. Then Susskind picked up a telephone and called Brooks Atkinson, the critic of the *New York Times*, who was waiting to give his assessment. Atkinson's view of *Suzie Wong* was considerably less upbeat than Susskind's.

He found it "flaring in style and sophomoric in viewpoint and on the artistic level of a comic book. It solves the problem of the expense account trade for the winter."

There was apparently no contingency plan for so dour a response. A call was placed to the *Herald-Tribune*'s Walter Kerr, whose judgment of the play was no more positive than Atkinson's. The script planned for the camera to focus on Merrick as Kerr's views were read, and so it did.

Merrick, embarrassed, could only bow his head. In some cruel stroke of fate, television captured him on the morning of his first critical defeat.

In addition to the unpredictably hazardous appearance on *Open End*, arrangements had been made for a "panoramic impression" of the play to be produced for the Ed Sullivan Show, a month after the opening. Original scenery and dances would be created for this capsulized narration of *Suzie Wong*. It was common for musicals to send performers to sing on the Sullivan show (two years later such an appearance would dramatically reverse the commercial fortunes of *Camelot*), but it was rare to feature a non-musical like this.

Merrick had made use of television as early as *Fanny*. At that time a mind-reader named Dunninger had a nationally televised program. On one of his shows, a camera near the stage door of the Majestic theater caught the cast lounging in their scanty Mediterranean costumes before a performance. Though blocks away, Dunninger was able to read the mind of one of the dancers. More important, TV viewers across the country got a glimpse of what was clearly a sexy musical.

In the fall of 1960 Merrick had even grander plans for TV. He planned to televise *Becket*, starring Laurence Olivier and Anthony Quinn, the very night it opened. The play would have been filmed beforehand. There would be live transmission of the audience arriving for the opening, after which the tape would be shown. The networks were reported willing to pay Merrick's $500,000 asking fee, but coverage of the 1960 presidential campaign precluded devoting a full evening to such an event.

Would such innovations have broadened the theater audience, which television was helping to shrink? It is hard to tell. It is very hard to make a theater piece work in either film or video, but, in retrospect, it seems a shame that as determined a figure as Merrick did not persevere.

Six weeks after *Suzie Wong* opened at the Broadhurst, Rodgers and Hammerstein's *Flower Drum Song* opened across the street at the St. James. (Kenneth Tynan dubbed the latter "A World of Woozy Song.") Merrick saw an opportunity to capitalize on his old antagonists' treatment of similar subject matter and had assistants pass out brochures to people waiting to buy tickets at the St. James informing them that "the only genuine Chinese show on Broadway" was at the Broadhurst.

By the time the Rodgers and Hammerstein show opened, Merrick had already opened four shows, the two "classy" failures, the tarnished success, *Suzie Wong,* and an import from Paris that brought him both success and cachet. On November 11, a few days after *Maria Golovin* closed, *La Plume de Ma Tante* opened at the Royale. The creation of Robert Dhery, probably now best remembered as the director of a satiric film of the early Sixties called *La Belle Americaine, Plume* was a revue of no intellectual or social pretensions. It fared better with the New York critics than many more serious efforts. Merrick himself called it "a sort of French *Hellzapoppin*," as apt a description as any.

Joseph Kipness, a producer and restaurateur, had discovered *Plume* in Paris and invited Merrick to co-produce it with him. It was an unmitigated success, despite the fact that it had no hit song and no album.

Plume was a collection of witty sight gags—a line of precision dancers thrown out of kilter by one errant member, a soprano growing a foot taller every time she sang a high note, a stripper's understudy wrestling with a problematic zipper while making her debut. The most memorable of the sketches, "Frere Jacques," showed a church belfry where a crew of monks began their morning chore of climbing ropes, Tarzan-like, to ring the bells. As they became more enamored of their tasks, their antics on the ropes grew more and more frenetic, and the bells rang more and more wildly.

Just as *Plume* had the virtue of being utterly comprehensible and enjoyable to New York audiences who spoke no French, it was similarly entertaining for the thousands of tourists who passed through the city and spoke no English. The little box that had humiliated Merrick the morning after *Suzie Wong* opened was changing audiences around the world. The box was image-oriented, not word-oriented, and audiences were becoming more attuned to visual rather than verbal communication. *Plume* may have been the first international hit to take advantage of the new orientation.

Of more immediate significance to Merrick and Kipness, after sixty-seven weeks on Broadway, *Plume* returned a 200% profit on an investment of $150,000.

HI
DEC
RECO

DAVID MERRICK
in association with
MAX BROWN
presents

ANDY GRIFFITH ★ DOLORES GRAY

in

DESTRY

RIDES AGAIN

also starring

SCOTT BRADY

with JACK PRINCE • LIBI STAIGER

Music and Lyrics by HAROLD ROME
Book by LEONARD GERSHE
Based on the story by MAX BRAND

Production Designed by OLIVER SMITH
Lighting by JEAN ROSENTHAL
Costumes by ALVIN COLT
Musical Direction and Vocal Arrangements by LEHMAN ENGEL
Orchestrations by PHILIP J. LANG
Dance Music Arranged by GENEVIEVE PITOT

Entire Production Directed and Choreographed by
MICHAEL KIDD

CHAPTER ELEVEN

LTHOUGH NO DAVID MERRICK opening was quite as surreal as that of *42nd Street*, during the good years they were evenings in which the excitement extended far beyond whatever happened onstage.

The night *La Plume de Ma Tante* opened, for example, Merrick's co-producer Joe Kipness thought he had made a killing. Rather than risk the critics' receptivity to this unconventional French revue, Kipness sold his interest in it to Mort Mitosky. It was, of course, Mitosky who made the killing. Merrick met Mitosky when Mitosky, a lawyer, was a consultant for RCA, and urged the record company to invest in *Fanny*.

In the few hours between the time the critics raced up the aisle and the early editions of the papers rolled off the presses, there was frequently a lot of horse trading at a Merrick opening.

Backers like Mitosky, a lifelong Merrick friend, would offer other backers a chance to recoup their investment on the spot. If anyone was nervous about losing money, here was a chance to alleviate that anxiety immediately, generally with some profit into the bargain. Even producers more seasoned than Kipness were likely to succumb to Mitosky's cajoling. (Shortly after *The Music Man* opened, Kermit Bloomgarden, in need of funds, sold Mitosky 20 percent of his share of it.)

Mitosky and others would also routinely approach the creators of a musical, who might be even more nervous than the backers about how well the opening had gone. For a flat fee, often a generous one, an uneasy composer or lyricist might consign Mitosky his royalties over the years.

This was the underbelly of the commercial theater, what went on in the shadows. What was visible to the casual observer was glamorous and exciting. For Merrick opening nights had evolved into a pleasant ritual, a periodic way of validating and celebrating his ongoing success. The presence of celebrities was a sign of his social eminence. The attention the press paid to Merrick himself confirmed his own growing celebrity.

Opening nights still required formal attire. Even the critics wore black tie. As part of the "game" critics would disguise their responses and remain stone-faced, lest anyone complain the next morning that their sour reviews were at variance with their apparent enjoyment of the show the night before. As Moss Hart put it, openings were the one occasion where the granite of their faces "resembled that of their hearts."

Byron Goldman would be seated just behind and slightly at an angle to Brooks Atkinson. Goldman scrutinized Atkinson's visage and was able to give the producer, pacing at the back of the theater, a thumbs up or a thumbs down as Atkinson hastened up the aisle during the curtain calls.

These two sides of the commercial theater, the surface glamour and excitement, and the underlying sense of a cockfight were both accentuated in anything associated with David Merrick.

Destry Rides Again, Merrick's next musical, was based on the great 1939 film starring James Stewart and Marlene Dietrich. It was, curiously enough, the first major musical shoot 'em up. Since the dramatis personnae were largely equestrian, it made it difficult to stable such a show in a Broadway house. *Destry*, happily, did not require any horses. It took place almost entirely in a saloon.

Merrick had shrewdly analyzed the appeal of Westerns. "The public takes its pick on Westerns," he said. "You can see a Western at a 42nd Street movie house and the audience takes it seriously. Or you can go to the Plaza and see the people who look at a Western in order to laugh.

"The same thing happened with *The Boy Friend* on Broadway—insiders saw it as satire and the people from Peoria took it as gospel. We hope to please everybody too. What *Guys and Dolls* did for Broadway hoodlums, maybe we can do for the American cowboy."

He asked Logan to direct, but the material didn't appeal to him. The direction and choreography were then given to Michael Kidd, who had choreographed *Guys and Dolls* and choreographed and directed the film *Seven Brides for Seven Brothers*. Kidd had a reputation as a stern taskmaster. After Robert Lewis, whose easy-going style on *Jamaica* had driven Merrick crazy, there was something appealing about the idea of a tyrant.

Merrick did yield to Logan's urging that Harold Rome do the score: "You can't make him a famous man and then just leave him." There were more cogent reasons for making Rome the composer. Among Rome's huge circle of friends was a man named Milton Rackmill, who was the head of both Decca Records and Universal Pictures. Universal, which produced the 1939 film, still held the rights. In making the deal with Rackmill, Merrick granted Decca the right to make the cast album.

In the decade since *South Pacific*, which opened on Broadway in 1949, cast albums had become enormously important to the profitability of musicals. In 1956, for example, CBS Records paid the entire cost of *My Fair Lady*, the then extravagant sum of $360,000, simply for the rights to produce the cast album.

One way to enhance a show's profitability was to cast TV stars. In the Jimmy Stewart role Merrick cast Andy Griffith, a TV favorite, who had appeared on Broadway a few seasons before in *No Time For Sergeants*. Because Griffith's musical skills were still something of a question mark, it was essential to have a solid musical performer opposite him in the role of Frenchy, the saloon owner.

Merrick had a great idea—Dolores Gray, an actress with comic skills and a belting voice often compared to Merman's. Gray was extremely careful about her career. She had enjoyed enormous success in London and Hollywood but had somehow never had the proper vehicle for stardom in New York. She didn't think *Destry* was going to be that vehicle. She had read the script very carefully and determined that her character was there for color, not really involved enough in the plot.

"The story is about Destry," she told Merrick, who was astonished she did not want to be in it. "Both the first and second act curtains are about Destry."

"I will have it rewritten," Merrick told her. "I'll change anything you want me to."

Gray was perplexed by his eagerness to please her. "David, you can't change the story," she insisted. "It's about the sheriff."

He had already changed the story. "We're not going to kill you off," he said.

"Why are you taking that out?" she asked him, remembering Frenchie's death as one of the high points of the movie.

"I don't want a downer for the audience," he said.

Gray told Merrick she could only be in the show if she were included in what promised to be its choreographic high point, a whip dance that indicated the kind of hostile welcome the cowpokes planned to give their new sheriff. Even if she participated in the dance for only four bars, she told him, it would give her character a darker color than that of being simply a saloon hostess.

Merrick had never made plot turns or character delineation part of his contracts. He had a meeting with Kidd, who agreed to the idea of including Gray in the whip dance.

"Fine," she said, when he reported Kidd's agreement to her. "But put it in the contract." He promised her that he would safeguard her interests in the course of rehearsal, but that he really could not include such material in a contract.

"I promise you, I swear to you I'll see it's done," Merrick said. "He won't break his word to me, and I won't break mine to you."

When Gray, with misgivings, succumbed to his persistent cajoling he was so delighted he sent her four dozen four foot long roses with a note, "If you knew how much I wanted you, you could have held out for anything. Love, David Merrick." (In 1986, when Gray went into the cast of *42nd Street*, she wired him, "If you knew how much I wanted to work for you again you could have held out for anything.")

By the time Gray had made her stipulations about the book for *Destry*, it had already proved a source of consternation. The original script had been written by Alfred Berter, a TV columnist and author. Merrick claimed Berter had never even submitted a draft. Berter claimed that he had but that he had received a letter from Merrick requesting the advance back as well as whatever had been written. This sort of acrimony was likely to frighten and anger Merrick's adversaries. The usual pattern was to stall as long as possible; then, when his opponent was tired of paying lawyers' bills, agree to some compromise settlement.

While he battled Berter, Merrick invited Leonard Gershe to write an entirely new book. Gershe had written the screenplays for the Hollywood musicals *Silk Stockings* and *Funny Face*. (He had also written the lyrics for "Born in a Trunk," which Judy Garland sang in *A Star Is Born*.)

Since Rome had already written the score based on Berter's book, Gershe's had to be fashioned around musical numbers he had no hand in shaping, which made his job very difficult. When he read his material to Merrick in Rome's Fifth Avenue apartment, Merrick embraced him with genuine enthusiasm. He offered Gershe a ride home in his limousine. As they drove through the city Merrick praised Gershe's work lavishly, calling it a masterpiece. Perhaps to counteract whatever rumors Gershe might have heard about what it was like to work with him, he declared he respected and cared only for creative people, not actors, who, he said, were simply willful children.

To prepare for her role in the whip dance, Gray went to a sport shop and bought a bullwhip. Working with it, she discovered, was grueling. The work fueled her anger and frustration when Kidd finally refused to allow her to be part of the number.

Couldn't she just crack her whip one time? No, he answered. Couldn't she throw her whip to one of the three henchmen? No. "Michael, this is supposed to be a pivotal character moment for me," she pleaded. He was unyielding.

As for Merrick, he was never available. Often he would be out of town. He also had several other shows in development, notably *Gypsy*, which would open six weeks after *Destry*. By the time *Destry* began its out-of-town tryout in Boston, Gray and Kidd were both at the boiling point. Nor did it help matters that she had virtually no relationship with her leading man, who was nervous about appearing in a musical.

After one of the performances Kidd and Gray had a heated argument in front of the cast. He called her a "slut." That word had been in the script. It had made Boston audiences gasp. She asked him to take it out. It had upset her when it was part of the show. It outraged her when Kidd applied it to her. She upped the verbal ante. She slapped him. He slugged her.

It made headlines. A *Herald-Tribune* reporter flew to Boston to report on the backstage rodeo. After a performance he saw Kidd accosted by Gray's mother, who slapped him hard across the mouth. A companion dragged her into her daughter's dressing room, from which she called out, "You haven't heard the last of this, Michael Kidd. I will kill you, Michael Kidd."

Normally it would be the producer's role in such a situation to restore peace and harmony. Merrick, however, refused even to fly to Boston. Gray's agent, Lester Shurr, pleaded with him, "You promised her a lot of things. The least you can do is go up there and back her up."

"Are you crazy, Lester?" Merrick told him. "I couldn't buy publicity like this for $5,000 a week. Let 'em fight it out."

By the time the show opened at the Imperial, Kidd and Gray had reached an uneasy truce. For opening night, 45th Street was filled with sawdust and, perhaps to compensate for the lack there-of onstage, a few horses. The reviews were solid if not ecstatic. "Who cares if it IS made from an old formula?" John Chapman wrote in its defense. "So is Old Grand-dad."

Kenneth Tynan noted that the musical missed the point of Max Brand's characters. The originality of *Destry*, he wrote, was that it was the first instance in the "celluloid history of the West [that] a town was cleaned up by an egghead. Whereas Shane came out of nowhere, Destry came out of law school." Griffith, he felt, was miscast. He was "not a shy, intelligent introvert set among dumb and brutish extroverts but a softhearted bumpkin set among hardhearted bumpkins."

The high point of the evening was clearly the number from which Gray had been excluded, the Whip Dance, in which three desperadoes filled the stage with the stinging, intimidating sound of cracking whips. "The trio marks out an electrifying space for itself," Walter Kerr wrote, "sends three crackling pinwheels of leather into the air, and turns the rhythms of Harold Rome's barn dance into a staccato, stinging, ear-splitting barrage."

Destry marked the beginning of Merrick's infatuation with high decibel levels for his musicals. Amidst his general enthusiasm for the show, Chapman complained that it had been "bugged with more mikes than the whole Soviet spy system owns. The Imperial, Mr. Merrick, is not the Grand Canyon; it's just a good theater."

If Merrick's shows over the years tended to sound extremely loud, especially to critics, it was not necessarily a matter of taste but of need. Merrick himself was a bit hard of hearing. The sound technicians had two settings, one for a normal audience, another—louder, of course—when they knew Merrick was in the house. On opening night, when Merrick was always in the house, the sound level was at its highest.

Destry paid back its investment and ran for a year, but it never achieved the popularity or respect it deserved. The honors that season went to the other musical the Merrick office produced, *Gypsy*, which had always found itself in the shadow of *Destry*, much as the young Gypsy Rose Lee had always found herself in the shadow of her favored sister, Baby June.

ALL I NEED IS THE GIRL

Lyrics by STEPHEN SONDHEIM

Music by JULE STYNE

DAVID MERRICK and LELAND HAYWARD

present

ETHEL

MERMAN

GYPSY

Book by ARTHUR LAURENTS

Music by JULE STYNE

Lyrics by STEPHEN SONDHEIM

Suggested by the Memoirs of GYPSY ROSE LEE

ALSO PUBLISHED FROM THE SCORE

MR. GOLDSTONE
LET ME ENTERTAIN YOU
ALL I NEED IS THE GIRL
EVERYTHING'S COMING UP ROSES
YOU'LL NEVER GET AWAY FROM ME
LITTLE LAMB
TOGETHER WHEREVER WE GO
SMALL WORLD
SOME PEOPLE

ENTIRE PRODUCTION DIRECTED AND CHOREOGRAPHED BY

JEROME ROBBINS

60¢

WILLIAMSON MUSIC, INC., & STRATFORD MUSIC CORPORATION
SOLE SELLING AGENT CHAPPELL & CO. INC., RKO BLDG. ROCKEFELLER CENTER, NEW YORK 20, N.Y.

CHAPTER TWELVE

A
LL THE YEARS Merrick had worked for Shumlin, even
during the years he had been putting *Fanny* together, he
had kept his pugnacity reasonably in check.
Success unleashed it.

He had not become a producer simply to arrange other people's triumphs. There was nothing selfless or self-effacing about
the job of producing as far as he was concerned. It was instead a
constant matter of self-assertion. The day-to-day work of producing, which involved constant negotiation, constant testing of
other people's wills, afforded him innumerable opportunities to
assert his own superiority over others. The years of waiting, the
years of building had been hard. But they had made possible the
release of the negative energies that flowed so naturally through
him. This was nowhere more true than in the matter of contracts.

To the layman a contract is a guarantee, a set of assurances that
have the support of the law. The lawyer takes a more imaginative
view of a legal document.

If he is a man of little or middling ambition he may share the
layman's conviction that the contract is a form of mutual protec-
tion. If, however, his ambitions are grander, if his pugnacity
exceeds his rationality, then he is likely to see a contract simply as
a basis for future litigation.

For Merrick, contracts were a means to control people, particularly people whose talents and achievements might have intimi-

dated lesser figures than himself. He began to explore the creative possibilities of contracts as he worked on *Gypsy*.

When Merrick read the memoirs of Gypsy Rose Lee, he immediately saw that the role of the stripteaser's ambitious mother would be perfect for Ethel Merman. Merman's last Broadway show, the 1956 *Happy Hunting*, had been the only failure in her nearly thirty-year career. It provided the disquieting proof that even with the biggest of stars a musical could not transcend a mediocre score.

Merman envisioned *Gypsy* as an affectionate salute to the now forgotten worlds of vaudeville and burlesque. So, initially, did Jerome Robbins, who had directed her in her last Broadway success, *Call Me Madam*, in 1950. Robbins, who would direct and choreograph *Gypsy*, immediately began putting a host of aged performers on payroll to advise him on what would be a retrospective of the lost arts of low comedy and urban folk culture.

It was Arthur Laurents who changed both their perceptions of what the show would be. In the memoir, Gypsy Rose Lee's mother is a woman of enormous charm. Stephen Sondheim observed that the actress who probably came closest to capturing the charm of the actual Mama Rose was Linda Lavin, who played the role on Broadway in 1990. But the Mama Rose of the musical was not the Mama Rose of the memoir.

Although he had fought with him during the production of *West Side Story*, their last collaboration, Robbins recommended Laurents to write the book for *Gypsy*. At first Laurents read Lee's book and was not interested. Then an agent who had known Mama Rose gave him an unvarnished version of the woman, which excited Laurents. He turned her into a quintessential stage mother and, more important, an American archetype, a woman whose hunger for success is so powerful she stops at nothing to achieve it vicariously through her offspring. She turns one of her daughters into a stripper to gain the fame and fortune she will never acquire on her own.

Laurents' caustic humor and his sharp sense of how to tell a story gave shape to what might have been a rambling tribute to old-fashioned forms of show business. It was Laurents who suggested that Sondheim, who had written the lyrics for *West Side Story*, do the entire score for *Gypsy*.

Merman objected: "He's a clever boy," she said. "But he can't write for me. He doesn't know who I am."

Merrick agreed. He had already offered the project to two composers who had written some of Merman's best songs, Irving Berlin and Cole Porter, but neither felt comfortable with the abrasive material. Merrick had also auditioned a pair of young songwriters, Cy Coleman and Carolyn Leigh. They wrote four songs for him, one of which was "Firefly." (When Merrick turned them down, they showed "Firefly" to Tony Martin, who made it a hit song.)

Finally Merrick approached Jule Styne, who, after many years on Tin Pan Alley and in Hollywood, had written several hit shows (*High Button Shoes, Gentlemen Prefer Blondes, Peter Pan,* and *Bells Are Ringing.*) He had also produced several shows, including the 1950 revival of *Pal Joey*, which made everyone (including Richard Rodgers, who had tried to dissuade him from reviving it) recognize its greatness.

Much of Merrick's success as a producer of musicals lay in his skill at matchmaking. At first the pairing of Sondheim and Styne seemed unlikely. Sondheim, twenty-eight, had studied composition with the eminent contemporary composer Milton Babbitt at Princeton. Styne, fifty-three, despite his Broadway success, was still thought of largely as a pop composer, having written many of Frank Sinatra's hit songs.

Despite the difference in their ages and backgrounds, the two hit it off remarkably well. "Steve was the first lyric writer who understood what I was doing," Styne said. "I'm not an accompanist for words. I'm a dramatist. For me the music has to come from the situation and has to capture it before the words are there."

Styne wrote the melody for a number that would appear near the end of the first act, in which Mama Rose's two daughters lament the fact their mother will not simply settle down, marry someone and let them leave show business. Styne took great care with the song that would become "If Mama Was Married." Aside from trying to impress the audience, Merman and Merrick, he also wanted to dazzle his new collaborator.

"I could have done a piece of crap; instead I did a waltz," Styne later recalled. "And Steve analyzed it perfectly. He felt that the music already established that Mama was not going to get married. He pointed to a certain measure in the score and said, 'You know what that note means? It ain't going to happen.'"

The score was finished in less than two months. Merman was so delighted with it that she asked Styne to accompany her to the Waldorf Towers so she could sing her numbers for Cole Porter. Porter, weak and ill, clinked the side of a glass with his spoon to register his enthusiasm.

Enthusiasm was always the response to *Gypsy*. The show gave its first public performance at a Sunday afternoon run-through on the bare stage of the Winter Garden. The invited audience, in addition to chorus members from other Broadway shows, included Mary Martin and her designer Mainbocher, Mr. and Mrs. William Paley and Janet Gaynor.

Jerome Robbins came out beforehand and explained that there would be no scenery or costumes. Nor would there be an orchestra, only a piano. It didn't matter. *Gypsy* received a tumultuous ovation from its chic audience.

The only apparently unenthusiastic response to the show came from Merrick. From the beginning of rehearsals until shortly before it opened, Merrick brought the full force of his negativity and contentiousness to bear on the show. The patterns of difficult behavior that eventually became standard on Merrick musicals began with *Gypsy*.

It began with the negotiations with the artists.

The conductor Milton Rosenstock had first met Merrick many years earlier in the bar at Sardi's. The two had remained cordial, and when it came time to talk about his contract for *Gypsy*, Merrick's approach to Rosenstock was civilized, even friendly.

"I'm glad you're going to be on it," he told the conductor. "I have to tell you I've admired you for years. However this is business. I'm giving you scale."

As Merrick made this declaration, Rosenstock noted, he had "a little smirk on his face." Rosenstock fought for more and wound up getting $100 a week more than scale. The negotiation, he discovered, was a Merrick ritual.

When Rosenstock began rehearsals, however, he was still without an actual contract. He thought it odd and mentioned it to Robbins, who, he discovered, also had no contract.

In fact no one had a contract, which disturbed Rosenstock. He went to confront Merrick in his office. "How come nobody's got a contract?" he asked him. "Are we going to open?"

Merrick gave him "the most quizzical look I've ever seen in my life," Rosenstock recalled. Merrick acknowledged that no one had a contract.

"Isn't it strange?" he said. "No one has left."

By denying his employees contracts Merrick was implying that they served at his pleasure. One reason, however, that there were no contracts was that technically the show could not proceed until there was approval from Gypsy Rose Lee's sister, June Havoc. Merrick had sent Fitelson, who was Havoc's personal friend and her sister's lawyer, to her with a blanket agreement in which she would sign away her rights to her "name, image and anything pertaining to them . . . in the theater, films and any medium yet to be invented" for the sum of one dollar.

Havoc felt that *Gypsy's* treatment of her life and that of her mother was a grotesque caricature. She had, after all, begun dancing at the age of two and all through her early childhood was making $1,500 a week on the Keith-Orpheum Circuit, headlining with the likes of Fanny Brice and Sophie Tucker. When she was two and a half the Seattle Times had called her "a second Pavlova." In Laurents' treatment, however, she was a coy amateur.

As for Mama Rose, Havoc felt, Laurents' rendering of the character was without nuance. "Mama was little, tiny, fragile, beguiling -- and *lethal*," she thought. "That's what everybody missed."

And yet here was Fitelson, her friend, standing over her offering her a pen, expecting her to give approval to "an utter and total dismissal of my life."

Havoc asked Fitelson if there were any lawyer he considered his equal.

He laughed.

"Louis Nizer," he said, referring to the most celebrated attorney of the day.

Havoc hired Nizer. She knew there was no hope of financial compensation. She also knew she would eventually give her approval for her sister's sake. If *Gypsy* travestied her life and her mother's, it sanitized that of her sister.

She knew that, however aloof her sister seemed about having spent a life in burlesque, it ate away at her -- "Why else should she have had ulcers growing within ulcers? The truth was that everybody loved Gypsy but Gypsy. This show cleared up everything. It made the image she dreamed of into a reality. It made her what she always wanted to be -- a pathetic little ingenue who made good."

Havoc had Nizer draw up a letter of agreement in which the creators of *Gypsy* would agree to certain things -- they would not, for example, depict Havoc beyond the age of seven; nor would they portray the two girls doing a sister act, which in fact they never did. Everyone signed the agreement. No one paid any attention to it.

The only lasting result Nizer achieved was the musical's subtitle. The show's depiction of the Hovick clan was so far from reality that he insisted they bill it as a fable, and in fact it is called "a musical fable."

The show was already in Philadelphia before Havoc signed the release. While waiting for her signature the younger sister was called Baby Claire.

(Three years later Havoc had a similar run-in with Merrick. She had shown her play *Marathon 33*, based on her experiences as a marathon dancer during the Depression, to Gower Champion, who wanted Merrick to produce it. She met with

Merrick, whom she found "more than unpleasant -- he was menacing." Again she was offered a contract in which she would give up any right to have a say in the depiction of her own life and in which she would also relinquish the guarantees contained in a standard Dramatists Guild contract. Merrick taunted her that they didn't need her; they only needed the script. This time she refused to sign.)

Even had there been contracts at the beginning of rehearsals, it wouldn't have meant much. Contracts were expedients for Merrick to gain whatever he wanted. He did not see them as threatening or binding—to him. (At a later date it would not have been possible to start rehearsals under such conditions. Largely as a result of litigation with Merrick, Equity refused to allow its members to begin work without contracts.)

A curious detail in Merman's and Rosenstock's contracts illustrates this attitude. After the show had run on Broadway almost two years, it went on tour, Merman's first cross-country excursion with a show. She had insisted when she agreed to the tour that Rosenstock be her conductor. In her contract it was specified that he was engaged for the entire length of the tour.

Rosenstock's contract, however, specified something else. At the time the tour began he was waiting to hear about a job in Hollywood. He had asked that his contract specify that should the Hollywood deal come through he was entitled to leave the tour. Merman's contract gave her what she wanted, Rosenstock's gave him what he wanted, though their respective demands were utterly contradictory. If Rosenstock's Hollywood deal failed to materialize, of course, nobody's interests would have been compromised.

But it did materialize. Rosenstock came to say goodbye to Merman, expecting a fond embrace. Instead she hit the roof. They compared contracts and discovered what had happened. Of course they had the option of suing Merrick, but that would take more time than they had to accomplish what either needed. Merrick invited suits. He was temperamentally and financially prepared for protracted litigation. The victims of his cavalier atti-tude toward contracts were not. In this case a replacement was found and Merman was mollified.

Over the years in contract negotiations he would appear to set great store by the size of type the actor would receive in the ad. He would think nothing of giving a handful of stars equal billing in their contracts. It would be up to the advertising agency to inform them that the billing they had been promised was impos-sible, given the space and design of the poster.

If contractual matters served as an ominous prelude, the cre-ative period could be marked by blowouts of operatic propor-tions. The years in which Merrick was a quiet, studious observer, swallowing his thoughts as an underling was supposed to do, were over. It gave him pleasure to be able to voice what he thought, and on *Gypsy* he grumbled constantly within earshot of Robbins.

Robbins was not used to this kind of treatment. He com-plained to Leland Hayward, Merman's agent and Merrick's co-producer. Robbins threatened to stop the work if Merrick came into the rehearsal room.

Hayward took immediate action. He called a meeting of the entire company and confronted Merrick. "I have something to say to you, David," he began, in the gentlemanly manner for which he was known—and for which Merrick himself continued to admire him long afterward.

"You're being negative," he said. "You're disturbing the rehearsals."

Merrick was startled by Hayward's bluntness. "Look, David, you got into this show for $10,000. Let's go upstairs and I'll give you a check for $10,000."

Merrick backed down. He agreed he would stay away. Once, however, at a rehearsal in a huge space that had been a nightclub called the New Amsterdam Roof, Rosenstock came across Merrick standing in the shadows.

"Look out, they'll catch you," Rosenstock joked.

Ignoring the tone of levity, Merrick asked, "How's it going?"

"They'll fix it," Rosenstock answered.

Merrick had ways to achieve retribution for this humiliation once the show was on the road. He would constantly offer to sell his percentage of the show to other backers (not, significantly, to Hayward). Then, if someone became serious about the offer, he would back down. It was done, very calculatedly, to give the impression that he had little confidence in the show.

He also postponed the New York opening. Carol Channing remembered visiting Merman in her dressing room after a performance in Philadelphia. "When is it coming in?" she asked Merman. "When that son of a bitch gives the OK," Merman replied.

In view of its legendary reputation, it is amusing to see how guarded many of the original reviews were. One exception was Walter Kerr, who called it "the best damned musical I've seen in years," for which he received "hundreds" of letters deploring his use of profanity. Another was Kenneth Tynan, the brilliant young Englishman who spent several seasons reviewing theater for *The New Yorker*. Tynan almost missed reviewing *Gypsy* because he had infuriated Merrick with his negative review of *Destry*.

Merrick forbade his press agent to send Tynan opening night tickets for *Gypsy*. He did not keep his decision a secret. Hayward offered to send Tynan a pair of his own, which Tynan accepted. Tynan, in fact, had a choice of seats. Laurents, Styne and Robbins also offered him tickets.

In 1959 all this made news. The *Herald-Tribune* assigned a reporter (the young Ed Kosner, who would later become the editor of *New York* magazine) to do a story about how Tynan got his tickets. Kosner had to track Tynan down in Paris to get a quote. The article ended with Tynan asking Kosner, "You don't really think this was worth a phone call, do you?"

Of all Merrick's musicals, *Gypsy* was the one that without question could be labeled "great." Though he had put the creative team together, the greatness had been achieved largely without him. That was a situation he made certain would never happen again.

CHAPTER THIRTEEN

MERRICK'S CAMARADERIE WITH the Royal Court and the British avant-garde did not preclude his having a similar relationship with the London commercial managements. In the Fifties the most prestigious of those managements was H.M. Tennent, Ltd., whose czar, Binkie Beaumont, had every reason to be pleased with the way Merrick had made a New York hit of *The Matchmaker*.

On the surface he and Merrick might have seemed a very unlikely match. The American was still nervous, still eager to be taken seriously. The Englishman dressed and behaved with an easy elegance, presumably the legacy of birth. Merrick longed to be thought Beaumont's equal, as much a gentleman, as much an arbiter of taste.

To his delight, he learned that Beaumont was not "to the manner born." Beaumont had achieved everything Merrick sought by his own efforts, not by the accident of birth. Had he not also been born into poverty? Most astonishing, considering how perfectly Beaumont fit into the British upper crust, had he not also been born a Jew? So Merrick had been informed. So London believed. It was not until many years after his death in 1973 that it was discovered Beaumont had invented both childhood poverty and Jewishness—they added some color to what he imagined was a colorless, thoroughly middle-class upbringing. But in the Fifties his affectations and Merrick's meshed perfectly, to their mutual economic advantage.

In 1958 Beaumont had a musical for which several American producers were competing, *Irma La Douce*, a Parisian show about a prostitute with a heart of gold. The likeliest contender was Robert Whitehead.

Whitehead, nowadays revered as the last of the "gentleman producers" and certainly Beaumont's equal in manners and polish, thought he had all but sealed the deal with Beaumont for *Irma*. The only unresolved matter was the casting of Clive Revill, who played the narrator as well as taking numerous small parts along the way. Revill subsequently became a popular performer in America, but he was unknown in 1958, when negotiations for *Irma* began. When Whitehead left Beaumont's office he thought *Irma* would be his with a little more amiable maneuvering.

When he got down to the street he realized he had forgotten his overcoat. Whitehead went back upstairs, knocked on the closed door of Beaumont's office, explained why he had come back and began to open the door. He was surprised to find sudden pressure on the other side of the door, as if Beaumont were trying to prevent him from entering. When he wedged the door open he saw why.

Seated on the sofa he himself had occupied only moments before was David Merrick. The normally imperturbable Beaumont stammered an alibi. Whitehead knew precisely what was happening. He retrieved his overcoat, slammed the door and refused to talk to Beaumont for many years.

Merrick, who was securing the rights to *Irma*, was for many years afterward the major importer of Beaumont's London hits.

Merrick was everywhere.

He was constantly forging alliances, constantly looking for talent he could use. In the next few years the Merrick office built an unparalleled record for productivity. One reason, of course, was the volume of shows Merrick imported from London. Another was the extraordinary talent pool Broadway then offered. In every area—performers, writers, directors—the level of talent and achievement was remarkable. It was never a case of finding the right person. It was always a tough choice because so many right persons were available.

Yet another reason for Merrick's apparent prolificacy was that projects begun many years before were finally coming to fruition. Throughout his career he was always optioning material, always planting seeds many of which never bloomed, but many of which took a long time to nurture and gestate.

Merrick had begun *Take Me Along*, for example, which opened in the fall of 1959, during the painful period when he was still waiting for Josh Logan to commit himself to *Fanny* in 1953.

In fact, it was an idea he had conceived as a young man in St. Louis, when he saw George M. Cohan in *Ah, Wilderness!* The story of a young man's coming of age in the seemingly sunlit years before World War I seemed a natural idea for a musical. The initial title was *Connecticut Summer* and its original writer John Latouche, who is best remembered for having written some of the lyrics for Leonard Bernstein's *Candide*. He had died in 1956.

Connecticut Summer was shelved until the right talent could be found to bring it to life. In 1957 there was a new composer-lyricist on Broadway, Bob Merrill, who was like Jule Styne, one of the few to make the transition from pop songwriter to theater composer. The show on which he had made the transition was, astonishingly, another musical adaptation of Eugene O'Neill.

Merrill had several hit songs in the early Fifties, including "How Much Is That Doggie In the Window?" and "If I Knew You Were Coming I'd Have Baked A Cake." This may not have seemed the most logical apprenticeship for musicalizing Eugene O'Neill, but Merrill proved his abilities by writing the score for a play that seemed even less a candidate for a Broadway musical than *Ah, Wilderness!* The latter play, a nostalgic look at pre-World War I America, had been written with the song and dance man George M. Cohan in mind and had been made into an MGM musical, *Summer Holiday*, which starred Mickey Rooney.

Merrill's first Broadway hit was based on a far less lyrical

O'Neill play, *Anna Christie*, which is about the return of a prostitute to visit her seafaring father, who has no idea how she has supported herself over the years. Merrill had originally intended to write it as a movie musical for Doris Day. Instead he and the veteran director-writer George Abbott turned this material into *New Girl In Town*, proving that O'Neill was more musical than anyone had imagined.

The morning after the show opened, Merrick phoned Merrill to congratulate him on his score. He made it a habit to phone people in their moments of success. Unlike some producers, he also phoned in moments of failure, to offer consolation on bad reviews they may not have deserved. If he ever wanted to employ them, it was the sort of gesture they would remember.

Shortly afterward, Merrick met Merrill in Shubert Alley. When Merrill looked at the somber, paternal figure in a black homburg and a black coat, who was very courteous and very terse, he felt an immediate bond. In Merrick he immediately sensed a father figure.

Merrick told him to reread *Ah, Wilderness!* When Merrill fell in love with the play, Merrick introduced him to Joseph Stein, whom he asked to adapt the play. The two men hit it off and spent the summer of 1958 working in Stein's house on Fire Island on what would be called *Take Me Along*.

Merrick hired two men who would be instrumental to the show's success, Jackie Gleason, at the height of his TV fame as the star of *The Honeymooners*, and the British director Peter Glenville.

In hiring Glenville, Merrick again aimed for prestige. To Merrill the very sight of Glenville conjured up Anthony Eden. Like many Englishmen then working in the theater, Glenville dressed elegantly and spoke in a cultivated accent that commanded immediate respect, particularly in New York. He was in fact the son of a famous English vaudeville team, which helped him appreciate Gleason.

O'Neill's young hero has read books by Carlyle and Shaw and two by Oscar Wilde. Glenville seized upon the last-named as a visual cue, suggesting that where the boy experiences his first hangover his dreams would be influenced by Wilde's illustrator, Aubrey Beardsley. The costumes for the number would be, like Beardsley's lithographs, entirely in black and white.

In 1959, the art nouveau work of Beardsley was as "out" as an artistic style could be, and Beardsley was a name known only to the cognoscenti. For all his aspirations toward "class," Merrick was not among those cognoscenti. He hated the Aubrey Beardsley ballet. At one point he stole the music off the musicians' stands. It was a ploy he would use to greater effect on later shows. This time he decided to replace it.

Glenville himself was dissatisfied with the choreography for the whole show, particularly his pet ballet. The choreographer, Onna White, who had not been his choice, had scored a great success a few years earlier with *The Music Man*, another musical set in pre-World War I America. Although her steps, Glenville felt, had an extroverted, bouncy zest, they were not right for *Take Me Along*. He told Merrick it was a "disgrace" and persuaded him to fire her and hire instead a young choreographer whose work he thought was very promising, Herb Ross.

With Ross making wonderful progress, Glenville decided to take a quick break in Cuba, a popular resort for show business people in the pre-Castro days. He had been there only a few days when he received a wire from Merrick ordering him to return immediately.

He was summoned to Merrick's office, where Merrick, with only a little awkwardness, told him the original ballets had to be restored. Since Merrick had agreed with the decision to fire Onna White, Glenville could not make sense of what seemed an arbitrary reversal. Nothing about their confrontation seemed rational.

When he had first met Merrick he thought of an American Proust, a sensitive fellow translated into a man of action and business. But he soon saw that the surface was misleading. He came to see Merrick as "a strange deep sea mammal swimming in extremely deep waters—occasionally you would see a spurt above the water. It was when you were having a row with him that he was at his least unfathomable."

Glenville analyzed the scene as follows: If Merrick could make Glenville lose control, Merrick himself would be entitled to lose his temper and carry the day. But Glenville refused to be pushed into such a trap.

Merrick tried to rile him by accusing him that he had "deserted" the show to take a vacation. Glenville suggested a compromise: restore the first act ballet and let Ross finish his work on the Beardsley piece. Merrick agreed.

Only later did Glenville discover what Merrick was too gentlemanly to articulate. The original choreographer was having an affair with one of the Shuberts, in whose theater the show would be housed. Her reputation was at stake, and her protector did not want it jeopardized.

In only a few years Merrick would not need to tolerate such awkwardness. He would be beholden to absolutely no one. Theater owners, other producers, stars—no one would outrank him. Right now he was expert at playing the game by the established rules. Increasingly he would make his own.

In Philadelphia, when the show was essentially "set" and already in performance, Merrill remembers standing at the back of the theater leaning on the rail behind the orchestra seats. Glenville was on stage working on some details with the dancers on the hated Beardsley ballet.

"I felt a finger like steel in my shoulder," Merrill recalls. "It was David."

Merrick, he remembers, then told him: "I've just come in from New York. I want you this minute to walk down the aisle and fire that son of a bitch friend of yours."

"David, you're the producer," Merrill said.

"No. I want you to have the pleasure," Merrick rejoined.

Merrill realized Merrick wasn't kidding.

Firing became an integral part of the ritual of producing a Merrick musical. Merrick could not fire anyone under contract unless formal legal provisions had been met. What he *could* do was make life so miserable for his victim that he would leave under his own volition. Then Merrick, as the newly aggrieved party, would indeed have the grounds to begin the legal maneuvers.

Merrill really understood none of this as he uneasily walked down the aisle toward the stage. He leaned over the orchestra pit. "Peter, I want to talk to you," he said awkwardly.

Glenville looked at him as one might at a pesky child. He was surprised to find the composer interrupting a rehearsal and insisted whatever it was could wait until later. Merrill insisted it could not. Glenville came forward to the apron of the stage. Merrill pointed to the back of the dark theater and said, "David's standing back there, and you're fired."

Merrill remembers that Glenville took only a few seconds before he asked, "Do you know anything about the weather in Jamaica?" And then Glenville said goodbye to Merrill, walked up the aisle, shook Merrick's hand and left.

Not all firings were final. It was most often a temporary measure to keep people down. By refusing to pay them, Merrick put them in a position where they had to sue to get what was rightfully, contractually theirs. The fact that he had "fired" them suggested some sort of incompetence or insubordination.

Herb Ross, in fact, had to sue Merrick to get his salary for *Take Me Along*. By the time the case came to trial Merrick needed him for something else. Virtually the day before Ross and Merrick appeared before the judge, Ross's agent received a call from Merrick's office offering him a job. Ross's lawyer came to court jubilant. How could his client be incompetent, he asked the judge, if Merrick was hiring him for another show? Merrick, straight-faced, asked the judge, "Your honor, am I to be penalized for giving this man a second chance?" He and Ross made an out-of-court settlement.

In fact the firings—as was certainly the case with both Ross and Glenville in *Take Me Along*—often came at a point where the creative work was almost completely finished.

Not always, of course. Joe Stein had been fired quite early in the proceedings. Shortly before the show went into production

Glenville wasn't confident that Stein could deliver the necessary rewrites. He wanted to hire Robert Russell, a friend, for the last draft.

Merrick used Glenville's complaints to his own advantage. He explained the situation to Stein. Stein complained to his agent, who had already spoken to Merrick. The William Morris agency, which represented Stein, also handled several others connected with the production, including Gleason.

Merrick's power was so great that he could influence William Morris to the disadvantage of its own client. The agency urged Stein not to make a fuss. They persuaded him it would be in his long term interest to maintain a cordial relationship with Merrick. (Ultimately another sixteen years went by before Merrick asked him to work again.) They even got Stein to settle for a 1% royalty rather than the standard 3% authors received.

While the show was on its pre-Broadway tour there was need for further revision. Stein himself was called in to do the rewrites. He was surprised and angry to find that the script that had theoretically been revised by Russell was essentially the script he had written. He made the necessary revisions and then demanded an arbitration to restore his full royalty. He was amazed to find that Russell was also only getting 1% royalties, meaning Merrick had secured the services of two writers for less than he would normally have to pay one.

The arbitrator acknowledged the unfairness of the situation but decided that since Stein had signed a document waiving 2% of his royalties he would be held to the terms he had once agreed to. On the way out of the hearing the disgruntled Stein ran into Merrick.

"You had a good case," Merrick told him. "If I had been your lawyer, you would have won."

Take Me Along opened at the Shubert Theater September 9, 1959, to enthusiastic notices. It had, after all, a great cast. In addition to Gleason there was Walter Pidgeon, in his Broadway debut, as well as Una Merkle, Robert Morse and Eileen Herlie. It had Oliver Smith sets that conjured up the lightness and innocence of a simpler America.

It was the third musical Merrick had produced that year. All had opened in less than six months, though several had been in the works for a long time. These were all his projects, not prestige products imported from England. Merrick had every right to act a little more cocky.

But Broadway always had pitfalls you could never expect. During the 1959-1960 season Merrick produced his first show that closed out of town. It was by John Patrick, whose *Willow and I* Merrick had co-produced as one of his first professional ventures. It was called *Jupiter and the Pagans* and starred David Wayne, who had scored a huge hit in Patrick's adaptation of the novel *Teahouse of the August Moon*.

Jupiter had been cast by a new member of the Merrick team, Michael Shurtleff. Shurtleff, a man who was as opinionated as he was knowledgeable, had worked for Jean Dalrymple, who ran the theater companies of the City Center. At the time he was working for Ethel Linder Reiner, the producer of *Candide*. Shurtleff made up his mind that he wanted to work for David Merrick. He laid siege to him. Once a week for about seven months he wrote Merrick a letter, discussing what was good and bad about his shows. He asked all his friends who knew Merrick to mention him to the producer. Finally Merrick's curiosity was piqued when he was at a dinner party in Los Angeles and Mrs. Daniel Taradash, the wife of the screenwriter, asked him, "Why don't you answer Michael Shurtleff's letters?"

When he got back to New York, Merrick called Shurtleff at Reiner's office and asked him to come over for a chat. Shurtleff told Reiner he would be gone for a little while. He arrived at Merrick's office at 1:00 that Friday afternoon and did not leave until 5:00. They talked about Merrick's shows, Shurtleff providing a more astute analysis of them than the critics. At an early age Shurtleff had trained himself "never to be a passive audience member."

Merrick, impressed, offered him a job immediately as his casting director, starting the following Monday. Shurtleff said he owed Reiner three weeks' notice.

"I don't like decency like that," Merrick told him but accepted his terms.

He was sent down the hall to Schlissel, who told him his salary would be $150 a week. Shurtleff thought it was too little but agreed to prove himself before demanding more. He told Schlissel he would work for two months at that salary, and if he had shown his value, he would expect a raise to $200. Otherwise he would quit. The last week of the "tryout" period, when no notice of the raise had been given, Shurtleff said to Schlissel, "This is my last week, isn't it?"

"I haven't had a chance to talk to David," Schlissel said. So Shurtleff packed his few belongings and left the office.

"I'm not going to shake your hand. You're a traitor," Schlissel said.

Monday, Shurtleff expected a call from the Merrick office. Nothing. Tuesday, nothing. Then Wednesday, when Merrick hadn't heard from him, he was rehired at the higher salary. Shurtleff became a member of the inner circle. When *Jupiter* was trying out in Boston, he joined a conference with Merrick, Schlissel and Hartley.

"Shurtleff, this is your first show. What do you think we should do with it?" Merrick asked him.

"Leave it in Boston," Shurtleff replied.

"You're the freshest kid I've ever had working for me," Merrick said. But they all knew Shurtleff was right. The play never reached New York.

A Merrick production that did reach New York with all the earmarks of success then floundered, illustrating just how treacherous the commercial theater could prove. In the spring of 1960 he produced a comedy Garson Kanin and Ruth Gordon had discovered in Paris, *The Good Soup*, by Felicien Marceau, a play about a woman who made a fortune in the world's oldest profession before devoting herself to higher pursuits. In the course of the play she reminisces about the compromises she made in her difficult youth. She appears on stage both as a mature woman and as her younger self. (Gordon played the older woman; the younger role went to Diane Cilento.)

The cast—which included Mildred Natwick, Sam Levene and Jules Munshin—was strong, the premise strong, the advance healthy.

The play failed because it aroused the enmity of one man, Walter Winchell. It was perhaps the only time in his entire career that Merrick was defeated by a titan of comparable power.

Winchell had been a potentate in New York for almost three decades. Like Merrick, he was a product of slums, in this case those of the Lower East Side. He too made his way by the adroit use of his tongue. His was sheathed in a gossip column, at one time the most widely circulated in the United States. He wounded enemies by printing gossip. He could control them by *threatening* to print it. Where many columnists adopted a tone of geniality and the breeziness of social aloofness, Winchell's style was abrasive and nasty, the voice of the little guy inflated by his own unexpected power.

Starting in the late Thirties, he also adopted the pose of the superpatriot, which reached hysterical proportions in the McCarthy years. By the Fifties he had been powerful for so long that he had lost any sense of mortal boundaries whatsoever. Among those he accused of being Red was the most popular woman in America, Lucille Ball. The allegation was entirely untrue, but Winchell was not used to making corrections or retractions, let alone apologies. He had gone too far. Newspapers began to drop Winchell's column in huge numbers. The only place it still mattered was New York.

In 1960, it turned out, Winchell still mattered very much. What aroused him about *The Good Soup* was a report—from an unnamed source—that its author had broadcast Nazi propaganda during World War II, had fled his native Belgium and had been tried in absentia after the war for deeds of collaboration; if he ever returned to his native land, Winchell reported, he would be forced to spend fifteen years in prison.

Many New York theatergoers were Jewish, who went to the theater all too often "not single spies but whole battalions." Many of the theater parties booked for *The Good Soup* were sponsored by Jewish organizations, likely to be sensitive to charges that the author was a Nazi collaborator.

Kanin and Merrick countered Winchell's smears by pointing out that Marceau was a naturalized citizen of France, which was scrupulous about investigating accusations of collaboration. Marceau's French citizenship papers had been signed, in fact, by no less a figure than Charles de Gaulle.

Marceau, born Albert Caret, had fought in the Belgian army until its surrender. He then indeed had gone to work in in a radio station run by the occupying German forces. Though he tried to dilute German news propaganda, his voice was heard broadcasting German communiques on the radio. After the war other radio station employees—administrators, technicians, musicians—were not tried, only the broadcasters. Marceau was one of them.

The broadcasters' defense was that the Belgian Minister of Communication had himself directed radio employees to stay at work when the Germans came. Shortly after issuing this order, the Minister fled to England. When he returned after the war he was named Minister of Justice. In a grotesque inconsistency, he refused to admit the order he himself gave to be used as evidence in the case of French language broadcasters, though six months later he did permit it as a defense for Flemish language radio employees.

Another piece of evidence in Marceau'sbehalf was that the Habimah, the national theater of Israel, had mounted one of his earlier plays, *The Egg*, and the Israelis were certainly as sensitive to allegations of collaboration as the French.

Facts were of no interest to Winchell. In one of his dispatches he wrote: "D. Merrick, *Good Soup* producer (written by a convicted Nazi in Belgium) was born David Margulois. Non-Aryan . . . Rabbis are now in the fight—not so much against the Nazi author but against show biz people who like money more than they hate Nazis."

Rabbis had indeed entered the fray, but not on the side of Winchell. When the Women's League for Israel cancelled two theater parties, Rabbi Jay Kaufman, vice-president of the Union of American Hebrew Congregations, the official organization of Reform Jews, issued a statement declaring that no entertainment should be judged on the basis of the political affiliation of its creator. "Judaism's ethical teaching forbids such trial by boycott," he said.

Rabbi Kaufman himself was more concerned with the apparent licentiousness of the play, which had caused much outrage during its Washington tryout. Describing the play as "frivolous and transitory," he questioned whether it was a suitable choice for religious groups' theater parties.

Merrick was delighted with Rabbi Kaufman's remarks. "Rabbi Kaufman is quite right in saying the play is frivolous, although frivolous with a point, and is designed only as entertainment," he told a reporter. "It is definitely not *J.B.* [an update of the Book of Job by Archibald MacLeish then on Broadway]. I'm glad Rabbi Kaufman brought up the point. I was beginning to fear that people might think *The Good Soup* was a political play rather than the comedy it is."

As for cancellation of theater parties, Merrick refused to hear of it. He would not refund any money. He would regard the cancellations as a breach of contract and would sue. Besides, he declared, "Some of these same people have been buying and selling merchandise like cars and cameras made by ex-Nazi manufacturers."

A few years afterward Marceau was elected to the Academie Française, an honor the French would not have conferred on a collaborator. But that was too late to save *The Good Soup*.

Despite these ordeals and a short run, *The Good Soup* returned 96% of its investment because of a film sale to Twentieth Century Fox and a successful pre-Broadway run in Washington. Recalling the struggle to save the play, Kanin said, "Merrick behaved very well, but with—for him—surprising naivete. He didn't take Walter Winchell seriously."

By the end of the year, in fact, Merrick showed he could take the episode in stride. In October of 1960 he had another show opening in Philadelphia, *Do Re Mi*, written and directed by Kanin, with lyrics by Betty Comden and Adolph Green and a score by Jule Styne. In his opening night wire to Kanin, Merrick wrote, "If Winchell does not find out that Jule is for Nixon, we're safe. Thanks for everything and Good Luck Tonight. Affectionately, David."

During the Washington run of *The Good Soup*, the Kanins invited Ruth's old friend Felix Frankfurter to dinner. The Supreme Court justice was an icon to Jews of his generation, a symbol of the heights Jews might attain in America. When Merrick heard the Kanins were going to have dinner with him, "he became all pale," Kanin remembered. "I know this is a terrible thing to ask, but would you let me go with you?" The Kanins were happy to oblige.

Merrick was already seated when the Kanins and Frankfurter arrived at the restaurant. Introductions were made, and dinner lasted a leisurely few hours. Merrick listened to the conversation, nodded and "never uttered one single word."

The next morning, when Frankfurter called to thank the Kanins for their hospitality, he asked, "What's the matter with your friend? Did I intimidate him in some way?" Kanin explained that Merrick was terribly shy.

Meeting Frankfurter may have reminded Merrick of his own beginnings and ambitions in the legal profession. With his degree from a St. Louis law school he might have done well back in the Midwest. But it would not have given him entree to the prestigious law firms in either New York or Washington. Although his mind was unusually agile and he frequently used his legal skills to win advantage on his chosen turf, he sensed the difference between that turf and Frankfurter's domain. He had come an extraordinary distance in the twenty years since he left St. Louis, but Frankfurter suggested a further distance he could not travel.

CHAPTER FOURTEEN

T WENTY YEARS HAD ELAPSED since David and Leonore had moved to New York. As there had been in 1940, there were voices in the spring of 1960 proclaiming the imminent death of Broadway. The jeremiads cited the dearth of new American plays (though they were grateful for the new British plays that arrived with such frequency, often thanks to Merrick).

The voices of despair were generally more concerned with plays than musicals. Often they were disdainful of the very idea of musicals. Which is why, in lamenting the state of Broadway, they ignored the fact that it was in the midst of a golden age of musical theater.

My Fair Lady and *The Music Man* were still in their initial runs. That fall there would be a revival of *West Side Story* (which had received mixed reviews at its debut three years earlier.) *Fiorello!*, one of the handful of musicals to win the Pulitzer Prize, opened that spring. *Gypsy* was completing the first year of its run in the spring of 1960.

Some of the same names that had been big in 1940 were still potent. Lindsay and Crouse, who had scored their big hit *Life With Father* twenty years earlier, had written the book for Rodgers and Hammerstein's *The Sound of Music*, which opened in the fall of 1959. Lillian Hellman, an acclaimed writer twenty years earlier, had her last major play, *Toys in the Attic*, produced in

At the Savoy in London, with Jeanne Gilbert.

the spring of 1960.

Many of the young artists who were beginning their careers in 1940 were now major figures. Both *Gypsy* and *West Side Story* owed much of their vision to Jerome Robbins, who had been a chorus dancer in 1940. So, back then, was Gower Champion, who, in the spring of 1960, directed and choreographed *Bye, Bye, Birdie*, a spoof of a musical style growing in popularity, rock 'n' roll, which Broadway could still afford to regard with amused condescension.

Unlike 1940, there were virtually no empty theaters. These days there were not enough theaters to hold the plays waiting to open, especially if, like Merrick, you were choosy about the houses in which your shows would play. In addition to the Broadway scene, there was great activity Off-Broadway. Along with plays by such avant-garde Europeans as Samuel Beckett and Jean Genet and a young American named Edward Albee, a musical called *The Fantasticks*, by Tom Jones and Harvey Schmidt, opened that spring.

Despite the jeremiads, this seemed like a lively and propitious time for the theater. It was certainly so for Merrick. In the course of the year 1960 he had 11 shows on Broadway, some holdovers from other seasons, others shortlived entries for the new season, still others "hits" that would keep Merrick's name in lights for some time to come.

On a hot July day in 1960 a bus lumbered up the driveway of a country house in Connecticut. Out of the bus piled a group of New Yorkers who had come up for the day to surprise the producer Alexander H. Cohen, who was celebrating his 40th birthday. The party was organized by his wife, the former actress Hildy Parks.

The passengers on the bus included Jason Robards and Lauren Bacall, Sidney and Gail Lumet, David Susskind, John Shubert of the Shubert Organization, Herman Levin, the producer of *My Fair Lady*, and other friends. One of the last to leave the bus, and a considerable surprise to Cohen, was Merrick.

Cohen and Merrick had known each other from the late Forties on. They had often spent time together in London, both having realized there was a great business to be done in importing British plays. They tended to be in London together when there would be a cluster of shows opening. They both flew BOAC. They both stayed at the Savoy. And they both traveled alone.

They would sometimes breakfast together at the Savoy to discuss what they had seen. Merrick had only one topic of conversation, the theater. "If you'd had a tape recorder, you could have learned a fantastic amount about show business," Cohen recalled. Once they had both been interested in producing the same show. Merrick suggested they co-produce it. Cohen had to fly back to New York and was grateful to Merrick, who offered to negotiate on behalf of both of them. He soon discovered that Merrick had negotiated only on behalf of Merrick. The show was *Look Back In Anger*.

"I came to see that he was a 24 ct. gold prick," Cohen said. But the two remained, albeit warily on Cohen's part, friends.

It was at the Savoy that Merrick met the woman who accompanied him on the bus to Connecticut. Her name was Jeanne Gilbert. She was an attractive blonde with a great sense of humor, a wealth of gossip and an unforgettable vivacity. A Kentucky girl, her roots were as poor as Merrick's. She, however, had risen from poverty not with his bitter edge, but with an earthiness and frankness that added to her charm. Despite her sophisticated veneer she would ironically refer to herself as "a hillbilly."

Jeanne had come to New York in 1948, when she was only nineteen, to model for the Barbizon Agency. In 1950 she married Justin Gilbert, the movie critic of the *Daily Mirror*. They had a daughter Kimberly. Jeanne divorced Gilbert in 1959. By the late Fifties she was already working in London as a press consultant to the Savoy Hotel.

Jeanne had blue eyes, perfect teeth and an altogether radiant smile. She wore very little makeup but what she wore she applied with great care. Invariably she wore her hair drawn back to show her face. Her demeanor was quiet and gentle, and, friends remembered, her look could melt you.

She was a perfect representative for the Savoy. She was popular with prominent Londoners and equally so with Americans, particularly the theater people who were extremely fond of the plush, conveniently situated hotel. When she left the Savoy the management gave her a huge party with an American-style brass band.

Merrick's relationship with her started casually. He preferred casualness in his dealings with women, which made it so convenient to have affairs with his own employees. As far as one associate could see, they were often "stupid women, caricatures, girls you wouldn't want to be seen with." But this was not always the case.

Just as friendship was difficult for him, so was intimacy. One-on-one relationships were difficult to sustain. He liked women who could, whenever he needed it, cheer him up. He didn't necessarily want to have to see them on a regular basis.

His approach to women was frank and straightforward. Ruth Kligman, who was the mistress of Jackson Pollock, described a date with Merrick in the first chapter of *Love Affair*, her memoir of her relationship with Pollock. "He was so smooth, like polished silver, and as cold," she wrote of Merrick.

As they drove in his limousine he did not whisper endearments in her ear. He talked to her of power: "We're the same kind of people, you and I, we are of the same cloth. We're both Jews and have that rare quality of knowing what the price is, and we are willing to pay it."

As the Nietzschean seduction continued, he stroked Kligman's leg and told her, "Most people are weak. It takes courage to admit that you are stronger than most. I know I am. I respect no one except myself . . . There is no such thing as unfair. It is simply a matter of inferiority and superiority. I know more than most people and I use it. I control . . . You must begin to see other people as puppets; you will pull the strings. If you don't control them, they will control you."

Apart from such conquests, he liked sexual *frissons* of another sort. One of his publicists, a man sometimes credited with devising the stunts for which Merrick took credit, was equally skilled at throwing wild parties, to which he would sometimes invite the gypsies from Merrick's shows.

Once one of the women who worked as a scriptreader in Merrick's office was at a cocktail party where she happened to hear the publicist discussing one of his upcoming bashes. One of the guests mentioned he was trying to find cardinal's robes to wear. The scriptreader, fascinated, asked if she might come. Merrick, who was standing nearby, refused to allow it. "No, no, no," he said. "She's a nice girl, and she works for me very properly."

Jeanne was an exception to the women with whom Merrick enjoyed casual sex, casual companionship. He enjoyed her company. She was a woman he was quite proud to be seen with. People who spent time with the two of them saw her as a civilizing influence.

Merrick wanted to be thought of as sophisticated, but he wasn't good at the things that implied sophistication—things like being a gracious host, negotiating a menu in French, or ordering wine with dinner. In a very gentle way she handled such chores for him. He had been too busy learning about the theater to be concerned with worldly matters. He never really cared about either food or alcohol. "He always ordered sparingly and never finished," Cohen recalled. "I never saw him drink except late at night in London. It would be a Stinger (half cognac and half creme de menthe) or a Campari and soda. And mainly he would play with the swizzle stick."

Jeanne helped him find his way around French menus. She smartened up his dress. She did so without ever making him feel insecure or self-conscious, perhaps because she knew that he was more serious about her than he was about the chorus girls. She was deeply devoted to him, and she was already pressuring him to divorce Leonore and marry her.

Merrick had no particular interest in rustic tranquility, which was yet another reason Cohen was touched that he had accepted the invitation to the country at all. Merrick was a man of the city.

"Once I asked David to come for a walk," Cohen recalled. "He looked at me and said, 'Where would you walk to here?'"

Whatever Merrick felt about wasting a Sunday in the country, Jeanne had a wonderful time that afternoon, so much so that she didn't want to leave. The Cohens invited them to spend the night. They all got up early. Jeanne and Alex went for a swim. Merrick, in the pinstripe suit he had worn the day before, watched.

Alex drove them back to New York. As he drove the two engaged in what would be a ritual of their years together, a morning quarrel. "She began the day asking him to marry her, and he wouldn't hear of it."

Jeanne's morning also began with a stiff drink. She had always been a drinker. She could handle it, but she drank a lot and in the next few years she would drink even more. Merrick seemed to intensify her need for alcohol. He could be charming one minute, testy, angry the next. But something about him got under her skin. Over the years she would undergo extraordinary abuse and coldness, but she never got over the fantasy that he wanted her as much as she wanted him.

There had been plenty of time for the two to see each other in London. Three of the shows Merrick would produce in the fall of 1960 were English imports. They opened in a little over a week. They were all hits, which meant that, with the holdovers from previous seasons (*La Plume de Ma Tante*, *Gypsy* and *Take Me Along*), he had six successful shows on Broadway simultaneously, a statistic he would maintain for several seasons to come.

On September 29, 1960, *Irma La Douce* opened to extremely favorable reviews. The show had run for four years in Paris in a tiny theater well off the beaten path. It had a score by the French pop composer Marguerite Monnot, a name Americans were unlikely to know, though they knew one of her greatest songs, "Milord", because it had been popularized by Edith Piaf. *Irma* had created a stir in her native Paris because the lyrics used slang so specialized even the Parisians required a glossary in the program.

Irma had crossed the Channel to London very quickly. There she proved equally popular. What made *Irma* a show of note, though no one sensed it at the time, was that—despite its saucy, endearing score and its "whore with a heart of gold" plot—it was very much an experimental musical. It used almost no scenery. Its cast consisted of all men except the title character. At a time when American musicals prided themselves on their psychological subtlety, *Irma* relied on old-fashioned touches from vaudeville and burlesque to tell its story.

None of this was surprising considering that *Irma* was directed in London and New York by Peter Brook, who began a cordial relationship with Merrick on this production and maintained it for many years. Brook found Merrick an agreeable man to deal with "as long as he feels you're on precisely the same wavelength as he is."

Irma cost $175,994. It had a cast of unknowns—the English Elizabeth Seal, Keith Michell and Clive Revill and such young American performers as George S. Irving, Fred Gwynne and Elliot Gould. None of these names was likely to draw a large advance, but well before it opened, it had begun to move toward a profit. The film rights were sold to Billy Wilder and the Mirisch Brothers for $225,000.

What most delighted Merrick about the New York reviews, a columnist reported, was that several critics and columnists had called it "dirty," an adjective he estimated would give the show a three year run. Walter Kerr began a Sunday column in the *Herald-Tribune*, "I must say this leaves me in a terrible position. I didn't much care for *Irma La Douce* and I don't think it's dirty. (My apologies to Mr. Merrick. I realize I couldn't have said anything worse.)"

This, it turned out, was the opening sally in a verbal war the two would keep up for much of the next decade. In any case Kerr's demurrals did not impede *Irma*, which ran for well over a year on Broadway and had a successful road tour before becoming a Billy Wilder film starring Shirley MacLaine, in which the songs were used merely as background music.

There were also two English plays that fall. One of them was expected to be a huge hit, the other was a huge gamble. The expected hit was Jean Anouilh's *Becket*, which starred Laurence Oliver and Anthony Quinn. *Becket* was Anouilh's retelling of the story of the rivalry between King Henry II and the Archbishop of Canterbury, which resulted in the infamous "murder in the cathedral." Peter Glenville, who directed the play, cast Olivier not as Henry II but as the Archbishop, reasoning that it would be hard enough for another actor to act opposite Olivier, let alone Olivier playing a king. Quinn was cast as the king.

Despite its stars, despite favorable reviews, *Becket* did not find an audience. For much of its engagement it was available on "two-fers," coupons that allow you to buy two tickets for the price of one. When it closed in January it was a flop.

Normally, because business was soft, Merrick would have closed it sooner. But by keeping it open a little longer, he made $37,500 for the production. There was a clause in Quinn's contract that specified he had to remain in the show for its entire Broadway run. Merrick knew that the Italian film producer Dino De Laurentiis needed Quinn to begin shooting *Barrabas*. In order to release the star from his Broadway contract, De Laurentiis paid Merrick $37,500, which meant that *Becket* lost only $100,000 of its $185,814 investment.

Because Olivier was still available, Merrick decided to send *Becket* on tour. For the road company Olivier would play the king and the young American actor Arthur Kennedy played Becket. At the suggestion of Alex Cohen, who arranged bookings for the 3,000 seat O'Keefe Center in Toronto, Merrick sent it there. The week it played Toronto the play broke the house record, grossing $100,104.24. That week, in fact, Merrick himself established a record. The combined grosses of his shows on Broadway and out of town were $389,714.24, the largest any producer had ever achieved in one week.

In April, when *Becket* won Tonys for Best Play and Best Set Design, Merrick brought it back to New York, this time at the Hudson Theater. In the smaller theater, business was very good. By the time it closed *Becket* had become, in *Variety*'s term, a "financial sleeper." From being $100,000 in the red in January, it was $40,000 in the black in June.

Just as he had cemented a strong relationship with Peter Brook, Merrick continued a solid friendship with Olivier. "A lot of people dislike David," Olivier once told Quinn. "I like him."

"Why is that, Sir Larry?" Quinn asked.

"The general consensus is that a leader should take care of the masses before the few," Olivier said. "He doesn't worry about the masses. He takes care of the principals."

Of the trio of English plays he imported that fall the one that mattered the most to him was the biggest gamble, *A Taste of Honey*, written by a young Englishwoman named Shelagh Delaney.

Delaney had been an usher at a theater in Manchester. She was disgusted by the artifice of a Terrence Rattigan play she saw there. Convinced she could write something better, she began *A Taste of Honey*. She was only nineteen when she finished it.

She sent it to Joan Littlewood, who was, along with George Devine of the Royal Court, the most important of the London figures challenging the "established" theater of the West End. In a cover letter Delaney wrote Littlewood, "I am sending the play to you for your opinion. Would you please return it to me, as whatever sort of theatrical atrocity it is to you, it means something to me."

Littlewood was so enthusiastic about the play she put it into rehearsal two weeks later. It opened at the Theater Royal in the East End of London May 27, 1958, then at Wyndham's in the West End February 10, 1959.

Delaney's play concerns a young woman whose aging mother is too obsessed with herself to worry about her. The young woman falls in love with a black sailor, who leaves her pregnant.

The closest her child will come to a live-in father will be the gentle homosexual who is the young woman's closest friend.

It was a harsh, unsentimental play, bleaker perhaps than *Look Back In Anger* because it had no intellectual patina to keep the audience at a distance from its protagonist's pain. Merrick found himself as deeply drawn to it as he had been to the Osborne play. He optioned it and brought back a script to show to the people in his office. The only one to share his enthusiasm was Michael Shurtleff.

Schlissel was angry when he discovered that Shurtleff was as eager to do it as Merrick. Schlissel dragged him into his office and told him, "The Shuberts hate this. Byron hates it. I hate it. If it weren't for you, he wouldn't do this play. The Shuberts won't even give us a decent theater. They're talking about the Lyceum."

Merrick forged ahead. In his whole career few plays meant as much to him as this one did. He had hoped to bring it in during the 1959-60 season, but first there had been a shortage of theaters, then, in the spring of 1960, a strike by Actors' Equity (which Merrick called "the best show last season"). Had he had any doubts about the play, either of these might have served as a pretext for cancelling the production. Even the discouragement of his most trusted associates could not dissuade him from producing it.

Shurtleff had assembled a remarkable cast. Angela Lansbury played the callous mother, Joan Plowright the young girl, and a young American actor named Billy Dee Williams played the sailor.

Because the Shuberts were not interested in it, even the out-of-town tryout was difficult to arrange. Instead of opening in one of the customary cities along the Eastern Seaboard, *A Taste of Honey* made its American debut in Cincinnati. It was part of a subscription series in a theater much too large for so intimate a play. Moreover Cincinnati, just across the Mason-Dixon line, was in many ways, a city with a Southern temperament. In 1960 its provincial, conservative audience was not likely to warm up to a play in which one of the first things they saw was Joan Plowright kissing Billy Dee Williams.

The opening performance was a nightmare. After the first act Shurtleff could bear it no longer. He left the theater and began walking forlornly down one of the main streets of Cincinnati. He became aware of a tall, somber figure walking across the street, looking aimlessly into shop windows. It was Merrick. Shurtleff debated whether he should cross the street and say something. But his own mood was too downcast for him to think of anything to say.

The next morning he saw Merrick, still withdrawn, still somber, getting into the first class section of the plane as he entered the economy section. When they got off the plane in New York they met in the terminal area and Merrick offered him a ride into town.

In the limo Merrick told Shurtleff, the one man who had shared his faith in the play, the reason *A Taste of Honey* mattered so much to him.

"I'll tell you if you tell no one," he said. "It's the story of my life."

A Taste of Honey was about a lonely, abandoned child defying the world, telling the world, as Merrick had made a point of doing much of his life, "I don't give a fuck if people like me."

By the time the show opened at the Lyceum October 4, it had found its rhythms—and its audience. At the opening Shurtleff saw even Schlissel crying. "It's a terrible play, isn't it?" Shurtleff teased him.

The critics hailed Delaney's bittersweet voice. The play built an audience, and the Shuberts, eager to capitalize on its success, moved it to the Booth, which meant that Merrick again had plays in four of the seven theaters on West 45th Street.

CHAPTER FIFTEEN

THE HIGH QUALITY that came to be associated with The Merrick Office was in no way apparent in the physical office that occupied part of a floor in the building over the St. James Theater on West 44th Street. The decor was as spartan as Shumlin's had been, its only novelty being a trapdoor from which you could look down eight stories onto the apron of the St. James stage and the front section of the audience.

The number of people Merrick employed at any one time rarely exceeded a dozen people. They worked in small offices that fed into a corridor that made a square and led you back to the entrance.

The furniture was cheap. When Helen Nickerson, who was Merrick's secretary for seventeen years, arrived in 1963, her desk consisted of a wooden board set atop two filing cabinets. Proper furniture did not arrive until 1968, when *Cactus Flower*, set in a smartly furnished dentist's office, closed, and the Merrick office claimed the scenery.

Although it was larger than the other spaces, Merrick's private office was not luxurious. What it was was red. There was a red fake Empire couch. The walls were red. There were some posters of Merrick's shows, which were invariably red. There were a few paintings, noteworthy less for their quality or subject matter than the fact that they too had important touches of red. The shade of red that Merrick preferred, Oliver Smith once sniffed, had "too

Backstage at the St. James during *Do Re Mi* with Garson Kanin.

much brown in it to make a real statement." The writer Sanford Dody characterized the office as resembling "the inside of an ulcerous stomach."

Next to the window that overlooked 44th Street was a baby grand piano, opposite which was a desk that was rather small. It was "classy" but not entirely practical. There was not enough room to pile many things on it, so the piles tended to grow on the nearby sofa.

Stan Freberg, who wrote a show Merrick almost produced, was convinced that there were temperature controls hidden within the little desk, which could turn up the heat of the room. This notion, however, belittles Merrick. He did not require technology to achieve his ends.

The red office was the heart of what was, in the early Sixties, an extraordinarily vibrant organism, unparalleled in its efficiency and prolificacy. Much of what the Merrick office produced in these years came from England, produced by Binkie Beaumont or the equally prestigious Donald Albery. But there were more domestic offerings than at any other time in his career, and there were an astonishing number of musicals.

Do Re Mi was a show based on Garson Kanin's fascination with the relationship between pop music, jukeboxes and organized crime. He wrote it as a novella and envisioned it as a movie. He first brought it to MGM, which, in the early Fifties, was too pre-occupied with Biblical spectacles, to take the project seriously. He tried to pitch it to Columbia Pictures as a vehicle for Judy Garland, who would play a young recording artist. "Surround her with the passe mugs, Edward G. Robinson, George Raft, etc., give her a snappy romantic leading boy, and then spice it up with specialty appearances by top recording artists such as Eddy Fisher, Jo Stafford, Peggy Lee, Joni James, etc., etc." Columbia was not interested.

In 1959 Congress investigated Teamster infiltration of the jukebox business. In a story that created headlines in all the papers, a witness described a gruesome incident in which a

Brooklyn coffee shop owner who wanted to remain independent of the mob was beaten by three goons while his screams were drowned out by music blaring from a jukebox. Riding the wave of public interest, Kanin now sold Merrick on the idea of doing *Do Re Mi* as a musical.

The material was tricky. The gangsters it described were not quite as loveable as those in *Guys and Dolls*. Kanin focused on a man willing to compromise himself in the jukebox business because it represents his last hope of success in a lifetime marked by failure.

To make this shallow, unlikeable man more palatable, Phil Silvers was cast. His nagging wife was played by Nancy Walker, a beloved character actress who had appeared in the Leonard Bernstein-Betty Comden-Adolph Green *On the Town*. Comden and Green wrote the lyrics. Jule Styne wrote the score. Kanin directed it, and it was choreographed by Marc Breaux and Deedee Wood.

In the early stages of *Do Re Mi* Merrick was embroiled in the details of importing *Irma La Douce*, *Becket* and *A Taste of Honey*. He was also mounting a small revue called *Vintage '60*, which had been a mild success out of town but was ruined by all the "improvements" made en route to Broadway. Additional material was added by nineteen writers, including the already established Sheldon Harnick and the young, unknown Fred Ebb. Its cast included a popular Fifties singer named Fay De Witt and two Broadway novices, Michele Lee and Bert Convy.

Finally Merrick could go to Philadelphia and devote his unique energies fully to *Do Re Mi*. One day he told Kanin that he liked what Comden and Green had done but that he knew their limitations. They would be incapable of writing the show's big numbers. At the same time he told Comden and Green he thought that Kanin had taken the book as far as he could but it clearly would not be far enough. Who, he asked them, could be called in to doctor the book?

As it happened, Kanin, Comden and Green were old friends and over dinner that night they laughed about Merrick's plot to set them against each other.

Camaraderie had saved Kanin, Comden and Green from Merrick's bitter spirit. His attacks on individuals required enormous resiliency and strength to withstand. He had watched the first dress rehearsal of *Do Re Mi*, whose costumes were designed by Irene Sharaff, who had won a Tony for her costumes for *The King and I*. She had won an Oscar for the film version of that musical and for *An American in Paris*. Within a few years she would also win Oscars for her work on *West Side Story* and *Cleopatra*.

Sharaff had sensed the adventurousness and darkness of *Do Re Mi* and pointed these qualities up in a palette of harsh colors. As the dress rehearsal ended, Merrick came down the aisle to where she was sitting with an assistant, making notes. He leaned down and thrust his face into hers. "Oh, Miss Sharaff," he said. "I loathe every single costume you've done for this show. You've probably ruined it." He then strode calmly up the aisle.

Kanin watched the moment in horror and went over to Merrick. "Why did you do that?" he asked.

"Oh, that'll shake her up a bit," Merrick chuckled.

Despite Merrick's antagonistic presence, the creators of *Do Re Mi* made an entertaining evening from subject matter that was essentially dark.

Do Re Mi received good to excellent notices. With one exception. The reviewer for the *World-Telegram and Sun*, Frank Aston, called it "an extravagant disaster." The *World-Telegram* was an afternoon paper whose first edition was published at ten in the morning. As soon as the paper arrived on his desk Merrick was on the phone with Aston's editor.

"'Disaster' is a prediction," he told the editor. "Right now, from my window, I can see the people lining up for tickets—the show is going to run for two years. Your notice is the greatest journalistic blunder since the *Chicago Tribune* announced the election of Thomas E. Dewey."

The editor was cowed. He admitted Merrick had a point. Merrick suggested he drop the review altogether from later editions. This the editor refused to do. Then Merrick suggested dropping the final paragraph, in which the critic had made his erroneous prediction, and softening the headline, which, surprisingly, the editor did.

It was a great instance of damage control. The first edition of the *World-Telegram* reached only eight per cent of its circulation. In subsequent editions the review was little more than a plot summary. "I think we were doing the reviewer a favor," Merrick said. "He's a good reviewer. But he made a mistake. At any rate this was all in a morning's work."

Do Re Mi seemed to be a huge hit. President-elect John F. Kennedy insisted on seeing it shortly after it opened, just before his inauguration. The only suitable seats for him were already in the hands of the president of a Jewish organization, which had booked the show as a theater party. In exchange for relinquishing the tickets, she insisted on giving them to Kennedy herself. A woman in the second balcony stood to get a better view of him and her foot became wedged in the seat. A house carpenter had to dismantle it to free her. A few weeks later Harry Truman came to see the show. When Ginger Rogers and Cary Grant came, chorus members searched them out during the show, for which the stage manager reprimanded them afterward. There was excitement on both sides of the footlights. This was what was meant by the magic of Broadway.

If *Do Re Mi* was a glamorous show, it was also an expensive one. It cost $479,738. By the end of the twelfth week of its run, *Variety* predicted it would require twenty-six more sellout weeks to be in the black. It ran for fifty weeks and had a long road tour, but it never fully recovered its investment. Musicals were getting more and more costly.

Merrick and Schlissel had begun to systematize the gamble they took on every show. The weighing of the gamble was one reason contracts were generally not ready at the start of rehearsals (and often not signed until opening night, when Merrick would affix his signature to them on the orange juice stand at the back of the orchestra section).

If Merrick thought the show had longevity built into it, he would offer the creative team a heavy advance and relatively low weekly royalties. If Merrick thought the run would be short, he would give them a low initial fee and offer them extremely generous weekly royalties.

It was the same with backstage expenses. When a show begins its Broadway run it has what is called a "yellow card," a list of the precise number of men required for the stage crew and their specific tasks. During the out-of-town tryout it was the job of the stage managers to make certain there were no needless hands on the show.

Merrick himself would attend a late dress rehearsal or a final preview out of town. He would sit at the stage manager's desk and keep an eye on every crew member, every job that needed to be performed, in order to make sure there was no featherbedding. Then, when the show arrived in New York and finalized its "yellow card" with the union—which specified the size of the crew for every subsequent professional production—there would be no waste.

When *42nd Street* moved from the Winter Garden to the Majestic, he almost closed it prematurely in a fight with the stagehands' union over the necessity of one crew member. It was one of those cases when his rage got the better of him. He told the union and Bernard Jacobs that the show was closed. (Jacobs still keeps a handwritten note to that effect in his desk drawer.)

When even Merrick realized his hubris he had Mitosky call Jacobs to intervene. Only the efforts of Jacobs and the Shubert Organization treasurer Phil Smith allowed the show to go on. But Merrick's insistence that the crew be reduced by one paid off in later years, when the absence of that salary was crucial to touring companies operating on slender budgets.

Merrick stagehands rarely got more than a minimum salary, but because no one equalled his level of production, they always worked. Occasionally when the crew was traveling to another city to set up a show Merrick would order the railroad to put on a sleeper for them. It may have been concern for their comfort; more likely it was his conviction that if they were well-rested they would be more productive and less likely to go into costly over-time. Crews working for other producers would arrive in a strange town at five a.m., left to fend for themselves. Taxis met a David Merrick crew to take them to their lodgings. Merrick's master carpenter, Ted Van Bemel, remembered that Merrick was, in fact, the first producer to give his crews paid vacations. Also he had a kind of loyalty to them. In 1975, when he was producing Tennessee Williams' *The Red Devil Battery Sign*, the director, Ed Sherin, was berating the stage crew when suddenly a solemn voice thundered from the back of the theater, "No one talks to *my* stagehands that way." He reserved that privilege for himself. Merrick forced Sherin to apologize to the crew.

Efficiency was a hallmark of the Merrick organization. It was achieved by a variety of traditional and untraditional means. Emanuel Azenberg, company manager for the 1963 *The Rehearsal,* recalled an incident at the first preview, when Merrick was in the theater. The Anouilh play has a false ending. The curtain falls, but then it rises again on a brief "coda." The porters of the Royale Theater, not being students of Anouilh's dramaturgy, did not know about this unusual touch. They began opening the doors to the street as soon as the curtain first came down. Azenberg raced across the back of the theater to stop them.

After the show Merrick, who had watched Azenberg's alacrity with pleasure, came over to him.

"Why did you do that?" his boss asked him.

"Terror, Mr. Merrick, terror," Azenberg replied.

Terror, even more than efficiency, was the grease that lubricated the Merrick machine.

For Merrick a long-running show was a kind of milk cow whose productivity he continually labored to increase. This involved constant re-negotiation with the creative personnel and sometimes the stars, to get them to accept a smaller percentage of their royalties, which would theoretically go to help promote the show.

As Merrick was fond of telling people, reviews were secondary. "I'll pound away at it as if it had had mixed notices—and get an extra fifty per cent mileage out of it. The good notices just get you off to a start for the first six weeks or so. After that, it's word-of-mouth."

On *Do Re Mi* Merrick asked the whole creative team as well as Phil Silvers to accept a half cut on their weekly royalties to create a fund of extra money for advertising, promotion and to help backers recoup their investment. It was customary on Broadway to ask the creators to forego part of their royalties during weeks when business was insufficient to meet the weekly nut; Merrick insisted on such cuts whether it was a sellout week or a dry one.

If they did not agree to his demands, he would purposely hold back on promotion and advertising. If agents hedged on the percentages he demanded, he would accuse them of wanting to "kill the show."

The weekly statements in which all these matters were theoretically clarified and itemized were, as early as *Fanny*, made purposely vague and uninformative, driving those entitled to royalties into fits of rage they were afraid to display openly before Merrick. The reason invariably given for the royalty cuts he sought was that the investors had to be paid off as soon as possible. But the weekly expenses were often inflated in a way that made it seem unlikely the investors would see their money soon, since the show was so expensive to run.

On the weekly expenses for *Do Re Mi*, for example, Jeanne Gilbert was listed as a press representative. "The fact is that Jeanne Gilbert is a particular friend of David's (a damn wonderful girl, but that is beside the point), and lives in London and has only spent very brief periods in the United States in the last couple of years," one of those who studied the weekly expense statement noted angrily to his agent.

"And just what services she has ever performed for *Do Re Mi* I do not know. Off hand I would say that any part of her salary or payments to her charged to us is not correct. But is there any way of finding out? Isn't this always thrown into general press charges?"

Merrick had asked Kanin, Comden, Green and Silvers each to contribute a third of their royalties "for the purposes of exploitation." This was a huge sum, but they knew if they withheld it there would be no promotion. If they did not give him just as much as he wanted, the promotion would be "inadequate."

Merrick's need to be in absolute charge was apparent from the very beginning of a show, from the first announcement of who would be involved. Should a reporter call one of the creators about possible casting and should he make the mistake of answering the reporter's question, he would receive a call from Merrick even before the item appeared in print. It would go something like this: "You want to take over the publicity? Fine. I won't have anything to do with it." The tone was hysterical. It admitted no compromise even on so slight a matter.

In the early stages of the show any attempt to defy his will would be met by another set of threats. Unless those involved complied absolutely with his ploys, Merrick would threaten to do the show as cheaply as possible to guarantee its failure. Anyone who had spent time with him knew how pathologically cheap he could be (they had seen, after all, the furniture in his office); this too was clearly no idle threat.

The tension before the show opened, crushing even under normal circumstances, was magnified a hundredfold in a Merrick production. There was the litany of Merrick's temper tantrums, his threats to close the show out of town, to take his name off it, to bring in other talent to replace the "inadequate" writers he already had. There might be a jovial little breathing space when the show opened, assuming, of course, that it was a hit. Then the new threats would begin, the need to trim the weekly royalties, sometimes to withhold them altogether.

A Merrick show, even a hit, could be a nightmare from beginning to end. The miracle was that under these circumstances it was possible to turn out work of unusual quality and refinement.

Such a show was *Carnival,* an adaptation of the MGM film *Lili,* itself an adaptation of a Paul Gallico short story about a waif

whose only friends are some circus puppets. The screenplay for
Lili was by a Hollywood pro named Helen Deutsch, who suggested it as a musical to Merrick in 1958. Merrick thought the
score might be written by Gerard Calvi, who had done incidental
music for *La Plume de Ma Tante*, but Calvi's English was too
weak for him to set lyrics sensitively. Merrick then suggested
Harold Rome, but Deustch insisted on Bob Merrill.

Merrill resisted the project because he feared having to create a
song that would rival the popularity of "Hi-Lily, Hi-Lily, Hi-Lo,"
the film's hit song. He was finally seduced by the material, a story
about a European family circus. One way to circumvent the "hit
song" problem, he thought, was to make the score as French as
possible, to avoid a Tin Pan Alley tone.

Merrick humored him. His collaborators, Gower Champion
and Michael Stewart, fresh from their success with *Bye, Bye,
Birdie*, did not. Each morning they came to Merrill's apartment
to listen to the score, always waiting to hear "the hit song."
Merrill would play them variations on French folk melodies.
Each afternoon they left unenthused.

One day, as he walked them to the elevator, he exploded.
"While you're waiting for this fucking elevator, I can write the
song I know you want," he said. He then improvised the tune of
what became "Love Makes the World Go Round." He sensed
their excitement immediately. "That's it," Champion crowed.
And with this unwitting triumph, Merrill knew his battle was
lost.

Merrick was determined to produce the show more austerely
than *Do Re Mi*, which was repaying its investment all too slowly.
He arbitrarily decided to budget *Carnival* at $200,000, less than
half of the $480,000 *Do Re Mi* budget.

"There is too much overproduction on Broadway," he told a
reporter a few weeks after "Carnival" opened. "I've been guilty of
it myself. But I now realize that ultimately it's the words and
music that count and not the sets. 'Do Re Mi' was so expensive
that I got furious. The whole thing got out of hand. I too generously gave everyone what they wanted.

"When I started on *Carnival*, I was determined to hold costs down. I treated it as though we were all starving and didn't have a dollar to spend. We got a young designer, Will Armstrong, who took the set order to a small company that charged less than the bigger companies.

"I could have raised $400,000 to do the show, but I knew [Robert] Griffith and [Harold] Prince have regularly shown it could be done for half. I think my tendency in the past has been to spoil the baby, sometimes to the detriment of the project. From now on I intend to do everything with lighter sets."

The show paid back its investment in twelve weeks. It opened four months after *Do Re Mi*, but by the time *Carnival* had recouped its entire cost, *Do Re Mi* had recovered barely half of its heavier investment.

Part of keeping costs down was keeping salaries down. Kaye Ballard, who had already achieved celebrity on Broadway, was hired for $650 a week. She also made a weekly appearance on the Perry Como show, which taped on Friday afternoons. It was written into her *Carnival* contract that should she arrive at the Imperial Theater as little as one minute late on Friday evening she would have to pay Merrick $750.

At $650, Ballard was making $400 more a week than Jerry Orbach. At a performance Merrick noticed Orbach's wife Marta standing at the back of the orchestra. During a dance number he pointed to a member of the chorus. "You see that guy?" he said to Marta. He's making only $100 less than Jerry. And you know why? Because of Jerry's agent." Merrick agreed to raise Orbach's salary to $350 if he kept it a secret from his agent.

Carnival was the beginning of Merrick's longest creative partnership, with Gower Champion. The two were a splendid match. Champion was as tough, even as cruel a taskmaster as Merrick but much better at concealing it beneath a wholesome all-American charm.

Champion, who had begun dancing as a boy, later studied in Hollywood with Ernest Belcher, who urged him to form a team with his daughter Marge, the lovely girl who had served as a model for the Disney artists who created *Snow White*. The two were married in 1947. Gower, who was short, could not do conventional lifts. Instead of the romantic routines that were standard for such teams, Gower devised comic, refreshingly self-satiric numbers.

He won a Tony in 1948 for his first Broadway directorial assignment, *Lend An Ear*, a revue which also brought acclaim to a young comedienne named Carol Channing. The Champions, starred in several of the great MGM musicals of the late Forties and early Fifties, such as *Show Boat* and *Lovely to Look At*. Champion continued to improve his directorial skills on a number of forgettable Broadway shows, but, with his innovative staging of *Bye, Bye, Birdie* in 1960, he was catapulted into the elite handful of Broadway director-choreographers.

In the early Sixties that elite included Jerome Robbins, Bob Fosse and Michael Kidd, all of whom had fearsome reputations as tyrants. Champion, though he gave the impression of being good-natured, was no exception.

When a show was in its early stages, Merrill recalled, Champion was all charm. Once rehearsals started, he became "imperious—absolutely steel," often forbidding the creators even to watch him at work. "His *mother* couldn't come to the rehearsal hall," Marge Champion, who was also his choreographic assistant, recalled. "If he could have eliminated me, he would have been happy."

An astute observer noted that Marge was actually an integral part of Gower's work. By himself, as was apparent when the two divorced in the early Seventies, his work could be mechanical and cold. But when they were together, when he devised his steps using her body, the work would be warm and beautiful.

Jerry Orbach vividly remembered arriving for his first rehearsal at an unused theater on lower Second Avenue. At the stage door he saw Charles Blackwell, the dancer from *Fanny* who now worked as a stage manager. Orbach greeted him heartily. Blackwell raised his finger to his mouth, shushed him and pointed inside toward the center of the stage. "Mr. Champion is thinking!"

Michael Stewart, who worked with him on many productions, referred to Champion as a "Presbyterian Hitler." Stewart, Orbach recalled, was "deathly afraid of Gower. If he had new lines of dialogue he would give me the line in a whisper and tell me to try it out during rehearsal. If Gower didn't say anything we'd leave it in."

Champion was a perfectionist. Even good reviews did not deter him from tinkering with a show that was on the road. *Carnival* got excellent reviews and enthusiastic audience response in Washington. Champion tinkered with it a little before its Philadelphia opening. The result was a limp audience response at the first performance there. Merrick was enraged. He backed Champion up against the wall of the theater, lifted the short man off the ground so the two men's eyes met and screamed at him to restore the show to exactly the condition it had been in Washington. The scene took place in front of the entire company. No one dared say a word until Merrick stalked off.

Champion simply disappeared for several days, returning only after he exacted a promise from Merrick not to come back before the opening. "Gower was the only one Merrick couldn't eat up or spit out: he could out-Machiavelli David," Merrill said.

Carnival's innovative nature was apparent as soon as the audience entered the theater and saw that the curtain was already up, a great novelty in 1961.

There was a tree in the foreground on an otherwise bare stage with a hazy, French-looking landscape in the distance. Instead of a conventional overture, Pierre Olaf, the wistful looking man who had been the chief bell-ringer in *La Plume de Ma Tante*, entered in clown costume. He sat next to the proscenium playing a smidgen of "Love Makes the World Go Round" on a concertina. Roustabouts drifted on, planted a center pole for the tent. Circus wagons and booths were carried on as the tent was raised. The orchestra began a proper overture.

It was an opening that required enormous precision. The assembling of the set was handled by actors as well as crew. What was being established, after all and above all, was a tone, not just a tent. When Harvey Sabinson, the press agent, realized how complicated the setup was, he came to the final dress rehearsal equipped with a press release he assumed would be necessary. It explained that the opening of *Carnival* would be delayed because of the musical's extraordinary technical demands. When he showed it to Merrick and Champion, they were offended. Sabinson watched the rehearsal, which went off without a hitch. He tore up the press release.

In 1961, at the annual Tony dinner, a ceremony that was not yet televised, Merrick received a special Tony for his contributions to the Broadway theater. A special Tony was also given to the Theater Guild. Some felt it was done to make Merrick's award "palatable."

The award, announced in advance of the dinner, was denounced by other producers, who felt the committee was honoring a packager rather than a producer. They also resented the fact that Merrick constantly gloated about his accomplishments. The Tony would make him even more unbearable . . . if that was possible.

"It's part of the needling techniques that I think are part of the business," Merrick said. "It's certainly not intended to be gloating. I just like to drive them wild." Nevertheless he displayed surprising decorum in accepting the award, neither gloating nor making quips.He always maintained an ambivalent attitude towards his fellow producers. On the one hand he wanted their respect. On the other he did not want to be part of their clique. The reason he asked to be seated away from other theater people at Sardi's was not because he feared they might overhear his dealings. He was too careful for that.

Instead, he told his then accountant Aaron Shapiro, he asked to be seated in Siberia, near the kitchen, as a way of snubbing his nose at those sitting at the choice tables near the entrance.

Shapiro noted he did not even look left as he entered—as any Sardi's regular would—to see who might be there. It was a way of asserting that his success was of a magnitude that transcended any need for daily status reinforcement.

One of the producers who publicly expresssed his annoyance at the special Tony was his old antagonist Kermit Bloomgarden, whom Merrick had outbid for the right to produce *Becket*. Bloomgarden had offered Anouilh an $11,000 advance. Merrick upped it to $15,000. Both these figures would have been considered extravagant only a few seasons before, and Merrick was blamed for the inflation.

At the time Bloomgarden may have been the "classier" of the two producers, but, a rival informed Anouilh that Merrick would be better at selling tickets. Having already enjoyed several prestigious, unprofitable short runs, Anouilh may have been enticed by the possibility of actually making some money.

"The theater was the last small island left where individual creative effort was still feasible, the one place where mass methods of movies and television hadn't completely taken over," a rival producer told a reporter.

"Merrick brought in the assembly line, the pre-packaged show with a big star, a name director and a name-this and a name-that . . . There's less and less room for the fresh, original and medium-sized. The real estate men have got the message.

The theater owner doesn't have to see your script any more before renting you his theater. All he wants to know is, 'Who's your star?' 'Who's your choreographer?'"

FUN DAY IN NEW YORK

SUNDAY IN NEW YORK

CHAPTER SIXTEEN

W HEN *CARNIVAL* WAS TRYING out in Washington, Merrick
invited the syndicated theater critic Ward Morehouse
and his wife Rebecca to see it. Morehouse had known
Merrick for many years. Though he periodically fell under the
same spells of anathema which Merrick placed on all members of
his profession, he and Merrick had a surprisingly good relationship. Merrick could be relaxed and amusing in Morehouse's company.

Jeanne Gilbert, who was also coming to Washington at
Merrick's invitation, drove down with the Morehouses. When
they arrived at the hotel Ward registered, while Rebecca chatted
with Jeanne. When he and Rebecca started to go up to their
room they saw Jeanne remain awkwardly in the lobby. Rebecca
went over to find out what was the matter. Jeanne laughed. "I'm a
little embarrassed," she told her. "I don't know if I'm registered as
Mrs. Merrick or Jeanne Gilbert."

It was typical of Merrick's thoughtlessness, his carelessness
where anything personal was concerned. The infinite attention to
detail that characterized his professional life did not carry over
into the personal arena. In some ways this was not hard to understand.

It took great control, after all, to be David Merrick, so much
control in fact that probably only David Merrick had the requi-
site reserves. It took great control to persuade those who came
into the red office that the man behind the desk, a man who still
bit his fingernails and never managed to keep them clean, was
indeed Merrick the great and powerful. Even the Wizard of Oz,
another Midwesterner who wielded great power in an alien city,

had considerable stage machinery at his disposal. Merrick had to rely entirely on the force of his own personality.

There were obviously times when he needed a release from the all-consuming demands of being David Merrick. At such moments he did not want the stress of a demanding personal relationship. Nor, alas, could he find relief in the traditional manner of the tired, harried American businessman— an evening at the theater.

Even the notion of "after hours" entertainment was difficult for him, since he managed to conduct business at all hours. Happily that very spring he had discovered a source of pleasure that had, among other advantages, the virtue of reinforcing his sense of belonging to an elite of New York businessmen.

One Sunday afternoon that spring, realizing that everything was going unusually well with a *Carnival* rehearsal, Bob Merrill decided he could take the afternoon off and visit his friend Alan Grant, who had a large apartment at Third Avenue and 57th Street. Merrill left Grant's phone number with the stage manager just in case any emergency arose.

Alan Grant was born and raised in a poor neighborhood in the Bronx. Fur had worked the same alchemy in Grant's social and economic position that show business had in Merrick's. Fur, like show business, was a way to advance in the world. The right skins attracted the right people. This, of course, was in the days before the wearing of fur had become controversial.

Grant's apartment was, in fact, a perpetual party. His wealthy, influential friends might stop by for a drink and leave with a new girlfriend. As someone who knew him said, "He wanted to be America's host. He was a tremendously big-hearted fellow who seemed to have every connection in the world. If a friend needed a green card for one of his employees, Alan could arrange it. He could get you theater tickets. He could fix your parking tickets. Sometimes he did it because he wanted something in exchange. Sometimes he did it just for the pleasure of it."

On this particular Sunday Merrill found himself surrounded

by "half the Ford model agency." In the middle of the afternoon Merrick called, wanting to know why Merrill had left rehearsal.

"Where the hell are you?" Merrick demanded. "I hear music. And I hear girls."

Grant became curious. Who was Merrill talking to? When Merrill whispered, "David Merrick," he saw a light go on in Grant's slightly crossed eyes. Grant asked Merrill to invite Merrick over. Twenty minutes later, Merrill recalled, "the door opened, and David stood there, eyes wide open."

Entree to Grant's apartment was not accorded everyone. You had to be successful to be a recipient of Grant's largesse. And in exchange for access to attractive young women, Merrick offered Grant the rare gift of friendship.

Friendship, like intimacy or love, was something for which Merrick had little capacity. He befriended many business associates, so they thought, only to turn on them. He was wary of people outside "the business" because he was shy and uncomfortable outside his own world. He was wary of people *in* "the business" because he didn't like the idea of trusting anyone.

But Grant, who once did time in Sing Sing for "grand larceny of furs," became Merrick's friend. He was one of very few people who could walk into Merrick's office unannounced—he would tell Merrick's secretary he wanted to surprise David. Merrick was not crazy about surprises, but she knew this was one he would tolerate.

Once, some years later, Grant was in a plane that went down in the Dutch West Indies. When Merrick ascertained that his friend was among the survivors, he flew down to make sure he was being given proper medical attention. It was one of the rare times anyone could remember him taking a trip for the sake of friendship.

Grant had the wherewithal to make the gloomy Merrick happy. "David was not an aggressive man with women," Merrill remembered. "He would come in, and there were always three or four women there, generally models, actresses, dancers from Vegas. He would enter and sit on the side. But he became a magnet.

"The women were not attracted to him just because of who he was. When you sat and talked with him he was spellbinding. It's odd. When a man never smiles and then he does—it's magic. David only smiled when he cared, and then it was devastating."

This craving for casual female companionship was not uncommon in the pre-feminist early Sixties. It is hard, in the wake of the Sexual Revolution, to recall how much tension used to surround sex. The women at Alan Grant's were willing to take gambles that might bring them short-term financial advantages which, with skillful management, might be converted to long-term gains.

For many decades, the American theater had profited from the tension surrounding sexuality. The theater became a kind of libidinal pressure cooker. The audience brought its fears and anxieties about sex into the dark auditorium, where, in the course of the play, they would be heated to a frenzy. The resolution of the play, like the turning of the valve atop the pressure cooker, provided a needed release.

Sometimes the release was effected through laughter. During the postwar era there were many comedies that centered on the burning question of whether or not a young woman should sleep with a young man to whom she was not yet married. (The notion that she would sleep with a young man she had no particular intention of marrying was not even conceivable.) While the question might be posed in a variety of ways, the answer was always the same. Such titillating diversions could not survive the "brutal honesty" of the Sexual Revolution. These plays depended on an audience's innocence and nervousness about sex.

Despite his lingering reputation as a crass commercial producer, Merrick, apart from *Clutterbuck*, (which was not really about sex since, after all, the characters were English) produced only one such comedy, Norman Krasna's *Sunday in New York*. When the play opened, in the fall of 1961, it already seemed old-fashioned. *Time*'s anonymous reviewer said "this type of play has long been outgrown by just about everyone whose first love was not a box office."

The young man and woman who had to decide the burning question were played by Robert Redford and Pat Stanley. At a matinee during the Washington tryout the characters Redford and Stanley played were standing in bathrobes discussing whether they ought to go to bed together. A New Jersey teacher who had—inexplicably—brought her students to see the play was afraid of the answer and instructed her charges to leave immediately. (If she had remained she would have seen that the answer was, as ever, negative.)

The noisy departure of the students created headlines in both Washington and New York and was immediately assumed to have been a Merrick stunt. He held a press conference to deny it. A Washington columnist who happened to have seen the students declared they did not look like anything that might have been recruited for the occasion by the William Morris agency. Merrick called the teacher an "old biddy" and invited the students to return as his guests.

Krasna described his play as "preachment for chastity." Krasna also denied that it was a stunt. "It is only because of Mr. Merrick's reputation as a kind of hoodlum that people believe that," Krasna told a reporter. "I mean hoodlum in the nicest sense. Please do not quote me as saying Mr. Merrick has a reputation as a hoodlum unless you point out that I said, 'in the nicest sense.'"

By this time Krasna had already gone several rounds with Merrick. There had been the usual fight over royalties. There had been a fight about a song Merrick asked Bob Merrill to write with the same title as the play. Krasna was afraid that if audiences heard a radio commercial with Merrill's song they would come expecting a musical and be disappointed.

One of the bittersweet pleasures of being associated with a Merrick project was that in addition to the constant, often ugly sparring that went on in private there was also the opportunity to joust in public, to trade barbs with the master in newspaper columns.

The media barbs had begun in earnest during *Take Me Along*, when Merrick and Gleason had traded quips for the benefit of columnists. The verbal nimbleness of both concealed an enmity that ran quite deep and was in no way feigned. Merrick had a simple reason for disliking Gleason. Gleason was being paid the highest weekly salary in Broadway history. Gleason, after all, was used to television money, which made Broadway salaries look paltry. He agreed to do *Take Me Along* only if he received $50 a week more than the highest salary ever paid to a Broadway performer. Alfred Drake had earned $5,000 a week to star in *Kismet* in 1953. Gleason got $5,050 six years later. Gleason also demanded a private car on the railroad that would take the cast for the Boston tryout. The car, he insisted, must be equipped with a well-stocked bar and a Dixieland band. Merrick complied, but added two more private cars so that the press could witness Gleason's "royal progress."

The two began their adversarial relationship playfully. At one point Gleason said of Merrick, "He's not a producer—he's a playground director. Every time I look at him I can visualize him with a medicine ball in his hand. Dealing with him is like playing hardball against a putty wall." On another occasion he said, "I made him smile once—I trained a fly to tickle his cheek."

Merrick, informed that his star had a stomach ache, told a columnist, "I sympathize with him deeply, because when Gleason has a stomach ache it's like a giraffe having a sore throat."

When Gleason left the show he announced he was going to play golf with Arnold Palmer: "I'm going to put Merrick's picture on my golf balls—I should be able to get anywhere up to 800 yards with that kind of imagination."

Gleason, at least, was a plausible adversary for Merrick. He was a huge success and a man with a tongue as agile as his opponent's. Peter Glenville, in fact, was convinced that Gleason was the pettier of the two. One of their non-publicized battles was over billing. In Gleason's contract it specified that Gleason's was to be the only name above the title. The wording, however, was that Gleason was appearing in "The Peter Glenville Production of *Take Me Along*." Gleason came to apologize to Glenville beforehand but he explained what his contract specified and told him, "I'm going to make the bastard honor my contract."

Merrick vs. Gleason was a fair fight. But, for Merrick to attack Anna Maria Alberghetti on *Carnival* was shockingly ungallant. That may have been precisely why he did it. Picking on a delicate young woman made him seem an unconscionable monster, a role he recognized had great publicity potential.

There was some justification for his sharpness with Alberghetti. She had asked him for permission to leave the show—barely four months into the run—to do film work, which was more lucrative. He could not tolerate such a breach of contract. Hence, he embarked on an astonishing campaign of vilification.

Alberghetti, born in Italy, had begun her career as an opera singer, a coloratura, making her Carnegie Hall debut at the age of thirteen. In the audience were Giovanni Martinelli, Giuseppe de Luca and an unknown compatriot who shouted, in Italian, during the encores, that she was an angel from Paradise. Her parents wisely pushed her career into television, where she quickly became a popular figure, explaining why she earned $2,000 a week in *Carnival.* Her salary may have rankled Merrick, for even before open hostilities began he started taking potshots at her privately. "Today is Anna Maria's birthday," he told his secretary one day. He pulled out his wallet, withdrew two single dollar bills and told her to buy Alberghetti some plastic roses.

In August, less than five months after the show opened, Alberghetti checked into a small, private hospital. Since Merrick would not release her from her contract she would have to reinforce her claim that she was too ill to perform.

Merrick's first strategy was to sing the praises of her understudy, Anita Gillette, so customers wouldn't feel they were being shortchanged: "If I'd known she was this good when we were casting, she would have had the part." Gillette, however, was leaving in ten days to play a role in a new musical by Howard Dietz and Arthur Schwartz, The Gay Life. Alberghetti's contract had another eighteen months to run.

The hospital had called her condition "fair." Merrick told a reporter, "There's nothing wrong with her. She'll be back shortly. As soon as *my* doctors get to her, she'll be OK."

Having impugned her honesty, he went on to denigrate her talent. To the gossip columnist Sheilah Graham, Merrick described Alberghetti as "my adorable little electronic star." He claimed that her voice would not project, an odd charge considering that she had been trained as an opera singer. At any rate, he told Graham, she wore an electronic mike taped to her chest, which was "hooked to an outside channel and sometimes the audience would hear police messages from the microphone. And one time when Anna Maria went to the powder room she forgot to turn off the gadget and the whole audience knew where she was."

With Anita Gillette.

Throughout this assault Alberghetti maintained a brave, dignified silence. When a reporter called her for a response to Merrick's praise of her understudy, she said she was "delighted" with Gillette's success: "Isn't that great. Anita and I are such good friends."

When she returned to work, Merrick sent her roses—wax ones—and arranged for photographers to see a man in medical whites heading toward her dressing room with a lie detector. Each stage of the drama was duly reported in the columns, so that readers were constantly reminded of what was happening backstage at "David Merrick's smash hit *Carnival.*"

Alberghetti enjoyed a revenge of sorts. At some point Merrick's caricature disappeared from the walls of Sardi's. Shortly afterward it was discovered hanging where she felt it belonged—above the toilet in her Los Angeles home.

This was the easy part, the enjoyable part of being David Merrick—the creation of a character as fascinating as those in the plays he produced. Merrick had taken the press's measure very early. "The day I picked up the paper and read that Mike Todd had been killed I knew I was in trouble," he once quipped, adding with obviously false self-effacement, "The press always needs a colorful theatrical figure, and I was afraid I would be next. Actually I was a very poor replacement."

In a city of seven newspapers, each with a host of columnists in constant need of items, Merrick was a godsend. There were, in fact, plenty of Merricks to go around. There was the ingenious Merrick, the publicity hound, who had thought up—or at least took credit for thinking up—clever stunts. He was the Merrick who had sandwich men parade around midtown wearing French berets and, around their middle, portable pissoirs like those you see on the streets of Paris, with posters for *Irma La Douce.*

There was the witty Merrick, the puckish Merrick, Merrick the merry prankster. These Merricks—which existed mainly in printer's ink—were a boon to columnists. They were also a godsend to their creator. They gave him a visibility that made him ubiquitous. These public Merricks "covered" for the actual Merrick, who was intensely secretive, his whereabouts unknown much of the time even to those who worked for him.

The actual David Merrick, whose attitudes toward women were not much more enlightened than those of *Clutterbuck*, seldom emerged from behind the camouflage of the many masks he wore for the press. Some, in fact, doubted that there was an actual David Merrick, a core human being. There had been a David Margulois, but Merrick used to boast that Margulois had died the night *Fanny* had opened and David Merrick had at last been accepted into the Broadway community.

The character of David Merrick was urbane, sophisticated and wry. What added the demonic piquancy to his profile—as he demonstrated in his badmouthing of Anna Maria Alberghetti— was his deliberate, unabashed cruelty.

On one occasion even Merrick became upset when the twisted, dark reality behind the twisted, dark mask was exposed. The renowned portrait photographer Arnold Newman had been commissioned by *Playboy* to photograph Merrick in January of 1961. He shot Merrick in the St. James Theater, where *Do Re Mi* had just opened. The portrait catches the wariness, the profound distrust behind the icy bravura. But when the photograph was printed the high contrast made Merrick seem unusually sick and unsavory.

Newman himself was upset at the way the photograph had been printed and had just begun to write Merrick a letter of apology. The phone rang. "Mr. Merrick would like to speak to you."

Newman was glad to have a chance to apologize in person. He did not get to utter a word. The receiver rang with expletives, concluding with Merrick's threat that the next time he saw Newman he would slug him in the jaw.

About a year later Newman's friend Harold Rome invited him to the rehearsal of a new show, *I Can Get It For You Wholesale*, in which there was a remarkable young woman, whom Rome described as "not much to look at but with a sensational voice." Entering the rehearsal studio in the New Amsterdam Roof,

Newman had trouble adjusting his eyes from the bright daylight to the blackened room. He took a seat, and, as his eyes became acclimated, became aware that someone was sitting two seats away. They turned toward each other at the same moment. It was, of course, Merrick. Each was somewhat startled. Rather than make good on his threat, Merrick faced straight ahead. So did Newman. The bully tended to be tougher on the phone than in person.

Garson Kanin had once discovered the same thing. Once, negotiating with Merrick, he was amazed that Merrick hung up on him. At that time Kanin too had an office in the St. James Building. He raced upstairs, ran past Merrick's secretary and into his office. Confronted with his boorish behavior, Merrick backed down and claimed he had only hung up as a joke.

During their limousine ride into Manhattan after the dismal opening of *A Taste of Honey* in Cincinnati, Shurtleff had asked him why he worked so hard at being disliked. He had answered frankly, "I discovered early on that I did not have a warm personality. Since I was never going to get anywhere with charm, I decided to be the most unlovable person around and see if that would work for me, and it has." A year after *Taste of Honey*, during the fall of 1961, Shurtleff had a play he wrote, *Call Me By My Rightful Name*, produced Off-Broadway. (The cast included two unknown actors, Robert Duvall and Joan Hackett, and a dancer making his acting debut, Alvin Ailey.)

In an interview in the Sunday *Times* Shurtleff had praised his boss and even confessed to a liking for him. The next day he was summoned into the red office. "Now, listen, I don't want any more of this going on," Merrick told him. "I have worked very hard to be the most disliked man in America, and I don't want you going around saying you like me. You're ruining my image."

Could Merrick have been serious?

"He was very serious." Shurtleff said.

7 OUT OF 7 ARE ECSTATICALLY UNANIMOUS ABOUT SUBWAYS ARE FOR SLEEPING

 HOWARD TAUBMAN — "ONE OF THE FEW GREAT MUSICAL COMEDIES OF THE LAST THIRTY YEARS, ONE OF THE BEST OF OUR TIME. It lends lustre to this or any other Broadway season."

 WALTER KERR — "WHAT A SHOW! WHAT A HIT! WHAT A SOLID HIT! If you want to be overjoyed, spend an evening with 'Subways Are For Sleeping.' A triumph."

 JOHN CHAPMAN — "NO DOUBT ABOUT IT. 'SUBWAYS ARE FOR SLEEPING' IS THE BEST MUSICAL OF THE CENTURY. Consider yourself lucky if you can buy or steal a ticket for 'Subways Are For Sleeping' over the next few years."

JOHN McCLAIN — "A FABULOUS MUSICAL. I LOVE IT. Sooner or later, every one will have to see 'Subways Are For Sleeping'."

 RICHARD WATTS — "A KNOCKOUT, FROM START TO FINISH. THE MUSICAL YOU'VE BEEN WAITING FOR. IT DESERVES TO RUN FOR A DECADE."

NORMAN NADEL — "A WHOPPING HIT. RUN, DON'T WALK TO THE ST. JAMES THEATRE. It's in that rare class of great musicals. Quite simply, it has everything."

ROBERT COLEMAN — "A GREAT MUSICAL. ALL THE INGREDIENTS ARE THERE. As fine a piece of work as our stage can be asked to give us."

Evgs.: Mon. thru Thurs.: Orch. $8.60; Mezz. $6.90; Balc. $5.75, 4.80; 2nd Balc. $3.60. Fri. & Sat. Evgt.: Orch. $9.40; Mezz. $7.50; Balc. $6.90, 5.75, 4.80; 2nd Balc. $3.60, Wed. Mat : Orch. $4.80; Mezz. $4.30; Balc. $4.05, 3.60; 2nd Balc. $3.00. Sat. Mat. Orch. $5.50; Mezz. $4.80; Balc. $4.30, 3.80, 2nd Balc. $3.00

 ST. JAMES THEATRE 44th St., W. of B'way

 MAIL ORDER FILLED THRU JAN. 1963

CHAPTER SEVENTEEN

I N THESE YEARS, everything and everyone yielded to Merrick's will—stars, writers, unions, the press. Only one thing eluded his iron control. Jeanne Gilbert.

Sometimes in the middle of the afternoon Merrick would tell Michael Shurtleff to stop what he was doing and go to the Manhattan Hotel, around the corner from his office. Jeanne was there drinking and making a spectacle of herself. Shurtleff was ordered to pick her up and take her someplace outside the theater district.

When Shurtleff got such calls late at night it was actually easier since Jeanne and Shurtleff loved dancing. They could go to a discotheque.

Jeanne still had friends in London, and occasionally Shurtleff would run into her there, where she seemed to preserve her equilibrium better. But when she was in New York, all the qualities that had made her a success in London—the charm, the wit, the intelligence—were subverted by her nearness to Merrick, her uncontrollable yearning for him.

Once, when Shurtleff ran into her, he saw that she had a black eye.

"Did he do that?" he asked her.

"No," she said. "I fell."

In his own way Merrick cared for her. She ran up debts. He paid them. Sometimes he would give her his car to ride around in.

The one thing Merrick would not do for her was marry her, and that was the only thing that mattered. He was, after all, still married. And frankly he had had his fill of marriage. He had married Leonore not just in another city and another time, but another world, a middle-class Jewish world where marriage seemed all-important. He now lived in a world beyond class, beyond religion, a world where everything was possible. In this world marriage seemed a foolish anachronism, a limit on his freedom that he would have to be crazy to accept.

In the fall of 1961 he turned fifty. Success had given him the opportunities of youth denied him as a young man. That he loved Jeannie there seemed no doubt. But that he would accept the yoke of marriage again was out of the question. It was more pleasant to focus on the women he met at Alan Grant's. It was, all things considered, even more pleasant to deal with Leonore, who was now quite resigned to her peripheral role in his life.

Moreover the real love of his life was his work. No woman could give him the feeling of excitement and power he derived from the everyday conduct of his business.

The conduct of that business was becoming more bizarre, more tyrannical. The morning before rehearsals began for *Subways Are for Sleeping*, he asked his creative team to meet him in his office. It was a Sunday. No one expected an invigorating pep talk or a lovely champagne brunch. They were were all veterans of Merrick shows—the book, lyrics and music were by Styne, Comden and Green, and the director was Michael Kidd, who won his spurs on *Destry*.

When the creators had filed into the office, Merrick asked them, "Do you know where your contracts are? They're on my desk. They're not signed."

He then threatened that he would not sign them until they complied with a list of changes he wanted made immediately. "He loved to torture people this way," Shurtleff, who watched the grim proceedings, recalled.

On earlier shows Merrick had trusted his creative team. Now

he began to see himself as a necessary catalyst for their efforts. His contribution was not to analyze the characters or the aptness of the songs. His contribution was to scream.

Subways was based on a collection of stories by Edmond Love, the rights to which Jule Styne had acquired in 1958. He thought the stories had the same insouciant charm and drollery that characterized *Bells Are Ringing*, his 1956 hit with Comden and Green.

But the characters in *Subways* were not the loveable eccentrics that Comden and Green had chronicled so successfully in their previous New York shows, *On the Town* and *Wonderful Town*. They were the people we now call "homeless," making their home in the subways. Even in 1961 their situation was nothing to sing about, although the score does have several dazzling Jule Styne songs, especially "Ride Through the Night."

The fact that the subject matter was not innately musical became increasingly apparent to Merrick, whose tirades grew in virtuosity.

During the Philadelphia tryout a young friend of Styne's had dinner with the composer at the Warwick Hotel, then accompanied him to the Shubert Theater for an early preview. At the back of the orchestra section Styne stood with Comden, Green, Kidd and the designer Will Steven Armstrong, whose sets had been one of the ornaments of *Carnival* earlier that year.

As the admittedly rough and uneven show passed before them, Merrick stood behind the creators muttering abuse at them. When the show was over he had them all sit at the back of the theater, and the muttering turned to bellowing. At one point he shouted at Armstrong, "The museum set is out!"

"It's the most expensive in the show and my best work," Armstrong retorted bravely.

"The scene is deadly," Merrick shouted. "The set and the scene are gone. The public can go to the Metropolitan Museum any day—for free!"

Throughout the coming weeks Merrick picked on his team individually and as a group, trying, as he did on *Do Re Mi*, to get them to abuse each other's work. With Kidd he campaigned for more and more dances.

"I remember once, after I put in a murderous 18 hour day—I not only had to rehearse spoken dialogue but work on rewrites with Betty and Adolph and invent new dance numbers—he began screaming at me to put in still more dancing," Kidd recalled. "I said I didn't have any handles for any more dance numbers.

"He wanted Act II to open with a dance. It used to open with Orson Bean meeting Carol Lawrence in a subway station and talking to her. Merrick shouted, 'The hell with handles. Find one. Make up a handle. But open the second act with dancing.'"

At this point Kidd said, "Mr. Merrick, you are yelling at me. Under these circumstances I find it hard to think creatively."

Merrick lowered his voice, well aware that he could be equally menacing when he spoke softly and icily. "I will request you quietly. Put in a dance to open Act II."

He constantly needled Green about his young wife Phyllis Newman, who played a beauty contest aspirant. Merrick was convinced the audience could never accept her as such. He seemed to take great pleasure in putting Green on the defensive about his wife. Comden felt compelled to defend both her partner and his talented wife. But the needling put great strain on their working relationship.

At one point they added a song for Newman called "I Was a Shoo In." The night they put it into the show the audience response was tremendous. Standing at the back of the theater, Comden burst into tears. She and Green hugged each other. At the intermission Merrick came up to Green and, as if he had been supportive of Newman along, said, "Well, how do we make the whole show about her? Then we'd have a hit."

In New York Newman won raves from the critics. The show itself was the least favorably received of all the Merrick musicals to date. The fact that it then ran for over a year and recouped 90% of its investments less than six months after its opening was thus solely attributable to Merrick's promotional talents, which were as varied and unceasing as his tirades.

The promotions began well before the show opened on December 27, 1961. The previous summer there had been ads in all the papers urging former winners of the Miss Subways contest to contact the Merrick office. In September they were invited to audition for the show. None was accepted. It didn't matter. It was about creating material for columns, and it achieved its objective.

The first week in November 2,800 green placards with white lettering began to appear in the New York subway system announcing *Subways Are For Sleeping*. There were no quotes around the words, nothing to indicate this was a show poster. Almost immediately transit policemen began to complain to the Transit Authority that the signs were encouraging people to sleep on the subways, an offense that then carried a $10 fine and up to thirty days in jail. The Transit Authority ordered them removed. That was what Merrick had hoped for.

He revealed that he spent $60,000 a year on subway advertising and declared that he was "astonished" by the removal of the signs. "The Transit Authority has no sense of humor," he said. "They're squares all right. That space belongs to me. I rent it all year long. It's just a teaser ad."

He declared the removal of the posters "a new form of censorship. As if we don't have enough." He suggested he might put stickers saying "A New Musical Comedy" over the offending posters, but the Transit Authority insisted they had to be removed altogether.

On November 13, 1961, Merrick offered the services of his lawyer to one Bruno Bella, who was arrested for sleeping in the subway and sentenced to ten days in the New York Work Detention Home on Hart Island. Bella, who was enjoying more square meals than he had in some time, told Merrick's lawyer, "Please tell my family, my friends and Mr. Merrick not to post any bail. I want to remain in jail. I need the rest."

In February, traditionally one of the slowest months of the year for Broadway business, Merrick sponsored a contest for photos of people sleeping in the subway, with prizes ranging from $25 to $250.

None of these stunts, of course, brought him the continued mileage of an idea he had been thinking about for some time, ever since the retirement of Brooks Atkinson at the end of the 1959-60 season.

In Boston it became clear that no amount of changes in the script or set could make *Subways* a hit. It was time, Merrick thought, to put the plan he had been devising into practice. He asked a young production assistant backstage at the Colonial Theater to find a Manhattan telephone book, not an easy feat in Boston.

The young man found one in a hotel and brought it back to Merrick, who ensconced himself in the box office of the Colonial with a yellow legal pad. He asked Merrick what he was doing and received a curt, "You'll see."

"His face used to light up when he was doing something nobody else would be able to think of," the young man recalled.

In the phone book (and with one excursion to New Jersey) Merrick had found seven men with the same names as the aisle-sitters of the seven daily papers. He had been aching to orchestrate this stunt for years but he had had to wait until Brooks Atkinson retired. There were sometimes several namesakes for the other critics, but there was only one Brooks Atkinson.

Merrick had his press agent Harvey Sabinson invite each of the namesakes and their spouses to dinner, either at Sardi's or the Oak Room of the Plaza, and then to see *Subways Are For Sleeping*. Each then contributed a favorable quote about the show (in most cases simply endorsing a favorable comment written by Sabinson.)

When the actual critics were as unenthusiastic about *Subways* as Merrick expected them to be, he prepared a full page ad with the quotes from their namesakes. So that he could not be accused of misrepresentation the ad included postage stamp size photos of the non-critics. Space for the ad was reserved, but the newspaper advertising departments were alerted that the ad might not arrive until just before press time, which meant that it could not be seen or approved through the normal channels.

Just at deadline time one of Merrick's advertising men arrived at the *Times* and the *Herald-Tribune* with the ad. At the *Trib*, it was immediately rushed into print. The ad man, however, had a twinge of guilt as he submitted it to the *Times*. He told a long-time associate there to make a print so he could check the ad before setting it into its final form.

"And," he added, "maybe call your counterpart at the *Trib* to ask if he knew that Richard Watts was black."

The ad man's conscience had saved the *Times* a major embarrassment. But it was too late for the *Trib*. One edition had already gone into print. Because the first edition was not large, the ad immediately became a collector's item. But it was seen by millions, since reproductions of it appeared in newspapers all around the country as well as in London, Paris, Stockholm and Tokyo.

Merrick defended it in his best deadpan style. "My own group of drama critics are real people, and I think far more representative of the tastes of the community," he declared. He also noted that his group of critics included a black, which the "real" group did not. Merrick went so far as to offer to "lease" his group to other producers.

The League of Broadway Theaters and Producers met to discuss whether Merrick, who over the years had joined and left the organization to suit his publicity purposes, should now be thrown out. They decided against it. (Richard Coe, the drama critic of the *Washington Post*, who reported the meeting, noted that the League's major achievement the previous year was to pressure the city government to remove a tax from theater tickets "and to pocket the difference without passing along so much as a mill of savings to the paying public.")

The advertising officials for the *Times* and the *Trib* expressed indignation.

Whenever the subject arose Merrick feigned innocence. "I think it is unfortunate that one edition of one paper carried it, but I don't see any real harm in it," he said. "It was a bleak day in January, and Broadway needed something to laugh at. I've sent gag ads before. There's nothing wrong with a good inside joke."

On another occasion he said he was "bowled over that anyone used it. It was just a private gag for the drama desks. I got bored with all those quote ads. I thought this would be a quote ad to end all quote ads. It was so downright outlandish.

"But I'm mighty glad these ads didn't run as scheduled in all the papers. Who could afford such a $25,000 joke?"

When the ad was denounced by the Better Business Bureau, Merrick asked, "What's that? Something like the Diners' Club?"

One of Merrick's hand-picked critics was indignant that all these voices had been raised against them. "What is so wrong with us that we can't be quoted with the complete respect Merrick gave us?"

John McClain, the critic of the *Journal-American*, interviewed his namesake, a meat packer in Old Tappan, N.J. "My wife goes to the theater every now and then, but I seldom do. We accepted the offer to attend *Subways* because it sounded like an amusing idea, and we had a good time."

As for the quote, "I don't believe I have to tell you the way they arranged the remarks that were credited to me, do I?" the meat-packing McClain asked his interviewer.

"I have a rough idea," the better-known McClain said. The stunt made a brief reappearance the following season when The Establishment, an improvisation group from San Francisco, publicized its New York engagement with an ad in which David Merrick was quoted as saying The Establishment's work was better than *Oliver* and *Stop the World*, the two musicals Merrick then had running on Broadway. The ad had a postage stamp size photograph of Merrick -- not the producer, but a Philadelphia postman.

Subways had the distinction of being the first Broadway musical to be picketed by the Congress of Racial Equality. CORE picked the show, columnist Murray Kempton explained in the *New York Post*, because it "could have truthfully portrayed Negroes in their ever expanding role in American life." He ended in high dudgeon: "One reason, I suppose, why Negroes wonder about white civilization sometimes, of course, may merely be because it deeds over its taste to David Merrick." For a man who craved nothing more than to be perceived as a villain, here was truly a laurel wreath.

From London that season he imported Terrence Rattigan's *Ross*, a play about Lawrence of Arabia, which starred John Mills. *I Can Get It For You Wholesale*, based on a 1937 Jerome Weidman best-seller, was the other Merrick musical in the 1961-62 season. Weidman turned his attention to the theater in the late Fifties, winning the Pulitzer Prize in 1959 for his musical about LaGuardia, *Fiorello!* The following year his agent, Harold Freedman, called Weidman and said David Merrick wanted to meet with him in a restaurant embedded in the Astor Hotel, which, though it defined the Eastward boundary of Shubert Alley, was an eatery totally ignored by the theater community, which made it extremely useful for a man who liked secrecy as much as Merrick.

Merrick walked into the meeting with the idea that Weidman should adapt *National Velvet*, a project he had been trying to activate for years, but he walked out with an agreement that he would produce *Wholesale* instead. Harold Rome, for whom the show was a congenial return to the milieu of his first hit, *Pins and Needles*, would be the composer and lyricist.

Wholesale, a tough show about the garment center, had a large cast, and a distinguished one. Lillian Roth played the mother of the slippery central character, Harry Bogen. Sheree North, once considered a possible successor to Marilyn Monroe, played Harry's mistress. Harold Lang, who had appeared in the historic 1950 production of *Pal Joey*, played Bogen's star salesman. The two most difficult roles to cast were Harry himself and a small comic part, his secretary, Miss Marmelstein.

While the show was being cast Peter Glenville passed through New York with his friend Laurence Harvey, who was touring the U.S. in the wake of his glowing notices for *Room at the Top*. Harvey was commanding the then astronomical sum of

$350,000 a picture, but he was eager to do *Wholesale* for a reasonable fee. It turned out that he was Jewish and had once worked as a delivery boy. "It's the story of my life," he said. Glenville, acting informally as his agent, told Merrick that Harvey could only sign for nine months.

Merrick blew up. "I am building something," he shouted. "These goddam movie stars—he's not even a movie star." Weidman, who watched the blowup, had a feeling that a lot of Merrick's tantrums were really the effect of Merrick having an argument with himself. It was his way of testing the effect of both sides. After he had gauged the effect, he could always backtrack and become reasonable. Except in this case there was no room to backtrack. Glenville and Harvey had already departed.

Weidman had a lingering regret about Harvey. Even if he had only stayed nine months, it would have created an interest in the show that would have made it run much longer.

The part eventually went to Elliott Gould, a young actor who had been in the chorus of *Irma La Douce*.

In one of the script revisions the character of Miss Marmelstein had been eliminated altogether. But Shurtleff had seen a young singer he thought would be perfect for the part and arranged an afternoon of auditions to see if the creators might reconsider. The young lady had a tendency to be late for everything. He told her to come at 3:00, assuming she would arrive at 3:30. If she were the final auditioner of the day, her talent would so outshine her predecessors', he reasoned, that Merrick would not ask the question he had on previous occasions: "Why are you bringing in this ugly girl?"

The penultimate auditioner finished before 3:30 and Shurtleff had to work hard to persuade Rome, Weidman and Arthur Laurents, who co-wrote the book and would direct the show, to wait for his final entrant.

She rushed in at 4:00. She had been delayed, she explained, by something that caught her eye in a thrift shop window. It was, in fact, the ratty raccoon coat that she was wearing. She also wore a commissar's fur hat that reminded Weidman of *Michael Strogoff,*

Courier of the Czar, a film his mother had taken him to as a child. The impression these thrift shop specials made was not enhanced by her unmatched shoes or her behavior.

"Is this girl sane?" Merrick asked Shurtleff.

"No," he replied.

"Why are you putting us through this?" Merrick asked.

"Miss Streisand, would you sing?" Shurtleff asked.

"I have to sing?" she said, her hand over her eyes, looking out into the dark, empty auditorium.

Miss Streisand sang two bars and stopped. She could not continue, she explained, unless she had a stool. A stool was brought for her.

Barbra Streisand—even the spelling of her first name was peculiar—then sang three bars and stopped again. She could not continue wearing her new coat. She removed it. Then she complained that the accompanist was playing in the wrong key. He was, of course, playing in the key in which she had always sung.

Rome, who was by this time fascinated by the girl, asked if she had an "up song."

"If I didn't have an 'up song,' would I be auditioning for a musical?" she told him.

Her up song was "Why Do I Love Arnie Weissberg," from an Off-Broadway flop. While she sang it everyone was in stitches, including Merrick, though as soon as she finished, in the best auditioners' style, they all pretended they had yawned all the way through it.

No stickler for etiquette, Streisand asked, "How'd you like it?" Amused at her effrontery, Laurents said, "It's OK."

"That's all you can say?" she challenged them. She was asked if she had a ballad. She sang "Too Long at the Fair" from the *Billy Barnes Revue*. Everyone was moved.

Weidman asked Rome, "Is she as good as I think she is?"

"Better," Rome told him.

Rome, Weidman and Laurents rushed to the stage, fascinated by this strange and extraordinarily talented girl. Merrick dragged Shurtleff to the back of the theater.

"How many times have I told you I don't want ugly girls in my shows?" he screamed at Shurtleff. "They love her," Merrick said, pointing to the others huddled around the woman who was perfect to play Miss Marmelstein.

"I want you to take her out and kill her."

Rome came up to Merrick and pointed out that a weak spot in the second act could be filled beautifully by a number for Miss Streisand as Miss Marmelstein.

"Miss Marmelstein has been out of the show for two weeks," Merrick countered. "Haven't you read the script?"

Weidman had sidled up to the pair, who were having a heated conference. Merrick glared at him. "I suppose you're going to back him up," he said.

Rome, who, after all, had now been working with Merrick for some time, instantly knew how to handle the matter.

"You can get her for scale,"he said.

"You're the most anti-semitic guy I know," Merrick shouted at him. "You've hired every ugly Jew in town for this show, and now you want me to hire this meeskite."

Rehearsing *I Can Get It For You Wholesale*, with Harvey Sabinson, Harold Rome and Jerome Weidman.

What Merrick hated even more than her looks, Florence Rome thought, was her blatant Jewishness. She could see him bristle when he heard Streisand talking with her pronounced Brooklyn accent or behaving in an abrasive manner. He had no choice but to go along with his creators' enthusiasm for her. But throughout the rehearsal period he would urge Laurents to fire her.

On the first day of rehearsal everyone felt a sense of discovery about her. At the first break Bob Schear, a young production assistant, went to talk to Lillian Roth.

"Who does that girl remind you of?" he asked Roth. Before she could answer, he asked her to write the name on a piece of paper. He did the same. They had both written the same name, Fanny Brice. Schear couldn't wait until the lunch break to race back to the office to tell Merrick.

He knew Merrick was beginning work on a musical version of the life story of Fanny Brice. The leading contenders for the part were Carol Burnett, Kaye Ballard and Anne Bancroft. Schear burst into Merrick's private office to tell him that the girl who had to play Fanny Brice was the new girl in *Wholesale*.

Merrick snarled back, "Not only is she not going to be Fanny Brice, but she's not even going to be in *I Can Get It For You Wholesale*. She was late to rehearsal this morning."

Schear was startled to hear this. It confirmed the rumor he had always heard, that Merrick had spies in every company, keeping him informed of the slightest details. Laurents, in fact, had assumed that Schear was the spy on *Wholesale*, but when Schear reported his conversation with Merrick, they both realized it must be someone else.

Streisand continued to be late for rehearsals. She continued to be difficult. She never won the hearts of the men who wrote the show. "I have dealt with revolting people all my life," Weidman said. "I began my career working in the garment center, after all. As far as I was concerned she had not earned the right to behave that way."

But her fellow cast members embraced her. Lillian Roth and Sheree North both took a maternal attitude toward her, encouraging her to respond to the attentions of her handsome leading man. Whenever they needed her and couldn't find her, someone would suggest, "Try Elliott's room."

Merrick, needless to say, was not interested in the amorous inclinations of his cast. He wanted the show to shape up. Unable to attend a run-through, he sent Shurtleff, who came back with a sheaf of notes. Merrick called Laurents into his office and fired off Shurtleff's criticisms.

Laurents, enraged, found Shurtleff and called him "a traitor."

Shurtleff was wounded by Laurents' accusations. He hadn't attended the rehearsal on his own initiative, he stressed. He had gone at Merrick's behest. Nor had he known Merrick would transmit his notes in so ungracious a style.

"Arthur, you know that David is a shithead," he pleaded in his own defense.

Shurtleff then went back to Merrick. "You're just so dumb, David Merrick," he said. "Here I am, able to communicate with the directors, and you're fucking it up."

Merrick smiled. "I'm just mischievous," he said. "I can't help starting trouble."

"Don't pull your pixie act on me," Shurtleff retorted.

Unabashed, Merrick sang his constant refrain about maintaining his reputation as the most hated man on Broadway.

Merrick continued to foment uneasiness and hostility among Rome, Weidman and Laurents. Shurtleff couldn't understand the pleasure it brought him, but he thought the twinkle in his eye was unmistakable when he said, "I'm just up to my old tricks."

From her first performance in Philadelphia until opening night in New York, Streisand stopped the show with her "Miss Marmelstein" number. The number was foolproof. The only time it didn't stop the show was well into the run, when she begged the musical director, Lehman Engel, to let her do it her own way. She took liberties with the rhythm, and the song got applause but by no means did it stop the show. Streisand immediately went back to doing it the way it was written.

Wholesale got mixed reviews; Streisand, superlatives. This was one time when Merrick injured himself by not signing the contracts in advance. He was now forced into giving her much more advantageous terms than the "scale" for which she had originally been hired.

Despite the sensation Streisand caused, despite the logical appeal of the show to a New York audience, despite the fact it got better reviews than *Subways*, despite a reasonably good run, when *Wholesale* closed the following season, it had unrecouped costs of $140,000 on its $275,000 investment.

That spring the Tony nominations for Best Featured Actress in a musical were performers from two Merrick shows, Phyllis Newman from *Subways* and Streisand. In those days the Tonys were announced at a dinner dance.

Merrick sat at the *Subways* table next to Newman. When the nominees were announced, he turned to her in his most graceless manner and said, "Streisand's going to win. I voted for her."

The timing was perfect. Seconds later, the winner was announced as . . . Phyllis Newman. Merrick was not fazed at all. He congratulated her as if he had been on her side all the time.

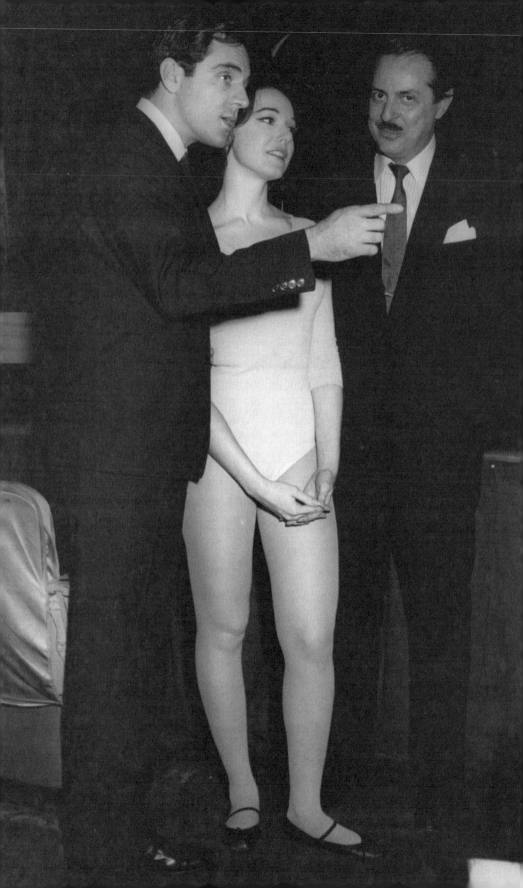

CHAPTER EIGHTEEN

MERRICK'S ICY BEHAVIOR toward Barbra Streisand was understandable, given her own abrasiveness. Nothing could explain or excuse his rude treatment of Phyllis Newman.

But then his attitudes toward women had never been particularly enlightened. Early in the run of a long-running Off-Broadway show in 1960 he took an interest in one of the young actresses who played the leading role. He came to see her several nights in a row and then, one night, while the cast was ready to go on he stood in the minuscule backstage area trying to persuade her to meet him afterwards. "Your fucking career will be over if you don't go out with me," he bellowed.

In 1967, he watched a rehearsal on the stage of the St. James Theater of *Stan Freberg Presents the United States of America*. Three women were doing a comic number. They became aware that Merrick, in the audience, was gesticulating toward them. "That one!" he shouted. "That one! The not too attractive one in the middle: You're very funny." Happily Dorothy Loudon, the woman in the middle, focused on the compliment rather than the manner of identification.

When his office was casting dancers for *110 in the Shade*, Merrick was adamant that he didn't want the "ugly, old women" Agnes DeMille used in show after show. He did allow her one of

With Anthony Newley and an urchin from *Stop the World–I Want To Get Off.*

her trusted acolytes, a veteran who understood her way of working and who could teach the young and pretty recruits he would add.

There would not be time for him to audition them individually. He had Schlissel station the finalists where he could survey them on a quick trip through the office. At one point one of the more talented dancers was signing a contract in the outer office.

"What are you doing?" he asked her.

"I'm signing a contract for *110 in the Shade,*" she said.

"No, you're not," Merrick said, ripping up the contract. "I don't have girls in my shows who look like they've just been in an auto accident."

A few years later, in the early days of feminism, a writer asked Merrick what he thought about the changing role of women. Merrick's reply was curt: "A woman's place is in the oven!"

He could be charming enough toward the young women he met at Alan Grant's, from whom he had reason to expect a few hours' or a few weeks of pleasure, without entanglements. Anything more complicated made him wary.

Even under the simplest circumstances, the charm and gallantry could wear thin. Once, Merrick drove Grant and Bob Merrill out to Long Island for a first meeting with three young women. When they arrived all three men were disappointed in the women's looks. They had not, after all, come for scintillating conversation.

Shortly after the men arrived one of the women asked for a cigarette. Merrick extended a pack. The girl, not very graciously, refused. She wanted one with a filter. In a display of excessive gallantry Merrick offered to drive to get her some. Merrill and Grant tried—in vain—to stop him, knowing he would not return. He didn't, and they had to hitchhike back to New York on a bitterly cold night.

In the summer of 1962 he was on the verge of fatherhood, a prospect that enraged him. Jeanne was pregnant. It was not an accident. It was her last, desperate attempt to get him to marry her. She confided what she was doing to a friend, who told her, "You can't do this—it's the lowest from of blackmail."

"Never you mind," Jeanne told her.

As far as Merrick was concerned, there was only one possible response. Jeannie must have an abortion. Grant knew of a clinic in Switzerland where abortions could be performed with safety even relatively late in pregnancy. Merrick arranged for her to be flown to Switzerland with money for her expenses.

Instead, she flew to the Far East, no one knew where. She wanted to have David Merrick's baby. By the time she got back to New York it was much too late even to consider an abortion.

Merrick's treatment of her grew worse. She drank more. Instead of wearing maternity clothes she wore tight, restrictive dresses—and corsets. Was it to avoid reminding him that she was pregnant? Was it at his insistence, so that people might not realize that she was pregnant? His increased hostility in no way diminished her love for him.

His professional rages intimidated people. His domestic rages—which rendered him a thoroughly loathsome human being—had the odd effect of making the women who loved him and with whom he was theoretically in love feel an almost maternal pity for him. It was, of course, a pity he neither sought nor relished.

Fortunately for the teams who wrote David Merrick musicals, none was scheduled to open while this painful drama was being played. Everything Merrick produced during the 1962-63 season was imported from London.

On October 3, 1962, Anthony Newley and Leslie Bricusse's *Stop the World, I Want to Get Off* opened at the Shubert. The show, which starred Newley, had been written in New York during a few months in the early spring of 1961, when Bricusse was there to write some special material for Beatrice Lillie. Merrick had optioned it during its pre-London tryout later that spring in Nottingham.

The New York reviews for *Stop the World* were by no means enthusiastic. Nevertheless, to Merrick's great pleasure, a long line appeared at the box office the morning the reviews appeared.

There were several reasons for that line.

One reason was very simple. By Merrick's orders, only one of the two available box office windows was open, which slowed the traffic considerably, deliberately making it irritating and time-consuming for people to put money in his pocket. Though they were a great nuisance to the people who stood in them, Merrick regarded long lines as a form of advertising, visible proof of a show's popularity.

Whatever the actual merits of its contents, Merrick knew that *Stop the World's* mildly experimental, mildly perplexing quality was outweighed by two first-rate songs, and he had made sure that those songs—"What Kind of Fool Am I?" and "Gonna Build Me A Mountain"—were well known even before the show opened. They had been recorded the previous summer by Sammy Davis, Jr., Robert Goulet, Vic Damone and Newley himself.

Even though the reviews were mixed, they reminded readers that *Stop the World* was the show from which two familiar songs came, and that was enough to make a lot of people willing to wait in unnecessarily long lines to buy tickets—a disturbing sign, perhaps, of the audience's diminishing expectations.

Stop the World was a greater financial success than either of the more ambitious shows Merrick mounted the previous season. A year after it opened, between the New York company, which starred Newley and Anna Quayle, and a touring company with Joel Grey and Julie Newmar, the musical had made $700,000 on a $175,000 investment.

Stop the World was not the only iconoclastic show to open that month. On October 17 Edward Albee, who had hitherto only written one-acts performed Off-Broadway, created a sensation with his play about domestic strife in academia, *Who's Afraid of Virginia Woolf?* On October 25, a Merrick import, *Tchin-Tchin*, written by a pseudonymous Frenchman called Francois Billetdoux, opened.

Tchin-Tchin, directed by Peter Glenville and starring Margaret Leighton and Anthony Quinn, was a series of scenes between a man and woman, both alcoholics, from two quite different walks of life. It was a play that aroused controversy in London, with estimations of its content ranging from a demonstration of "pure behavior" to "an exposure of the degrading effects of alcohol" to an allegory of Christian salvation. In New York the reviews were less cerebral, praising the play cautiously and the performers warmly.

Like *Stop the World, Tchin-Tchin*, which managed a six-month run, traded on intellectual vagueness, a commodity that, for a few years at least, had surprising marketability.

Later that season Merrick imported Charles Dyer's *Rattle of a Simple Man*, a subtle variation on an old theme, the encounter between a virgin and a whore with a heart of gold. The virgin in this case was a man of forty-two, played by Edward Woodward. Tammy Grimes played the whore, and George Segal had a small role. Richard Watts, of the *New York Post*, noted that the production was "a reminder of the importance to the theater of expert professionalism in production. We have had too many examples this season of the havoc wrought by careless craftsmanship in staging, even when the script has merit. For all the deftness and taste in the writing, Mr. Dyer's play might have seemed paltry and vulgar if it hadn't been cast and staged with artful appreciation." Though many charges might be leveled against Merrick, even the slightest of his productions would be marked by "expert professionalism."

The grandest of Merrick's London imports that season was *Oliver!*, Lionel Bart's musical adaptation of Charles Dickens' *Oliver Twist*. It had been produced in London by Sir Donald Albery, a descendant of the distinguished English theater family. His grandfather, James Albery, had written Henry Irving's first great success, *Two Roses*. It was Sir Donald who had taken an obscure play by an Irishman residing in France from a London fringe theater and restaged it at the Criterion in the West End, where the critics first realized *Waiting for Godot* was a major theater work. He had produced Graham Greene's first play, *The Living Room*, and had transferred many of Joan Littlewood's productions (including *Oh, What A Lovely War!* and *A Taste of*

Honey) to the West End. Like Merrick, he had analyzed the theatergoing audience and was the first English producer to recognize the value of tourists—particularly American tourists—to the British theater.

America heard a hit song long before the show reached our shores. "As Long As He Needs Me" would be sung by the husky-voiced, powerful English actress Georgia Brown. Instead of just releasing the single, the American cast album was widely available well before the show opened in New York. The *Variety* ad announcing the album featured not the poster art of *Oliver!* but the increasingly familiar profile of its producer, which occupied half a page of vertical space.

Oliver! made its American debut not in any of the traditional tryout cities but rather in Los Angeles, where it played seven weeks. The show went on for seven weeks in San Francisco, then three each in Detroit and Toronto before opening in New York. The long pre-Broadway tour allowed the show to repay its investments well before it reached the New York critics.

Oliver! finally opened in New York on January 6, 1963, during a long newspaper strike. All the advance publicity and the already available record album now became vital assets if the show were to survive. The publicity items that would normally have filled the columns of seven daily papers to keep readers aware of the new musical had to be replaced by heavy advertising on radio and TV. *Variety* noted that Merrick had a record-breaking ad bill for the new show: $133,488 during its first four months on Broadway, roughly $3,000 a week.

Even when he saw the show in London, Merrick knew one thing would have to be changed. Clive Revill played Fagin, the villain of the piece, as a brash caricature. For America, where Jews constituted a large part of the theater-going audience, Fagin would have to be somewhat less brazen. The wisdom of Merrick's decision was borne out in 1985, when the show was revived with Ron Moody, who played the role in the film version, doing a more blatantly Jewish Fagin; it closed almost immediately.

But apart from this significant change of emphasis, there was little Merrick could do to imprint *Oliver!* with his "creative" stamp. To prove to himself that *Oliver!* was *his* show, Merrick decided to "improve" the music, the area in which he knew the least.

The musical director for *Oliver!* was Don Pippin, a young conductor who had first come to Merrick's attention when he replaced the musical director of *Irma La Douce*. Pippin desperately wanted to conduct *Oliver!* in New York. During the summer before the show went into rehearsal he phoned Merrick's secretary repeatedly for an appointment. He was constantly put off. Then one morning suddenly she called. Someone had broken an appointment for that afternoon at two. Could he come in then? Of course he could.

Pippin arrived promptly and was sent into the red office. The man sitting behind the little desk showed him no recognition at all. He read papers while Pippin stood in front of him feeling foolish. After what seemed to Pippin like an hour, Merrick, without even looking up, said, "Yes?"

Pippin, unable to contain his enthusiasm, asked if he could conduct *Oliver!* As if he hadn't even heard the question, Merrick went back to the papers on his desk. Then, after another seemingly interminable pause, he asked, "Why should I give it to you?"

"Because I love the show and nobody will do it as well," Pippin blurted out.

Merrick's response, barely looking up, was simple. "OK, it's yours." Pippin sensed that this offhand treatment was a deliberate game, that Merrick probably surmised what Pippin was after and decided he would be a good conductor but he would never give him the pleasure of saying so. He preferred to make people squirm.

If Pippin thought his job would be simply shaping the orchestra and the singers, he was wrong. Immediately Merrick had a task for him. In London the show had been scored for an intimate orchestra of less than twenty pieces. But the union contract for the Imperial theater, where *Oliver!* would open when *Carnival* closed, required twenty-five musicians, to be paid whether they played or not. Merrick was not in the habit of paying anyone to do nothing. He wanted Pippin to reorchestrate it for the larger number.

"Do you think that's wise?" Pippin asked.

"Why don't you think it's wise?" Merrick glowered in a way that made Pippin realize there was no point in questioning Merrick's thinking. "I want twenty-five men in that pit," he said. "But keep the feeling of intimacy."

Merrick did not hear the new orchestrations until the recording session for the cast album, which was made in a Baptist church with excellent acoustics. "Why does it sound different?" he asked Pippin. Pippin diplomatically reminded him that he had demanded the larger orchestra.

"Can you make it sound smaller?" Merrick asked.

Pippin was able to do so by having several instruments in each section remain silent. At no point during the evening were all twenty-five musicians playing at once.

When *Oliver!* played its first preview in the Imperial, Merrick found himself disturbed by the light emanating from the orchestra pit. He ordered the musicians to turn their lights off. Pippin pointed out they couldn't read music without their lights. Merrick was also annoyed by the fact he could see the hair of the French horn player. "Tell him to get a haircut," he ordered.

Then Merrick had a better idea. If the pit itself were lowered, it would solve the problem of the lights and the horn player's offending hair.

A quick study of the foundations of the pit showed that it could be lowered considerably on the audience side but no more than eighteen inches on the stage side. That night a team of carpenters lowered the pit. It meant that the musicians would be slanted steeply in the direction of Pippin, who would be below rather than above them. This could be solved, Pippin thought, by standing on a stool. But, he was informed by an assistant, "Mr. Merrick doesn't want you to stand on anything."

The only way the musicians at the high back of the pit could see him was for him to wear shoes with eight-inch lifts. After the next performance Merrick came backstage beaming. He didn't notice that Pippin was taller than he had been a few days before. He was pleased at the restructuring he had ordered.

"You see, it sounds better with the pit lower," he told Pippin. Pippin could not help but agree.

It had cost $10,000 in one night's overtime, but, as far as Merrick was concerned, it was worth it. If only his problems in the outside world could be resolved with the cash and fierce determination that rendered everything tractable in the theater. Just around the time *Oliver!* opened Merrick's major problem in the outside world materialized. Jeanne's baby was born prematurely. It weighed barely three and a half pounds. The man who waited outside the delivery room, pacing nervously in the time-honored tradition of expectant fathers, was not the father. It was Jerry Orbach, one of the many members of Merrick's entourage who had become Jeanne's close friend. During the delivery Merrick made a brief appearance, and then left.

When he told one associate that Jeanne's baby had been born premature and woefully underweight, he quipped, "With my luck, it'll live."

Jeanne named the baby Cecilia Ann. When the baby finally came out of the hospital, Jeanne arranged a christening for her. Merrick had never taken his Jewishness very seriously, but there was something humiliating about attending a christening in a church for a child that was his own flesh and blood.

When he arrived at the church—late—he went to the pew where the obstetrician who had delivered and cared for the baby, Dr. Norman Pleshette, was sitting.

"You and your miracles!" he hissed at Pleshette.

Afterward there was a reception in Jeanne's apartment. At a certain point little Cecilia Ann was handed to her father. The sight of the man in the pinstriped suit holding the infant was, one of the guests recalled, "ludicrous." Shortly after he handed the baby back to her mother Merrick fled the apartment and did not return for weeks.

When he eventually came back, a few weeks later, it was with flowers. He had decided finally to propose to Jeanne. His decision was based, he told an associate, on some atavistic Jewish patriarchal feeling. It was, he said, "the Jewish father in me," though his own father had transmitted pitiful little such feeling to him.

A more important reason for his decision to marry Jeanne was that he learned that another beau of hers, a lawyer, was going to marry her so that the child would have a father. He could not tolerate the thought that someone else would be the father of his child. So he finally gave in to Jeanne's fondest wish. They were married by a justice of the peace in Elkton, Maryland.

It was not only utilitarian reasons that propelled him toward the altar. When Marta Orbach registered surprise at Merrick's formal commitment to Jeanne, he smiled at her and said, "Well, Marta, fucking sometimes leads to kissing."

His marriage with Leonore was finally terminated on January 11, 1963, only five days before their 25th wedding anniversary. It had been a deep disappointment to her that he had never wanted children, and it seemed especially cruel that the reason they were now being divorced was because he had fathered a child with another woman.

Leonore received a $90,000 settlement and an annual alimony of $26,000. A clause specified these payments would cease should she marry someone with an annual income over $200,000. Over the years he gradually raised the yearly sum to $50,000.

His oldest friend, Rabbi Pilchik, tried to persuade Merrick to restore to Leonore the full amount of the inheritance she had given him on their wedding. By then the $150,000, a fortune in 1938, would have been a pittance to Merrick. He refused.

Some of her friends urged her to get a high-powered lawyer and go after him. She was too proud to involve herself in nasty litigation. Curiously, their relationship remained amicable. She continued to invest money in his shows. When, a few years later, Merrick brought his widowed sister Sadye—much against her will—from California to New York to be a grandmother-figure for Cecilia Ann, he found her an apartment not far from Leonore's. The two women resumed the slight friendship they had known in St. Louis. He paid for the two of them to take a Mediterranean cruise together.

Well after the divorce, Leonore clung to her "title." Alexander Cohen recalled that when she phoned him, she would identify herself to his secretary not simply as "Leonore Merrick," but as "Mrs. David Merrick."

 with apologies to Thomas Gray

ELEGY WRITTEN IN SHUBERT ALLEY
for ST. VALENTINE'S DAY

The Kerr-few tolls the knell of parting play
  The weeping actors pitiful to see
The playwright homeward plods his weary way
  And leaves the street to darkness and to me.

Now fades the glimmering marquee in the night
  And all the air a heartbreak stillness holds
Save where Sardi mourners, drained of fight,
  In Angel voices toast the play that folds.

For nevermore the blazing lights shall burn
  For hungry people with an evening free
No flacks' full cries will serve to make them turn
  To live Broadway instead of dead TV.

Perhaps in Shubert Alley's dark is laid
  Some heart once pregnant with celestial fire
A heart that Merrick's marvels seek to aid
  And wake to ecstasy the Larchmont squire.

 EPITAPH

Large is his virtue, and his soul sincere
  Fame its recompense does largely send.
He gives the Theatre all he has, a sneer,
  When what the Theatre merits is a Friend.

We in the theatre need friends, Walter.
Have a heart.

DAVID MERRICK

CHAPTER NINETEEN

WHEN MERRICK ARRIVED in New York in 1940, the city had eleven daily newspapers. The consequence of the prolonged newspaper strike of 1962-63 was that, within four years, only three were left: the august *Times*, the working class, conservative *News* and the middle-class Jewish *Post*.

The most sophisticated and literate of New York newspapers, the *Herald-Tribune*, died in 1966. That year the *Journal-American* and the *World-Telegram & the Sun*, which appealed to a variety of constituencies, merged with the *Trib* to form an unwieldy amalgam, the *World-Journal-Tribune*, which ultimately appealed to no one and met its end in 1967.

In the Fifties and the early Sixties, when a show opened, the press agent called sources within the composing rooms of each of these papers to find out what the reviewers had written. He kept careful score. The judgment of the man at the *Times*, then as now, carried the most weight, but his negative opinion could be outmaneuvered if at least three other reviewers—virtually any three other reviewers—liked the show.

To have only three newspapers at all left very little room for maneuvering. The death of four newspapers diminished the importance of the printed word in the nation's largest city. The death of newspapers also diminished—beyond calculation—the vivacity of the city's public life. The sharpness of public debate, the common store of verbal wit, the image of an urbane, complex metropolis: all these existed in newspaper columns in a way they could not on video screens.

Both newspapers and the Broadway theater grew out of a cosmopolitanism that was on the wane. The *News*, for example, always had extensive coverage of high society; it attracted society readers with its right-wing editorials, and it gave its working class readership enticing glimpses of high life. Often this mix resembled *News* photographer Weegee's famous image of a bag lady ogling two dotty-looking grande dames arriving at the Metropolitan Opera. But this contrast was the essence of New York, which fiercely blended high and low.

In his eagerness to project the carefully wrought image of David Merrick, Merrick aspired to and depended on an urbanity that was alien to television. Television was not about sophistication; it radiated a mood of suburban recreation rooms. It was an equalizer, reducing high and low alike to the level of the banal chitchat of the increasingly popular talk show. Merrick seldom made TV appearances. Television did not enhance him the way the printed word did. The medium itself worked against the pretensions he had set himself. Its growing importance could only imperil his.

During the 1962-63 season Merrick capitalized on what he had learned the season before—that nothing excites the press as much as attacks upon itself. Nothing had given him the notoriety that the ad for *Subways Are For Sleeping* did. He resolved to build on it. Astute strategist that he was, he focused his attack on the two most important reviewers: Walter Kerr of the *Trib* and Howard Taubman of the *Times*. If he feuded with these two the other papers would certainly take note. If he engaged in repartee with, say, Frank Aston, of the *World Telegram*, who would care?

Merrick had never tangled with Taubman's predecessor, Brooks Atkinson. This was understandable. Although some of Atkinson's colleagues had a clubby, barroom conviviality, Atkinson had an aloof manner, that of a Brahmin whose breeding prohibited him from hobnobbing with the untouchables who surrounded him. Moreover, in his writing he had an impeccable Yankee integrity that kept him somehow above the fray.

On the other hand, since his "promotion" from chief music critic to chief drama critic, Merrick had always taken a dim view of Taubman. After reading Taubman's negative review of *Subways Are For Sleeping*, which opened about fifteen months after Taubman had been the first string critic of the *Times*, Merrick sent him a wire: "Thank God. At last you've had an opinion."

He asked a waiter in a Greek restaurant in the theater district to translate a quote from Taubman's review of *Stop the World, I Want to Get Off* into Greek. He then had the waiter read the translation back in English and realized the waiter had softened some of Taubman's remarks. Merrick insisted on an accurate translation. The waiter demurred, then said, "OK, but I warn you, Greek waiters who read this won't want to buy tickets to your show." The effort was academic, since the *Times* refused to run the ad with its critic's quote in Greek.

On the Johnny Carson Show Merrick called Taubman "an incompetent hack" and "a blind idiot." When Taubman and the *Times* indicated they might sue, Merrick sent Taubman a private letter of apology. It is surprising that the comments, which were indeed ugly and abusive, were aired, since the show was taped beforehand, not "live." In retrospect it is even more surprising that a feud between a theater producer and a newspaper theater critic was deemed worthy of national network television. Of Merrick's tasteless performance, Kenneth Tynan observed, "Perhaps he's had a feud too many." Lee Solters, one of Merrick's earliest press agents, would sometimes be asked by other clients to mount a campaign *a la Merrick*. What that meant, he would tell them, was going after the press. He seldom found takers.

Although it was especially important to keep the *Times* critics on their mettle, lesser beings did not escape Merrick's notice. It was during the '62-63 newspaper strike that TV critics first came to his attention. Merrick squabbled with them very little because their reviews tended to be upbeat and not very influential. He did take on one of the few who was genuinely literate, Edwin Newman, from NBC.

Merrick's approach was a strong offense. "He's what I call a 'Hey, you!' critic. His editor says, 'Hey, you! Go out and cover that show.' He could just as well be the washroom attendant." In 1966 he withheld Newman's tickets for the Hugh Wheeler adaptation of Shirley Jackson's novel, *We Have Always Lived in the Castle*. Newman threatened to buy tickets. Merrick issued a counter-threat, using a legalistic argument: "If we give free press tickets to a critic, that's inviting criticism. But if a critic buys a ticket and then adversely comments on my private property, I want equal time."

The legality of Merrick's approach was questioned by an FCC spokesman, who pointed out that the equal time policy only applied to issues of public importance, to which Merrick replied that a Broadway show was indeed "of public importance."

Of the various feuds Merrick conducted with critics none was more entertaining than the ongoing one he had with Walter Kerr of the *Trib*. In 1958 Merrick optioned *Goldilocks*, a musical spoof of the early movie industry when it was still centered on Long Island, with book and lyrics by Walter and his wife Jean, the author of *Please Don't Eat the Daisies*. They had an agreement with Leroy Anderson to do the score. Merrick tried to dissuade them from using Anderson. He wanted to pair them with the team that had written *Happy Hunting*, Ethel Merman's only flop. The Kerrs would not desert Anderson. They withdrew the project (and were furious when Merrick announced that *he* had dropped the option).

Merrick's skirmishes with Kerr may have stemmed from an informal survey he once did with questionnaires in the Playbill asking audience members which critics they relied on in deciding to buy theater tickets. Kerr ranked high.

Once, displeased with Kerr's negative review of *Becket*, Merrick had the review of the same play by Richard Watts of the *New*

York Post set in *Tribune* type and format. Though the Watts review was an ad, it looked as if it were part of the paper. The subterfuge, like the *Subways* ad, slipped by the *Tribune* advertising department.

Several of Merrick's sallies against Kerr occurred during the strike, when normal outlets for publicizing his shows were unavailable. Things were so topsy-turvy that Merrick arranged to review *Oliver!* himself on WNEW radio. He gave the show a tongue-in-cheek rave. Then he went on to condemn the radio station for permitting him to do so. He also announced he would apply for membership in the New York Drama Critics' Circle, since he had now joined the profession.

Merrick tried to prevent Kerr from reviewing *Oliver!* He was annoyed because Kerr had panned both his earlier entries that season, *Stop the World* and *Tchin-Tchin*. On a CBS radio interview Merrick said that "with sleeping pills so expensive, insomniacs should read Kerr instead. If the *Trib* does not survive the current strike, it would at least have the benefit of putting Kerr out of work."

Merrick forbade his press agent to send Kerr tickets to review *Oliver!*, but when Kerr threatened to come with another critic, Merrick relented. Such public battles often had a mollifying effect on the critics involved. Not wanting to appear the "heavy" that Merrick had portrayed them, they often were gentle on the show. Not Kerr. He knocked *Oliver!* on the radio.

Oliver! was critic-proof. Merrick sent Kerr a photograph of the long lines at the box office. Kerr thanked him for sending him photos of "David Merrick's mother." Merrick then said he had interviewed people on line. They told him they decided to buy tickets after hearing Kerr's pan.

At times the feud with Kerr could be quite congenial. They had known one another personally, after all, since *Goldilocks*. At one point Merrick declared he would only give the critics a single ticket. In the seat next to them he would plant a "well-proportioned starlet." Except for Taubman: Merrick himself would sit next to Taubman, "helpfully holding a flashlight for note taking."

As for Kerr, he found it necessary to separate him from his wife Jean because he was convinced that she was "nudging" him and thereby exercising too great an influence on him.

Kerr responded enthusiastically to this charge. "First, she does nudge me, nudges me all the time," he wrote. "And do you know why? She likes me, that crazy girl. Surely, Mr. Merrick, someone, somewhere has liked you well enough to give you a little dig in the elbow. No? Ah, well.

"Then there are other type nudges. Sometimes she nudges me because I am sitting on her coat. And sometimes she nudges me to pick up her program, which has slid from her lap onto the floor at my feet . . .

"I must also put into evidence a recent occasion when I asked for a nudge, though not from my wife. For the first time in all my years on a newspaper I found myself seated exactly next to Brooks Atkinson, who has so recently surrendered his claim to an aisle seat. In my delight at seeing him and in what may have been an excess of sparkling good humor, I leaned over and said, wry fellow that I am, 'Nudge me if you see anything you like.' Is it possible that one of Mr. Merrick's friends mistook my wife for Brooks Atkinson? (Mr. Atkinson is on the slight side and wears a mustache; my wife is tall, and does not.)"

Jean Kerr was, of course, a figure of stature in her own right. Her comedy *Mary, Mary* remains one of the longest running non-musical plays in Broadway history. Well before Merrick's allegations about her undue influence on her husband, *Please Don't Eat the Daisies* had been a nationwide bestseller. But for many years afterward, she observed with rueful amusement, whenever the Kerrs went to London, she was invariably introduced as "the woman who nudges her husband."

During the newspaper strike Merrick paid Kerr the great tribute of printing an elegant-looking valentine devoted to an attack on him. Inside was an "Elegy Written in Shubert Alley for St. Valentine's Day" (with apologies to Thomas Gray.)

The valentine read:

> The Kerr-few tolls the knell of parting play
> The weeping actors pitiful to see
> The playwright homeward plods his weary way
> And leaves the street to darkness and to me.
> Now fades the glimmering marquee in the night
> And all the air a heartbreak stillness holds
> Save where Sardi mourners, drained of fight,
> In Angel voices toast the play that folds.
>
> For nevermore the blazing lights shall burn
> For hungry people with an evening free,
> No flacks' full cries will serve to make them turn
> To live Broadway instead of dead TV.
>
> Perhaps in Shubert Alley's dark is laid
> Some heart once pregnant with celestial fire
> A heart that Merrick's marvels seek to aid
> And wake to ecstasy the Larchmont squire.

EPITAPH

> Large is his virtue, and his soul sincere
> Fame its recompense does largely send,
> He gives the Theater all he has, a sneer,
> When what the Theatre merits is a Friend.
>
> We in the theater need friends, Walter.
> Have a heart.
>
> David Merrick.

Antagonizing the press was a surefire way to get space, even out of town. When *Subways Are For Sleeping* was on its tryout tour in the fall of 1961, it would open in Boston the same night that the Netherlands Chamber Orchestra would mark its Boston debut. Cyrus Durgin, the first string critic of the *Boston Globe*, wanted to cover the chamber group. He planned to send his second string critic, Kevin Kelly, to review *Subways*.

Kelly had fallen afoul of Merrick the previous spring for not having liked *Becket*. Merrick announced he would give no tickets to Kelly. So Kelly went to Philadelphia and bought a ticket for the final performance there. Alongside Kelly's favorable review of the show was a story by Durgin explaining what had happened. The opening of a David Merrick musical thus became a news event in Boston. (After he read Kelly's review, Merrick sent him a bottle of champagne, addressed to "the greatest drama critic in the world.")

Merrick maintained a good relationship with some of the out of town critics, particularly Elliot Norton of the *Boston Globe* and Richard Coe of the *Washington Post*. The out-of-town critics, Merrick felt, could sometimes provide useful insights. By the time the New York critics saw a show it was too late to fix it. After Coe had panned *Fanny*, Merrick prohibited Harvey Sabinson from giving him tickets for *Epitaph for George Dillon*. Sabinson had not complied, and Coe, who had not liked *Look Back in Anger*, wrote one of the few enthusiastic reviews for *Dillon*, after which he became Merrick's friend. Once, Coe wrote a profile of Merrick in which he noted that he had attended the Washington opening of *Mack and Mabel*, gone back to the office to pan it and then joined Merrick and his wife Etan for dinner.

Merrick's essential complaint with critics was that they were out of touch with the audience's concerns. For this reason he looked kindly on John Chapman, who, he said, "writes for the readers he has. The other morning paper critics don't write for their readers. They write for each other, or for what they are sure is a personal following of superior intellect."

However much he yearned to be seen as classy, he knew it would not help his shows at the box office if they were so perceived. Alec McCowen, who starred in his production of Christopher Hampton's *The Philanthropist,* remembered seeing Merrick read the review in the *Times*. "A 'literate comedy,'" he scowled, slamming down the paper and stalking off.

"If you think an audience is looking for literary value, they're not," he told an interviewer in the spring of 1962. "From six to nine, they're looking for entertainment . . . That's the whole point of my squabble with the critics—they have no relation to entertainment.

"You know, I've been toying with a new idea. This season I opened four shows in one week. Next year, I could open all four in one night. That would keep Walter Kerr out of three of them. I'd have one arty show, to decoy the first string critics, and I'd get the sports writers for the others. They'd just review them as entertainment."

CHAPTER TWENTY

O N MAY 24, 1963, several U.S. astronauts made an official visit to New York after a triumphant flight into space. There was the traditional ticker tape parade, a visit with Mayor Robert Wagner at City Hall, and a visit to a Broadway show.

The show was *Stop the World—I Want To Get Off.* When the motorcade arrived at the Shubert Theater, 3,000 people were waiting to cheer the astronauts and their wives. Standing just in front of the huge crowd, beaming, was the celebrated producer David Merrick, who greeted the group and personally escorted Gordon "Gordo" Cooper and his wife Trudy to their seats.

To complete the New York experience, the astronauts were taken to a glamorous nightclub, the Eden Roc, after the show. It turned out they didn't enjoy their evening very much. As Walter M. Schirra, Jr., put it, "Maybe if I'd been briefed for a few months on going far out, I'd have enjoyed it."

Schirra, in fact, had wanted to see the Neil Simon-Cy Coleman musical *Little Me,* which starred Sid Caesar. His wife had wanted to see *A Funny Thing Happened on the Way to the Forum. Stop the World* was no one's first choice for an evening at the theater—except, of course, for David Merrick, who had been working for months to arrange their visit.

The evening at *Stop the World,* with all its attendant publicity, had been the work of a new man in the Merrick office, Alan Delynn. Delynn was a mysterious figure in the Merrick organization. Unlike Schlissel, who knew more about the nuts and bolts of every show than Merrick himself, Delynn appeared to have little to do with anything businesslike. Unlike Hartley, whose personal magnetism could be depended on to solve the myriad artistic problems every show presented, Delynn alienated as many people as he charmed. Jeanne Gilbert called him "the slitherer."

A young woman who worked as his secretary, Elizabeth Kaye, described him as "someone who dangled people in front of you." More important, he could apparently deliver what he dangled. One of the Harvard intellectuals who advised President Kennedy once called to arrange a date for Kennedy with a Las Vegas performer, one of Delynn's assistants recalled. It was arranged.

Delynn and Merrick were a kind of Tweedledum and Tweedledee, a close observer remarked, because the latter had no real sense of himself, and the former didn't really believe he existed.

In his need to reassure himself of his own existence, Delynn had devised a list of famous people he referred to as "The Flimsy." The term may have referred to the fact that Delynn was using the flimsiest of excuses to phone these important people. Sometimes he had met them at parties. Sometimes he had met them in his previous job as an assistant to Huntington Hartford. Sometimes he had never met them at all. In addition to show business people, the list included the names of socialites like Marietta Tree and Judy Peabody.

His assistant's job was to go down The Flimsy and leave word that "Alan Delynn called." Sometimes they ignored him. Sometimes they returned his calls. If famous people returned his calls, then, yes, he did exist.

Just as he dangled celebrities in front of Merrick, he dangled Merrick in front of others. Once he asked Merrick and his third wife, Etan, who were in Los Angeles, if they would like to have dinner with Blake Edwards and Julie Andrews. The Merricks said yes. At some point during the dinner Andrews gestured toward Delynn, whose name she had clearly forgotten. She shot a help-less glance at Edwards, assuming he would remember Delynn's name. Edwards sheepishly shrugged his shoulders.

If the Kennedy White House was quick to return his calls, it may have been because he was personally friendly with Kennedy's sisters. Once, during a reception there, during which each of the guests was introduced to the President and Mrs. Kennedy by a member of the protocol staff, the President stepped out of the receiving line to give Delynn an affectionate jab in the ribs.

Whatever else he did for Merrick, if he could arrange a coup like the astronauts' visit to *Stop the World*, Delynn was a valuable asset. For Merrick was no longer merely a local celebrity. The *Subways* ad had given him national press. As early as 1959 he had been profiled—though not as attractively as he wished—in the *New York Times Magazine*. In the next few years he would become a truly imperial figure, and, as such, he needed courtiers to reinforce this position. Delynn filled the bill admirably.

The pressure of working in the Merrick office was not offset by the negligible salaries he paid. In the spring of 1963 his secretary of several years had quit. A possible replacement was told she had three weeks, until the boss came back, to clean up the mess he had left in his wake.

She found a huge pile of mail on his desk and immediately set to work sort it out. She came across an astonishing number of unpaid bills and was told her new boss didn't like to pay any bills union regulations did not require him to pay. When the mount-ing total was high enough he would offer his frantic debtor some percentage of the amount owed—in cash. The system generally worked.

On the day of his return she was terrified of what he might say, but she thought the polite thing to do was smile at him, regard-less of his manner. Her smile, rather than the fearful look many such applicants had shown, slightly unnerved him. He liked it.

Someone had suggested it might be a good idea for her to wear a red dress. Later that day Michael Stewart was in the red office and asked Merrick, "How do you find her in this room?" But Merrick liked the fact she had worn the color that meant so much to him. He liked the fact that she had organized the mess he had left and which had grown in his absence. And so Helen Nickerson spent the next seventeen years working for him.

Born to a wealthy, well-connected San Francisco family, Nickerson had come to New York in the late Forties with theatrical aspirations. She had studied with Sanford Meisner at the Neighborhood Playhouse. She had done a lot of work as a radio actress just as the field of radio drama was disappearing. Like many aspiring actresses, she needed a second job and had found employment as a secretary.

Her youth in upper crust San Francisco gave her a knowledge of certain things Merrick never managed to acquire. Someone who watched her from the beginning of her association with him observed, "She was the taste of David Merrick. He would send Helen out for Christmas presents. She would pick out exquisite things. She gave him an aura of class. If the gift was cheap or impersonal you knew he had chosen it himself. Anything Helen picked would have had good taste." Anything Helen picked would have had good taste.

The first time Merrick sent her on such an errand was to find an opening night gift for Anthony Newley for *Stop the World*. Nickerson went to Steuben, where she selected a crystal vase she knew was overdone, but which she also knew—for that very reason—would appeal to Newley. It did. After seeing Newley's excited response, Merrick delegated her to do more of his shopping. What allowed her to be exquisite was his annual burst of generosity. One year, in fact, the gifts for all the important people in Merrick shows, which had been assembled and wrapped, were stolen the day before Christmas. Merrick sent Nickerson out to replace as many of them as she could before the holiday with no thought to the expense. The only one she was unable to replace was a sapphire pin she had found at Tiffany's with the precise color of Julie Harris's eyes. If Jeanne Gilbert added class to his private life, Helen Nickerson provided the same touch for his public image.

She was also a conspirator in her boss's strategies. One of Merrick's favorite ploys was to raise a telephone conversation to fever pitch, in which he was screaming and being screamed at. At a certain point, to insure that he had the last angry word, Merrick would slam down the phone. The party at the other end would call back, frantically wanting to finish the conversation. If he were lucky, Nickerson would connect him to Schlissel, who would win whatever points Merrick was after. Otherwise he would be told by Nickerson, in her most businesslike voice—a continuation, perhaps, of her radio skills—that Mr. Merrick had suddenly been called out of town.

There was about her a kind of primness and formality that could be intimidating in their own way. She herself observed that though he screamed unrestrainedly at male agents no one handled him more effectively than some of the female agents who carried themselves in a deliberately old-fashioned, "rigidly ladylike" style. Women like Audrey Woods or Leah Salisbury, she recalled, would come to see him in elegant hats and white gloves. After a discussion of terms, they might say something very dignified like, "No, Mr. Merrick, I can't accept that for my client. I'll go back to my office and let you think about it." Invariably, Nickerson recalled, he would cave in to their demands.

If Nickerson was annually delegated to embody his generosity, she was more frequently required to reflect his imperiousness. "You'd get into your office at 9:00 in the morning," someone who had extensive dealings with Merrick recalled, "and even before you had a chance to take your coat off the phone would ring. It would be Helen. 'Merrick wants to see you,' she'd say, in an icy tone. Not, 'Mr. Merrick,' but 'Merrick.' You felt like a little kid summoned to the principal's office."

Being "well liked," after all, was not part of the Merrick plan. It was Bloomgarden who had produced the play in which Willy Loman expounded on how far you could go in America by being "well liked." Merrick preferred to be feared. He also wanted respect, and one of the reasons he commanded it was both the precision and the elan with which his organization could function under sometimes unimaginable strain.

CHAPTER TWENTY-ONE

I N THE FALL OF 1963 there were more dark theaters on Broadway than there had been for decades. A group of concerned and eminent theater people, tired of simply lamenting the state of the theater, decided to do something about it. They enlisted the help of the attorney John Wharton, who, more than twenty years earlier, had founded the Playwrights Company. Wharton devised a complex legal structure that would enable a not-for-profit corporation to provide financial aid to the commercial theater. It took almost five years for the organization to be incorporated as the Theater Development Fund.

TDF was born out of a sense of despair about the commercial theater, a despair more profound than the one that had inspired the issue of Theater Arts that outlined the Broadway theater's woes in 1940.

There was, however, no despair on the eighth floor of the St. James building that fall. There the Merrick Office was making plans to produce nine shows.

As had become his custom, he produced half these shows in very quick succession during the fall. From England he imported two plays, Jean Anouilh's *The Rehearsal*, with Coral Browne and Keith Michell, and John Osborne's *Luther*. The latter introduced Albert Finney to American theater audiences at just the time he and Tony Richardson made a huge splash with the film *Tom*

With Albert Finney and Tony Richardson at the opening of *Luther*.
With Tallulah Bankhead and Tab Hunter at the opening of *The Milk Train Doesn't Stop Here Any More*.

Jones. He produced a Brecht play, *The Resistible Rise of Arturo Ui.*

For the first time he produced a play by his fellow refugee from St. Louis, Tennessee Williams, *The Milk Train Doesn't Stop Here Any More.* He produced *110 in the Shade*, Tom Jones and Harvey Schmidt's musical version of *The Rainmaker*, their first show since *The Fantasticks.* He also produced an adaptation of Ken Kesey's novel *One Flew Over the Cuckoo's Nest* that starred Kirk Douglas.

All these shows opened in barely two months during the fall. Later that season he brought *Foxy*, a musical version of Ben Jonson's *Volpone* that starred Bert Lahr, to Broadway. (It had originally been produced in the Klondike by Robert Whitehead, whose other commitments made it impossible to supervise its journey to New York.) For several years Merrick's office had been developing the musical based on the life of Fanny Brice, *Funny Girl.*

It was Merrick who sent Bob Merrill to Palm Beach, where he knew Jule Styne was beginning to work on the score. Originally the lyrics were to have been written by Stephen Sondheim, but Sondheim withdrew because he could not envision Mary Martin as Fanny Brice. Styne's "chance" encounter with Merrill in Palm Beach led to their collaboration on the score. Several months before it opened Merrick sold his interest in it to his co-producer, Ray Stark, who happened to be the late Brice's son-in-law. "Life is too short to deal with Ray Stark," Merrick declared.

Of these, two were *success d'estime*—*The Rehearsal* and *Arturo Ui.* The Brecht play was produced in association with Neil Hartley as a gesture of gratitude to Tony Richardson, who had provided the Merrick office with so many hits. It starred Christopher Plummer and had, among other virtues, a background score by Jule Styne, who evoked the jazz he knew as a young man in Chicago for this bitingly satiric depiction of Hitler as a Chicago gangster.

The play was not really Broadway fare. During previews it attracted an extremely appreciative audience—students, theater lovers, intellectuals who knew and admired Brecht. Night after night they gave the play tumultuous ovations. But the opening night audience consisted of the same people who had been attending openings for decades. Instinctively they knew Brecht was not their friend. They were, in fact, the sort of theatergoers Brecht himself despised. For them the play was cryptic and repugnant. Their response was cold and hostile, which affected both the opening night performances and the unenthusiastic reviews. *Arturo Ui* did find a vocal audience. Sylvia Schwartz was deluged with phone calls, largely from students, begging Merrick to keep the play open. When she passed on their pleas, her boss's response was simple: "Sylvia, tell them to buy tickets."

Cuckoo's Nest was not even a *success d'estime*. Despite its Hollywood star, it flopped. Kesey's book was an early manifestation of what would later be considered a Sixties spirit. Even when the play was revived in a more congenial Off-Broadway setting, in 1972 (only three years before the film version), it flopped.

Milk Train was also a flop critically and financially—for the second time. It had originally been done at Gian-Carlo Menotti's Festival of Two Worlds in Spoleto, Italy, in 1961. Roger Stevens saw it there and brought it to New York, where it opened during the 1962-63 newspaper strike and closed after sixty-nine performances. One reason Merrick may have been eager to produce it again was to succeed where Stevens had failed.

Richardson was eager to direct the play. Williams had done a revised version of the play for the Barter Theater of Virginia in the summer of 1963. Richardson was enthusiastic about the revisions. He did not share the enthusiasm of the author and the producer to see Tallulah Bankhead as Flora Goforth, whose courtship with death the play describes. But he was willing to accept Bankhead if the others would accept Tab Hunter in the role of the young man Flora calls the Angel of Death.

In retrospect Neil Hartley realized this was "camp casting," but everyone thought that both names would be box office draws. The audiences the play attracted during its out-of-town tryout were specialized. They consisted, Hartley said, of "middle-aged women who felt emancipated by Tallulah and gay young men imitating her. The critics all mentioned the audience. They picked up on the—as it were—homosexual cloud that hung over Tallulah."

The last stop before New York was Baltimore. All through the run there the playwright wept over the beauty of his play. But the director was not happy with the way the production had gone. Nor, it turned out, was the producer, who arrived the Saturday before the show was to move to New York.

Milk Train was supposed to open at the Brooks Atkinson Theater on Wednesday, January 1, 1964. Sometime after Merrick's arrival in Baltimore, Schlissel notified the management of the Atkinson that the booking was cancelled. No reason was given. Only Merrick could have broken a contract in so peremptory a manner, knowing the theater owner would be unlikely to sue, lest he lose Merrick's bookings in the future.

As it happened, no litigation was necessary. Later that same evening Schlissel rescinded the cancellation. Merrick had been dismayed by what he saw in Baltimore. It was too late to re-direct the play before the New York opening. Besides, Richardson had already flown back to London to try to patch up his faltering marriage to Vanessa Redgrave.

While it was standard for Merrick to threaten to close a show before it got to New York, this time he meant it. However he felt he owed Williams the chance to decide the fate of his play. Williams thought it would kill Tallulah, who was already extremely ill, if they didn't open it in New York. Merrick decided to go ahead with the opening.

There was one preview in New York, attended by a predominantly gay audience, which gave Tallulah huge ovations. "If we had this audience every night, we'd have a smash," Merrick told Williams. The next night, however, the traditional opening nighters were as unresponsive to it as they had been a few months earlier to *Arturo Ui.*

The critics, having missed the chance to pan it the season before, compensated this time. One dismissed the star with the curt, "Miss Bankhead was hoarse and unhappy." *Newsweek* said the role of the Angel of Death "is walked through by Tab Hunter, an actor hitherto used by the movies as a form of catnip for pubescent females." As for Richardson's direction, *Newsweek* said, "The whole play was chastened to a Brechtian coolness which made it seem wholly alien to Williams' sensuous imagination." After five performances, *Milk Train* closed.

Merrick's association with Richardson ended around this time. Merrick told Peter Brook that he was going to withhold Richardson's pay for one of their productions. Richardson, he assumed, would sue him. He would let Richardson dangle a while, then offer to pay half. Richardson, he was confident, would accept.

He knew perfectly well that Brook and Richardson were close friends and that doubtless Brook would pass on the strategy to Richardson. It didn't matter. The scenario played itself out exactly as Merrick predicted.

1963-64 was a particularly auspicious season to produce musicals because, if they succeeded, they would run into the spring when the New York World's Fair would open. Merrick had scheduled three musicals, the first of which was *110 in the Shade*, the story about a spinster in a parched Southern town that had been made into a film starring Katharine Hepburn.

Merrick's personal grievances wound up in the way of his professionalism. The leading role of the charlatan who promises the town rain required an actor of great charm and vocal power. Among those being considered was Howard Keel, the star of many great MGM musicals of the Fifties. Keel was willing to appear at the audition so the producer could see he was still in good physical shape, but he felt his reputation was sufficient that he should not have to sing. Merrick took this as a personal affront. He insisted that if Keel came to an audition he would have to sing. Keel told Merrick he would arrange a screening of any of his films. Merrick refused to consider him.

At one point Hal Holbrook was going to play the part. Holbrook, a thorough professional acclaimed a few seasons before for his portrayal of Mark Twain, might have made it work.

But suddenly Robert Horton became available. Horton was a TV star with limited stage experience and vocal ability. His major virtue, in the eyes of Merrick, was that he had recently been hired by Richard Rodgers, whom he still viewed as an enemy. (There had been a brief reconciliation, arranged by Logan, when Rodgers and Hammerstein asked him for help promoting their unsuccessful *Pipe Dream.* In exchange, a few years later, Merrick asked them if they would put an insert for his *World of Suzie Wong* in their *Flower Drum Song* programs. They refused, claiming a statute of limitations on gratitude. He resumed his former attitude of hostility.)

Rodgers had engaged Horton for a show he wrote with Alan Jay Lerner called *I Picked A Daisy,* which was cancelled shortly before *110 in the Shade* went into rehearsal. (*Daisy* was resurrected a few years later when Lerner and Burton Lane wrote it as *On A Clear Day You Can See Forever.*)

It gave Merrick pleasure to take on an actor his rival had had to let go. Merrick bought out Holbrook's contract and put Horton into the role. Horton never felt comfortable in it.

Joseph Anthony, who had directed both the Broadway production of *The Rainmaker* and the film, directed the musical. Agnes DeMille did the choreography. Even Jerome Robbins acknowledged DeMille as the great pioneer in the use of dance to further plot and character in the Broadway musical. Her legendary status and her own authoritarian demeanor did not deter Merrick from needling her during rehearsals. He would walk through the rehearsal room mumbling, "Agnes DeMille is over the hill. Agnes DeMille is over the hill."

Tom Jones, the writer, was disturbed by Merrick's comments on the developing show: "It was very infrequent that he had creative suggestions. But when he did, the next day he might say just the opposite. He was disturbingly inconsistent and much more likely to trust the opinions of the men's room assistant than his own staff.

"We had the feeling we were working with a deranged person,

but also someone who could use derangement for his own amusement and his own purposes.

"We would have a conference and sometimes he would fly into a rage. As he left I felt he had enjoyed it. But sometimes it was my impression he couldn't control it. He would start with a genuine grievance. Then he'd build it up. He'd play with it. And then he'd get trapped in it."

Jones felt Merrick's eagerness to upset his creative team stemmed from a "basic theory that creative people were too often too easy on themselves. They felt sympathy for each other, encouraged each other, were warm toward each other.

"His own temperament was to create doubt, fear, chaos and uncertainty—to counterbalance this warm support. His theory was, 'Hit 'em hard. The world is tough. Audiences are tough. Critics are tough.'"

On shows where the creative staff had a pre-existing rapport or were individually strong, Merrick's divisive techniques did not interrupt the flow of ideas. Here, however, no one was strong enough to withstand his constant assaults. The scapegoat turned out to be DeMille.

She knew something was the matter when, just before a preview one evening, Nash who had opposed hiring her, came over to her at the back of the theater and extravagantly praised her work.

"I think I've just received the kiss of Judas," she told the stage manager, whom she saw a moment later. She knew that just before he had seen her, Nash had had dinner with Merrick. Sure enough, after that performance Merrick informed her that all the dances were being cut. She protested that they were only in their formative stages. None of her fellow creators came to her defense. No one knew what to say. Anthony, who, more than anyone had been responsible for her being hired, actually broke down crying.

110 in the Shade opened October 24, 1963. It received good but not great notices. As Jones observed, "By then a hit wasn't enough for David Merrick. A smash hit was approaching The Right Thing."

Much the same was true of *Foxy*. It got good reviews, especially for Lahr's performance, but by the time it opened, *Foxy* was, in effect, a stepchild.

Merrick had found his smash hit. It was a musical based on *The Matchmaker*. It was called *Hello, Dolly!* For many years it was the show with which he was most closely identified. In the public's mind he was not the producer of Anouilh or Brecht or Williams, not the man who brought Osborne's work to America, but the man who produced *Hello, Dolly!*

Merrick was doing more serious plays not simply because of Richardson's enthusiasms but because he had found a way to soften the economic blow that inevitably resulted from producing serious theater. In 1959 he had established the David Merrick Arts Foundation. The Foundation invested in Merrick's shows, starting with *Gypsy*, and the profits established a fund that could be used to produce plays that seemed bad commercial risks. By the late Sixties, interestingly enough, many of the plays the Foundation backed turned out to more successful than the supposedly "commercial" ventures.

Producing through the Foundation softened the blows of financial failure. The losses were heavy—in the space of barely two months it lost $200,000 on *Arturo Ui* and $80,000 on *Milk Train*. Happily, the flops sponsored by the Foundation did not need to be listed on the prospectus every producer must issue to prospective investors in his shows.

The cynical saw the Foundation as Merrick's revenge against Uncle Sam: Foundation money is not taxed. Others saw it as part of his ongoing desire to associate himself with "class," even to see himself as a philanthropist. In many ways the David Merrick Arts Foundation was a precursor of the not-for-profit theaters that dotted the landscape from the Seventies onward. Merrick's foundation drew its funds not from corporate sponsors but from his own commercial efforts. Moreover, like not-for-profit theaters of today, which profit when their productions are transferred to commercial venues, sometimes when a play initially presented by the Foundation would move to a different theater, as part of Merrick's constant juggling, it would be re-incorporated as a commercial production.

Profits from the Foundation were donated to the theater departments of two schools, Brandeis and Catholic University in Washington. The Brandeis connection was its president, Abram Sachar, whose family Merrick knew in St. Louis. Sachar had given Eli Pilchik his first job.

The choice of Brandeis as the recipient of his benefactions seems to go beyond this personal association. He could just as easily have donated Foundation moneys to either of his alma maters in St. Louis, to any of the universities in his adopted city or to any number of theatrical charities. This was one of the few instances where he associated himself with a specifically Jewish institution. Success had made it possible for him to acknowledge his roots, however obliquely, (and then, lest his gesture seem too parochial, to balance it with donations to a school representing another religion.)

The Foundation also helped him produce the quantity of work he liked to produce. "By producing in quantity I can buy advertising in quantity," he once told an interviewer. "I have a theory that you can sell shows using the Madison Avenue technique. I reason—if you can sell all sorts of merchandise that they do sell with all these ridiculous campaigns—that I can certainly try that technique in selling my lovely plays. And I sold some rather literate and articulate plays that way. Believe it or not. They weren't all *Suzie Wong*."

By this time in his career Merrick was like a juggler who sets a group of dowels spinning, then sets plates whirling on top of them. Professionally, plate spinning now seemed a breeze. There was, however, one plate that he never could keep on balance. That was Jeanne. Marriage had not made her easier to deal with. Nor, of course, had it had any such effect on him.

As it had before they were married, their day would begin with a fight, the effects of which were visible when Merrick arrived wearily, testily at the office around ten. Shortly thereafter Jeanne would phone. He wouldn't accept the call. This aggravated both her frustration and his irritation.

Sometimes Jeanne would have a liquid lunch at Sardi's making a spectacle of herself while her husband tried to conduct business. Sometimes her friends kept an eye on her during opening nights, when she was just as likely to create an embarrassing scene.

Leonore had accepted the limitations of what she might expect from him. Jeannie kept imagining she could get more. She had seen what limitless energy he had. She had not understood that he saw no point in investing that energy in private matters. Who would see it? Whose perception of his ability, his greatness would be enhanced? Jeanne's? Why would *that* matter?

You perform plate spinning in a ring surrounded by people—mostly strangers—whose applause you crave. You don't do it in your own living room.

CHAPTER TWENTY-TWO

ROM THE MOMENT he acquired the rights to present *The Matchmaker* on Broadway in 1955, Merrick was convinced Wilder's play would make a great musical. After the success of *Carnival* in 1961 he was convinced that Bob Merrill was the man to deliver the score.

He and Jeannie took Merrill and his steady companion for cocktails one evening shortly after *Carnival* opened. In the midst of a convivial evening Merrick brought up his idea of doing *The Matchmaker* as a musical.

"You'll do the score, and Gower will direct," Merrick said matter-of-factly.

In an equally matter of fact way Merrill said, "No, I won't. I'll never work with Gower again."

Merrick was at first taken aback. He knew the two men had almost come to fisticuffs during their work on *Carnival*, but he saw that as normal backstage behavior.

"Yes, you will," Merrick said jovially. "And you want to know why?" he added. "Because writers are whores."

Merrill laughed but stood his ground.

Then his girlfriend said, "David's right," echoing Merrick's words. "Writers *are* whores."

Whether or not she intended to endear herself to Merrick, her words accomplished the exact opposite effect. Many had noted the suddenness with which Merrick could change from an amiable, teasing fellow to a raging tyrant in next to no time. The effect was like being at sea, with the weather balmy and agreeable. At sea, if a squall arose, you could see it in the distance and gauge its speed as it came toward you. In Merrick's eyes there was no warning—the squall would arise instantaneously.

This was one of those occasions.

"How dare you!" Merrick shouted at her. "I can say that because I'm his boss. I'm not supposed to be in love with him. I never want to see you again."

The squall now raging out of control, Merrick turned to Merrill. "Get her out of here," he yelled. "I don't ever want to see her again."

It was a side of Merrick that Merrill had never seen. He knew this was not a jest. This was not the controlled, dispassionate anger he sensed when Merrick made him fire Peter Glenville. This was the real thing. He helped his girlfriend up and left.

Merrick's rage implied a certain deep loyalty. It was the same paternalism Merrill had noted in him all along, but the intensity of the rage was unprecedented in their relationship.

It unsettled Merrill, but it did not change what he had told Merrick. He was not going to work with Champion again. (It would take a decade for him to change his mind.)

Merrill's adamant refusal annoyed Merrick. He was not one to mess with new talent. Once he had used people who brought him success he was eager to use them again. He was not interested in discovering talent. Michael Shurtleff, in fact, had urged him to hire Gower Champion before the latter's whopping success with *Bye, Bye, Birdie*. The morning after *Birdie* opened, Shurtleff couldn't help going into Merrick's office to point out Champion's glowing notices.

Merrick, unfazed, said, "Yes, I see. We let other people take the chance. *Then* we take them."(Similarly, Claibe Richardson, the composer of *The Grass Harp*, was taken by his agent, Gloria Safire, to play some songs for Merrick, who was very complimentary. "What does that mean?" Richardson asked Safire afterward.

"It means that after you've had your first hit, he'll hire you," she said.)

Champion and Michael Stewart, both of whom Merrick hired for *Carnival* after their success with *Birdie*, were enlisted to do the direction and book for the musical based on *The Matchmaker*.

There was a brief moment when it seemed as if Champion might not be available to direct the musical, which by then had a full book and score. It was then entitled, *Dolly, That Damnned Exasperating Woman*. Merrick toyed with the idea of giving the project to Harold Prince, who, after a decade as an extremely successful and innovative producer, had begun directing musicals. The score was auditioned for Prince, who decided he did not want to do it. He did, however, give the creators a bit of free advice—get rid of that awful song, he told them, by which he meant a number called "Hello, Dolly." Shortly afterward, fortunately, Champion again became available.

Stewart began working on the book without a composer. The men who had given Merrick his previous hits were busy on other projects. Merrick called Jerry Herman, a shy, eager-to-please young songwriter who had scored a great hit in 1958, when he was 26, with a revue called *Nightcap*. It was performed at a Village nightclub called The Showplace (where its cast included Charles Nelson Reilly and Estelle Parsons.)

In 1961 Herman wrote a musical about the young state of Israel called *Milk and Honey*. It starred two opera singers, Robert Weede and Mimi Benzell, and the great favorite of the Yiddish theater, Molly Picon. When he heard Merrick had come to the Martin Beck to see *Milk and Honey* Herman was understandably nervous. He was doubly thrilled when, shortly afterward, he received an invitation to the producer's office to discuss the musical version of Wilder's play.

Herman entered the red office with no little trepidation. Merrick's reputation had preceded him. Herman was struck by the dark hair and the furrowed brow, which gave him a sinister look. After a little chitchat, Merrick got down to business, explaining he intended to do *The Matchmaker* as a musical.

"I like very much what I heard at the Martin Beck, but it's an operetta," he said. "I need somebody who can write Americana. *Milk and Honey* was so ethnic."

"Mr. Merrick, that was my assignment," Herman pleaded. He could see Merrick was not convinced. This was a Friday. He told Merrick he would write four songs based on moments in the play to show him he could compose "Americana."

Herman raced back to his Village walk-up, read the play and selected four scenes to set to music. He made his songs as American as he knew how. Monday he called Merrick and asked if he could play them for him.

"He probably thought I had four 'trunk songs,'" Herman recalled. But Merrick could see the material was right for the show. (Three of these audition songs, in fact, remained in the final version: "Dancing," "I Put My Hand In" and "Put On Your Sunday Clothes.") Merrick was also impressed with the speed with which Herman worked.

"Kid, the show is yours."

Perhaps because he was a relative neophyte, Herman had more contact with Merrick than many songwriters. During his first few meetings he was "absolutely cowed" by him, but gradually he began to see that the "gruff, tough" manner was a pose, and that it got results. But if you challenged him, he might back down.

"He would tell me flat out whether he liked something or not—and why," Herman recalled. "He didn't like a song I wrote for Vandergelder. He felt I was straining for comic effect, not getting to the heart of the character. I wrote 'It Takes A Woman' after that, which was a much better song.

"He likes toughness in people. He admires a writer's ability to be told, 'That's lousy,' and to be able to come up with something new that's better."

When the bulk of Dolly Levi's songs were written, Merrick asked Herman to play them for the woman he wanted to be his star, Ethel Merman.

After her triumph in *Gypsy*, Merman was wary of taking on a new role that might seem anticlimactic. Now, in her early fifties, she was reluctant to sign on for a new Broadway show under any circumstances. "It's like taking the veil," she told her friends.

Herman played his score for her, and she told Merrick she would think about it. As it happened, Donald Brooks, the eminent Seventh Avenue designer who, throughout his career, created dresses for women of the theater and designed several Broadway shows, was fitting Merman's costumes for a TV special when she gave Merrick her decision.

After a few pleasantries, she told him, "I've given it a great deal of thought. It's been on my mind for weeks now. In my heart and in my head, even though Jerry has said he would do some additional songs, I just can't do it.

"No, David. I want you to know in my whole history I've created every role I've ever played. This is Ruth Gordon's role. I'm not about to be the musical version of Ruth Gordon."

For anyone who had seen Gordon in *The Matchmaker* it was true. The impression she had created was indelible.

This left Merrick and Champion in a quandary. Their second choice was Nanette Fabray, a singer who had developed a huge following from television. But neither Merrick nor Champion found her entirely engaging for the role.

One person neither of them wanted was Carol Channing. Champion had directed her in an amusing revue called *Lend an Ear*, which had opened in Hollywood in 1946 and then been brought to New York. It was Champion's first Broadway credit and led to his first Tony. From *Lend an Ear* Channing had gone into *Gentlemen Prefer Blondes*, which made her a star, even landing her on the cover of *Time*. (Channing felt she had earned Champion's disfavor by agreeing with Oliver Smith, who produced *Gentlemen Prefer Blondes*, on Agnes De Mille as the choreographer over Champion.)

After her huge success in the show that introduced "Diamonds Are A Girl's Best Friend," Channing replaced Rosalind Russell in *Wonderful Town*, which she then took on the road; in Chicago the redoubtable Claudia Cassidy called her a "genius." She won personal raves for her performances in two Broadway shows in the next few years, *The Vamp* and *Show Girl,* but the shows themselves were short-lived. George Burns presented her in Las Vegas and the two toured together. Later she presented her night club act in the Empire Room of the Waldorf-Astoria and in similarly elegant clubs all across the country. Merrick himself caught her act in Minneapolis, where he first mentioned the possibility of the musical based on *The Matchmaker* to her.

If he and Gower both had reservations, they were based in part on the fact that Channing was as much a perfectionist as Champion.

Merrick eventually softened. He invited her to his office to discuss the project. They talked about her unsuccessful shows since *Blondes.* Channing said one thing she had learned from her flops was that, "You have to have one man who is a benevolent despot." As far as this show was concerned, she told Merrick, "You have to have a Gower Champion."

"We have Gower," Merrick took pleasure in informing her. "But he doesn't want you."

He also told her his own reservations about what she tended to do: "I don't want that silly grin with all those teeth that go back to your ears."

Channing refused to take offense. Channing had become passionate about the role of Dolly Gallagher Levi. She noted it was the one thing Thornton Wilder had added to the Nestroy play on which he based *The Merchant of Yonkers.* In Dolly, Channing held forth, Wilder had poured his intense belief in the need to affirm life.

Channing also saw the role as another way of expressing one of the important themes in *Our Town.* At the end of that play the young husband George throws himself on the newly dug grave of his wife Emily, and the dead admonish him, "You don't go to the grave with your lovely young bride—you stay with the living."

As Channing saw it, Dolly Gallagher was an Irish woman born on Second Avenue who fell in love with Ephrem Levi. Her years as Mrs. Levi "turned her into a Hadassah lady, and she turned into Ephrem when he died." She based her accent on the rhythms of the turn-of-the-century New York Irish as modified by the Jewish Levi.

In the summer of 1963 she was performing Shaw's *The Millionairess* for the Theatre Guild. Merrick took Champion to see her and they met her in her hotel afterward. There she auditioned by reading from *The Matchmaker*. They discussed the role until five in the morning. It was overpowering. The role was hers.

Channing felt Merrick was especially won over: "I was the symbol of his own ego," she felt. The months between her casting and the show's opening would be grueling, but Channing—like Bob Merrill—felt Merrick's attitude toward her was essentially paternal and benevolent. (Years later, when she invited him to the premier of *Thoroughly Modern Millie*, she felt awkward watching her own performance. He must have sensed her insecurities. Slowly he put his arm around her and held her throughout the film. Not knowing the critical response to her work would be favorable, she looked at him and said, "At least I still have you." He responded, "You'll always have me.")
During the rehearsal period, Merrick would drop in once a week to see how things were progressing. But by the fall of 1963, when he was mounting five other shows, he did not really catch up with *Dolly* until it began previews in Detroit. He arrived in Detroit shortly after the dispiriting opening—and closing—of *Arturo Ui*. He tended not to be optimistic under the best of circumstances when he went to see shows out of town. The Brecht misadventure left him particularly grim.

What he saw did not cheer him up. The show was not yet in focus. The audiences were not enthusiastic. The Detroit reviewers doubted it would even reach New York. One headlined his review, *Goodbye, Dolly*.

Merrick responded in his classic fashion. He began screaming. "You've got one number—'Hello, Dolly!'—and that's it," he told Herman and Stewart. "If this show becomes a hit, it'll be for all the wrong reasons," he told Marge Champion, who worked as

Gower's assistant. As he had been on *Do Re Mi*, he was particularly vicious toward the costume designer, perhaps because changes in costumes tend to be less expensive than changes in the sets. And he wanted changes.

Merrick's tirade left Freddy Wittop, whose costumes had in fact captured the comic spirit of the piece perfectly, deeply humiliated. Herman tried to rally him. He pointed out to Wittop that the generally cool Detroit audiences had invariably applauded after the "Put On Your Sunday Clothes" coda, in which the chorus donned new clothes.

"Freddy, listen to me," Herman told his disconsolate colleague. "There's no music, just a vamp. There's no dancing. There's no dialogue. Who do you think they're applauding?"

Merrick became "maniacal." He threatened to close the show in Detroit. Champion, however, decided he would not stand for Merrick's tantrums. If Merrick wanted to close the show, he told him in front of the squirming cast, that was fine. He would buy Merrick out.

It was a gesture of bravado, but after Merrick stomped out Champion went to the writers, to Channing and other members of the cast and asked if they would contribute to buy the show from Merrick. They all felt the show had great potential and were willing to contribute money to save it from Merrick's wrath.

Faced with this revolt, Merrick backed down, as he had when Leland Hayward made a similar offer in the early stages of *Gypsy*. He would remain the producer. In that capacity he began giving Champion advice. Champion snapped. And in his classic fashion he left town. He informed Neil Hartley, "When Mr. Mustache leaves, tell Marge, and I'll come back." Marge knew that Gower had gone to Ypsilanti, Michigan, where he divided his time between agonizing in his hotel room and going to the movies. After three days Merrick left. Champion returned.

Before his standoff with Champion, Merrick had worked on the others. Shortly after he arrived in Detroit he called Bob Merrill, who had listened to the score in its very early stages and praised it. Merrill had also made some suggestions to Herman and Michael Stewart in exchange for which he received a percentage point of royalties from the show.

Merrick told Merrill he was planning to close the show in Detroit. "Protect your one percent," he warned him. "Get on a plane Friday and work the weekend."

Merrill protested he could not come. He was writing the lyrics for *Funny Girl.* Besides, he knew how tense everything was when a show was out of town. "Does Gower know I'm coming?" he asked. "Does Jerry know I'm coming?"

"Absolutely," Merrick told him. "They *want* you to come."

This, of course, was not true at all. When Herman saw Merrill in the lobby of his Detroit hotel, a look of horror came over him. Merrill realized immediately that Merrick had lied. But as long as he was there he felt he should make some observations about the show. He thought the book was strong and that the show was not as far as Merrick thought from its final shape. The parts he felt the strongest about were the closing of the first act and the opening of the second.

Herman himself had expressed doubts about the last number in the first act, "Penny In Your Pocket," a song sung by Horace Vandergelder at an auction at which he had acted stupidly. David Burns, who played Vandergelder, sang the song beautifully, and there had been a solid choral accompaniment. Herman sensed that the act was closing with the spotlight on the wrong character. At that point the audience wanted to know more about Dolly, not her prey.

"You need an explosion at the end of the first act," Merrill told Herman. He thought there was something about the idea of a parade that would be an attractive way to end the act. (Only later did it occur to him that parades were heavy on his mind—he was also writing a lyric for *Funny Girl* that pleaded, "Don't Rain On My Parade.") As for the second act, though Merrill will not confirm it, it is generally known that he wrote "Elegance," which opens the act on a spiffy and gracious note.

Merrill didn't fully crystallize the "parade" number. That was precipitated by another set of songwriters, Charles Strouse and

Lee Adams, who had written *Bye, Bye, Birdie*. At Merrick's invitation they wrote a song for *Dolly*, which was called "Before the Parade Passes By."

The number was sent to conductor Peter Howard from New York. Howard showed it to Herman, who was crushed that Merrick, who had been so supportive of him, now seemed to be peddling percentages of the score wholesale. He took the idea and wrote his own version, the one that finally closed the first act.

Herman completed his work at three in the morning. He woke up Channing and asked her to come to his room. He played the song for her and she assured him it was just what the moment needed. The next morning he played "Before the Parade Passes By" for Merrick and Champion. Both approved. Champion turned to Merrick, "You know, David, this requires a new set, a new group of lavish costumes." Without hesitation, Merrick told him to go ahead. Champion discussed his ideas with Smith and Wittop without consulting Merrick. "David didn't know what the bill would be," Herman recalled. "But he was an artist. He could have said, 'Do it in front of the railroad drop.' But he wanted to give the audience a show."

Recalling the harshness of those weeks in Detroit, Herman said he later found Merrick's behavior amusing. "Back then I was young. I thought I was going to be replaced. But we all had standard contracts. He couldn't have replaced us. The threat of replacing you was a way he had of bringing out your best work."

After considerable rewriting, *Hello, Dolly!* moved on to Washington, where it was received enthusiastically. *Dolly* now looked like it might be a huge hit.

When it opened at the St. James on January 16, 1964, that hunch was confirmed. *Hello, Dolly!* received ecstatic notices. In the traumatic months following the assassination of President John F. Kennedy, *Hello, Dolly!* was the perfect antidote to melancholy. The score had great appeal. Channing's performance was effervescent. Smith's lavish sets and Wittop's costumes evoked a more innocent, happier New York. If any musical was likely to raise the spirits of its audience, it was *Hello, Dolly!*

And so it did. For almost seven years.

Normally when a star leaves a musical, he or she is replaced by a talented but lesser known performer. Merrick took a more aggressive stance on cast replacements for *Dolly*. When one star left, he replaced her with another, insuring that the show would remain a draw, since even people who had seen it might want to see it again with another beloved performer. When Channing took the show on tour, she was replaced on Broadway by Ginger Rogers. Rogers was followed by Martha Raye, who was succeeded by Betty Grable. (At one point Merrick talked to Jack Benny about taking over the role in drag, opposite George Burns. Benny liked the idea but only wanted to do it for a week.)

Another tantalizing prospect for the role of Dolly was Bette Davis. The idea was proposed by a young agent at General Artists Corporation (which, after several mergers, became ICM). The young Englishman, Lionel Larner, was reprimanded by the head of his department. "You're crazy," he told Larner at a staff meeting. "Merrick will never go for that."

Nevertheless, Larner proposed her and was astounded to receive a telephone call from Tokyo. It was Merrick, very quiet, very polite.

"Are you serious about Bette Davis?" Merrick said.

Larner assured him he was. Merrick said he was "very interested."

Davis was initially receptive, but by the time Larner arranged a meeting with Gower Champion she had cooled on it.

"It's a fifteen minute show," she told him. As far as she was concerned it was all about the title number.

Ginger Rogers missed a lot of performances. Merrick and Schlissel devised a way to protect less sophisticated audience members from knowing that they were not seeing the star. In those days Actors' Equity required that if a performer was going to be out of a performance, the producer could either post a notice in the lobby or make an announcement before the performance began. Merrick and Schlissel decided it would be more advantageous to make the announcement before the performance.

The announcer would welcome the audience to the show and state that the role of Mrs. Levi (omitting the first name, which might have tipped them off that the part in question was the title role) would tonight be performed by Bibi Osterwald. As the announcer began Osterwald's second name the conductor gave the downbeat. Also, at that precise moment, the box office window slammed shut. This minimized the need to refund money to disgruntled patrons. This came to be known as The Ginger Rogers Cue.

Audiences had no reason to complain about the substitution. Osterwald was a splendid performer. Moreover it had been so many years since anyone had seen Rogers even in films that many did not know the difference. It was Osterwald who complained to Equity about what was happening. Equity ruled that henceforth if a performer was absent the audience had to be notified *both* in the lobby and from the stage.

Mary Martin opened the show in London later that year. She was scheduled to take it to Moscow in a cultural exchange. Merrick was on the plane with the cast flying to Russia via Seattle. When they arrived in Tokyo Merrick left the plane to take an urgent phone call from Helen Nickerson. The Moscow engagement was cancelled. In this spring of 1965, America was rapidly building up its forces in Vietnam. The Soviets had cancelled the musical as a gesture of anger.

Without a moment of hesitation, as if it had been a contingency he had planned for, Merrick told Nickerson to have Alan Delynn call the White House. He was going to take *Dolly* to perform for the GIs in Vietnam. Delynn arranged it within an hour, and the plane took off for Saigon.

In a mere five days one of Merrick's most trusted lieutenants, Willard Shaffar, who had worked for him as both electrician and Man Friday since *La Plume de Ma Tante,* made all the necessary arrangements, including a Japanese orchestra to record the score—there was little likelihood of picking up a pit band in

Saigon. By the time Merrick arrived, Shaffar had even arranged a party on a Saigon rooftop to console the disoriented, nervous cast. As the sun went down and the enemy bombs began to be heard in the distance, Merrick surveyed the Saigon skyline and smiled. "Willard, isn't this sensational?" he said.

Within hours of the change of plans Merrick had also arranged for NBC to follow the *Dolly* company around Vietnam. News coverage of the tour was extensive. If, in the year since *Dolly* opened, newspaper readers all across America had forgotten about *Hello, Dolly!*, they were now reminded of it with a vengeance.

For the next six years, during which Merrick's fortunes began to change, *Dolly* was always his steady girl. She remained a steady source of income and, for Merrick, a steady source of pride. For *Dolly*, his ballyhoo knew no bounds. He allowed the Democrats to sing, "Hello, Lyndon" at their convention in the summer of 1964 and then threatened to sue the Republicans when they sang, "Hello, Barry" at theirs, both items garnering a lot of publicity. He donated 10,000 recordings of Carol Channing singing "Hello, Lyndon!", accompanied by the composer, to raise funds for Young Citizens for Johnson.

The title song was the subject of litigation. The composer of a Forties hit, "You Are My Sunflower," charged that "Hello, Dolly" began the same way his song did. The suit was settled out of court. More important, Louis Armstrong, who had made a hit of "Sunflower," made an even more gigantic hit of "Hello, Dolly!"

Looking back, *Hello, Dolly!* seems the last of the innocent American musicals, the last musical to reflect the unbounded optimism that characterized America before it plunged into the Vietnam war.

For one thing, the musical idiom in which *Dolly* was written was on the verge of being passe. In January of 1964 the song at the top of the charts was "I Wanna Hold Your Hand" by an English group called The Beatles, who would make their first

American tour in February. *Dolly* outlasted The Beatles in one sense—they gave their last public concert in 1966—but it was overshadowed by them in another. British rock eclipsed the musical style that had served Broadway for many decades. Young people's record collections would henceforth be filled with rock 'n' roll rather than original cast recordings.

The year that *Dolly* opened, 1964, was still a relatively innocent year. Even drugs, which did so much to change the hopeful face of America, seemed unimportant back then. In the spring of 1964 New York held its first World's Fair since 1939. It was an event that all seven of the local newspapers trumpeted with intense provincial fervor.

The excitement over the Fair was so great that a man who had been banned from New York for three years wrote a letter from his exile in Pittsburgh to the judge who had passed the sentence begging permission to return home for a few days to see the Fair.

At a performance of *Hello, Dolly!* taped for the NBC special. Next to Merrick is Biff Liff. Down the row is Sylvia Schwartz. In front of Merrick is Jack Schlissel.

In retrospect the sentence seems very odd, even unenforceable. What was the crime that merited it? The man had been convicted of possession of a small amount of heroin, an offense apparently so heinous that the *Times*, which reported the vignette, withheld the criminal's name. The judge, touched by the miscreant's eagerness to see the Fair, generously granted him his wish.

The New York in which that happened seems as naive as the city *Hello, Dolly!* nostalgically evokes. Very soon it would all change.

CHAPTER TWENTY-THREE

NOT EVERYTHING WAS INNOCENT in the spring of 1964, even in the theater, even in connection with *Hello, Dolly!*

The previous fall Louis J. Lefkowitz, the attorney-general of the state of New York, had held explosive hearings—Merrick called them "the best show of the season"—documenting corruption in the Broadway theater. Some of it had to do with kickbacks on set construction. But the most disturbing revelations had to do with "ice."

It was estimated that the black market in Broadway tickets was $10 million a year. Evidence of the naivete of the period emerged in the revelation that the Internal Revenue Service was looking into ticket scalping for possible tax law violations. The IRS had a suspicion that "the persons who shared in these proceeds" were not reporting it as income. Imagine!

The hearings disclosed that an actress had sold her two nightly house seats to a broker for $10,000 a year. A coordinator for CBS, which had produced *My Fair Lady* and thus was entitled to fourteen house seats per performance, found that provision insufficient to satisfy the demand of clients who wanted to see the show. Even though CBS had access to a certain number of prime seats, once that supply was exhausted, she had to ask the box office. The box office, however, made its prime seats available to

At the "ice" hearings.

brokers. The brokers charged about $50 a seat when top orchestra seats were $6.90. A percentage of this money obviously found its way back to the box office—so there would have been a loss of customary income for box office personnel to sell CBS tickets to their own show. The CBS coordinator regularly purchased four or five extra pair a week from brokers.

It was not only in New York that "ice" crystallized. Once, when one of Merrick's Broadway hits was about to come to Boston, the box office manager informed Merrick with considerable glee that the entire run was sold out. What should have delighted Merrick aroused his deepest suspicions. He knew that the manager had a relative who was a ticket broker. If Bostonians believed tickets were scarce the manager and the broker stood to make a fortune in "ice," none of which would go to Merrick.

The manager saw no reason why he should not sign the document Merrick demanded guaranteeing revenues for the sold out run, which Merrick and Schlissel had already calculated to the penny. The "ice," after all, would not only cover these revenues but would give him and his relative huge profits. By satisfying Merrick he would get the meddlesome producer off his back. He and his relative could proceed unsupervised.

A few days later with collegial bonhomie Merrick showed the manager the full page ad in the *Boston Globe* announcing "SORRY, BOSTON—ALL SOLD OUT!!!" Wasn't the manager pleased to see that Merrick had devised a way to keep pesky customers away from the box office? Furthermore he refused to take any more advertising. Why bother, if the run were indeed sold out? The manager glumly assented.

Instead of the windfall the manager and his relative anticipated, they had to cough up an enormous amount of money to cover the guarantee. To do anything else would not only be an admission of dishonesty but would guarantee the next Merrick hit would not be booked into that theater.

To flout Merrick was to risk these subtle but Draconian reprisals.

The day after *Hello, Dolly!* opened Lefkowitz announced he

was proposing legislation to "eradicate the evils" of the theater both on and off Broadway. The announcement came seemingly in the nick of time, since the rave reviews for *Dolly* were likely to precipitate a huge blizzard of "ice."

Lefkowitz's minions were stationed unobtrusively in the lobby of the St. James Theater scrutinizing those waiting in line to buy tickets. By 10:00 the morning the reviews appeared there was a line of three abreast at the box office. Until the windows closed that evening the line never numbered fewer than 100 people. Merrick, who could see the line from his office above the marquee, sent a wagon with coffee and cake for his customers. Clearly he had softened since *Stop the World*. Perhaps more important, *Dolly* did not need as much publicity. The line out to the street would have been gratuitous.

Merrick alerted Lefkowitz's office that interspersed among the legitimate ticket buyers were "diggers," who were employees of New Jersey ticket brokers. They would buy several pairs of choice orchestra locations for some future performance, then repair to a nearby hotel, where they would quickly change clothes and get back in line. The ticket sellers at the St. James recognized them. When a box office employee spotted a "repeater," he would signal one of Lefkowitz's men, who would ask the person for identification. His picture would be taken and he would be handed a subpoena. The procedure was done quietly enough that normal patrons were unaware of the box office drama.

Hello, Dolly! was another of those shows in which Merrick had announced that there would be no tickets for brokers. By now brokers understood this defiant posture to mean that the tickets for brokers would be extremely costly. The New York brokers had no choice but to comply—if they didn't they would lose their customers. The New Jersey brokers were more numerous and less controllable; hence Merrick's zeal for Lefkowitz to police them.

In March Lefkowitz sponsored a bill requiring theater owners to supply a list of everyone involved with ticket sales. The legislation would have given him the authority to suspend anyone caught dealing in "ice." The bill passed the State Assembly.

However it was never voted on by the state Senate because Majority Leader Walter J. Mahoney considered it "too restrictive." The *Times* reported that there had been intense lobbying by the Treasurer and Ticket Sellers Union, Local 751. The group had always been surprisingly undemanding in salary demands, presumably on the understanding that producers and theater owners could pay them less provided they could supplement their income with "ice."

The stalemate of Lefkowitz's legislation left the practice of "ice" to flourish. By May it was reported that a ticket for *Hello, Dolly!*, which sold at the box office for $9.60, could be had through scalpers for $25. (Interestingly, it was not the highest priced ticket in town. Tickets for *Oliver!* were scalped for $27.50. The demand for the Dickens musical may have been increased by the number of families in New York for the World's Fair.)

In May, however, three ticket brokers were indicted by a grand jury on charges of scalping. Two production aides were also indicted for kickbacks. News of the indictments sent a shiver through the theatrical community. Who would be next? Who was spilling the beans?

Lawyers for the Shuberts were amused that Merrick came to see them. He laid out a hypothetical situation in which a producer might be ratted on by a trusted confederate. The parallels between the hypothetical producer and Merrick and the hypothetical confederate and Schlissel seemed remarkably close.

Just before news of the indictments broke, Neil Hartley announced he was leaving Merrick's employ. The departure seemed sudden and even inexplicable. This season, after all, Hartley had been accorded a rare honor; his name had been permitted equal billing with that of the David Merrick Arts Foundation in producing *Arturo Ui* and *Milk Train*. Why, when Merrick had shown him such favor, was he going to leave?

The ostensible reason was that he had a better offer. Over the years Hartley had established a close friendship with Tony Richardson, who had often asked him to join his film production company. With the worldwide success of *Tom Jones*, Richardson's standing offer was indeed one Hartley would have been foolish to refuse.

But there was another reason. Between the public hearings Lefkowitz held in December and the indictments handed down in May, rumors flew furiously through the theater community on who was and who was not in on the "ice" for Broadway shows. For the first time Hartley realized just how much money floated through the Merrick office. For a long time he had turned down Tony Richardson's offer to join him in his film production company. Richardson's offer was $15,000 a year above what Merrick was paying him. Hartley decided to take it.

Normally Merrick took departures from his office as a matter of indifference. Not Hartley's. It did not, however, occasion a fit of Merrick's famous anger. Merrick felt genuinely wounded. Never mind that Hartley was the victim of his own dishonest, disloyal treatment. How could Hartley leave an organization to which he contributed so much?

For years afterward whenever he saw Hartley, who prospered in his new position with Richardson, he would invite him to rejoin the Merrick office. Hartley would always laugh—politely—at the suggestion. "Don't you miss Jack?" Merrick would ask him, with genuine sincerity, thinking the prospect of seeing the hatchet man might lure him back. Merrick and Hartley remained surprisingly cordial, but the professional association was never renewed.

Another man who did not prosper from *Dolly* was Max Brown. Along with Byron Goldman, he had been Merrick's very first backer, who had sustained faith in him from the beginning, years before even *Clutterbuck*. Brown had given him space in his office when he finally left Shumlin.

But you couldn't be a friend of Merrick's unless you could read the fine print, and Brown had not paid attention to some small print in the release sent to all backers of *The Matchmaker*. And his friend never pointed out the clause whereby he relinquished any claim to profits in a musical version of the Wilder play.

Gratitude and friendship, though they had never played a major role in his life, now mattered even less. Similarly, the Theater Guild, which had co-produced *The Matchmaker* with him, shared in none of the profits of *Hello, Dolly!* They had assumed Merrick was negotiating with Wilder on behalf of both of them. Merrick's contract with Wilder only benefited Merrick.

A few years earlier, the conductor of a Merrick musical happened to be reading a Louis L'Amour novel, *Flint*, in which he came across a character description that he thought suited Merrick perfectly: "His life had not fitted him for living with people. As a predatory creature he had been successful; as a human being he was a failure. He had invited no friendship and offered none."

CHAPTER TWENTY-FOUR

FOR SOME TIME NOW Merrick had thought he deserved the cover of *Time* magazine. He was, after all, in his own sphere, a potentate equal to those of the world leaders, the businessmen and certainly the show business figures that *Time* had accorded that honor.

For God's sake, Carol Channing had managed one fifteen years before!

Harvey Sabinson was assigned the mission. Although Merrick used several press agents on every show, by the early Sixties it was Sabinson who coordinated their activities.

Sabinson acted as a cushion between the other press agents and Merrick. One publicist remembered that Sabinson had a red plastic garbage can next to his desk. Even when the door was closed, the others knew Merrick must be on the tie line because they could hear Sabinson kicking away at the garbage can. The frequency and intensity of the kicks grew as the conversation went on.

Sabinson was a short, trim, balding man who gave an impression of great affability. He was like the father of the bride greeting guests extra-enthusiastically as a way of suppressing his realization of how much the wedding has cost. Sabinson was a perfect facade for Merrick, gracious where his boss was gruff, congenial where his boss was contentious. Many attributed the emergence of the shy Merrick as a public figure in the late Fifties and early Sixties to Sabinson's ability to get him quoted.

Just as he tried—not always successfully—to shield his press agents from Merrick's wrath, Sabinson tried to be a buffer between the world at large and the man who delighted in rankling people.

When Nathan Cohen, a Toronto critic known for being as acerbic as he was obese, died, one of the Toronto papers called Sabinson to see if Merrick wanted to eulogize Cohen. Sabinson thought it unlikely.

There was no reason for Merrick to have had any fondness for Cohen. Once, after panning one of Merrick's shows, in which he felt most of the humor was inadvertent, Cohen said one of the funniest lines in the show was in the program. He was referring to the opening line of Merrick's biography, which described him as "the most vital force in the theater today." Cohen's observation on this was, "Now *there* I assume the humor is advertent."

Sabinson tried to dissuade the Toronto reporter from seeking a quote, but the man was persistent. So Sabinson had to ask Merrick for a statement about the death of his adversary. "The fat's in the fire," he replied, a piece of wit he may have remembered from the script of *Fanny*.

The previous season had been relatively quiet, understandable after the exertions of 1963-64, when Merrick himself admitted he had overextended himself. A mere five shows opened in 1964-65, four of which were imported from England. *A Severed Head*, by Iris Murdoch and J.B. Priestley, was a respectable flop, a success in London only tepidly received in New York. *Pickwick*, a musical starring Harry Secombe, was also a failure. Joan Littlewood's controversial anti-war musical, *Oh, What A lovely War* ran from September 30, 1964 to January 16, 1965, bringing with it prestige, if not profit.

Another Newley-Bricusse show, *The Roar of the Greasepaint, the Smell of the Crowd*, was sold, like its predecessor on the basis of one song, "Who Can I Turn To?", which Tony Bennett recorded well before the show arrived from England. Merrick had seen it in Liverpool and snapped it up even before the reviews, luckily for Newley and Bricusse. The show received such caustic reviews it never reached London.

Merrick arranged another extremely long pre-Broadway tour (the show even played Albany!) because Newley was a draw regardless of what critics said. The show's investment might be recouped even before the Broadway opening.

He also hoped to tighten the show before it reached New York. He made it clear to Newley, for example, that he hated the way he performed one of his numbers. Newley persisted in playing it *his* way.

One night Merrick gathered all the music from the orchestra stands and appeared in Newley's dressing room. "You see this number?" he asked. "Well, it's out of the show. I own this music. And if you don't do the show my way, 'The Joker' [one of Newley's best received numbers] will be cut tomorrow night." Newley acquiesced.

Building on what he learned from *Oliver!*, Merrick persuaded RCA to cut and release the cast album before the Broadway premiere. On the basis of the one song, the album sold 100,000 copies even before the opening May 16, 1965. *Roar* had an $800,000 advance. It closed at the end of the year after a run of 231 performances. Not bad for a show that closed on the road in England.

The one homegrown product during this season was a play by Pulitzer Prize winning novelist Edwin O'Connor, the author of *The Edge of Sadness* and *The Last Hurrah*. O'Connor's play, *I Was Dancing*, was brought to Merrick by Garson Kanin, who thought its leading role would be perfect for his old friend Burgess Meredith. Meredith would play an aging vaudevillian who, in old age, wants to move in with the son he hasn't seen in twenty-one years.

O'Connor may have seemed the answer to what would be a continuing quest for Merrick in the next few years—to find an American Playwright who would be *his* the way Arthur Miller had become Bloomgarden's or Hellman had been Shumlin's. O'Connor did not turn out to be that playwright. The play's respectful notices drummed up no enthusiasm at the box office.

For Kanin the experience was doubly disheartening. He saw that his friend Meredith, after a long stay in Hollywood, had lost his theater skills. He could not be heard. He treated the text cavalierly, sometimes omitting words, sometimes substituting his own.

Meredith was hardly the only problem. Kanin was disturbed by the tendency of other members of the cast to insert the phrase "you know" in the midst of the text. It was a sign of things to come. It showed a disrespect for the writer, a casual disregard for the discipline of acting. "You know" was a foreshadowing of the notion of "doing your own thing" that would mark theater and society in the coming years.

But for 1965-66 the portents were much better. Merrick would import an unusual, iconoclastic production from London by Peter Brook, which was entitled *The Persecution and Assassination of Jean-Paul Marat as Presented by the Inmates of Charenton Under the Direction of the Marquis de Sade* (generally shortened to *Marat/Sade*). He would bring over John Osborne's latest success, *Inadmissible Evidence*, starring a 28-year-old actor who had caused a sensation in London, Nicol Williamson. He would present Lauren Bacall in a Parisian farce, *Cactus Flower.* He would bring in a new play from Dublin, *Philadelphia, Here I Come*, by a new young writer, Brian Friel. He would also present *Hot September*, a musical version of *Picnic*, directed by Josh Logan. With the exception of the musical and the Bacall vehicle, all the projects would be produced by the Foundation.

Hot September had been adapted from *Picnic* by Paul Osborn, who had helped with the book of *Fanny* and who had adapted *The World of Suzie Wong.* The score was by Kenneth Jacobson and Rhoda Roberts, pop song writers who had no experience in the theater. The score contained one song that is in the classic style of the Broadway musical, "Golden Moment," but neither the score nor the book captured the poignant spirit of *Picnic*.

After three weeks in Boston, Merrick closed the show October 9, 1965, at a cost of $500,000. The money had come from two sources, RCA, which had put up $450,000 in exchange for the right to record the cast album, and Columbia Pictures, which put up the other $50,000. No film was produced. Only a "pirate" album came out, many years afterward.

John Osborne's *Inadmissible Evidence* was yet another attack on postwar England, this time characterized as an alcoholic, failing barrister, played by Nicol Williamson.

At its first preview in Philadelphia the play ran past 11:00, when the last trains were leaving for the suburbs. During the last half hour of the play a steady stream of patrons rushed out to catch their trains. After the performance Merrick raged at the director, Anthony Page: "Tell that son of a bitch [Osborne] to get his ass out of the Algonquin and work on it." Merrick demanded that a half hour be trimmed from the play.

A week later he and one of his press agents, Max Eisen, took the train to Philadelphia to see the tightened version. The play did not end at 10:30. There was still a stream of people leaving during its final half hour. The play had not been trimmed a whit. Merrick was livid. He stormed backstage and fired Page.

When Williamson heard what had happened he told Merrick if Page was out he would go too. Williamson owed his career to Page, who had discovered him in a theater in Scotland and brought him to London.

Williamson was holding a can of Budweiser. His sense was that Merrick, behaving belligerently, was fairly demanding to be insulted. When Merrick contemptuously taunted Page that the show was bound to be a dud—"Turkey lurkey," he sneered—Williamson said to Merrick, "I won't stoop to spit in your eye," and flicked the beer at him. Merrick then lunged at him. Williamson socked the oncoming figure in the jaw. In some versions he even threw Merrick into a nearby garbage can. What most interested Williamson in recalling the incident was that no one in Merrick's retinue attempted to stop him or to help Merrick.

A week went by before any word of what had happened appeared in the press. Eager as he was to publicize his plays, particularly his *serious* plays, what happened in Philadelphia was something Merrick was understandably not eager to spread around.

But word got out. An item about the incident appeared in the *Philadelphia Bulletin*. The day after, Rex Reed, in his first flush as a celebrity journalist, arrived in Philadelphia to interview Williamson, who told him the whole story: "I'm afraid people in America are going to remember me only as the bloke who pinned one on Merrick and not the actor I really am. Well, the papers exaggerated. They even had me sleeping all night in the railroad station, on my way back to England. Hell, I just went bowling. I didn't really hurt him, didn't even hit him right. I figure this fist smashing into his face gave him and the play $100,000 worth of publicity."

Williamson was right. This time Merrick didn't need to stage a ruckus to publicize an Osborne play. In fact, he had rehired Page only an hour after coming to blows with Williamson. Once Merrick had calmed down, Page explained that he had only been waiting for the playwright to arrive before introducing the proposed cuts. When Osborne arrived the following night he approved the cuts. The show went on.

Even Williamson eventually felt the cuts improved the play. "Now I don't get so tired, and I'm giving a better performance than I did in London," he told a New York interviewer. Tom Prideaux, the critic for *Life*, who saw him in the role in both London and New York, felt the latter performance was much stronger.

Merrick also managed to get revenge. Despite strong reviews, *Inadmissible Evidence* did not attract sizable audiences. As usual, Merrick demanded that everyone take pay cuts to contribute to a fund to publicize the show. Williamson refused, and Merrick forced his benefactor Page to get Williamson to agree to the cuts.

"Tony Page came to see me and absolutely *begged* me to accept the cut. It was pathetic. I haven't forgiven him for that and I never will."

Although other producers regularly shopped London for plays to bring back to New York, no one made the short journey across the Channel to compete with Merrick for French commercial fare. (In the early Sixties the plays of Genet enjoyed great vogue Off-Broadway, but they did not fit in with Merrick's dictum: "I'm less interested in Theater in the Round than in Theater in the Black.")

In 1965 he came across a boulevard comedy called *Cactus Flower*, by Pierre Brillet and Jean-Pierre Gredy. The title refers to a desert bloom that is always prickly and only occasionally flowers. This was a description of a woman who works in a dentist's office, an unlikely setting for a romantic comedy. The dentist, a playboy, only belatedly discovers romance within close proximity of his drill.

Merrick commissioned Abe Burrows to adapt the play for Broadway. Burrows had written the books for such musicals as *Guys and Dolls* and *How to Succeed in Business Without Really Trying*. He was also Broadway's best known "doctor."

The most obvious star to play the difficult, late-blooming nurse was Lauren Bacall, who projected toughness both on and off the stage. Bacall had become a Hollywood star at a very early age. She had also become part of Hollywood legend by marrying Humphrey Bogart. After Bogart's death in 1957 her career lost momentum. She had moved back to her native New York and, during the 1959-60 season, she appeared in a short-lived comedy called *Goodbye Charlie*, by George Axelrod. Bacall was a draw on the road, but the New York critics, while respectful of her, panned the play, which closed despite her presence. She had not achieved her objective, which was to change her image. She was still thought of as Mrs. Humphrey Bogart.

By the time of *Cactus Flower*, five years later, she was Mrs. Jason Robards, Jr., but she still had not achieved a Broadway reputation of her own. Initially Merrick did not want Bacall for *Cactus Flower*. He wanted Rosalind Russell. But Burrows knew he could write dialogue Bacall would deliver perfectly.

"I don't want her," Merrick told Burrows. "She's a tough bitch." Burrows persisted. Merrick agreed to accept Bacall on one condition, that she sign for two years. If she did prove a draw, he might as well make the most of her. Because her box office appeal had proved weak in *Goodbye Charlie*, she was vulnerable when Merrick negotiated her salary with her agent. For Bacall it was a wise career move. A hefty salary was less important than the vehicle that might firmly establish her as a theater presence. *Cactus Flower* was that vehicle. That her star power had waned was clear to advertising man Fred Golden, who remembered walking down the street with Merrick and Bacall. It was Merrick rather than Bacall that passersby asked for autographs.

Bacall knew the material in *Cactus Flower* was right for her and she was determined to make the most of it. During rehearsals Burrows marveled at her professionalism. She had the reputation of being a prima donna, but he discovered she was simply a perfectionist. Her good humor was especially valued during the tryout in Washington, when her leading man, Joseph Campanella, was fired and replaced by the much savvier Barry Nelson, who proved a better straight man for her. The replacement benefitted the show, but it was not without considerable adjustments for her.

Her hard work paid off. When the show opened in New York she received a rapturous ovation from the audience and bouquets from the critics.

Success, unfortunately, brought out her sour side. When a friend congratulated her in her dressing room after the performance, all she could muster was, "That son of a bitch has me signed to a two-year contract at a fixed salary. And he won't give me a limousine."

Their barbed relationship was good for publicity throughout the run. Though he was no more solicitous toward her than he was to any of the actors in his shows, he did send her a silver bowl from Tiffany's for her first Christmas in the show. It was engraved, which meant she couldn't take it back.

When her son graduated from Andover Academy, she insisted she must miss a matinee to attend the ceremony. She resented the fact that "he made me crawl to him" to ask permission. On the understanding that there be no publicity, lest patrons not buy tickets for that performance, he let her go, insisting that she be back for the evening show.

Throughout the run Merrick was grateful that Bob Ullmann, one of the press agents who worked for Sabinson, enjoyed a working rapport with her. Merrick had a channel to Bacall but could keep his own contact to a minimum. Whatever hostile remarks she made to the press, as far as he was concerned, were good for business.

Once, walking down Park Avenue, Ullmann was startled to feel a firm hand on his shoulder. He whirled around and was surprised to see a dapper, grinning Merrick.

"How's that bitch?" Merrick asked him.

As the sole backer of *Cactus Flower* (he had not even permitted Bacall to buy a unit), Merrick had made a killing even before the show opened. It had cost him $125,000. A month before the opening, he made a deal with Columbia Pictures, who paid him $250,000 plus a percentage of every profitable week's gross until the sum of $750,000 was reached in order to gain the film rights.

Few productions of the 20th century have generated more excitement than Peter Brook's staging of *Marat/Sade*, Peter Weiss's play about revolution and madness.

During the early Sixties Brook had been experimenting with a group of actors at the Royal Shakespeare Company with new techniques, new approaches to theater, significantly based on the French actor Antonin Artaud's theories about The Theater of Cruelty.

A young actress described the Theater of Cruelty Project as "an experiment to see how far the human body could go in movement and sound." The actors did exercises to communicate with sounds rather than words. After several months of intense private work they presented a private performance of an extended improvisation, which was attended by an audience that included Laurence Olivier, Edith Evans, Kenneth Tynan, Harold Pinter and John Osborne.

In the improvisation the young actress, whose name was Glenda Jackson, played Christine Keeler, then making headlines during the Profumo Case. First she read some lines from the recent trial that had enveloped some of Britain's most powerful figures in scandal. In the improvised drama Keeler was sent to prison, where she was stripped. She took a bath onstage and changed into prison clothes. Then the bathtub was turned upside down. It became the coffin of John F. Kennedy. Jackson, having doffed Keeler's prison clothes, was now playing Jackie Kennedy, receiving bishops and politicos at the Kennedy funeral.

Just around the time Brook was developing the Theater of Cruelty Project, a manuscript arrived at the RSC. *Marat/Sade* was by the 49-year-old Peter Weiss, a German Jew who emigrated to Sweden early in the Hitler regime. Brook saw that it would be the ideal text with which to test the power of his experiments.

When Sabinson was in London during the summer of 1964 he chanced to pass a rehearsal hall where Brook's company was working on *Marat/Sade*. Struck by the novelty and power of what he saw and heard, he placed a transatlantic call to Merrick, who surprised Sabinson with the news that he had already optioned it for New York. Unbeknownst to his own publicist, Merrick had already been there.

This extremely complex production required an ensemble; and Brook insisted the 35-person cast must be brought over *in toto*. By now Merrick fairly relished his skirmishes with Actors' Equity. A member of the Equity Council suggested Merrick wanted the all-English cast because it would be cheaper than hiring an American one. He was only obliged to pay them English Equity minimum, $200 a week, considerably less than American Equity. "It is not actual greed which lies behind his attitude," the

Council member conjectured. "Nor even a yen for absolute power; but a real psychopathic hatred of the American actor and a desire to crush and destroy him."

Other voices at Equity responded to the request with less paranoia. *Marat/Sade* opened at the Martin Beck December 27, 1965 with all thirty-five English actors.

Along with their tickets, reviewers received a press release from Sabinson that read, "Peter Brook, director of the Royal Shakespeare Company production of *Marat/Sade*, has asked me to advise you that the first act of the play runs one hour and twenty-six minutes and the second act thirty-five minutes. Latecomers will not be admitted to the theater once the first act has started.

"Mr. Brook also requests that you remain in your seats because the play does not end where it seems to.

"Mr. Brook further adds that any hostility this might engender in you be directed toward him and not the producer David Merrick, who should be left to enjoy the good will of all men during this period of peace and temporary cease-fire."

Merrick himself had described *Marat/Sade* as "his Christmas package to Broadway." Though even the title must have suggested there was irony in his remark, the opening night audience was clearly not attuned to irony. They behaved even more boorishly than they had at *Arturo Ui* two years before. Large groups rose to leave before the end of the play "as if they were hurrying to get the best restaurant table," Brook recalled. During the final moments of the play an actor actually shouted to the audience to "shut up" when they began applauding tentatively a scene in which the inmates, aroused to violence, began marching forward and singing. "The audience began to clap as if it were the finale of a musical," Brook said disgustedly.

When the performance was over, Merrick was nowhere to be found. He had smelled the air of failure over this iconoclastic venture. Then, lo and behold, at the subdued cast party, Merrick arrived with a fresh white carnation in his button hole. He had already read the reviews. This time the critics showed better taste than the first nighters. They had perceived the depth and daring of Brook's production.

The next morning a long line appeared at the box office of the Martin Beck. No one was more astonished than Merrick. He immediately had Helen Nickerson send coffee and donuts over to those in line. Even with the reviews he had not expected to find an audience. "It was when he still did shows because he believed in them," Nickerson recalled.

Incredibly, *Marat/Sade* became a "hot ticket." Brook and his company eventually agreed that the play was more rewarding to perform in New York, "where people accepted and believed the proposition that man is a potential lunatic more than in London, where it was not so much a play about revolution, war and madness as an exhibition of theatricality."

Merrick's extraordinary season finally accorded him the honor he had so deeply sought: the cover of *Time*. A jubilant Sabinson reported the news to his boss, expecting that Merrick might break out a bottle of champagne.

Instead, Merrick erupted in anger.

There were, after all, two Merricks. There was the public Merrick, the man in the pinstripe suit—elegant, witty, belligerent, assured. That, however, was the facade for the other Merrick—the man Shumlin saw battling to conceal and control his sensitivity, the man agent Irving "Swifty" Lazar called "the most insecure person I ever met in my life, a man with no sense of inner security."

The public Merrick loved to see his legend celebrated in print. He knew that he was playing a role. Peter Brook once said of him, "Of all David's qualities the one that stands out is his cool enjoyment of his role. He carries out his beliefs to such an extent that they become pure." As he himself once told a Newsweek reporter, "I put on everything and I put on everyone."

But the man behind the mask didn't want reporters investigating what lay behind the carefully built facade. He didn't want them to know about his ignominious years in St. Louis. It was amazing how, despite all his success, St. Louis still rankled him. Once Marvin Stuhlbarg, who had spent so many holidays with him as a child, decided to visit Merrick when he came to New York. He went to Merrick's office and was informed Merrick was not in. But the door to Merrick's private office was slightly ajar and he could hear Merrick's voice. He decided to walk in.

Merrick was startled to see him. He was even more startled to be upbraided by Stuhlbarg for not having kept in touch with Sadye. "What's the matter with you?" Stuhlbarg asked. Merrick could only phumpher.

"Dave, I remember you when. As far as I'm concerned, you're still Dave Margulois," Stuhlbarg continued, perhaps not even knowing that nothing made him angrier than to be called Dave. Nevertheless, he bore with it for almost half an hour.

When Stuhlbarg left the office he was aware that the employees were staring at him rather as the keepers of the Babylonian lion pits must have stared at Daniel. They were even more amazed to learn that Merrick had authorized him to receive *free* tickets to one of his shows. The confrontation, they realized, must have been profound.

Worse than *Time*'s looking into his background, he didn't like the idea of anyone prying into his relationship with Jeanne Gilbert. He didn't like the idea of anyone prying into his relationship with Jeanne Gilbert. He dreaded the thought that someone would find out that Cecilia Ann had been born out of wedlock.

But it was too late. All the resources of *Time*—including those of an aggressive young reporter named Kitty Kelly—were now thrown into finding out whatever could be found out about David Merrick. In the case of Miss Kelly, who interviewed him during one of his trips to London, he wired *Time* in New York, "Get this cunt off my back." They sent back a telegram deploring his use of the offensive word.

At first Merrick did little to cooperate. Then he saw an advantage to allowing himself to participate in the story. To forestall any revelations about his miserable childhood Merrick took *Time* writer Brad Darraugh, who would write the story from the myriad materials assembled by reporters all over the country, out to lunch and told him many unpleasant details of his life—off the record, thus preventing him using them in print.

Ultimately the cover story, which appeared at the end of January, 1966, was a valentine. It began on an extravagant note: "This one-cylinder Barnum, this tower of sneers in tasseled shoes, this Shubert Alley Catiline, this mustachioed thane of the sceptered aisle, this Greek god, this other Edam, this papier-mache genius . . ." The story largely chronicled his phenomenal success. Nothing untoward was said about Jeanne or Cecilia Ann. The researchers had uncovered and interviewed a former Merrick girlfriend who lived with her mother in Atlantic City, but nothing about her appeared in print.

Although the tone might occasionally be tongue in cheek, the article was exactly what Merrick had wanted, recognition on a high journalistic level of his achievement. It noted that since 1954 he had presented 37 shows on Broadway. Twenty-two had been profitable, eleven enormously so. On an investment of $7 million he had grossed $115 million and shown a net profit of $14 million for his investors. There was every reason that the public Merrick should be pleased.

It was, however, the other Merrick who shaped his response. The other Merrick was outraged at the amount of space given to the early years in St. Louis. For some men the ascent from poverty might have been a point of pride. For Merrick it continued to defeat him. Despite the fact no genuinely revealing insights were given into his private life, Merrick gave vent to unparalleled rage.

For several months Merrick had been having cordial discussions with the young director Ulu Grosbard about another Peter Weiss play, *The Investigation.* The play about Auschwitz consisted of testimony from the Nuremberg trials arranged for solo and choral reading. This was hardly likely to be big box office, so Grosbard, who controlled the rights, was thrilled when, entirely out of the blue, he received a phone call from Merrick, who said he was interested in producing it.

They had several serious meetings in the months before the

opening of *Marat/Sade*. Grosbard suspected Merrick was positioning himself so that, should *Marat/Sade* be a success, he would have another Peter Weiss play waiting in the wings.

During their meetings Merrick was at his most charming, though Grosbard was appalled at the way Merrick reviled one of his employees during these otherwise delightful conversations. "If I had been working for him and he treated me that way in front of a stranger, I would have walked out on the spot," Grosbard commented.

The day the *Time* story appeared Grosbard received a phone call that floored him. It was his erstwhile producer shouting obscenities into the phone, declaring that if *Time* would treat him this way he would no longer be a producer of serious theater. He would have nothing whatsoever to do with *The Investigation.*

Grosbard was flabbergasted. Was Merrick so outraged? Was the *Time* cover story a pretext for getting out of a project he had no intention of carrying forward anyway? A few weeks later he received a conciliatory call from Biff Liff, who now played the Intercessor role Neil Hartley used to play. Merrick regretted his anger, Liff told Grosbard. He was still interested in doing the Weiss play. By then Grosbard had found other producers—Emanuel Azenberg and Eugene Wolsk, both of whom had worked in Merrick's office—and wanted nothing more to do with Merrick.

Eventually Merrick's rage subsided. After all, he hated much of what the press wrote about him. If he couldn't find grounds for complaint in the text he would bemoan the pictures that accompanied it. One of the few pieces that had pleased him, he told an associate years later, was an article in *Screw* magazine by a woman who had slept with him. She had described his penis as "not long but broad" and commended his performance. She had apparently had nothing to say about his childhood in St. Louis.

A letter from Jo Mielziner commiserated with him on the tone of the *Time* piece, but Mielziner assured Merrick that most readers would find it an admiring profile, which indeed it was.

Merrick came to see Mielziner's point. He dropped a jocular note to the publisher asking if the entire staff of the magazine was on LSD.

It turned out that what he mainly took exception to was the cover drawing, which was hardly flattering. It was neither the stolid portrait *Time* gave wealthy businessmen or politicians nor the lighthearted caricature that might befit a raffish showman. It was an uncannily accurate portrait of a brooding, wary, deeply disturbed man.

Merrick wrote *Time* he would sue "for defamation of caricature."

February 10, 1966

Mr. Stanley Kauffmann
New York Times
229 West 43 Street
New York 36, New York

Dear Mr. Kauffmann:

     At your peril.

          Sincerely,

          David Merrick

CHAPTER TWENTY-FIVE

HOWEVER MUCH THE PRIVATE Merrick may have seethed at his imagined wounds inflicted by *Time* magazine, the public Merrick was riding high. Only a few weeks after the cover story, Merrick scored one of his major coups against the press, probably his most impressive victory next to the *Subways Are For Sleeping* ad.

It was connected with the New York opening of *Philadelphia, Here I Come*, by a young Irish playwright, Brian Friel.

Stanley Kauffmann became the theater critic of the *New York Times* during the 1965-66 season. Kauffmann, an intellectual of high standing, had written criticism of theater and film for highbrow magazines, including *The New Republic*. Kauffmann was also a man of the theater. In 1957 he had directed two friends, Frances Reed and Philip Birnoff, in a production of an Italian play, *Lease on Love*, at the New Hope Playhouse. They had invited David Merrick to see it. He had no interest in transferring it to New York.

Kauffmann's accession to the *Times* suggested that the Old Grey Lady of 42nd Street had recognized that the American theater, bolstered by avant-garde contributions from Europe, required a more thoughtful kind of criticism than had been standard on New York daily newspapers.

Arthur Miller once pointed out that when he came into the

theater in the Forties the newspaper reviewers tended to be reporters at heart. (Even Brooks Atkinson, instead of remaining on the theater beat during World War II, had elected to cover the war in China.) The older generation of newspaper reviewers, Miller pointed out, came to their positions after the sort of journalistic apprenticeship that might have made them crime reporters or editorial writers.

As a result their taste tended to be closer to that of their readers than it was in the Sixties and afterward, when, Miller lamented, the reviewers came to their jobs with an academic preparation and orientation. Such background had been the rule on "little" magazines like *The Nation,* for which Harold Clurman had been the critic, the *Hudson Review,* which employed the young John Simon, or *The New Republic,* whose theater critics included Kauffmann, Eric Bentley and Robert Brustein, but it had not been true of New York daily newspapers until the *Times's* appointment of Kauffmann.

Kauffmann had been in his position for several weeks before he requested, early in January of 1966, that he be allowed to review shows at the final preview. This would give him time to reflect on the intellectual issues the playwright raised. The creators had spent years preparing the play he saw. Was it fair to treat it on deadline like a reporter covering a fire? Seeing a preview would give him a chance to do proper credit to the performers, the design and the direction, which was not always possible in the rush to meet a deadline only two hours after the opening night performance.

As long as reviewers thought of themselves as newspapermen, the pressure of meeting a deadline had been considered an integral part of the job. Critics were seated along the aisle so they could literally dash out as soon as the curtain fell to begin writing their reviews.

Because the deadlines were tight, the more conscientious editors would stand at the back of the theater so their reviewers could begin writing their notices in longhand during the final moments of the play. The editor could go back to the office and begin setting the opening lines in print while waiting for the show to end and the reviewer to race back to the office to finish.

Sometimes the excitement of the opening night performance became part of the review. When John Chapman reviewed *The Matchmaker*, for example, he wrote, after a quick description of the play in the first paragraph, "This perfect entertainment opened last evening at the Royale Theater, and if the stony-hearted stage manager hadn't finally ordered the curtain held down and the house lights turned up, the audience might be there this morning cheering. I'd rather be there than where I am at this moment of turning in a report. For cheering on a typewriter offers difficulties. The machine goes clackety-clack when I want it to go 'Yeeow!'"

This, of course, was not the sort of review Kauffman would be filing for the *Times*. Nor would it have been suitable for the first play he was permitted to review from the final preview, Edward Albee's *Malcolm*, adapted from a James Purdy novel. When Kauffmann had made his request on behalf of himself and other critics to the League of Broadway Theaters and Producers, its then president Harold Prince was adamantly opposed to the idea, but he would not forbid other producers—in this case Richard Barr—to accede to Kauffmann's request.

When Kauffmann put in his formal request for final preview tickets for *Philadelphia, Here I Come*, the tickets arrived with a typewritten note signed by Merrick. It read, "At your peril."

Kauffmann later discovered that Merrick had been so intent on keeping him "fresh" for the opening that he even prevented him from reading the play in advance. He dispatched an employee to the Drama Book Shop to buy the six available English copies. (Kauffmann, in fact, did not even know it had been published.)

When Kauffmann arrived at the Helen Hayes Theater on February 15, the night before Friel's play was scheduled to open, the marquee was dark. The performance had been cancelled, ticketholders were informed, because a rat had been discovered in the generator. Kauffmann was especially grieved on behalf of his wife, when the pair became a public object of curiosity in front of the theater. He phoned the managing editor of the *Times*, to report the peculiar circumstances surrounding the cancellation. They agreed it would be a mistake to put a spotlight on the incident. But later, *Times* reporters were scurrying through bars in the theater district, trying to locate members of the cast and crew who might have information on what happened. The *Times* had in fact, become Merrick's eager accomplice in publicizing the pre-curtain drama.

The next morning the *Times* reported this odd event on its front page. Early in the story Merrick made it clear that he was not averse to the idea of critics attending previews. "I don't think it will help them," he said. "I don't think they know what they're doing anyway. My opinion is that it won't make any difference whatsoever, even if they cover seven nights in a row. They can attend as many performances as possible—previews, openings, post-views. So far as I am concerned, they can also attend rehearsals."

The reporter who covered the cancellation of the final preview did note an inconsistency. Although the marquee was dark, the lobby of the theater was lit. The owner of the theater issued a statement that any technical difficulties must have been with the show's own electrical equipment. The theater's equipment was in perfect order and would certainly be able to function for the opening that night.

Asked to comment, Merrick said, "What do I know about electrical equipment? I only know about the quality of a play, the cast, the director, the effect of lighting, not how they achieve it."

The "rat in the generator" incident received considerable coverage. *Time* used it as a pretext to dub Merrick "the *adulte terrible* of Broadway."

Whatever innocence Merrick feigned the day after the rat was discovered was dispelled in an interview with Dick Schaap a few weeks later in the *Herald-Tribune*. Schaap asked Merrick when he began to suspect he might have generator trouble.

"When I went to Viet Nam with *Dolly* last year," Merrick told him. "I talked to officers there about ambush tactics. Guerrilla warfare fascinated me, and I wondered if it could be used against the enemy. . . For about two weeks I had a premonition that something might go wrong with the last preview of *Philadelphia.* I guess I'm a mystic. By Monday I was really afraid something might happen, so we stopped selling tickets for Tuesday. My worst fears were confirmed. At 7:45 Tuesday night my technicians informed that a large rat had gotten into the generator. It was, I discovered, a large white rat."

Kauffmann himself assumed that his grey hair may have qualified him for the sobriquet, but another *Times*-man said White Rat was a nickname for Clifton Daniel, the editor who had encouraged Kauffmann to attend previews. If so it indicates the depth of the "intelligence" Merrick gathered on "the enemy."

At the conclusion of the interview Merrick asked Schaap, "What's a generator?"

Shortly afterward Merrick was in London and happened across a pile of remainder copies of a novel called *The Philanderer,* whose author was none other than the *Times*'s Stanley Kauffmann. Published in the U.S. by Simon & Shuster and in England by Secker & Warburg, it was the subject of an obscenity trial in England in 1954. (The book was not deemed obscene.) Since it was being remaindered, Merrick bought 100 copies of the book. He sent eighty-nine to reviewers and editors across the country, ten to the top brass of the *Times.* All the copies were signed, "Compliments of David Merrrickk," calling attention to the redundancies in Kauffmann's spelling of his name.

Kauffmann had written a tepid review of *Philadelphia, Here I Come,* but it almost didn't matter. He had served another purpose. He had helped Merrick put a play by an unknown writer from Dublin on the front page of the *New York Times.*

He was able to mastermind this sort of event with aplomb. He had proven his ability to adapt to new conditions during the Philadelphia run of *Philadelphia, Here I Come.* One of the local

TV stations had a reporter and camera crew outside the theater to interview members of the audience as they left. Merrick himself got into line and declared it was one of the best plays he had ever seen. The TV reporter had no idea who he was. Moments later it didn't matter. One of Merrick's publicists, Bob Ullmann, using a huge shears, had cut the cable. In any case the footage wound up on the cutting room floor.

Events in his private life were now beginning to happen beyond control.

To a certain extent Jeanne had always been beyond his control. What had begun as a genuine love affair had turned inexplicably into a marriage. Once married they both found living together a strain.

Jeanne Gilbert remained Mrs. David Merrick until October, 1966, when they were divorced in Juarez, Mexico, on grounds of incompatibility. When she left his apartment she amputated the sleeves of all his Savile Row suits—the sleeves facing the wall. He could easily look at his enormous closet full of suits and not realize anything was amiss until he put one on.

She left in a fur coat and galoshes, which she claimed was all she had when she married him. In her settlement she received $50,000 a year plus the assurance of a sum of $300,000 each to her and Cecilia Ann. The child received a Park Avenue apartment in her own name. (It was two floors above the one Merrick would later occupy with his third wife.)

On October 13, 1966, she took out an ad in the Public Notices section of the *Times* announcing "My husband, David Merrick, having left my bed and board, I will no longer be responsible for his debts. Mrs. Jeanne Gilbert Merrick." It was the sort of prank he might have devised.

Jeanne's obsession with him never faded. A year later her friend Rebecca Morehouse mentioned that Merrick was coming to have drinks with her and Ward. Jeanne begged to be invited. Rebecca acquiesced. Merrick arrived, jovial and charming. Drinks were poured. Conversation flowed. The doorbell rang. It was Jeanne.

If either of the women imagined the sight of her after a long absence might soften him, they were wrong. His face turned ashen, he muttered a few words and left.

The rancors he harbored were too deep to be smoothed over with conventional politeness. The game-playing he could indulge in if a show or a business deal were at stake was out of the question with his personal life.

CHAPTER TWENTY-SIX

I F AT THE BEGINNING OF 1966 *Time* had accorded Merrick its
highest honor, by the end of the year *Time's* editors were concerned. What was happening to Their Man? an internal
memo wanted to know.

It was indeed embarrassing. After the brilliant 1965-66 season
the fall of 1966 was a huge disappointment. There were several
ambitious plays, all of which had quickly closed. There was a lavish musical with two big stars that was floundering out of town.

What indeed had happened to Merrick?

It was not the personal troubles. The 1963-64 season, in
which he had presented eight shows (and had laid the groundwork for *Funny Girl*), was in its planning stages during the
tumultuous period when Cecilia Ann was born. He could shut
his private world out with little difficulty.

What made Merrick a different man by the end of 1966 was
the fact that he was the same man. There had been a remarkable
consistency to the theater from the time he dreamed of entering
it in the Thirties to his arrival in New York in the Forties and to
his ascendancy in the Fifties and early Sixties. It was a period of
consistency and coherence, and Merrick had known how to
exploit it. Strangely, he did not see how his world was changing.
He had spent so much energy fashioning a self to function in the
theater he knew so well that he was understandably averse to

fashioning a new one for what might be a passing fad.

He had built his career by an almost uncanny sense of how to foresee or, when necessary, how to manipulate the public taste. He had not gauged how much the public was changing, how much "his" public was becoming outmoded. A man who had striven to project an elderly somberness from an early age, he was an unlikely convert to the burgeoning "youth movement."

In November of 1966 he would be fifty-five years old. In January of 1967 *Time* would name as its "man of the year" the entire generation under twenty-five, who, *Time's* editors imagined, were bringing a new idealism to bear on a troubled world.

The times were, as a popular song declared, "a-changin'." The Vietnam war had begun to cast its shadow over everything American, not least the idea of "entertainment." The younger generation of actors, writers, and directors—following a notion established by intellectuals as early as the Fifties—had come to regard Broadway as an epithet.

Commercial theater was regarded almost as a contradiction in terms. To be pure, theater had to be separated from commerce. Young people presented their plays in cafes, in lofts, in converted warehouses, not in anything that a conventional bourgeois audience might consider a theater.

Nor were they interested in "entertaining" their audiences. It was more important to instruct them, sometimes even to punish them. They must not be allowed to forget that their values had created an odious war in Southeast Asia and iniquitous racial conditions at home.

For the younger generation Merrick was the producer of the long-running *Hello, Dolly!*, which, by the fall of 1966, starred Ginger Rogers. The cult of old movies, even the cult of Astaire and Rogers, had yet to take hold. She was merely a has-been star, and the idea of casting her in a silly musical made Merrick the apotheosis of what was wrong with the American theater.

The younger generation conveniently overlooked the fact he had brought *Marat/Sade*, the avant-garde work that more than any other crystallized their ambitions, to New York.

A few months after *Time*'s cover story, *Newsweek* weighed in with a profile of Merrick in which the New Republic's drama critic Robert Brustein admitted to a "grudging admiration" for Merrick's "shameless hucksterism."

"By reducing every theatrical function, including reviewing, to a link in the cash nexus, he is discrediting Broadway more effectively than a battalion of minority critics," Brustein said. "Perhaps deep down within his press agent's heart, he is as bored with the commercial theater as the rest of us."

Being a villain was hardly a role that displeased Merrick. In 1968, for example, he would place an ad in *Variety* alerting the theater community that "In the October issue of *Esquire* there appears an article written by me in which I hoped to offend everybody. If I have omitted anyone, please believe me, it was an underslight. I meant no offense. To these, my humble apologies. David Merrick."

What mattered more than the insults of a Brustein was his own increasing record of failure. In the fall of 1966 his first offering was another play by Brian Friel, produced under the auspices of the Foundation. In *The Loves of Cass McGuire* Ruth Gordon played an Irish woman who had gone to America and become an alcoholic. After forty-two years she returns to Ireland, where her family treats her cruelly. It was a distasteful story, and even Gordon's skill could not make it endearing. (Nor could Merrick's own attempts at rewriting the second act. Inserted during previews without the knowledge of the playwright, they were promptly excised. It was one of his rare attempts at creative participation.) The play opened October 6 and closed two weeks later.

On October 19 Merrick presented an adaptation by Hugh Wheeler of a Shirley Jackson novel, *We Have Always Lived in the Castle*, a grisly story about a teenager who murders her parents. Directed by Garson Kanin, starring Shirley Knight and Alan Webb, the play lasted a week.

In January of 1967 he produced Pauline Macauley's *The*

Astrakhan Coat, a drama about a thief and killer and his twin assistants, who make a fall guy out of a gullible young waiter.

Only ten years had elapsed since Merrick discovered Osborne and made an important author known on this side of the Atlantic. But theater was changing so quickly, so radically that his tastes and instincts no longer seemed in sync with the times. One American critic dubbed Macauley's play "mod," a catchword of the time; another called it "camp," a trendy word just coming into vogue, which the critic probably did not understand.

Even the critics, it appeared, were bewildered by the changes around them. "Mod" and "camp," though they may have persuaded the critics themselves that they were "with it," persuaded no one to see *The Astrakhan Coat*, which lasted slightly more than two weeks, despite a cast that included Brian Bedford, Carole Shelley and Roddy McDowell. The cast had become despondent on the road when their director, an alcoholic, once fell asleep giving them notes after a performance. They discovered that, regardless of the critical response, Merrick intended to keep it open only long enough to secure the movie rights.

Merrick's most successful play that season was by a former stand-up comic named Woody Allen. Merrick co-produced *Don't Drink the Water* with Jack Rollins and Charles Joffe, who went on to produce all of Allen's films. It was about a Newark caterer trapped in an Iron Curtain country where he is accused of being a spy. With the inimitable Lou Jacobi as the caterer, the play was a big hit.

Merrick scored a moderate hit with the musical *I Do! I Do!* an adaptation of Jan de Hartog's play *The Fourposter*, which follows a married couple from youthful innocence to severe old age. The musical was by Tom Jones and Harvey Schmidt, the creators of *The Fantasticks*. Despite the unpleasantness of their experience with Merrick on *110 in the Shade*, they, like many others, decided his skills were worth putting up with his tirades. When he offered them the material, they took it. The show starred Mary Martin and Robert Preston and was staged and choreographed by Gower Champion.

For the first time in Broadway history a 25-piece orchestra would not be in the pit. It would be concealed backstage, an innovation generally attributed to rock musicals, but which began with Jones and Schmidt's tender score.

Possibly for the last time, Marge and Gower Champion, who would soon be divorced, performed their act at the opening night party in the Rainbow Room. For a young Englishman, Lionel Larner, the image of the Champions dancing with consummate wit and elegance before a black-tie audience, with the lights of Manhattan sparkling below, crystallized why he—and many others in the room, including, perhaps, the producer—had come to New York in the first place.

The most exhaustive press coverage of the season was reserved for Merrick's first colossal disaster, an experience he himself dubbed his "Bay of Pigs." Merrick had shows close out of town before. None had closed in previews on Broadway. None had stars of the caliber of Mary Tyler Moore and Richard Chamberlain.

Breakfast at Tiffany's was indeed a very remarkable failure.

On a plane together, Merrick was badgering Merrill about doing a musical version of *Casablanca*. Merrill was unenthusiastic about having to compete with people's vivid memories of the classic film. Looking across the aisle, he saw someone reading Truman Capote's *Breakfast at Tiffany's*. And Merrill heard himself saying that Capote's novel would stand a better chance as a musical than *Casablanca*. So the surreal history of this musical began.

Merrill began working on the score. He persuaded the versatile screenwriter Nunnally Johnson to do the book. Both agreed it was important not to sentimentalize the story of Holly Golightly, a woman who lives off the generosity of wealthy men.

Merrick had asked Joshua Logan to direct. When Logan read Johnson's book he thought the approach to the material had been too tough. Johnson, knowing Logan's close association with Merrick, assumed Logan's word would carry great weight. Johnson bowed out. Then Logan also bowed out, opting to work on the ill-fated *Hot September* rather than wait for a new writer.

In the wake of the huge success of *Cactus Flower*, Merrick asked Abe Burrows to write the book. Merrick saw the Capote story as a glamorous evocation of sophisticated New York. Burrows, however, stuck closer to the original cynical and dark material.

The disparity between the two views of the book was not immediately apparent because the book was not finished by the time they went into rehearsal. Burrows, a popular toastmaster and eulogizer, was too busy on "the circuit" to finish the second act.

But wasn't Burrows the theater's most often sought after "doctor?" He had fixed other people's second acts out of town. It seemed silly to worry about whether he could fix his own.

Merrick had persuaded the author himself, Truman Capote, heady with the success of his book *In Cold Blood*, to hang around the rehearsals. Oliver Smith recalled the sight of the aloof Merrick and the tiny Capote as "Lewis Carroll time." But the two, so different in every way, hit it off surprisingly well: "Merrick beguiled Truman, and Truman charmed David." As for why Capote would have trusted his most famous and celebrated story to Merrick, Smith thinks it was simple: "Truman was greedy. He admired Merrick's success."

The show opened in Washington to mixed reviews, though the audience seemed to enjoy it. Merrick resorted to his usual remedy: he screamed. This time he even screamed at his favorite designer, Oliver Smith.

Smith had designed half a dozen shows for Merrick, beginning with *Jamaica* in 1957, most recently creating the elegant turn-of-the-century New York of *Hello, Dolly!* There had been very few arguments on any of the shows Smith did for Merrick. On *Take Me Along* all the masking for the sets was in green. At a certain point Merrick, inspecting the sets, said to Smith: "I hate that green." Undaunted, the tall, aristocratic Smith replied, "I happen to like green." Merrick said nothing but turned away, "as if he were talking to an idiot."

Smith had created a modest drop curtain with an impressionistic painted exterior of Tiffany's. Merrick was looking for the real thing. He wanted Tiffany's on 57th Street. Merrick, prevailed, and against his better judgment, Smith created a realistic-looking Tiffany's.

"It was a very heavy set. It looked like something out of Karnak. But David just adored it."

The sets were the least problematic part of what was still entitled *Holly Golightly*. By the time the show reached Philadelphia, where the reviews were harsher, something very disturbing happened. The audience had turned on the show. "I've never seen an audience as vitriolic as the one in Philadelphia," Smith recalled. "They even booed Mary Tyler Moore."

Their hostile response was not entirely unreasonable. Moore was a beloved TV star, pixie-like, pert, always endearing. When Audrey Hepburn played the kept woman in the film version, she sacrificed none of her charm. Moore was not allowed to play the role that had made her an adored figure on TV. She had to play a dark version of Holly for which she was not really suited.

"She gave the impression of a square-jawed girl who should have been working at Prudential, not taking things from men," Merrill recalled. "She was a dream to work with, inexhaustible. She was a good egg, but you always had a sense you knew you weren't getting all of her."

Moore knew instinctively why the audiences hated her. Here was their fantasy daughter swearing—a shocking thing in 1966. She was acting not like a sophisticated kept woman but like a high class hooker.

In deference to the audience's hostility, Burrows tried to sweeten the character. But it was too late. Merrick knew it. Drastic measures were required and, without consulting anyone, Merrick took them. One night, after a dispiriting performance in Philadelphia, the beleaguered Bob Merrill heard a knock on his hotel room door. When he opened it, there was Merrick.

"Bob, I want you to take a ride with me," Merrick said cryptically.

He then escorted Merrill to an elevator and took him to his own suite in the penthouse of the hotel. As Merrick opened the door, Merrill saw in the distance a figure lounging on a chaise longue with his hand upraised in greeting.

"Meet Edward Albee," Merrick said.

As early as Washington Merrick had been speaking to Albee about rewriting the book. In Washington Merrick had told Merrill that Burrows didn't want to continue with the show. Merrill was disappointed but he understood Burrows' frustration and dissatisfaction. Years later he found out from Burrows that he *had* wanted to continue, but Merrick was intent on ousting him.

Merrick's explanation for this unconventional choice of a bookwriter was, "Why drown in two feet of water? We might as well swim out and take our chances."

In theory Albee would rewrite the book and Burrows would continue to direct. In Boston, however, Albee gave an interview to Kevin Kelly of the *Boston Globe* in which he disparaged Burrows' work. "All those awful jokes will be thrown out, and I hope to substitute some genuine wit. The characters, from Holly down, will be redefined, and she won't have any of those borscht-circuit lovers she's saddled with now."

When he read the interview Burrows felt he had to withdraw. With him departed much of the cast's spirit and hope. He was replaced by Joseph Anthony, who, three years earlier, had directed *110 in the Shade* and had vowed he would never work for Merrick again. When Merrick asked him to direct *Breakfast at Tiffany's*, Anthony asked, "How will I explain this to all the people I've sworn to I'd never work for you again?" "Tell them you did it for the money," Merrick replied.

Albee had never worked on a musical before, but he did not consider this a drawback. He would bring new ideas to the form.

When he showed the dialogue he had written to Merrill, the latter was dismayed by the huge quantity of it. He explained to Albee that musical audiences were not used to so much dialogue. They would be riffling through their programs, fidgeting in their seats, waiting for the next musical number during such long scenes.

"They've never seen an Edward Albee musical scene," Albee told Merrill grandly.

Soon audiences were given their opportunity to see Edward Albee musical scenes. Their response was much as Merrill had predicted. The Albee version began with a scene in which Sally Kellerman, playing a secondary character, Madge Wildwood, delivered a long soliloquy, which ended with her stretched out on the stage, sobbing. The audience was immediately hostile.

The audience, as became common in the Sixties, had to be taken to task for its intransigence. "Audiences apparently expect a musical to be noisy, they expect to see people jumping up and down," Albee told an interviewer. "Of course it's difficult to over-haul old elements."

He said he wanted the acting to be more naturalistic. He want-ed the singing to avoid the extroverted Broadway style. He want-ed the numbers re-orchestrated so they would not build to the kind of climax that begged for applause.

One of the "old elements" that was overhauled was the notion of a female chorus. Albee summoned the chorus girls to the the-ater on a Sunday. Many had gone back to New York on their one day off in weeks. They trudged up to Boston, where Albee lined them up on stage and walked around them, scrutinizing them as he stroked a cat he had in his arms. He decided to fire most of them, retaining only a few to play hookers.

Throughout the frantic gestation period Merrick remained gal-lant toward Mary Tyler Moore. She was traumatized by the hos-tility she felt from the audience. Worse, there were rumors that Tammy Grimes and Diahann Carroll were being groomed to replace her, but there was apparently no foundation to these reports. Merrick continued to treat her solicitously.

No one seemed able to alter the show's catastrophic trajectory. One night in New York one of the characters spoke her line, "I need a lawyer." Someone in the audience shouted back, "You don't need a lawyer; you need a doctor." When this performance ended, Moore threw herself on the floor, sobbing, "What have I done wrong?"

In its final incarnation the musical became a Pirandello-like exercise in truth and fiction. Was Holly a real character, or was she merely the imagined creature of the Richard Chamberlain character, who was now a writer? Not that Albee's book lacked reality. He had Holly being punched viciously in the stomach by an FBI woman, after which she lost an illegitimate child.

Cast members began calling the show *Who's Afraid of Holly Golightly?*

Merrick realized he had made a miscalculation of epic proportions. Whether he had initially regarded Albee as a "classy" way to rectify the adaptation of an undeniably classy writer; whether he thought this would be a way to make Albee the American writer whose career he would nurture; whether he he had just made a gamble wilder than he was used to making, Merrick knew it was hopeless.

On December 15, knowing he would have to refund $1 million in advance ticket sales, he closed *Breakfast at Tiffany's*. The final performance was a matinee. When word spread through the theater community that Merrick was closing the show that afternoon, there was a stampede on the box office. In an act of loyalty, Schlissel stationed himself at the box office to prevent people he recognized from buying tickets. He didn't want them to have the pleasure of seeing his boss's most humiliating failure.

Merrick himself took the failure with surprising grace and equanimity. He joked that he closed the show at the behest of the retailer Tiffany, who had gotten word that Cartier's was underwriting the musical to embarrass its competitor.

A few days after the show closed, a White House aide called Merrick to get his personal permission to use "Hello, Dolly!" for a holiday show being done in honor of President Johnson. The caller extended his sympathies to Merrick over *Breakfast at Tiffany's*.

"Oh, but you're the one who needs the sympathy," Merrick said. Referring to the huge tax break the flop would give him, he quipped, "Seventy-five percent of the loss was yours."

Well after the debacle Albee remarked that the musical taught him what it was like "to watch a dictator being disappointed in preconceived notions." The dictator, he clarified, was not David Merrick, but rather *the audience*, who ran around at intermissions saying, "Where's David Merrick? How *dare* he give us anything like this?".

Merrick himself had always behaved with remarkable compliance toward *that* dictator. How many times had writers and composers been upbraided because of the chance remarks Merrick had seized on in the lobby or at the bar across the street from the theater. Once a writer's sister-in-law happened to sit next to Merrick at a rehearsal. The sister-in-law made some casual negative remark. It was like tossing a lit cigarette into a gas tank. Merrick blew up, storming toward the stage, screaming at the bewildered actors for a line to be changed immediately.

Merrick knew the audience was changing. If, in retrospect, his decision to bring in Albee as a "doctor" for a Broadway musical seems bizarre, to Merrick it may have seemed a way to keep on top of current trends. Earlier that fall Hal Prince, who had produced such shows as *Pajama Game* and *Fiddler on the Roof,* had continued his fledgling directorial career with a musical about—of all things—Nazi Germany. *Cabaret* became a blockbuster hit. The musical theater, Merrick saw, was striving to become "relevant," and Albee certainly seemed a useful teammate in the chase after that cause.

CHAPTER TWENTY-SEVEN

R ELEVANCE WAS NOT on everybody's mind in the fall of
1966. It was certainly not a pressing issue for Truman
Capote.

In January of 1966 *In Cold Blood*, his "non-fiction novel"
about two ex-convicts who murdered an entire family in rural
Kansas, had been published. The success of that novel had transformed Capote from a New York coterie writer into the most
publicized author in America. This transformation may also have
persuaded Merrick to do the musical of *Breakfast at Tiffany's*,
which was first announced for Broadway in February of that year.

Like Merrick, Capote had come from the hinterlands with
dreams of conquering the glamorous metropolis. Capote, who
arrived five years afterward, had made a name for himself well
before Merrick. Like Merrick, Capote had been no slouch at publicity. But his dreams of glory had been grander and more precise.
As early as 1945, very shortly after his arrival, he had told his
friend Leo Lerman, long an *eminence grise* at Conde-Nast, that if
he ever amassed a lot of money he would throw a great masked
ball to which he would invite the upper echelons of New York.

In 1956, when *My Fair Lady* opened, he saw what the ball
would look like—it would be all in Black and White, like the
costumes in the Ascot scene his friend Cecil Beaton had designed
for the show. With the huge critical and financial success of *In*

Cold Blood, the moment he had been awaiting for twenty-one years had arrived.

On November 28, 1966, Capote, ostensibly repaying the generosity of his neighbor Kay Graham, who had thrown a party in his honor the year before, gave a ball for 450 people in her honor at the Plaza Hotel. (Because he was besieged with calls from people not on his list, some of whom threatened suicide, at the last minute he added another eighty people.) Invitations to his Black and White Ball constituted proof of one's standing in New York society the way admission to Mrs. Astor's ballroom, which could only accommodate 400 people, did the century before.

Whereas Mrs. Astor's guest list was limited exclusively to Society, Capote's was eclectic. There were elements of what used to be known as Society (a Rhinelander, several Vanderbilts and an Astor); many more from Cafe Society (the Agnellis, Henry Ford II, Princess Lee Radziwill), and a generous helping of people in journalism and the arts: Andy Warhol, Marianne Moore, Noel Coward, Marlene Dietrich, Sir Isaiah Berlin, Candice Bergen, Anita Loos, Janet Flanner and Frank and Mia Sinatra.

Many on the guest list were people Merrick had once employed: Tallulah Bankhead, Jerome Robbins, Thornton Wilder, Tennessee Williams, Stephen Sondheim, Betty Comden, Adolph and Phyllis Green, S.N. Behrman, Peter Glenville and Lauren Bacall. A few were fellow producers, like Robert Whitehead, Harold Prince and Leland Hayward.

A number of the people attending were associated with *Breakfast at Tiffany's,* then still floundering toward Broadway: Abe Burrows, Edward Albee and Alan Delynn. The stars of the musical, perhaps because they were merely television celebrities, were not on the guest list, suggesting that Capote had invited no one out of a sense of mere obligation. Hence there was nothing spurious about the presence of the producer of *Breakfast at Tiffany's.* In fact Merrick felt confident enough about his presence there to break one of the rules. Single men were not to bring dates, but Merrick brought a young actress named Jane Alexander.

Merrick had come a long way from the days when he and

Leonore were excluded from the Logans' A List. In the eyes of Capote, who was, in 1966, the ultimate arbiter, Merrick and the Logans, not to mention the Richard Rodgerses, were equal. It was, all things considered, a miraculous ascent in barely a dozen years.

Capote's party inspired Merrick to greater generosity than people were accustomed to seeing in him. The party was "always shimmering," he told Charlotte Curtis, the society editor of the *Times*. "It was never still, nor was there a static moment. I guess you'd call this a rave review." Merrick told Curtis he would give his own party next year and that he would ask Truman to help him.

A few weeks after the party Merrick had closed *Breakfast at Tiffany's*. Whether, in the wake of that disaster, Capote would have been eager to collaborate with Merrick on party planning seems a moot point.

The Black and White Ball was the last glittering gesture of the New York that the two provincials had come to conquer. Even a year afterward the estimated $20,000 Capote spent on his party would have been considered scandalous. Though the price of the women's masks was reported (Adolfo's custom-made masks ranged from $65 to $300, Halston's from $50 to $600), the cost of their dresses was not, suggesting that even then, even before Vietnam cast its shadow on everything American, the public might not have been able to stomach what the wealthy spent on party duds.

Probably even such pundits among the guests as Walter Lippmann and James Reston could not have imagined how quickly everything would change, how American aspirations, once unabashedly upward, would turn downward. Could one of the Vanderbilts at the party, for example, have imagined that in only a few years she would be engaged in the manufacture of blue jeans?

Capote's ball was one of the final rites in the cult of the goddess Success, and it seems significant that Capote drew his image of how to pay her obeisance from a Broadway musical. The very look of Broadway was part of the shrine at which Capote and Merrick were ardent worshippers.

For Capote, the Black and White Ball was the beginning of a downward spiral that would end only with his death nineteen years later. He never wrote anything else that demonstrated the literary talent that culminated in *In Cold Blood*. In fact, a large part of his later career was devoted to attacking some of the society matrons whose presence had lent distinction to the Black and White Ball.

For Merrick, however humiliating the closing of *Breakfast at Tiffany's* had been, there was still every reason to feel confident, every reason to believe the goddess still favored him.

He had recently concluded an agreement with RCA Victor, which was willing to entrust $1.5 million to him under a two-year arrangement whereby it would automatically have the right to issue original cast albums of his shows. The crop of musicals to which RCA obtained these rights was, with the exception of *I Do! I Do!* a rather lackluster harvest. No album was made of *Breakfast at Tiffany's*, which was a pity, since the score, which can be heard on pirate tapes, seems vintage Merrill.

Even the closing of a $1 million musical made no noticeable difference in his financial prowess. He was putting eggs in other baskets. Ever since *The World of Suzie Wong* he had sent road companies of his shows to Las Vegas, where they invariably did extremely strong business. In 1966 he began to make his presence felt there in grander ways. He acquired five points of the Riviera Hotel. "That's like owning five per cent of Chase Manhattan," a columnist explained.

Although he had not really been harmed by the string of failures he experienced that fall, they made him aware that he should pay attention to Alan Delynn, who was constantly advising him that the real place for his talents, the place where the business skills he had developed over the years would really reap dividends was Hollywood.

Earlier that year an Al Hirschfeld caricature of him had appeared in the *New York Times*. It depicted Merrick—unmistakable with his mustache and diabolical eyes—in a Santa Claus costume and beard tiptoeing away from the scene of a crime. He had set fire to a Christmas tree and the toys underneath it.

Merrick appeared to take great umbrage. He sent a note to Hirschfeld threatening a suit for libel. He fulminated against what he considered a malicious drawing. Probably his anger was intended merely to put Hirschfeld off guard, for that year on his Christmas card, there was the Hirschfeld drawing. Needless to say, Merrick had made no effort to obtain proper permission or to pay Hirschfeld any sort of royalty.

Hirschfeld had in fact captured him the way he wanted to be seen—malignant, unrepentant. The use of the drawing on a Christmas card was itself an act of thievery. Sending it to friends and colleagues was a way of flaunting the fearsome reputation that he had built.

CHAPTER TWENTY-EIGHT

MOST OF THE MEMBERS of Merrick's staff did not see their positions as creative. They were subordinates whose job was to follow the commanding officer's orders. Though Alan Delynn was careful to describe himself to others as an unabashed yes man, perhaps he felt his overall obsequiousness entitled him occasionally to make creative suggestions. Though he was not eager to entertain other people's suggestions, Merrick seemed receptive to Delynn's, even when they proved catastrophic. As they did with a musical called *Mata Hari*.

Mata Hari was the invention of Martin Charnin, who had begun his career as a dancer in the original cast of *West Side Story*. Charnin sensed his future was not in performing but in writing, and as early as 1958, when Merrick was still casting about for a writer for his musical version of *Ah, Wilderness!*, Charnin had auditioned for him, unsuccessfully.

In 1967 Charnin and his collaborators, the bookwriter Jerome Coopersmith and the composer Edward Thomas, envisioned an anti-war musical centering on the career of the World War I spy, Mata Hari.

He was very impressed that Merrick responded to his idea in the spirit in which it was presented. Other producers he'd approached had only been able to imagine it as a spoof. (One suggested he write it as a vehicle for Bert Lahr and Nancy Walker.)

At a time when the office seemed out of touch with the disquieting mood of America embroiled in Vietnam, "Mata Hari" seemed as close to "relevance" as the Merrick office was likely to come. It juxtaposed, for example, a scene of Mata Hari and her French lover enjoying the high life in Paris with a scene depicting the wretchedness of trench life at Verdun.

Merrick was not averse to keeping up with the temper of the times. But his interest in anti-war statements was not as strong as his overall interest in bank statements. Delynn suggested a director who would make *Mata Hari* relevant to profit margins. Merrick hired the man without consulting Charnin.

The man was Vincente Minnelli. It did not matter that Minnelli had not worked on Broadway in thirty years or that even his Hollywood musicals were pure glitz, by no means "relevant." Merrick, who found himself succumbing more and more to Delynn's constant urging that he should set his sights Westward, hired Minnelli, who was celebrated for such extravaganzas as *The Band Wagon* and *Gigi*, to direct what its authors had conceived as an uncompromising show about the folly of war.

To make matters worse, Minnelli and his wife Denise were enthusiastic about Marisa Mell, a young Austrian actress, to play the title role. She had done almost no theater. She could neither sing nor dance. Her acting was adequate—and no more—for the screen, and virtually untested on the stage.

All this seemed less important than the fact that she was ravishingly beautiful. That was enough for Merrick, who approved the Minnellis' choice. No one even bothered to find out if she knew how to dance. Choreographer Jack Cole auditioned her shortly before rehearsals began and reported, "She has big German feet, but we can get away with it."

To assure that *Mata Hari* would not be a visually barren work—bare stages and leotards were becoming increasingly popular in the theater in 1967—Merrick hired Jo Mielziner to do the sets and Irene Sharaff for the costumes. He encouraged them not to stint on anything.

Whatever misgivings Charnin and his colleagues had about Minnelli, they were thrilled about the way he discussed their work. "He was the best possible director of that musical *in a living room*," Charnin recalled.

They were perplexed by the fact that he seemed caught up in little details about the decor and the costumes and didn't seem concerned about the overall thrust of the piece. "We needed someone who understood the book and not the costumes," Charnin said, but at the time they knew Merrick believed in him, and for a while that was enough. For Charnin, it was thrilling to have a producer who was not constantly worrying about having to raise money, who seemed so supportive of a serious work. Trust seemed to be the least thing Charnin could offer in exchange.

Until the first day of rehearsal.

The large cast was assembled on the bare stage of the Cort Theater. They were excited by the prospect of being in the show that would bring the great Minnelli back to Broadway. Minnelli, a diminutive man who did not have a diminutive sense of himself, greeted them crisply and then asked the stage manager to have all the participants in the first scene come onto the stage. As the actors did so, he went down into the audience and took a seat on the aisle in the second row.

He looked up at the actors onstage and shouted, "Action!"

No one moved. No one had been given any direction, and Minnelli had apparently not remembered that in the theater there were no assistant directors to move the actors around. That was *his* job. The helplessness of the cast reminded him that the theater was different, and, almost reluctantly, he began to do the blocking.

Like Merrick, he had a passion for details. He indulged Mielziner and Sharaff in a way no one had ever indulged them, and Merrick, having decided that Minnelli was the man for *Mata Hari*, refused to deny him anything. Ultimately Marisa Mell would have twenty costumes. Getting her in and out of them would require three dressers. The budget grew by leaps and bounds, but, for once, Merrick didn't seem to care.

As rehearsals proceeded, Charnin noticed that Minnelli favored the scenes depicting the decadent life Mata Hari led in Paris and spent next to no time on the battle scenes. The show made parallels between her "career" and that of a young French conscript. An especially important juxtaposition was that of Mata Hari making love to her French lover for the first time and the frightened soldier killing his first German. Minnelli spent "endless amount of time on the position of the bedsheets in the Paris scene and no time on the parallel scene in the trench."

On top of this there was no sense that the company was being molded into a team. Mell seemed to have no rapport with her co-star Pernell Roberts, and he, a professional dismayed by her inexperience, made no effort to bridge the gap between them.

On another front Irene Sharaff created such intricate costumes that Jack Cole's dancers had difficulty moving in them. Cole went onstage and ripped the specially stitched costumes apart at the crotch to provide his dancers the freedom they needed. The five-week rehearsal period was so chaotic there was no time to get an overall view of the show. The creators did almost no rewriting because they had no sense of where the show needed work.

Mata Hari was one of several musicals the Merrick office was producing that fall, the others being *How Now Dow Jones, The Happy Time* and *Stan Freberg Presents the United States of America*, a theatrical version of a satirical record Freeberg had produced in 1960.

If Merrick took a "hands off" attitude toward *Mata Hari* he approached Freberg's piece with more ideas than usual. Unfortunately for Freberg, his show was rehearsed on the stage of the St. James, except, of course, for Wednesday afternoons, when *Hello, Dolly!* played there. This saved Merrick the cost of a rehearsal studio and enabled him to drop in frequently.

"Take Lincoln out of the Civil War," he advised Freberg on one occasion. "He doesn't work." When Freberg protested, Merrick assured him the audience would not miss him. "Oh, sure, *you'll* miss Lincoln, I'll miss him, a few history teachers maybe, but the average person . . ." He also felt there were not enough strong women in the Revolutionary War and suggested moving Barbara Fretchie from the Civil War to the earlier war. Freberg said, "David, we can't rewrite history."

Merrick reacted philosophically: "Why not? We can do anything we want in the theater." Freberg was actually relieved when the show closed in rehearsals.

Throughout the rehearsals of *Mata Hari* Charnin begged Biff Liff, to persuade Merrick to fire Minnelli. Liff knew Charnin was right, but he was not about to convince Merrick that Minnelli had been a disastrous choice. On many projects Merrick was willing to listen to advice from almost anybody. But not this time.

If on many of his musicals Merrick took a cruelly negative position, on Mata Hari he remained resolutely optimistic. Once, after a depressing run-through, Merrick left the Cort with his lieutenants Liff and Schlissel. By the time they had turned the corner onto Broadway Liff could restrain himself no longer and began to voice some of his misgivings about the show.

Merrick blew up. "You're a Cassandra! This is going to be one of the greatest musicals ever."

Truth to tell, Merrick had his own doubts, which he confided to almost no one. But every time he went to see Minnelli to lay down the law, the director exuded all his immense charm, which totally defused the anger that Merrick was normally so quick to display. Merrick would return to his office, cowed.

On the surface Merrick remained as loyal to Minnelli as he had been a decade earlier to George S. Kaufman. But Kaufman had been hired to do the fine tuning on a show that had already been a hit in London. He had not had to build it from scratch. The loyalty that had been a virtue in 1957 was now an extreme liability.

How extreme became clear at the first public performance, Friday, November 16. Delynn, relying on the Washington contacts that had served the Merrick office so well in the past, had arranged that the first preview of *Mata Hari* would be a glamorous one. It was a benefit for the Women's National Democratic

Club, chaired by the president's daughter, Lynda Bird Johnson, and her fiance, Chuck Robb. Among the guests was the Deputy U.S. Ambassador to South Vietnam, Robert Komer, and his wife. These guests were probably not going to be receptive to an antiwar musical. What they saw, however, was the sort of disaster that provides unwitting and incomparable entertainment.

Mielziner had designed such huge sets and so many of them that it was impossible to store them all inside the theater. Some had to be kept in the alley. Bringing them on and off the stage made the technical side of the show a nightmare. During the performance they crashed into each other in full view of the audience. In a particularly embarrassing moment, the sets began moving too soon. Mell and Pernell Roberts were standing on the balcony of an alpine chalet singing a love song. As they sang rapturously about feeling closer together, the sets began to move, bearing the two parts of the balcony, and the lovers, to opposite ends of the stage.

The problems that evening were not just technical. As Mell prepared to make her first entrance the many jewels encrusted on the legs of her costume became enmeshed. Instead of coming on like a seductress, one of the most famous femmes fatales of the century, she entered with mincing steps—like a traditional Chinese woman whose feet have been bound.

In one scene Minnelli had devised a lovely effect in which the stage would go completely black. All that would be visible would be the tip of Pernell Roberts' cigarette. Somehow that night Roberts forgot to bring the pack of cigarettes onstage. The effect was lost.

The clincher came at the very end of the show. Mata Hari has been captured by the French Secret Service. She is tied to a stake and shot by fifteen French soldiers. As the smoke cleared the slumped body of Mell became visible. What also became visible was that her bottom eyelash had wiggled off and was slowly making its way down her cheek. Concerned perhaps at the impression she would make on her Creator, the dead Mata Hari raised one of her limp arms to try to put the lash back in place.

With Marissa Mell.

Had so many other things not gone wrong that night, the audience might have booed. But this simply capped the evening and drew hysterical laughter as the curtain fell.

The curtain had gone up at nine in the evening after a speech in which Merrick, noting that Democrats were "known for tolerance," had assured them that if it lasted until one in the morning he would give them all their money back. He had nothing to worry about. The curtain had fallen by 12:15. It had been a long evening but hardly a boring one. Had *Mata Hari* fulfilled its polemical intentions, it might have angered the audience. Instead it provided them unexpected diversion and a season's worth of cocktail party conversation.

Merrick himself, concealing his rage, remarked that if they could sell it as a parody and reproduce this catastrophe eight times a week, they might have a hit.

After the debacle, Minnelli assembled the cast onstage. He neither chided them nor tried to boost their morale. He had one note for them. In the scene in the first act in which the Parisian women carry Galeries Lafayette shopping bags, he told them, it was *essential* that they carry them so the audience could see the labels.

That was his final word to the cast. When Charnin came the following Monday morning to watch rehearsals he was startled to see no lights on backstage. None of the cast was there. The doorman informed him that "Mr. Merrick will not allow you to rehearse." There would be no further rehearsals, no rewriting. The show would finish its sold-out four-week run in Washington and die there.

Recalling Merrick's debacle of the year before, Richard Coe headlined his review of the show, "And Dinner at Cartier's?"

Fortunately there were other irons in the fire. John Kander and Fred Ebb, the creators of the previous season's hit, *Cabaret*, had written a warm, affectionate musical called *The Happy Time*, which starred Robert Goulet.

It was directed by Gower Champion. By this time the relationship between Merrick and Champion had settled into a ritual. Champion explained to Kander and Ebb that there would come a time when he and Merrick would have a blowup. He would threaten to leave. Merrick would withdraw, and they would continue working. The confrontation took place as he predicted, almost as if the two had a tacit agreement that the showdown was a talisman to guarantee success.

How Now Dow Jones, observed other rituals. Veterans of Merrick musicals were accustomed to being told that Mr. Merrick would not appear until the final dress rehearsal. They knew, however, that he was often hiding in the shadows, watching them work. Once, at two in the morning, the *How Now* dancers were rehearsing on the stage of the Imperial under the supervision of choreographer Gillian Lynne.

Suddenly from the balcony a voice bellowed, "This is the worst piece of shit that has ever been seen on an American stage." Merrick made his way downstairs, bellowing as he approached the stage on which the dancers trembled.

"You, out," he shouted, pointing to a dancer in the front row. "You're fired," he shouted to another. After four dancers had been fired, he ordered the four in the rear to move forward. However random his firings may have seemed, they showed his intuitive understanding. The dancers he fired were all essentially "serious" dancers, oriented more toward ballet than musical comedy. The ones in the back were theater dancers who knew to smile at the audience, which was what Merrick wanted.

The fact that the "serious" dancers were in the front with the theater dancers relegated to the back suggested another firing was in the offing. Gillian Lynne was next to go. She was replaced by a young choreographer named Michael Bennett. Merrick also brought in the old master director George Abbott. Somehow Merrick and Abbott had never crossed paths before, even though both had expressed admiration of the other's work. Abbott was able to "doctor" *How Now* satisfactorily. It even had a hit song, "Will Everyone Here Kindly Step to the Rear?"

There had been a time when every Broadway season would

generate a dozen songs that made the Hit Parade. That time was over. The ballads, the novelty songs that had been staples of Broadway scores—easy to take out of context, easy for the average American to sing or whistle—were no longer in vogue. Portable radios and earphones had eliminated the necessity for the man on the street to sing or whistle. He could now carry the definitive performance with him.

Besides, in rock music, you were not supposed to sing along. A number was written by the performer for his own use. He was not crooning a love song. He was making a statement about American life. These were not songs Tony Bennett or Sammy Davis Jr. could use in their lounge acts.

An example of the new music was making a stir in a new theater far from the beaten track. On Lafayette Street just below Astor Place Joseph Papp, who had been presenting Shakespeare for free in Central Park, had opened a new theater. It was in the Astor Library, a building scheduled for demolition. Papp had persuaded the city to renovate the building and rent it to him for $1 a year. In exchange he would give the citizens of New York lively, stimulating new theater. Papp's theater would not be for the stuffed shirts who went to Broadway shows. His was a theater for everyone, hence the title, the Public Theater.

His first offering was a musical called *Hair*, which had originally been presented in Texas. It was novel not only for its overt anti-war politics, but also for the grungy attire of its cast and for its infectious score.

When *Hair* moved to Broadway it also offered a little nudity, and it seems worth noting that though Merrick was an unabashed purveyor of commercial fare, the only nudity in his productions had been a brief look at Britannia's breasts in *The Entertainer*. However adventurous his own private life was, Merrick was careful about what he put on the stage. During the final dress rehearsals he would frequently sidle over to his master carpenter, a family man named Theodore Van Bemel, to ask him if there was anything in the show he found offensive. If so, it would be removed. When he produced *Turtle Necks*, a play by

Bruce Jay Friedman starring Tony Curtis, the director, Jacques Levy, decided to experiment with nudity while the play was trying out in Detroit. Nudity sold tickets, but Merrick ordered him to remove the innovations. The cast was clothed while Merrick was in Detroit but bare again once he left. When the company arrived in Philadelphia, the next stop on its journey to New York, the marquee on the theater did not read *Turtle Necks*. It read *One Night Stand*. It was the producer's ironic way of letting them know the show would not come to Broadway.

The one time he toyed with nudity was in *A Patriot For Me*, John Osborne's 1969 play about homosexuality in the Austrian army during the early part of the century. The production starred Maximilian Schell. Merrick wanted Schell to appear naked in a scene where he lies in bed with another man, played by the actor Noel Craig. Schell refused. At some point Schell complained to the costume designer, Freddy Wittop, that a mink coat he wore in one scene ought to be more luxurious. Wittop passed the complaint along to Merrick, who told him to inform Schell that if he were naked in the earlier scene he could have a more luxurious mink in the later one. Schell learned to appreciate the mink as issued.

Hair was an entirely different order of entertainment from *The Happy Time, How Now Dow Jones* or even the well-intentioned *Mata Hari.*

It was even further removed in spirit from the musical that redeemed Merrick that season, at least in his own eyes and, perhaps more important, at the box office. That show was, *mirabile dictu, Hello, Dolly!*

A year and a half after *Dolly's* Broadway opening Carol Channing had taken a company out on tour. Soon companies of varying degrees of extravagance were crisscrossing the country. In the summer of 1967, when racial turmoil was enveloping American cities, Merrick had what seemed an outrageous idea. Why not an all-black company of *Hello, Dolly!?*

This was not the sort of thinking the civil rights movement was encouraging. It was, in almost every way, a giant step backward. But it provided dozens of jobs for black performers. (Among those in the cast were Morgan Freeman and Clifton Davis.)

And Merrick had a great choice for the title role—Pearl Bailey. Bailey herself had mixed feelings about doing theater at this stage in her career. She was used to performing her own shows in the more lucrative area of nightclubs. She was also aware that Merrick's concept was not what seemed useful to blacks in this difficult year.

But the tour was scheduled to begin in Washington, and she was thrilled at the idea that she would be performing in a theater where, as a child, she would not have been allowed to come through the front door. So she said yes.

When the show was in previews in Washington, Merrick came down to attend a matinee. Bailey was a brilliant performer but a willful and sometimes difficult one. If she felt the audience was not responding to the show, she ad libbed her own. Even when the show worked on its own terms, she added her own "third act" during the curtain calls, a little chitchat with the audience.

The afternoon Merrick attended *Hello, Dolly!* in Washington Bailey performed the show as written—magnificently. The audience gave her an uproarious ovation. As the audience rose to its feet (standing ovations were not yet a common occurrence in the theater) Merrick walked down the side aisle of the theater, his jaw agape all the way.

With this kind of performance he could give the New York production a boost in the arm and extend its run indefinitely. Although Merrick had built his early reputation on getting the maximum mileage out of a show, none of his hits had run long enough to set any records. With Pearl Bailey as Dolly, that suddenly became a possibility.

A week after he attended the matinee in Washington Merrick took a full page ad in the *Times* to announce "The Event of the Century," the arrival of an all-black cast of *Hello, Dolly,!* headed by Bailey. The response was unprecedented. A four-year-old musical that had been on the verge of closing was suddenly a hot ticket again and "ice" was forming on the box office windows.

Bailey's tenure as Dolly Levi was a stormy one. Like Ginger Rogers, she tended to miss a lot of performances. But The Ginger Rogers Cue was no longer applicable. Bailey was too familiar a figure for that. The frequency with which she missed performances came to Merrick's attention and he decided to strike a deal with her.

As she described it in one of her lengthy curtain speeches, "Honey, David took me to lunch today. 'Course, we had to stand up—we went to Nedick's. But he did take me to Tiffany's. Bought me a bauble. he said, 'You pick out a bracelet—we'll make a deal. I'll pay for it, you don't miss any more performances.'"

She later told a member of the cast she had crossed her fingers when she struck the deal. Her attendance record remained spotty.

Nevertheless the Broadway arrival of Bailey as Dolly, in November of 1967, was a huge blow to Twentieth Century Fox, which had paid $2 million plus a percentage of the grosses for the movie rights to *Hello, Dolly!* But the film could not be released until after the Broadway show closed.

Merrick, gloating over his coup in prolonging the run, announced, "After Pearl, it'll be Liberace. In that red dress. Coming down that staircase." The film had cost $25 million to make. Fox was in the midst of a huge downward spiral, both artistically and economically. In theory *Dolly* might have helped stem the financial decline.

Tooting his own horn, Merrick jibed at the film. "I think the show is better now than when it first opened. I think they've made a big mistake. Who's the big box office draw now? Poitier. If they'd waited they could've got Poitier." This, of course, was a dig at the star they did get, his great un-favorite, Barbra Streisand.

Eventually Merrick agreed to accept $1.85 million so that the film could be released in December 1969, when the Broadway production was still running. The sum was considered smaller than the interest fees for holding back the release of the film.

Who could blame Merrick if he displayed little interest in adapting to the times? He would never have produced *Hair*. When it was moved to Broadway in 1968 he went to see it with the Kanins. Only Ruth stayed for the second act.

Yet here he was succeeding—almost unimaginably— with the absolute antithesis of *Hair*. He was still nominally a liberal, and his own record of forcing the stagehands' union to hire blacks back in the Fifties had been exemplary.

What had given him this great new success, however, was bucking what was considered correct racial thinking for the time. Merrick had never followed other people's rules. It was increasingly clear to him that there was no reason why he should.

VOCAL SELECTIONS from "PROMISES, PROMISES'
AS RECORDED ON THE UNITED ARTISTS ORIGINAL CAST ALBUM

DAVID MERRICK
presents
A NEW MUSICAL
Promises, Promises

Book by **NEIL SIMON**
Based on the screenplay "The Apartment" by
BILLY WILDER and **I. A. L. DIAMOND**

Music by **BURT BACHARACH**

Lyrics by **HAL DAVID**

Starring **JERRY ORBACH**
JILL O'HARA   EDWARD WINTER

with

PAUL REED   DICK O'NEILL   NORMAN SHELLY
VINCE O'BRIEN   MARIAN MERCER   MILLIE SLAVIN
ADRIENNE ANGEL   BARBARA LANG   DONNA McKECHNI
and
A. LARRY HAINES

Settings Designed by   Costumes Designed by
ROBIN WAGNER   **DONALD BROOKS**

Lighting by   Musical Direction by
MARTIN ARONSTEIN   **ARTHUR RUBINSTEIN**

Orchestrations by   Dance Arrangements by
JONATHAN TUNICK   **HAROLD WHEELER**

Associate Producer **SAMUEL LIFF**

Musical Numbers staged by
MICHAEL BENNETT

Directed by
ROBERT MOORE

[a] **United Artists Records**

A publication of EDWIN H. MORRIS & COMPANY, INC.
By arrangement with BLUE SEAS MUSIC, INC.—JAC MUSIC CO., INC.

CHAPTER TWENTY-NINE

I T WAS NOT ONLY the sensibility of the theater that was changing. It was also the technology.

Merrick stayed abreast of technology because there was a financial advantage to doing so. He welcomed the computerization of backstage mechanisms for several reasons. One was that computers could guarantee the precision that was a hallmark of a David Merrick show. Another was that computers could significantly reduce the number of men on a show's Yellow Card.

The stagehands' union was well aware of the advantages computerization offered a producer. Merrick was convinced that the union wanted to sabotage *Promises, Promises,* on which twenty-seven automated motors could be handled by a single stagehand. During previews each night two of the machines would break down. Merrick resolved nothing like that would happen opening night.

The orchestrator Jonathan Tunick remembers seeing Merrick arrive at the opening at his most immaculate, his most jovial. "Don't worry, boys, I've paid off the critics," he said in his grandest manner. Having given a splendid display of confidence and insouciance, in full dress attire, he removed a fire ax from its post and spent the entire evening in the basement, the machines in clear view, making sure no human "mishaps" threatened their functioning.

Although technology made some things easier, it couldn't solve all the problems of a musical. In the case of the 1968 musical *Promises, Promises*, the tone was utterly contemporary. Many American musicals are set in an exotic clime or a period that evokes nostalgia. *Promises, Promises* was set in the present. The up-to-the-minute costumes were by Donald Brooks, whose first encounter with Merrick had come at the beginning of the decade, when the Merrick office was still producing the still untitled musical based on the life of Fanny Brice.

The director was then Bob Fosse, who asked Brooks to prepare some designs. Brooks worked furiously to show the transformation from poor girl to wealthy star. Fosse then brought Brooks to meet Merrick in the red office. Fosse and Merrick sat on the sofa as Fosse explained the sketches to Merrick, who was guarded about assessing them. One by one, Merrick flung the sketches to the floor. The presentation over, Fosse got off the couch and got down on his knees and put the sketches back in the portfolio.

He then looked Merrick in the eye. "David, you never do this to an artist's work," he said. Brooks was awestruck by Fosse's sensitivity and nerve. Shortly afterward Merrick sold his interest in what became *Funny Girl* to Ray Stark and Fosse was no longer associated with the project.

Six years later Schlissel called Brooks to a production meeting for a musical based on Billy Wilder's Oscar-winning film *The Apartment*. The screenplay would be adapted for the stage by Neil Simon. It would be directed by Bob Moore and choreographed by the young man who replaced Gillian Lynne on *How Now Dow Jones*, Michael Bennett. The sets were by Robin Wagner on his first assignment for Merrick.

Brooks found Merrick respectful and supportive. After the show had been running for a year, Brooks went to see it and found it "unbearable"—his designs, he felt, were already out of date. He offered to completely redesign the costumes at no charge. Merrick was flabbergasted at the offer, but he quickly, shrewdly realized that if the women's skirts were made longer, as Brooks proposed, the show would have to be rechoreographed. He declined Brooks's offer.

The score was by Burt Bacharach, whom Merrick had approached at a party at the height of his fame as a pop songwriter to do a Broadway score.

Bacharach's eminence in his own world did not grant him immunity from Merrick's badgering techniques. In New Haven Robin Wagner saw Merrick corner Bacharach and his lyricist, Hal David.

"You people cannot write theater music," he berated them. "If I don't have a new song Friday night—and if it doesn't stop the show, I'm getting new composers."

David, whose memories of Merrick are entirely benign, remembers that for much of the New Haven engagement Bacharach was in the hospital with pneumonia. (Which is why, he thinks, pneumonia figures in the lyrics.)

He would receive daily calls from Merrick: "Is he really sick? Is he faking? We need a song."

Then the hysteria would escalate: "Should I bring Leonard Bernstein in? Who should I bring in? We've got to get the song going."

David had been working on the lyric to "I'll Never Fall In Love Again," and when Bacharach was released from the hospital he set it within a few hours. It went in that night and fulfilled Merrick's demand that it stop the show.

Bacharach and David wrote another song on the road, "Turkey Lurkey Time," which everyone liked except Merrick—until, that is, at a preview in Washington, John Kenneth Galbraith, who had come to the theater with Jacqueline Kennedy Onassis, told him he loved it. "From that moment David loved it too."

The innovation on *Promises, Promises* had to do with the changing style of pop music. It was becoming increasingly "engineered." The man in the sound booth blending voices and instruments was growing in power. He was, in the pop world, as much a "designer" as those who created the sets and costumes on Broadway.

Before *Promises, Promises* the man who controlled the musical sound in the theater was the conductor. He set the balances, he guided both the singers and the orchestra. What Bacharach wanted, however, was not the traditional Broadway sound but the pop sound that fit the music he had written. To achieve this the orchestra was placed backstage, as it had been in *I Do! I Do!* The conductor could not be seen by the actors.

The man who molded the sound was at the back of the theater, modulating the sound through a sophisticated amplification system. In a few years, with the advent of rock musicals like *Jesus Christ Superstar*, the amplification would become increasingly loud, the sound less and less "natural": but the changeover of the traditional Broadway sound to one more akin to pop music began with *Promises, Promises.*

Merrick himself, at the opening night party for *Promises, Promises,* had proclaimed Bacharach "the first original American composer since Gershwin." His music, Merrick said, had "more emotion than the music that came out of Vienna and Strauss. Young people understand it. For older people it may be an acquired taste."

The increasing use of amplification had many consequences. When Merrick imported John Osborne's *A Patriot For Me*, it starred Maximillian Schell, a hugely popular film star. To take advantage of Schell's popularity, Merrick booked the play into the Imperial, a house normally reserved for musicals.

To make sure the intimate play filled this large house, it was heavily amplified. Sound systems were still primitive on Broadway shows, designed mainly to give the actors' voices a slight boost in reaching the upper balcony (though most actors still had had vocal training that made amplification unnecessary). The amplification on *Patriot* was not understated, and immediately critics sensed there was danger. The hollowness of the sound was apparent, especially to ears not yet hardened to the omnipresence of amplification.

Patriot was noteworthy for reasons other than its electronic sound. Based on an incident in Austrian history, it was one of the first Broadway plays to deal frankly with the issue of homosexuality. Merrick had optioned it shortly after it opened in London in 1965, but he did not mount it until after the 1967 Off-Broadway *Boys in the Band* proved the subject of homosexuality was commercially viable.

By the late Sixties, Merrick was no longer a constant presence on the shows he produced. The producing itself seemed to operate as if by automatic pilot. In effect he went through the routine of being David Merrick, of importing a certain number of plays from London, of mounting a certain number of musicals for tired businessmen. But there was increasingly less pleasure or profit in it.

During rehearsals he would no longer hover in the background. He might attend a rehearsal late in the game. Everyone would be aware of him. Many knew him only by his forbidding reputation. He would speak only to one of his trusted lieutenants. His notes would immediately be implemented.

His costume—the pinstripe suit—heightened the effectiveness of these brief appearances. For all his success, close associates noted, Merrick was still a man who seemed uncomfortable, ill at ease, in his own body.

This essential discomfort made the theatricality people had noticed as far back as high school useful and necessary. An employee of the Shubert Organization remembered that when Merrick arrived for a meeting he would make a point of closing the door behind him, as if the matter they had to discuss was not just a question of show business, but one of such importance that the utmost secrecy and discretion was required. It was a charade, but, for those who knew Merrick, an oddly ingratiating one.

He still savored fights. When he imported Christopher Hampton's *The Philanthropist* in 1970, the first order of business was arranging with Equity for Alec McCowen to repeat the leading role he had created in London. By then McCowen, whom Merrick had imported for *The Matchmaker* (before Ruth Gordon and Tyrone Guthrie became embroiled in a battle over the role, which eventually went to Bobby Morse), had become a major theater star. There was no question but that Equity would accede to Merrick's demand.

A few days later Merrick informed Biff Liff that they were going back to battle for Victor Spinetti, another British actor not well known to the American public, although he had won a Tony for *Oh, What A Lovely War.* Liff thought it impossible that Equity would acquiesce on this actor and told Merrick it would be a waste of time.

"Don't you see—this is the fun of it," Merrick told him. They went to plead their seemingly hopeless case before Equity, and, of course, Merrick won.

Merrick had won so many battles that he now carried great weight, the weight he had earned from his astute judgments, from his phenomenal success.

Though he cultivated the image of himself as a reckless, boorish, selfish vulgarian, more and more people who worked in the theater saw that this was a pose. In 1968 there was a strike by Actors' Equity, one of the many strikes that plagued the administration of Mayor John Lindsay. Lindsay invited members of Equity and representatives of the League of New York Theaters and Producers, including Merrick, to settle their grievances at Gracie Mansion. Lindsay felt that of the various strikes settled there—the subway strike, the garbage strike, the taxi strike—this one had the fewest histrionics.

Within the League itself Merrick was regarded as a troublesome maverick. Once, in an effort to stem declining ticket sales, the League voted to change the curtain time from 8:30 to 7:30, hoping more people would go to the theater if they got out early. Merrick went along with the plan for a few months, then resigned from the League and changed the curtain time of his own shows to 8:00. It delighted him that in all the stories about his withdrawal from the League the papers had to mention all of his shows.

Merrick also took pleasure in disrupting business meetings of the League, a way of agitating his fellow members. (If there was any question that his belligerence was deliberate, he dispelled it years later when, like a naughty boy trying to win back an irritated parent, he asked Irene Selznick, "Wasn't it more fun when I was at the meetings?")

Nevertheless, his negotiating skills were useful to the League in dealing with the common enemy. Even the enemy valued his work as a negotiator. Larry Blyden insisted that it was Merrick, not Lindsay, who had been instrumental in bringing the two sides together.

Merrick himself said "the actors' training and natural hardiness served them well during the final eight-hour session. Actors always have to be very dramatic, and I suppose they just wore me down. About three a.m. you begin to make concessions that you might not make when you're not tired."

Merrick was a master negotiator, and one of the things he had learned was that you must never give your opponent the feeling you have won everything. His bluster about being too tired to fight—which no one who knew him took seriously—was a graceful way of covering the fact he had won all the points he considered important but left the actors with a feeling that they, too, had achieved victories.

Needless to say, Merrick did not always play the negotiator's role with finesse. He was once sent to bargain with ATPAM, the union that covers box office personnel, publicists and company managers. He had joined ATPAM during his Shumlin years.

Merrick began his negotiations with ATPAM by declaring, "You're all a bunch of thieves." One of the ATPAM negotiators became livid. "You're a member of ATPAM," he cried in a ringing tenor. "That means you're a thief too."

Merrick beamed his most devilish smile.

"And so I am," he thundered. And proceeded to negotiate.

With the passage of time and Merrick's growing involvement in other enterprises, he ceased to play a role in such negotiations. They would be handled largely by the theater owners, who were not as careful or as equitable—let alone as amusing—as he was. The theater owners often conceded things to the unions that would be onerous to producers, who had to pay the freight.

In some sense he was resting on his laurels. In a year-end column John Chapman noted wistfully, "I cannot recall David Merrick having thrown a stink bomb at a single critic. Is he getting old, soft or becoming genial? I hope not genial. Bring back the old Merrick! With him gone we are left with Edward Albee as the only dedicated critic-hater—but he has never been much fun." He remained feisty and acerbic. He dismissed the *Christian Science Monitor* as "a trade paper." During the strike he told Equity he would desist from importing English actors if they could get the *Times* to drop their British critic. The London-born Clive Barnes had assumed the chief critic's mantle in the 1967-68 season. Over the years he and Merrick got on amicably, and when Merrick praised his fairmindedness on a TV talk show Barnes said, facetiously, that it would ruin his reputation.

But, as his participation in the strike negotiations indicated, he had become a kind of elder statesman, a quirky one perhaps, but one whose word was heeded.

Binkie Beaumont, the quintessence of taste, relied heavily on Merrick's observations about the theater. Keith Baxter was once in a play trying out in Brighton and remembered how pleased Beaumont was that Merrick was coming to see it, not only because he might transfer it to New York but because he might have useful comments about the play itself. Merrick did have useful comments, but the writer and director were not interested in them. The play, whose title Baxter has forgotten, never even reached London.

Even with plays that had been successful in London, Merrick was not shy about making suggestions for New York. Often those suggestions strengthened the play significantly. One such case was Tom Stoppard's *Rosencrantz and Guildenstern Are Dead*, which opened under the auspices of the Foundation on October 16, 1967.

Stoppard's dazzling writing was a sensation in both London and New York. Here was a young writer, born in Czechoslovakia, who had mastered the English language and who brought to the stage a wit that harked back to a more literate time. In England the very idea of the play and the original use of language were enough. At first Merrick took a hands-off attitude though he knew that New York would lose patience with a wordy play, even if it were brilliant.

When the play opened in Washington it was icily received. "Tedium Ad Nauseum" was the headline of one of the reviews. Merrick too was struck by how monotonous it sounded. If the three leading roles were put on a graph, he asserted, they would all come out as one line.

There was nothing that could be done with the interpretation of the two title characters. For the play to come to life, he said, the Player King had to be reinterpreted. Robert Edison was playing the part in a poetic vein. When he refused to change his performance Merrick fired him. A young actor already playing a minor role in the production, Paul Hecht, succeeded Edison. His electrifying performance gave a new vitality to the whole play. Even Stoppard, who flew over to see it, stood at the back of the National Theater in Washington and said, "I never dreamed it like this."

With an already strong play Merrick could be useful. A weak play aroused his destructive instincts. In the spring of 1968 he produced a play Tennessee Williams had written in the Fifties, *Kingdom of Earth*. Substantially revised, it was now called *The Seven Descents of Myrtle*. The production starred Estelle Parsons, who, the year before, had won an Oscar for her supporting role in *Bonnie and Clyde*.

By the time Merrick agreed to produce *Myrtle*, it had been almost six years since Williams had had a success. The last of his plays that did well on Broadway was *Night of the Iguana*, which opened in December of 1961. Since then *The Milk Train Doesn't Stop Here* had flopped twice. Several of the plays he had written in the interim were produced in Europe but not in New York.

By this time Williams himself was in the unhappy condition in which he would remain submerged for the rest of his life. He drank. He took pills. Doctors had prescribed the medication but he was not always careful of the dosage. He made no effort to determine which pills ought not be taken with which. The overall effect was to leave him incoherent and morose. But, whatever his condition when he arrived, Merrick always made a point of having him ushered into his private office.

If the producer from St. Louis made a deliberate effort to control the way the press presented him to the public, the writer from St. Louis had done just the opposite. Ever since *Time*, in a profile in the early Fifties, had labeled him a "pervert," Williams, a naturally shy man, had been ill at ease with the press. The effect was to encourage them to present him as a degenerate, which, in turn, influenced the way the public saw his plays.

They were not treated as the work of a great poet but rather as the outpourings of a man who had lost control of himself. Moreover, by contrast to the new voices from Britain and even such new American voices as Albee, Williams seemed a bit old-fashioned.

Jose Quintero, who directed *Seven Descents of Myrtle*, had made a success of an earlier Williams play, *Summer and Smoke*. He had gone on to achieve a brilliant reputation on the basis of his revivals of Eugene O'Neill, productions which elevated the author's reputation. He was thus a logical director for the now sorely underrated Williams. But he resigned from *Myrtle* shortly before it was to open, citing "sadistic" interference by Merrick. "Poor Joe," Merrick countered angrily. "He finally got a live author and a strong producer. Apparently it has overwhelmed him."

Merrick continued importing plays from London, like the odd *Keep It in the Family* (which starred Maureen O'Sullivan and Karen Black) or *Rockefeller and the Red Indians* (a spoof of Westerns that had been produced in London under the title *The Wind in the Sassafras Trees*). It had had a decent run in London. In New York it lasted two nights.

He found another hit in Paris, *Forty Carats*, by the authors of *Cactus Flower*. This time Jay Presson Allen did the adaptation and Julie Harris was the star. The opening night critics were unreceptive. Happily, Walter Kerr, who began to write for the *Times* when the *Trib* folded and began to write Sunday reviews when Barnes began daily reviewing, liked *Forty Carats* a lot.

Using the ploy he had succeeded with earlier, Merrick had Kerr's piece set in the typeface used by the daily *Times*. Placed prominently in the Tuesday *Times*, it seemed like the opening night review. That night the audience responded to the show with an enthusiasm they hadn't shown since previews. Afterward word of mouth helped the show to a healthy run.

As he had done with *Dolly*, he replaced Julie Harris with stars rather than good actresses. June Allyson took over the role and gave good performances, though very often she did not go on. From the minute the play was announced Zsa Zsa Gabor proposed herself for the part.

When business with the ever-absent Allyson was waning, Merrick, uncharacteristically, showed up at an audition for a small part because he knew that Jay Presson Allen would be there.

"Do you think it's time to prostitute the show with Zsa Zsa?" he asked her. It was the most direct, economical way of explaining his position, as well as being witty.

At first she was thoughtful. Then she laughed. If it would buy time she was agreeable. Zsa Zsa was hired.

Merrick still had no gift for finding original plays. He turned down the opportunity to produce Leonard Gershe's *Butterflies Are Free*, despite his friendliness toward Gershe during *Destry Rides Again*. When Byron Goldman produced the play and it became a hit, Merrick chided Gershe: "You should have pressed me harder."

He never read plays and he was reluctant to act on the judgment of those he hired to do it for him. When Judy Bryant, who read scripts for him, recommended a play by Robin Maugham called *The Servant*, he showed no interest. A few years later it became a hugely successful film with Dirk Bogarde.

The closest he came to finding an American playwright of

interest was Woody Allen. After the great success of *Don't Drink the Water*, during the 1966-67 season, he produced *Play It Again, Sam*, which starred Allen and Diane Keaton in 1969. Allen was able to use Merrick's image for his own comic purposes when he told a reporter, "Mr. Merrick is giving me no author's percentage. Instead I get the orange juice and Hershey bar concessions in the theater . . . I don't care what they say about Mr. Merrick. To me, he's a Santa Claus—with a luger."

And, of course, though many of the hits Merrick produced were of secondary quality and interest, his great hit *Hello, Dolly!* just ran and ran. After Pearl Bailey left the cast in 1969, it reverted to an all-white show, and Phyllis Diller took over the lead. In 1970 Merrick finally persuaded Ethel Merman to assume the role that had been written for her. Jerry Herman brought out some of the songs that had been written expressly for her.

Originally she was only supposed to do it for six months, but in September, she agreed to do it for the rest of the year so that *Dolly* could overtake *My Fair Lady* as the longest-running show on Broadway. (Her reward for staying on and helping Merrick break the record was a closing night gift of two bottles of indifferently chosen champagne.)

If Merrick was indeed an elder statesman of the theater, it was of a severely diminished institution. Each season during the Sixties, more and more theaters remained dark. For Merrick this was not yet a worry because his own track record remained remarkable. In 1969 he boasted to an associate that he had municipal bonds worth $20 million. This, the colleague knew, was a way of letting him understand that the $20 million represented a fraction of his holdings, since municipal bonds are what the wealthy use as a kind of nest egg, a way to invest paltry sums "just in case."

The money, however, never gave him a feeling of ease outside his own world. In the summer of 1969 he spent a few weeks on Martha's Vineyard with Cecilia Ann. The summer before he had accepted an invitation from the Kanins to spend a little time with

Leaving the custody battle, with Etan

them in Edgartown. One of the first things he asked when he saw the little town, still unspoiled in the Sixties, five years before it became the backdrop for *Jaws,* was if they thought it would be a good place to send his daughter and her governess. The Kanins thought it would be a wonderful place for a city girl to spend the summer.

Merrick had won custody of Cecilia Ann in an ugly custody battle with Jeanne. To vanquish an already broken woman, to wrest her baby from her, knowing the child would simply be put in the care of professionals was as heartless a victory as Merrick would ever win. He claimed he could do nothing for Cecilia Ann unless he had custody of her.

Cecilia Ann required special care. It could have been the heavy drinking her mother did during pregnancy. It could have been the tight outfits Jeanne wore—either at Merrick's insistence, so people would not know she was pregnant, or at her own initiative, not to remind him of her condition. In either case it soon became clear that little Cecilia Ann was mentally retarded.

At first he had wanted to minimize his contact with the child, but more and more she laid claim to his emotions in a way no one else had. Linda Otto, who worked in the Merrick office, remembered hearing his baby talk to Cecilia Ann on the phone, an unusual sound to emanate from the red office. The baby softened even Schlissel, who kept cookies in his desk for her occasional visits. Her welfare became a matter of deep concern to her father.

Through the Logans he found out about special schools and institutions for retarded children. He knew that she would require special care all her life and in the process of the inevitable divorce with Jeanne, he made special provisions for their daughter.

But now, faced with abundant evidence that Jeanne was not a good mother, he had to win custody of Cecila Ann.

Among the witnesses Merrick presented was the novelist Barbara Taylor Bradford, whom Jeanne had befriended when Bradford came to New York in the early Sixties. Gilbert had introduced Bradford to the lively world of show business and cafe society. Now Bradford testified that she was an unfit mother.

"That's the kind of friends she had," Merrick sneered. That Jeanne was a negligent mother was, alas, beyond doubt. She had been similarly neglectful with her daughter by Justin Gilbert. Merrick had arranged for that daughter to go to Brandeis, but she dropped out and disappeared from sight.

Nevertheless it crushed Jeanne to see Bradford bolstering her husband's already unbeatable case. It seemed gratuitous.

In the courtroom with Jeanne, holding her hand and feeding her tuna fish sandwiches, was Jerry Orbach's wife Marta. The Orbachs had been at the hospital when Jeanne gave birth to Cecilia Ann. One Christmas, when Jeanne was in an alcoholic recovery center, the Orbachs had gone to visit her and brought her a little Christmas tree. A few nights later they saw Merrick at a Christmas party. "You're a young attractive couple," he told them. "Don't you have better things to do than visit drunks?"

He could see they were stunned. He leaned down and said to Marta, "Nevertheless that was a beautiful thing to have done."

He gave her a quick kiss on the cheek and walked away.

Now Marta felt compelled to be at Jeanne's side as the child was litigated from her. Marta herself had been the subject of a vicious custody trial as a little girl in San Francisco and knew what Jeanne and her daughter would be going through.

But she didn't want to hurt her husband's career. So she thought she ought to call Merrick. She began explaining to Helen Nickerson why she was calling.

"This has nothing to do with Jerry," she said. "I was the child in a custody case . . ."

Nickerson interrupted her. "I know," she said. "My father was your mother's lawyer."

Nickerson remembered the case well, not simply because it was a celebrated case at the time but because Marta's mother could not afford to pay her father. She was, however, a talented artist and paid him by painting his portrait, which still hung in Nickerson's apartment.

Even Marta knew that Jeanne was not a good mother. But she felt that there was something brave about Jeanne's presence in court. Rather than crumble before Merrick's lawyers, she had to make an appearance.

"She was a Southern belle hanging on to the last vestige of good manners," Orbach recalled. "The only way she could show she was a good mother was to put up what she knew would be a losing battle."

That summer Merrick himself came to spend some time with his daughter, for whom he had rented a suite in a hotel near the Kanins' house in Edgartown. One night they were all invited to a barbecue at the William Styrons, one of the social centers of Martha's Vineyard. The guests were all impressed to meet the famous Broadway producer and his six-year-old daughter. As on other occasions, when he was surrounded by eminent people from worlds other than his own, Merrick was polite, subdued and not very talkative.

For Cecilia Ann that summer meant the discovery of butterflies. As her father watched, the little girl ran along the beach, her governess not far behind, chasing butterflies.

CHAPTER THIRTY

ONE OF THE BEWILDERING phenomena about *Mata Hari* was that absolutely nothing had been under control, an exceedingly rare thing to happen on a David Merrick musical. Part of it was the fault of Minnelli. He was so damned charming, so seductive that Merrick could refuse him nothing.

When it became apparent that things had gotten perilously out of hand, Merrick had moved in to exercise authority in one area where he thought he was still in command—his star, the beautiful and not very talented Marisa Mell. There were limits to what he could do with her on stage, but he thought he could put his foot down on what she did offstage. Even that proved beyond his ken.

He took a particular dislike to the man she was seeing.

"Why are you going out with that pimp?" he once asked her.

She was annoyed. She had no intention of dropping the man she was seeing—a man who, after all, exercised considerable power in Hollywood—simply to please the producer of this bizarre and pointless musical. No doubt she passed the insult on to her boyfriend.

The boyfriend came to have a great deal to do with the producer, and the insult may have guaranteed that, from the beginning of their relationship, there was bad blood between them.

The boyfriend's name was Robert Evans, a strikingly handsome man who had enjoyed a brief, lucrative career as a child actor. He had then worked for several years in the garment business of his brother Charles Evans, whose firm, Evan-Picone, was a Seventh Avenue powerhouse. As a young man he had returned to Hollywood. Norma Shearer had spotted him by a swimming pool and recommended him to play her late husband, the producer Irving Thalberg, in the 1957 *Man of a Thousand Faces.* In 1960 he had begun producing.

In 1966, when he was thirty-six, he was appointed a vice-president at Paramount in an effort to combat charges that the company lacked youth. By 1970 he was head of production at Paramount, with whom Merrick had a contract to produce several films.

Temperamentally he had much in common with Merrick. He had once told an interviewer, "I don't want a director to talk with me and then leave and say, 'Gee, what a nice guy.' I want him to say, 'That bastard! That son of a bitch!' Because they always come back and say, 'Well, you were right, let's talk.'" Two men so eager to alienate and enrage their colleagues, however, were not likely to become chums.

Merrick had begun visiting Hollywood on a regular basis in the Forties, when he was still working for Shumlin. By the time he started working there he had alienated some of its most influential people. The powerful agent Irving "Swifty" Lazar, who worked on both coasts, despised him. "He just was not a gentleman. He was a tough, unrelenting fellow who always acted as if he was mad at everybody. There was never a time when he would soft pedal anything. He operated only in one gear.

"He had utter contempt for contracts. What he depended on was the reluctance of people to get into lawsuits. He traded on that, and he had lawyers who encouraged him. Most people are wary of lawsuits. He thrived on them."

Billy Wilder, another pillar of Old Hollywood, also despised him. Merrick turned two Wilder films, *The Apartment* and *Some Like It Hot,* into stage musicals; the 1968 *Promises, Promises* and the 1972 *Sugar*, respectively. Wilder found Merrick relentless while in pursuit of these properties, indifferent once he had landed his quarry. Wilder eventually made deals for them only to get Merrick off his back. He would discover years later that he had in fact deeded Merrick *all* the rights in both properties. Wilder admitted Merrick could be charming in his campaign to secure the rights, but added, "I'm sure even Hitler was charming when he courted Eva Braun."

With his prodigious talent for alienating both young and old, Merrick began what became an increasingly frustrating, unrewarding chapter in his career, an attempt to overwhelm Hollywood Merrick-style.

Paramount contracted him to produce as his first film one of his own plays, Robert Marasco's *Child's Play*, which Merrick had presented on Broadway in 1970. Merrick himself joked that *Child's Play* was an on-the-job training program: "I should have paid Paramount tuition I learned so much."

Its plot about dark goings on in a Catholic boys' school was the sort of adolescent hocus-pocus that generally does not translate well to the screen. Merrick suspected Paramount was attracted to its supernatural element because of the great success in 1970 of *Rosemary's Baby*.

Merrick had wanted William Friedkin to direct. Friedkin had successfully translated *The Boys in the Band* to the screen. Evans thought Friedkin was "a bum" and refused to let Merrick hire him. This censure turned into a boon for Friedkin, who directed instead a picture called *The French Connection*, which made a fortune for Twentieth Century Fox and won "the bum" an Oscar. Years later Merrick was delighted to point out that Evans only hired Friedkin after the staggering success of another piece of hocus pocus called *The Exorcist*. None of the films Friedkin made for Paramount in the wake of *The Exorcist* turned any profit.

Merrick said both Joseph Mankiewicz and Alfred Hitchcock were interested in *Child's Play*. Evans pronounced them both "over the hill."

Eventually they agreed on Sidney Lumet, whose career alternated between gritty portraits of New York life (*The Pawnbroker, Serpico, Prince of the City*) and adaptations of theater, ranging from *Long Day's Journey Into Night* to *The Seagull.* Among Lumet's virtues, as far as Merrick was concerned, was his reputation for bringing in pictures on time and on—if not under—budget.

Another virtue was that he had worked with the man who would star in *Child's Play,* Marlon Brando, whom Lumet had directed in one of his pivotal films, *The Fugitive Kind.* In 1971 Brando's career was floundering in Hollywood Limbo. Brando still carried a mystique in New York and among some moviegoers. But in the eyes of the industry he was, like Manckiewicz and Hitchcock, a has-been, an actor who represented more trouble than he was worth at the box office. (A year later his appearance in *The Godfather* would change that.)

Lumet was aware that if Brando became unhappy he was perfectly capable of "walking through" a film without giving a real performance. He also knew Merrick and Brando had not hit it off: "That man is impossible, Sidney," Brando told him.

But he felt Brando was taking *Child's Play* seriously. He was asking questions, Lumet felt, "not destructively, but to get his own inner-logic in order."

On the first day of rehearsal Brando asked a question about a lapse in logic in the script. Lumet had an assistant call Merrick. "The question struck me as completely sensible. I don't remember what it was, but it was something on the order of, 'Why didn't he just call the cops?' He felt there was a tremendous hole in the script.

"You can never have a hole in a melodrama. Marlon simply wanted to plug the hole."

Merrick's response was typically suspicious: "Well, there he goes with his destructiveness again. You tell him at rehearsal tomorrow that he is to play the script he accepted."

A few nights later, after a long day of rehearsal, Lumet received a phone call from Brando wishing him well but saying he had instructed his lawyers to disengage him from the project.

Merrick told the press that he had fought with Brando because the latter wanted him to fire David Rounds, who had won a Tony for his performance of the same role on Broadway, in favor of his old friend and former roommate Wally Cox, whose career had been in a permanent tailspin since his TV appearance as Mr. Peepers in the early Fifties.

Lumet was unaware of any such altercation. He believed Brando when he said he could not work under the conditions Merrick had established. Lumet was not happy either: "He's one of those people who think by creating crises you get good work. I take exactly the opposite approach. Tension is not a spur to creativity. Athletes get hurt when tension is there."

Lumet was also aware of how little Merrick understood the business of making movies. *Child's Play* was being shot in Tarrytown, New York, in the Convent of the Sacred Heart. (When Lumet originally had shown Merrick the location Merrick pronounced the room "too big." Lumet assured him that in movies size is totally changeable. When Merrick saw the same room in rushes, he told Lumet it looked "marvelous.")

One day Lumet told the production manager he would need a crane for certain shots. The crane would have to be brought up from Washington. The next day Lumet found out Merrick had cancelled the order, simply because he felt it cost too much. Lumet informed him the crane was essential for the location and asked to see Merrick's "shot list" (which is nothing more than a breakdown of the screenplay into scenes and camera angles.)

Merrick had no idea what Lumet was talking about. The crane was brought up.

Brando was replaced by Robert Preston. *Child's Play* opened and shut so quickly almost no one noticed it. For Lumet, the tragedy was that the film's nosedive into obscurity carried with it what he considered a great performance by James Mason.

Merrick's Hollywood debut ran concurrently with another drama, an attempted takeover of Twentieth Century Fox.

By the time he began contemplating Hollywood as a new territory to conquer, he already had a considerable financial interest in it. By the beginning of 1971 he was the major stockholder of Fox, a dubious distinction since the company was in catastrophic financial condition (in part due to its problems with Merrick on the release of *Hello, Dolly!*). He owned between 200,000 and 225,00 of Fox's eight million common shares.

In 1969 he had been given a promissory note assuring payment of $1,850,000 by 1972, in exchange for which Fox was allowed to release the film of *Dolly* in December, while the show continued its run on Broadway.

Fox lost $21.3 million in the first nine months of 1970. Among the big losers was *Hello, Dolly!* but it was not Fox's only turkey that year. Inspired by the colossal success of its *Sound of Music* in 1965, Fox had embarked on a series of movie musicals, all of which bombed.

Even such runaway successes as *Butch Cassidy and the Sundance Kid* and *M*A*S*H*, both low budget films that were extremely profitable, could not pull Fox out of the red. By the end of 1970 Fox's losses totaled $77.4 million. Because about $67 million worth of bank and insurance company loans had fallen into default, the company was now on the verge of bankruptcy. Merrick's note for $1,850,000 was feeling more and more like paper.

In addition to protecting his own vested interests, Merrick had personal reasons for wanting to take over Fox. It would give him enormous satisfaction to see its longtime chairman, Darryl F. Zanuck, deposed. Zanuck had insulted him in public. At the 1970 annual meeting Merrick had asked Zanuck if he could use one of the microphones on the dais since the one provided for shareholders did not seem to be working. Zanuck looked at him, chewed on his cigar and said, "Mr. Merrick, it will be a long time before you make it up to this dais."

This was the sort of provocation Merrick relished. In the early months of 1971 newspapers buzzed with reports that Merrick was allied with MGM's president James Aubrey and other insurgent stockholders to attempt a takeover of Fox.

"For three cents I mobilized an entire corporation," he boasted to friends. That was the cost of the stamp he used for the letter requesting a list of stockholders, a list available to any other stockholder. His name on the letter, however, had forced the company to hire a corporate public relations firm and a team of lawyers expert at thwarting unfriendly takeovers, both costly measures for the already beleaguered Fox.

Zanuck was so convinced Merrick would stop at nothing to wrest control of the company from him that he also hired private investigators to tail him. The knowledge that his every move was being reported back to Zanuck brought Merrick huge enjoyment.

He liked the idea of nurturing Zanuck's fears of his unorthodox behavior. Every time he drove away from the Beverly Hills Hotel in a chauffeured limousine Merrick made a point of throwing himself to the floor of the car as if he were nervous about being tailed.

He sensed the naivete of his opponent, who had imagined that Merrick might be visiting allies of whose existence Zanuck's forces were unaware. Any business Merrick wanted to conduct—secret or not—could be done on the telephone. It could even have been done from New York. But he loved the idea that his simplest actions could create such consternation. He traveled far more widely and more often than necessary in order to exercise his tails.

Merrick's supposed ally, James Aubrey, with whom he met in January of 1971, was MGM's third president in 11 months. Nicknamed "the smiling Cobra," Aubrey had achieved great notoriety as the president of CBS from 1959 to 1965. Aubrey had been tapped to bring MGM under control after the unwieldy company had undergone three proxy battles.

Aubrey was one of the very few men in the entertainment business whose behavior could make Merrick look decent and humane. One of Aubrey's priorities when he arrived in late 1969 was to reduce the MGM payroll by about forty percent. One of his assistants asked if it might not be better to institute the cuts after the holidays.

"What holidays?" Aubrey asked.

Aubrey met with Merrick, Richard Brandt, president of the Trans-Lux theater chain, and David Factor, of the Max Factor Company. He proposed a merger with Fox that might help both MGM and Fox. Fox rejected the offer. At that point a proxy battle was set off between Zanuck and a group of dissident shareholders. That group included his own son Richard and Richard's co-producer David Brown.

Both sides courted Merrick, who behaved, a management negotiator recalled, "like a chameleon." It was hard to know where his loyalties really lay.

Zanuck was now a figurehead, the last of the great moguls from the golden years of Hollywood to have any position in the industry. The day to day running of Fox, however, was no longer in Zanuck's hands. It had been given to a young East Coast financial expert, 41-year-old Dennis Stanfill, with whom Merrick had a civil, entirely businesslike relationship.

While Merrick talked business with Stanfill he delighted in playing on the elder Zanuck's irrational fears. That Zanuck feared him—to a point that made no sense—there was no doubt. Zanuck was once sitting with his son and David Brown on a beach in Acapulco. The three were discussing Merrick's intentions in hushed tones. All three wore bathing suits, and there was no one near them. But Zanuck was convinced their conversation was being bugged by agents of Merrick. He insisted they swim out from shore to continue their chat.

At times the elder Zanuck was mistrustful even of his son's closest associate, Brown. He knew that Merrick and Brown had known one another for a long time in New York and imagined that Brown might be a double agent. "How do we know that David is not in his employ?" he once asked his son. Ultimately Brown and the younger Zanuck discovered that they were indeed being bugged, not by Merrick but by the forces led by Zanuck's father.

Eventually Merrick and the elder Zanuck agreed to meet.

Although Zanuck kept a suite in the Plaza Hotel, he was afraid that Merrick might have it bugged. Zanuck would not go to Merrick's office. Nor would he meet him in any of Merrick's numerous Manhattan apartments. The two rented a random room in the Plaza to have their discussion "with no seconds and no bugging."

The outcome was that Merrick sided with the elder Zanuck. Despite his early resentment, he saw in the aging tycoon a kinsman, a man who had created himself anew in the fertile soil of Hollywood just as he himself had done on Broadway. Both were the products of poverty. Both had become snobs—insistent that everything they represented had to be regal.

Merrick came to respect, even to like the old man. Whatever his misgivings about how Zanuck had treated him, he hated the insurgents even more. Except for Zanuck and Brown, they were not even show business people. Merrick saw them as greedy opportunists, wealthy men eager to bask in the media spotlight you get from making movies rather than, say, ball bearings.

In February of 1971 he agreed to remain neutral in the proxy battle. The agreement with the Fox management included, among other things, a guarantee that Merrick's $1,850,000 promissory note would be paid. Merrick denied there was any connection between his agreeing to stay out of the battle and the guarantee for the money owed him.

The rapprochement with Zanuck was his first and last significant victory in Hollywood.

CHAPTER THIRTY-ONE

I F MERRICK WAS FASCINATED by grand old men like Zanuck, he was also terribly aware of the generation gap, the chasm of twenty years that separated him from the men he was dealing with in Hollywood—men like Aubrey and Stanfill and Evans.

Joel Thurm, who worked in the Merrick office for most of the Sixties, before becoming a successful Hollywood TV producer and casting director, joined the organization at a time when everyone wore jackets and ties. One morning he decided to wear platform shoes, bell bottom jeans and a marine dress uniform jacket. Merrick arrived, dressed immaculately. He looked at Thurm and then declared, "No matter what anybody says, you wear that."

Merrick could appreciate the charm of the burgeoning youth culture, even if youthfulness was never a quality people associated with Merrick. The look he had cultivated starting in high school was of a mature, successful banker, not a young man on the go. Now he had to reverse gears. He made some discreet inquiries about plastic surgery. New York, as a Jet Set capital, had a wealth of cosmetic surgeons, but Merrick was loath to have his rejuvenation the subject of local gossip. He opted instead for a highly recommended surgeon in a private Swiss clinic.

Merrick was, in all things, a perfectionist. He drove his tailor crazy with little details every time he had a suit made. (He drove him crazier by never paying him, assuring him that the publicity he got by being known as David Merrick's tailor was worth more than the steep fees he charged.)

If he was fastidious about his suits, how much more demanding was he about his face. Unhappy with the results of his Swiss sojourn, he had some touch-up work done by Dr. John Converse, one of the most fashionable Park Avenue plastic surgeons.

As early as the mid-Sixties he had begun to fret about the loss of his hair. At one point he summoned Harvey Sabinson to his office to show him an article in *Parade* about hair transplants. He offered to pay for Sabinson's transplant if they did it together; but the latter had been bald long enough that he knew people would joke if he suddenly sprouted hair.

Merrick could not accept the fact that in a few years the image he had worked so hard to build would be undone by the natural incursions of time. A bald Merrick would not be the imposing figure he had been groomed for.

He ordered a toupee from a Hollywood wigmaker whose clients included Fred Astaire. The toupee was well made, but Merrick never bothered to learn how best to wear it. He threw it on. Moreover, with the passing years he became increasingly careless with it, never bothering to send it to be cleaned.

People were amazed that someone who went to such pains to create an image could be so cavalier about his "rug." Some sensed that it was a way of showing his contempt for people, a way to suggest that his power was so great he did not have to worry about conventional niceties like wearing a wig properly.

Neither the rejuvenation of the face nor the embellishment of the cranium gave Merrick the youthful image that might have made him more acceptable in Hollywood. Nor was he about to go bare-chested and wear gold chains. No one really expected him to do so, but they expected some loosening of his gloomy visage, some relaxation of his formal manner to suit the "laid-back" style of Los Angeles. He continued to dress as if he were on his way to Wall Street. He didn't play tennis. Hollywood had always made sharp distinctions between insiders and outsiders.

Merrick did nothing to ingratiate himself to the insiders.

He was a man approaching sixty. In other times he might be reaping the harvest of a lifetime devoted singlemindedly to the theater. The culture had changed with astonishing rapidity. It was now a youth culture, based on a rejection of the middlebrow tastes and interests of the older generation.

Throughout the late Fifties, when Merrick was building his reputation and his audience, the first readers to receive bulletins about a new show, the first to be offered a chance to send for tickets were not the readers of the *New York Times*, but rather those of the *Saturday Review of Literature*.

At the height of its success, in the late Fifties, the *Saturday Review* had about 600,000 subscribers nationwide, all of whom were attracted to the arts. One reason given for its great surge of readership in the late Forties and Fifties was that it was the first magazine to feature regular reviews of LP recordings, both classical and jazz.

These were the people who were likely to be interested in a play by John Osborne or Shelagh Delaney, in the directorial efforts of Peter Brook, or even in a musical based on Eugene O'Neill or Thornton Wilder.

By 1971 *Saturday Review* was floundering. That year Norman Cousins, who had guided the magazine for thirty-one years, its greatest period of influence and financial viability, retired in disgust. The new owners of the magazine moved its editorial offices to San Francisco. The magazine went through numerous restructurings in the next thirteen years. Its ultimate demise in 1984 was proof positive of what had been clear thirteen years earlier: the great middlebrow audience that sustained it—and that sustained the theater of David Merrick—was a phenomenon of the past.

In New York young people were not interested in the theater at all. They hadn't even bought *Hair*. That vicarious sensation was for the older generation, who still saw the youth rebellion from the outside. With its mild rock score, its harmless attempts at social satire and its ten seconds of nudity, *Hair* exploited the middle-aged audience's desire to spend a few hours as tourists in the land of the young.

Young people simply didn't go to the theater. "We [in the theater] are fighting a rear guard action, and I'm standing on the beaches of Dunkirk," Merrick declared. "And there is much more glamour in film than in the theater.

"Young people didn't go to *The Sound of Music*—but they stand shivering in line to see *The Graduate* and *Blow Up*. We on Broadway keep chasing the creative talent off to the films. Writers get more excitement out of writing for films, more money and more security. What more could they ask for?"

If the young went to the theater at all, they went to avant-garde productions like *Che*, a 1970 Off-Off-Broadway piece that offered the then novel spectacle of simulated sodomy. The play had been closed on charges of obscenity. Merrick was called as an expert witness in the subsequent trial, and he agreed that the play was obscene. He called it "patently offensive, vulgar, lewd and very dull." He said the playwright, Lennox Raphael, "had no talent whatsoever and should seek vocational guidance."

But he knew that in the theatrical climate of 1970 *Che* mattered more than anything that interested him. That year he imported Peter Brook's harsh, gymnastic production of *A Midsummer Night's Dream*. Brook's dark, abrasive vision of Shakespeare's fairy play suggested that in London, too, there was to be no smooth transition from one generation to another. Brook, the ultimate iconoclast, understood what younger people wanted. (This production, which featured such unknown actors as Ben Kingsley and Alan Howard, would be the last quasi-"conventional" theater Brook did before he devoted himself entirely to experimentalism.)

Not everything Merrick produced was aimed at bridging the generation gap. In the fall of 1970 he produced a ripping revival of Noel Coward's *Private Lives* starring Tammy Grimes and Brian Bedford.

Merrick's old friend and London associate Binkie Beaumont was, in the world of the youth culture, completely at sea. Beaumont had come to prominence with his grand productions of the classics, starring actors like John Gielgud, Ralph Richardson and Edith Evans. Aside from the high level of the acting what people remembered about these productions was the supreme elegance of the sets and costumes, all of which reflected Beaumont's infallible taste. Even in London such theater now seemed entirely old hat. Beaumont had cultivated none of the younger, vital writers. Nor the younger, grittier actors.

Even Merrick, across the Atlantic Ocean, had maintained a closer tie with the Royal Court than Beaumont, though in 1969 he jeopardized that tie needlessly by trying to outbid Alex Cohen to bring David Storey's *Home*, with Gielgud and Richardson, to New York. In England at the time a handshake could be as valid as a written contract. Merrick tried to offer the Royal Court more generous terms than Cohen after the latter had shaken hands with the management. The management, not so radical as to be oblivious to the value of a dollar, tried to renege on Cohen. He sued and won. The English judicial system reiterated the legal validity of the handshake.

If youth had altered so radically the face of theater in New York and London, what impact would it have on Los Angeles, a city where the altars of youth were tended with almost fanatical devotion? The answer was not long in coming. Los Angeles is a city where everything can be determined in The Grosses. Zanuck's multimillion dollar musical extravaganzas languished at the box office. A $400,000 film called *Easy Rider* took in $30 million.

When Merrick had first arrived in New York he had "studied" the theater. He had applied himself to the resources of the theater collection of the New York Public Library. To study the movies he simply went to them. Though he could have seen them in the comfort of plush screening rooms he preferred standing in line with other paying customers. The only way you could really gauge their impact, he thought, was to experience them with real people. That was where he saw the young people who were not going to the theater. That was how he understood the vitality of the movies in the culture that had changed so radically in the Sixties.

He observed the difference between the opening of a film and the opening of a play. "An opening on Broadway, even if it's an unheralded play or a flop, is exciting. If it's a hit there's nothing like it. A Broadway opening is an event. The opening of a picture is rarely glamorous. If it's a charity benefit, maybe they'll get out the klieg lights and light up the sky. But most of the time it opens somewhere on Third Avenue at noon on a Thursday and 150 senior citizens turn out. That's about it."

His embrace of the youth culture went beyond standing in line at Cinema 1. He had found a new female companion, Etan Aronson, a young Swede with a diminutive figure and a face of gamine poignancy. He met the former airline stewardess at a party given by Dr. Frederick Atkins, the partner of her then beau. Atkins, a man of mature years, was a pioneer of sorts, one of the first to cash in on one of the mainstays of the youth culture, The Diet Book.

Years later, during a long and turbulent divorce, Merrick spread the rumor that she had asked a friend that night which were the wealthiest men in the room. Two were pointed out to her, one a wealthy lawyer, the other Merrick. According to the rumor, for a few months she slept with both unbeknownst to the other while making up her mind that she would pursue Merrick. It was a story that sounded familiar to Etan. She had first heard Merrick tell it about one of Alan Jay Lerner's wives. Those who knew Etan discredited the story. Moreover anyone who saw the two together knew that the electricity between them was genuine.

They were married in September of 1969. Three weeks later, at his suggestion, they got a Mexican divorce. Once again marriage had transformed Merrick into a hostage. Once released from marriage's constraints, their prison again became their home.

Merrick did not want the marriage publicized. Before they were wed he introduced her to friends as "the future ex-Mrs. Merrick." After they were wed he didn't introduce her at all.

Once, when Binkie Beaumont was staying with Irene Selznick, Merrick came to discuss business with him. Selznick invited him to stay for dinner. He asked if he might include a guest. When he went to the telephone in another room Beaumont became very excited. A devoted gossip, he had heard that Merrick had married again. Now they would meet the new wife. The young woman had been instructed to enter through the service entrance. Whether or not Merrick introduced her by name—Selznick could not remember—he certainly never introduced Etan as his wife.

The new Merricks lived in the same apartment building as Cecilia Ann and her governess, Nan Patterson, who had once worked for Deborah Kerr. With the hauteur of the true nanny, Patterson once got into an argument with the woman she knew as Merrick's girlfriend. Etan was outraged that this servant would treat David Merrick's wife with such contempt. Patterson was not convinced that Etan was Merrick's wife until Etan went back to her apartment to get her marriage certificate. (Needless to say she did not show her the divorce certificate of three weeks later.)

Etan thought of herself as a "flower child." Her earlier affairs had taught her about material comforts, but in many ways, in her early years with Merrick, she maintained a Sixties simplicity, wearing unaffected dresses with monotonous regularity. Nan Patterson dressed with unusual flair. When they would meet in the corridor Merrick would praise Nan Patterson's outfits pointedly, looking awkwardly at Etan's comparatively drab outfits.

Had she been a golddigger, as he later maintained, she would have been eager to spend his money on clothes; moreover, having had a brief taste of what it was like to be Mrs. David Merrick, she could have used the occasion of the Mexican divorce to exact a financial settlement and begin an easier life.

But Etan had opted for the long haul. If the youth culture had this kind of strength and indomitability, perhaps it was a worthy object of Merrick's fascination.

CHAPTER THIRTY-TWO

F OR MOST OF HIS CAREER Merrick was used to taking out full page ads and sometimes double page ads in the *New York Times*. By the early Seventies his power and fame were such that he could achieve great effects by purchasing minuscule amounts of space on the front page.

On Christmas Eve of 1971 he purchased a tiny ad that simply stated: "MY CHRYSLER IMPERIAL IS A PILE OF JUNK. (signed) David Merrick."

The ensuing brouhaha, the *Wall Street Journal* later declared in a front page story, had made Merrick "the Ralph Nader of the limousine set."

Merrick had bought the car several years before (he and Chrysler—pre-Iaccoca Chrysler, to be sure—could not even agree on the date the car was purchased), and he claimed it had spent more time being repaired than it did on the road.

Merrick's claims and Chrysler's counterclaims became so well known that *Harper's Bazaar*, as part of a fashion layout, showed a young couple leaving a car declaring "Whatever David Merrick says about the Chrysler Imperial, I like it."

In the wake of Merrick's complaint ad, the *Times* was deluged by other consumers wanting to place similar ads. The newspaper decided to stop running them. Merrick suggested they devote a

Merrick at an opening, with Etan.

whole classified column to such ads—"a complaint column where people could sound off about their toasters, their air-conditioners and everything else. Hell, the *Times* is almost bankrupt, they need all the money they can get." The *Journal* hastened to point out that the *Times* reported a $9.5 million profit in 1971. Merrick liked to complain about the *Times* because he was a stockholder and frequently aired his grievances at the annual meetings.

Merrick prepared a cartoon ad in which a horse was pulling a large car labeled Chrysler toward a junkyard. The caption read "Good Riddance!" and was signed, in very large letters, "David Merrick." The *Miami Herald* ran it. Most other newspapers to which it was submitted refused it. A third ad, a little two-by-four in which Merrick exhorted: "CHRYSLER? Try it—you WON'T like it!," was submitted to the *Journal*, which rejected it.

In September of 1972 he took a similar tiny ad on the front page of the *Times* to announce "It's difficult to be a Dem in '72." The two-line ad prompted the *Times* to interview him on his political views. A life-long Democrat, Merrick, who had written a tongue-in-cheek negative review of the Republican convention of 1968 for the *Washington Post*, had decided four years later to support Nixon.

Several days later Dore Schary, the former head of MGM, was interviewed responding, point by point, to Merrick's remarks. What had begun as a little joke had escalated into serious political debate.

On the East Coast the Merrick mystique was as powerful as ever. Perhaps with his next project—a film version of F. Scott Fitzgerald's *The Great Gatsby*—Merrick could bring the other Coast into line. The story of a Midwesterner who creates a new identity, conquers New York but remains a loner, an outsider, seemed an ideal property for Merrick, who had followed a remarkably similar path.

It was Delynn who urged him to acquire the rights to the novel. One of the names that appeared on The Flimsy, the infamous list of people to cultivate, was that of Scottie Lanahan Smith, the daughter of Scott and Zelda Fitzgerald, whom Delynn introduced to Merrick. Merrick applied all his charm to Scottie, who gave him the screen rights to *The Great Gatsby*. She was apparently unaware of Artie Shaw's rights to do a Broadway musical. (The litigation between Shaw and Merrick dragged on for years. In 1977 Shaw received $118,200 from Merrick and Paramount, a fraction of the $5.4 million for which he had sued.)

Around the time *The Great Gatsby* was supposed to start shooting, Merrick's nemesis, Bob Evans, suffered a humiliating personal loss. In the summer of 1972 his wife, Ali MacGraw, ran off with Steve McQueen, with whom she was shooting a film called, ironically, *The Getaway.*

For Evans the Fitzgerald film became a way to lure his wife back. She was supposed to play Daisy opposite Robert Redford in the title role. The contracts had been signed, the rest of the cast hired, the costumes begun, and an estate in Newport had been hired for location shooting. Once she became unavailable Evans lost interest. Citing problems with the costumes, he postponed the production, a loss of $500,000 to Paramount.

If he could not work on the film with the woman he loved he did not want to co-produce it with a man he loathed.

Merrick, however, had drawn up the contracts personally, with his inimitable attention to detail. They left Evans no loophole for disengaging him from the picture. More important, Merrick by then had the complete confidence of Scottie Lanahan Smith, who made it clear to Evans there would be no picture without Merrick's participation.

Evans took a new tack. Quoting a line from Paramount's blockbuster hit from the previous spring, he actually told Merrick, "I'll make you an offer you can't refuse."

Merrick found this a pathetic way for two adults to begin a conversation, but he heard Evans out. If Merrick would let him produce *Gatsby*, he would let Merrick produce *Paper Moon*, a new film by Peter Bogdanovich, who had achieved a huge critical and commercial success with *The Last Picture Show.* He would also let Merrick produce the sequel to Francis Ford Coppola's *The Godfather*. Both of these films would become huge hits. Merrick spurned the offer.

"You might find a dead horse in your bed if you talk like that," Evans told him. Merrick did not back down. He wanted to produce *Gatsby*.

Evans pulled rank on Merrick. He tried to urge Charles Bludhorn, the head of Gulf and Western, Paramount's parent company, to cancel the production completely. Merrick was not averse to this development. He went to Bludhorn himself and offered him $1.5 million—in cash—to secure the rights from Paramount so he could produce the film himself. Bludhorn, a man of Teutonic steeliness, was unmoved.

His refusal drew out Merrick's persuasiveness and charm. "I don't understand," Merrick told him. "Paramount is a public company with stockholders. How can you turn down a million and a half dollars you may never see again?"

Bludhorn was direct: "Because you could make it for another studio, and if it was a smash hit, we'd look ridiculous. I'd rather throw away a million and a half of the stockholders' money than have that happen."

This was a decision Merrick could respect. He, after all, had thrown away almost the same amount to close *Breakfast at Tiffany's* in previews.

It was left to Merrick to pick up the pieces. He was amused to receive a phone call from the agent Freddie Fields, who offered him Steve McQueen for the title role. It was, Fields stressed, the only way Ali MacGraw would appear in the picture. Merrick had no particular interest in keeping MacGraw, whose acting talents had nothing to do with her being in the picture in the first place. He found it typical of Hollywood's idea of loyalty that among Fields' other clients was the actor who had already been cast as Gatsby, Robert Redford.

The elimination of MacGraw meant that a new Daisy had to be found. Bludhorn wanted Faye Dunaway, but the other actresses tested included Candice Bergen, Katharine Ross, Cathy Lee Crosby, and Lois Chiles, whom Merrick described as "Evans' girlfriend of the minute."

None of the others impressed the Paramount executives, and Dunaway did not help her case by acting like a prima donna. She arrived at 8:30 a.m., spent four hours having herself made up and her hair set, all the while sending her staff out for Coke, yogurt and vitamin B. When she emerged at 12:30 she demanded a closed rehearsal, the only candidate to do so. She had problems with her lines. Then it was time for lunch, for which she undressed, reset her hair and kept the crew waiting another hour.

Still, she might have gotten the part had not an unlikely contender, Mia Farrow, made a personal plea to the director, Jack Clayton, to test her for the role. Clayton was angry that the cast thus far had been presented to him as a fait accompli. While he doubted she could manage the role, he nonetheless arranged what Merrick considered "a second rate test, with borrowed costumes from a costume company and a long wig." Despite these handicaps, Farrow's test impressed Clayton deeply.

Merrick's initial response to Farrow had also been skeptical: "She was a little skinny thing with short hair. That's not the way Fitzgerald described Daisy." When he saw the test, however, he felt she had "filled out physically and she was a woman with an aristocratic look we hadn't been able to find."

Evans, Bludhorn and Frank Yablans, the head of Paramount, would watch the tests and then convene with Merrick and Clayton.

Bludhorn set down the order in which each would give his opinion: Clayton, Merrick, Evans, Yablans and finally Bludhorn himself. Both Clayton and Merrick voted for Farrow. Evans, thinking Bludhorn wanted Dunaway, voted for her. Yablans voted for Farrow. Then Bludhorn analyzed each of the tests. Merrick was impressed by the analysis, "considering he's a businessman, not a film maker." Bludhorn too voted for Farrow.

The vote could only intensify Evans' hatred for Merrick.

Merrick was amused because he knew the contest left Evans in a quandary—whether he wanted the film to succeed and humiliate MacGraw; or to fail and humiliate Merrick.

There had been no one comparable to Evans in New York. When Merrick produced a show he was his own head of production, often his own financier. He was accustomed to launching attacks, not to having to watch his back or to mount rearguard offensives.

Even Yablans had misgivings about Evans. He took Merrick to "21" to warn him, "When Bob makes up his mind that he's after something he's a very determined fellow, and you're going to have a terrible time of it on this picture. So I give you fair warning. It's going to be a nightmare."

Evans' preferred field of battle, Merrick discovered, was not the studio, where he had already been outmaneuvered, but the Bel Air social circuit, where he poisoned people against his adversary.

If Evans had been Merrick's only enemy, the filming of *Gatsby* might have been a pleasant experience. But Merrick's capacity to arouse animosity created other difficulties. Clayton, a director admired for his studies of the changing English class system, was as much an autocrat as Merrick, or, for that matter, Gower Champion. His chain smoking gave him a nervous air. His constant downing of brandy and sodas did not make him more pleasant. Also, he wore a Bedouin knife taped to his right leg.

Clayton was convinced the film would be a disaster. He had little confidence in the cast that had been selected for him. He doubted any of them were real actors.

Like Champion, he did not like to have his work observed. Merrick had imagined he might spend the summer of 1973 charmingly in Newport watching the shooting of the film. He and Etan spent some time on the set. Clayton was nasty. He once threw a chair through a mirror as part of a tantrum. Once, when Merrick came to him with a suggestion, Clayton shouted, "Don't speak while I'm talking or I'll have you thrown off the set." Merrick withdrew.

He even managed to put a diplomatic face on it: "All good directors are sadists. I won't put up with it from mediocrities, but for genius I'm willing to be a doormat."

Although Merrick told an old associate he would have liked to kill Clayton, he was unfailingly complimentary to him in the press (and the two later announced they would work together again on a film version of Jessamyn West's *Massacre at Fall Creek*, a project that then fell through).

The original screenplay for the *The Great Gatsby* had been written by the author of one of Merrick's greatest flops, *Breakfast at Tiffany's*, Truman Capote, by then well down the road to self-destruction. The screenplay was a disaster. Francis Ford Coppola was brought in to do the revision. Clayton made so many additions to Coppola's screenplay that Merrick felt he was entitled to share the on-screen credit.

When the production moved to London for indoor shooting, Merrick felt himself isolated. Only one person on the set talked to him, Raymond Gow, the hairdresser. Gow had begun his career in the theater, and the two had that shared love as the basis for conversation and a friendship.

Merrick was not destined to be treated like a mogul in either Hollywood or London. The stiffness that served him well in the West End only offended people in the film world. Once, in the commissary of Pinewood Studios, on the outskirts of London, Merrick was having lunch with a group of British film people, including David Niven, Jr., the son of the actor, who has occupied various executive positions in the film industry.

At a certain point during the lunch Merrick got something lodged in his teeth and tried to use his cloth napkin to dislodge it. From the other end of the table, Niven, like a nasty schoolboy, shouted, "What have you got in there, David? Why don't you let us all see it?"

Merrick was red-faced but quiet. No one would have dared jeer at him like that in New York. Here, however, he felt the wise choice was not to make a fuss.

The morning the final print of *Gatsby* was shown at Pinewood Merrick and Etan drove out in a limousine. They were shown to Clayton's private office. Clayton greeted him with a sneer. He was already drinking and invited the others to join him. He jibed at Merrick's refusal to imbibe during the day. Resignedly, Merrick gave in to Clayton's taunts and joined the others.

Throughout his career he relished confrontation, but it was invariably confrontation when he had all the cards, not when it was a fair battle. His experience on *Gatsby* taught him when confrontation was futile.

Evans was not among those who saw the first print. When he learned, however, that Yablans and Bludhorn were pleased with it, he began expressing pride over "his" work.

Merrick was justifiably angry that *Time* magazine, which devoted a cover story to the film, ran a sidebar on Evans. Evans had persuaded them that he was the producer, and they had profiled him as such. A week after the film opened, at a luncheon given by the Television Academy of Arts and Sciences, Merrick

Merrick at the opening of The Great Gatsby, flanked by Robert Evans and Frank Yablans

got some revenge against both Evans and *Time*. He quipped, "I thought Robert Evans was the producer [of the film] . . . by some mistake my name got on the print."

At the opening night party at the Waldorf-Astoria in New York, Evans paid a grudging tribute to Merrick, but Merrick omitted any mention of Evans in his speech. When someone asked if the omission was deliberate, Merrick asked, "Was he there? I didn't see him." They had been seated at separate tables, about a foot apart.

When the film opened in Los Angeles a radio interviewer asked Merrick to straighten out the conflicting stories on who had done what on the production. What exactly was Evans' position? the interviewer asked.

"Why, I believe he's Paramount's vice-president in charge of procurement," Merrick said in a solemn, deliberate tone of voice. Noting the stunned reaction of the interviewer, he explained, "His job is to procure scripts, procure actors . . . "

He could not control his hatred of Evans. "Bob's interested in girls," he told the interviewer. "He's also interested in other people." The interview was never aired.

Although he was justly wounded by the callous way Evans and others had treated him, nothing upset him more than the way the studio executives handled the profits of *Gatsby*. Why, their wizardry with figures rivaled his own cavalier weekly accounts to his Broadway backers.

In 1975, a year after the picture opened, Merrick sued Paramount, demanding $7 million plus $500,000 in "exemplary damages" plus ten per cent of any further funds generated from the distribution of *Gatsby*. He claimed that Paramount had "wrongfully interfered" in the production, inflating the negative cost. He claimed that other items were "fraudulently" included in the production and that the delay incurred by Evans' postponement of shooting had cost him $1 million in theater projects he had been unable to push forward. He also charged that Paramount had not given its "best efforts" to distributing the film and that its financial statements to him had been "fraudulent and substantially false."

The case was resolved nine years later, in 1984. Paramount was ordered to pay him $6 million.

CHAPTER THIRTY-THREE

ONE SUNDAY IN SEPTEMBER 1973, while Merrick was in London for the final shooting on *Gatsby*, Schlissel needed to check something at the office. When he arrived he was disturbed to find the door unlocked. Worse, when he got inside his own office, he found several chairs and a sofa had been slashed.

Schlissel and his boss had a reputation for toughness in the theater; but there was, after all, a larger world in which what passed for toughness in the theater was not very tough at all.

Schlissel had a very good idea who might have been responsible for the break-in. And it made him nervous.

He immediately called Frank Weissberg, who was the attorney for Joe Kipness, with whom, fifteen years earlier, Merrick had produced *La Plume de Ma Tante*. Kipness had a reputation as a conduit for Mafia money in the days when theater was still regarded as a potentially profitable investment. Schlissel was convinced Kipness had engineered the new design of his upholstery.

Although over the years Schlissel had become an accomplished actor in negotiating for his boss, he was quite unable to conceal his anxiety when he spoke to Weissberg. He knew that Merrick and Kipness had been in contention over a new musical Jerry Herman was writing. The show was called *Mack and Mabel* and concerned the professional and amorous relationship of the slapstick genius Mack Sennett and his great star Mabel Normand. Herman, who, for various contractual reasons, had not worked with Merrick since *Hello, Dolly!*, had a verbal understanding with Kipness about the show.

In the spring of 1973, however, Kipness had been preoccupied with a musical called *Seesaw*. He sold his interest in *Mack and Mabel* to Merrick. In addition to a percentage of the profits, Kipness felt he was entitled to producer's billing. As a restaurateur who had made his name and personality part of the product (one of his restaurants was called Kippy's, the other Joe's Pier 52), Kipness found billing on a Broadway marquee a useful form of free advertising.

Merrick absolutely refused. Equally important, they had not yet come to terms on Kipness's financial share in the show, and their conversations on the subject became increasingly heated. Schlissel was convinced the late-night visit to Merrick's office represented a frightening escalation of hostilities. Weissberg assured Schlissel he would find out whether his client had anything to do with the break-in.

Weissberg went to see Kipness, whose pudgy face and frame and easygoing nature were a perfect camouflage for an understructure of reinforced concrete. "Listen, you fuck, tell me what's what," Weissberg sallied.

Kipness beamed. "I thought it was time to send them a message," he told Weissberg.

On the basis of his conference with Kipness, Weissberg was able to reassure Schlissel. "I see no reason to believe Kipness had anything to do with this, and he's assured me it won't happen again," he told him.

In fact, Kipness's crew had bungled Operation Merrick. Their mission had, after all, been to ransack Merrick's office. Instead they had ruined the cheap furniture Schlissel had been trying to get rid of for years. At last he was able to furnish his office comfortably.

A few months later Merrick asked Weissberg to arrange a meeting in his office with Kipness. Weissberg, who was about to leave for a vacation in Florida, thought it would be a waste of everyone's time. Merrick insisted the meeting would be productive. Merrick, his attorney, Ben Aslan, and Biff Liff arrived in Weissberg's office.

There they found Kipness, who had every reason to gloat, having put his adversary on the defensive. Merrick, on the other hand, perhaps encouraged by his opponent's inability to control his rage, assumed his best deadpan.

Aslan began a pompous speech defending Merrick's position, but saying nothing specific about the financial terms in contention. Weissberg, who had initially feared nothing would come of the meeting, heatedly asked Aslan to come to his point. Aslan insulted Weissberg.

Kipness could restrain himself no longer. "No one attacks my lawyer," he thundered and walked over to where the short, pugnacious Aslan stood and picked him up by the scruff of the collar.

As Aslan and Kipness screamed at each other, Merrick motioned to Weissberg, and the two retired to Weissberg's library. As soon as they closed the door Merrick began laughing, a kind of cackle, as Weissberg remembers it. "I always knew someone would do that," he told Weissberg.

He then explained that the reason he could not yet come to terms with Kipness was that he hadn't been able to get Gower Champion to agree to work on *Mack and Mabel*. As soon as that happened, the terms would be easily arranged.

Kipness would eventually get a ten per cent share of the profits and one per cent royalties on an investment of $30,000. But no billing.

In the midst of his frustrating altercations with Evans, it was refreshing to be back in the theater, where things could be settled so directly, so much more amusingly.

During the next few years he would be able to juggle a full theater schedule, some more work in Hollywood, and even another attempted takeover—this time in league with Norton Simon—of Twentieth Century Fox.

Though they were busy and profitable years, they were also a time when his tendency toward cruelty grew more marked. Perhaps it was a way of reassuring himself, in the wake of his deflated profile on the West Coast, that his absolute power back East was all he really needed.

For the last few years he had been largely absent from the theater. In 1971-72 he had produced four plays, two of which—a British import, *Vivat, Vivat Regina*, with Claire Bloom and Eileen Atkins, and *Sugar*, the Jule Styne-Bob Merrill musical version of Billy Wilder's *Some Like It Hot*—were hits. He had imported a Feydeau farce from Canada, *There's One in Every Marriage*, and a play by the young American playwright Michael Weller, *Moonchildren*, from the Arena Stage in Washington, D.C.

Vivat, a drama about Queen Victoria, would be the last play Merrick would produce with Binkie Beaumont. Throughout the late Sixties Beaumont had seen his empire crumble. He was oddly less in touch with the more adventurous London theater than Merrick, who, until the legal battle over David Storey's *Home*, had nurtured his longstanding relationship with the Royal Court. The exquisite productions of classics at which Beaumont excelled had been supplanted by the brilliant productions by the Royal Shakespeare Company and the National Theater.

In these years Beaumont found it increasingly difficult to raise money. Merrick, who had courted Beaumont when he needed him, deserted him when it seemed to offer no financial advantage. Help—in the form of American capital—came from the American producer Arthur Cantor, who suggested that it might be easier to raise money if the investors were offered a series rather than an individual production. Beaumont agreed. *Vivat* was part of that series and the most likely candidate for export to New York.

Beaumont saw *Vivat* as a way to ingratiate himself again with Merrick and asked Cantor to make him a co-producer. Cantor spoke to Merrick, whose financial investment would not be great but who insisted on billing above Cantor's. Cantor refused, but Merrick eventually considered the show worthwhile enough to give Cantor equal billing.

In addition to those of Beaumont and Cantor, another name, that of Michael Codron, was contractually required to appear on all posters. Codron controlled the rights to the play. What Codron did not control was the size of his billing: Merrick, who did not like clutter in the area of the poster where producers' names were listed, gave Michael Codron extremely small print. This was a grave miscalculation, since Codron would soon play the role in the West End that Beaumont had once played, and, after this experience, he had no intention of working with Merrick again. At one point, several years later, Merrick tried to use Cantor as an intercessor with Codron. Codron refused to speak to him.

The techniques Merrick had developed to goad his creators into doing their best work were now being used for no other purpose than to provide Merrick himself with sadistic pleasure.

Peter Stone, who wrote the book for *Sugar*, recalled that as the musical made its way to New York nothing filled him with more dread than to enter the stage door and see, hanging on the hat-tree just inside, a homburg. Merrick was in town.

In Washington one day, Stone was summoned to the telephone. There was Merrick's familiar, somber voice, with a simple message: "You're fired. Get out of town."

Stone knew this was part of the modus operandi of a Merrick musical, but somehow he imagined he might be exempt. Stone, who later became president of the Dramatists' Guild, also knew that firing a writer was not quite so easy to do. He called his friends Cy Feuer and Ernest Martin, whose firings were legendary. They had terminated George S. Kaufman from *Silk Stockings*. Well, Feuer explained to Stone, not exactly.

Since you cannot fire a writer without going through a rigorous legal procedure, the more efficient method is to make his life so miserable that he leaves of his own accord, which was what Kaufman had done. And what Merrick wanted Stone to do.

The process of making Stone's life miserable began immediately.

That night Stone noticed, in his own house seats, Neil Simon. Simon was startled to see him. Merrick had told Simon that Stone had walked out on him. Simon did not want to get into the middle of a set-to. He left his revisions of the first few scenes with Stone and went back to New York.

Simon was succeeded by many other writers, including, Stone thought, the whole staff of Rowan and Martin's *Laugh-In*. "Merrick got a special rate from Amtrak to ship them in," Stone later quipped.

To tighten the screws Merrick would have a meeting of the creative staff every morning, at which he would deliver a blistering speech about how awful *Sugar* was and how all its problems could be attributed to one man. He pointed to Stone.

But Stone stood his ground and eventually won Merrick's grudging respect.

Stone was not the only object of Merrick's torture. At a certain point Styne and Merrill, the composer and lyricist, were startled to see Jerry Herman in Boston. He had written two songs for *Sugar*. He had only done it, he told them, because of his affection and gratitude for Gower. The songs, like Simon's revisions, were not used. For Herman there must have been a slight feeling of revenge to be called in to "help" Merrill the way Merrill had been summoned to "help" him on *Hello, Dolly!*

During the Washington tryout Merrick dispatched Biff Liff to inform Styne and Merrill that he was taking them off "per diem." Liff arrived as the pair were having dinner at the Watergate Hotel. He sat down beside them. "Stop eating," he admonished them. "You're off per diem."

Since Both Styne and Merrill were veterans of the Merrick wars, they smiled at him. "Have some ice cream, Biff," Merrill offered.

For a while Merrick refused to return any of the creative team's phone calls. Finally they begged Liff to go to Merrick to arrange a conciliatory meeting.

"You see, Biff? They finally called me," Merrick said. "It shows they need me."

Naturally Champion was not immune from Merrick's machinations. Merrick informed him he could be either the director or the choreographer of *Sugar*, not both. At first Champion opted for choreographer. That night Robert Moore arrived in Washington. The next night it was Gene Saks. Champion decided he would rather be the director. That night Merrick brought in Donald Saddler to replace him as choreographer.

Merrick was especially angry at Champion because of the sets, which Champion had worked on closely with Jo Mielziner. When the company first saw them in Washington, everyone was dismayed. They were in shades of brown, which everyone, including Champion, agreed was not really a helpful color for comedy.

"I am going to junk every piece of scenery on that stage," Merrick informed Champion. "It will be redesigned and you will pay for it."

Mielziner, one of Merrick's earliest allies, was stunned to find Robin Wagner in Washington. Wagner had, of course, been assured that Mielziner not only knew but was grateful he was coming to do the new sets for *Sugar*. In fact, although he had no idea he was being replaced, Mielziner told Wagner, he was "actually relieved" to see him. Twenty years had passed since Merrick had written to Mielziner sympathizing with him for being on the receiving end of Shumlin's screams. Merrick had surpassed his mentor.

Although the new designs were completed quickly, the construction of the sets would take time, which allowed Merrick to extend the out-of-town tour as well as the agony of everyone involved in *Sugar*.

Because he was expending so much energy on *Sugar* he had little time to devote to another show he produced that spring, Michael Weller's *Moonchildren*, which he imported from the Arena Stage in Washington.

At one of the final rehearsals in New York, Weller felt a paternal arm around his shoulders. "I see Pulitzer here," Merrick told him. "Maybe a Tony. Of course you have to cut twenty minutes."

Weller, who felt the show had worked well in Washington, suspected Merrick's concern about the twenty minutes had more to
do with paying the crew overtime than with any perceived audience discomfort.

At the rehearsal Weller told Merrick it would be easy. "Just cut
scene six," he said.

"You're a pro, kid," Merrick told him.

When Merrick mentioned Weller's proposal to his staff, he
learned that scene six was the pivotal scene in the play. Weller
had outmaneuvered him. But that simply meant that when box
office response to the play, which elicited thoughtful reviews, was
weak, Merrick simply closed it.

During the 1972-73 season, while he was overseeing *Gatsby*,
Merrick had only one Broadway production, Tennessee Williams'
Out Cry, a quick flop. More annoying than the flop—his third
with Williams—was a confrontation with the board of directors
of the Repertory Theater of Lincoln Center.

The battle with the Lincoln Center board was as ugly as his
battles with the Hollywood moguls, possibly more so since this
was about his own turf. When Lincoln Center was planned, it
was going to provide new homes for the Metropolitan Opera, the
New York Philharmonic, the New York City Opera and the New
York City Ballet. A building was also planned for a repertory theater.

By the fall of 1972 two managements—led by Elia Kazan and
Robert Whitehead, then by Herbert Blau and Jules Irving—had
failed to sustain theatrical life at the Beaumont, and the board of
directors of Lincoln Center was at a loss. The theater was com-
monly regarded as a great white elephant. Merrick in a sense was
coming to its rescue when he proposed to rent the small theater
under the Vivian Beaumont, The Forum (later renamed the
Mitzi Newhouse), to present new works. Merrick's vitality should
have been welcomed under such moribund circumstances.

He went to meet with the board of directors, who, in
December of 1972, consisted almost exclusively of bankers,

stockbrokers, investment consultants and attorneys. The chairman, Clarke Coggeshall, was vice-president of the First National City Bank. The only show business representatives on the board were the theater owner Lucille Lortel, the sometime actress Dina Merrill, a former Broadway producer named Sherman Ewing, and Michael Burke, president of the New York Yankees.

For the most part, however, the board consisted of men who had been born in pinstripes. His own fraternal uniform, which he had worn as vestments since high school, might have identified him as one of their own. They, however, made it clear they wanted no part of him.

Though Merrick had never been successful presenting new American plays he might have made a serious contribution to the development of new drama at Lincoln Center, which was free of the pressures of Broadway economics. Merrick might finally have found his Arthur Miller or Lillian Hellman. We shall never know. But at a time when the alternative theater movement denounced everything David Merrick stood for, he himself stood ready to extend his resources for their experiments.

In fact the board had never been particularly devoted to serious theater. Even before the Beaumont opened, when Elia Kazan and Robert Whitehead were putting together an ambitious first season, the board was negotiating secretly with Alexander Cohen to present Rex Harrison in some revival. As Arthur Miller had remarked, "They wanted a show in there at which you could really *dress.*" Given this mentality, no proposal from Merrick or anyone else was likely to have interested them.

Merrick came back to his office in a rage, fulminating against "those anti-semitic sons of bitches. They think they're so fucking fancy," he fumed. Clearly, they had hit a very raw nerve. They had reminded him of the David Margulois he had left behind in St. Louis, where, he once recalled, "the little theater was run by the Busches and the rich families, and I couldn't get near it. If you were from the other side of the tracks, no matter what you had on the ball you were ignored."

In fact there was a less emotional reason why Merrick's proposal was rejected. Because of both union regulations and structural reasons, the Beaumont and the Forum could not be leased separately. They were a package. This somehow Merrick could not understand. No matter how many times John Mazzola, then the executive director, explained the matter to him, Merrick repeated one refrain, "I want the Forum."

The rejection made it seem as if, after all these years, he was still an outsider.

To add insult to injury, the *Times* was beginning to snipe at him. Both the Beaumont and The Forum were, a few months later, handed over to Joseph Papp, a man who could match Merrick in terms of both temper and ego. (As for temper, in fact, Papp had once so enraged the City Council, at whose behest he ran the Public Theater for $1 a year, that they threatened not to renew his contract. He had asked Merrick to intercede for him, which Merrick, very graciously, did, never even receiving a thank you from Papp.)

Unlike Merrick, Papp made no effort to conceal his ethnicity or his class origins, which discounts Merrick's paranoia about anti-semitism. He fairly flaunted them. He made no attempt to dress or act like the men on the board. They wore banker's gray. He wore "mod." In the "radical chic" mood of the times, this was an asset, both in the eyes of the pinstripe boys and, apparently, those of the *Times*. In reporting on Papp's accession to power at Lincoln Center in March of 1973, Mel Gussow wrote, "In recent years, Mr. Papp has become new York's most visible producer—far outstripping, for example, David Merrick."

Similarly, a few months before, in reviewing Merrick's film version of *Child's Play*, *Times* critic Vincent Canby had referred to Merrick as "Broadway's Joseph Papp of yesteryear."

In 1973 Merrick had been preoccupied first with salvaging, then with producing *The Great Gatsby*. As a result the 1973-74 season was the first in almost twenty years that the Broadway season did not contain even one new show produced by David Merrick.

In June of 1974 there was a gathering at Princeton University humbly billed as the First Annual Congress of Theater, or FACT. Most of the Congress consisted of rhetoric, as representatives of the vibrant alternative theater railed against the commercial theater they imagined they had supplanted. "The capitalist pig theater must go!" exulted Julian Beck, one of the founders of the Living Theater. "We rejoice in its death."

Joe Papp, of course was there. "The commercial theater needs financial support because it is ailing, and they want to exploit the energy and purity of the non-profit theater."

The most conspicuous representative of the "capitalist pig theater" was David Merrick, who was seen sleeping during several of the panel discussions.

Rocco Landesman, then a Yale theater teacher, later the head of the Jujamcyn Organization, one of the three major Broadway theater owners, reported on the event for the *Times*. He noted that when Merrick "dragged himself to the podium, the delegates visibly braced themselves in their seats."

Merrick noted that two of the most important producers in the country—Hal Prince and Roger Stevens—were not in attendance. (It was the first time he had paid Stevens such a compliment.) He thought they were smart to have stayed away.

"The Congress, it seems to me, is a lot of hot air," he declared. "I was going to give you some specific advice about how to get more money for the theater but I see no point in that now. I really do have to get back."

He had their number. According to Landesman, "The words stung all the delegates, whether they were from the profit or the non-profit theater, from New York or from regional theaters, and one after another they exhorted Merrick to tell them his secrets."

All Merrick did was discuss his own lack of success dealing with foundations and with government agencies. He had teased them and forced them to exhibit their own need for and hunger for money. Even from these avowedly enemy forces he had wrested a sense of himself as an elder statesman of the theater.

Mack and Mabel, which opened October 6, 1974, was received tepidly by the critics, and, despite the presence of Robert Preston and Bernadette Peters, it only ran for sixty-four performances, returning nothing on its $800,000 investment.

A few weeks after the Herman show opened, Merrick presented *Dreyfus in Rehearsal*, about a bedraggled Warsaw troupe of Jewish actors in 1933 rehearsing a play about the Dreyfus affair.

He would collaborate on *Dreyfus* with Garson Kanin and Ruth Gordon for the first time in almost a decade, since Kanin directed *I Was Dancing*. And though the relationship was one of the oldest he had forged in the theater, still Merrick went to special pains to torment Kanin on the percentage of his royalties. When a representative of the Dramatists Guild called Merrick to confirm a previously agreed upon percentage, Merrick flew into a rage, denying he had ever suggested such a number. When the bewildered Kanin then called to find out what happened, he was told that Merrick was out of town and would be for months, a blatant lie. When *Dreyfus* closed very quickly, the Merrick office was unusually unpleasant about forwarding Kanin's royalties.

If he was treating an old *friend* like Kanin so cruelly, it hardly seemed surprising that he treated Tennessee Williams, whose plays had brought Merrick neither prestige nor money, with unusual coldness.

In part, Williams had brought on Merrick's wrath himself. In these years, when New York seemed to delight in minimizing his importance, Williams had found a new audience, a new respect in London. In 1974 *A Streetcar Named Desire* was revived in the West End in a production that starred Claire Bloom. It was directed by Ed Sherin and produced by Bloom's husband, Hilliard Elkins. Williams thought he had found the team that might bring him success again in New York.

Elkins, he decided, was the man to produce his new play, *The Red Devil Battery Sign*. The only hitch was that it had already been optioned, for some time in fact, by David Merrick. In a foolish attempt to wrest the rights away from Merrick, Williams' agent, Billie Barnes, neglected to inform Merrick that the option was about to lapse. This was both discourteous and unprofessional.

It may, however, have seemed the only way to get Merrick to give up the rights.

Merrick, after all, was like the proverbial dog in the manger. He didn't want the bone, but he certainly didn't want anyone else to have it either. In the case of *The Red Devil Battery Sign*, he had expressed no particular enthusiasm for the play but he wouldn't allow anyone else to have a success with Williams when he had produced three Williams flops. Williams' great friend, Lady Maria St. Just, became exasperated. "What's the matter, David?" she confronted him. "Don't you have the money?"

He seemed to choke on her words. But in the spring of 1975 he went forward with the play.

For Barnes to imagine he could pull a fast one on Merrick was the height of folly. It was an act of betrayal that would require an especially torturous revenge. Meanwhile the property itself was a useful tool with which Merrick could torment others.

The Shuberts, for example. They might need to be reminded of who David Merrick was. The Shuberts had, over the years, become a generic term, like Doge or Senator. Neither of the current occupants of the office was an actual Shubert. Gerald Schoenfeld and Bernard Jacobs, who had toiled for many years as lawyers for the Shubert Organization, had ascended to the presidency and chairmanship respectively in 1972, along with a man named Irving Goldman, who resigned in scandal a few years later.

The Shuberts had, in fact, been deferential to Merrick. They had known him practically since the beginning of his career. What may have irritated him, however, was the fact that two lawyers had brought themselves to a position of power theoretically greater than his own. *The Red Devil Battery Sign* provided a pretext to instruct them on theatrical hierarchies.

The Shuberts had taken an interest in a project being developed by his nemesis, Joe Papp, at the Public Theater. The musical about the life of gypsies, those unsung heroes of the musical theater, was being directed by Michael Bennett, who had done the zippy disco choreography for *Promises, Promises* and gone on to choreograph two Hal Prince-Stephen Sondheim musicals, *Company* and *Follies*. The score for Bennett's musical, which was called *A Chorus Line*, was by lyricist Ed Kleban and the Oscar-winning composer Marvin Hamlisch. The show clearly had Broadway possibilities. The Shuberts thought it would fit nicely into the Shubert Theater.

The only problem was that the Shubert Theater had already been booked for the spring of 1975 by David Merrick for *The Red Devil Battery Sign*. This was an odd choice of theaters since the Shubert was ideal for musicals, too big for an intimate play, even one that starred Claire Bloom and Anthony Quinn. Right next door was the Broadhurst, whose proportions made it a much more suitable choice for a dramatic play.

Logic was entirely on the side of the Shuberts, who asked him if he would move his play to the Broadhurst. When Merrick left his office one winter morning to go across to do battle with Jacobs, logic was nowhere in his armory. The fight he had to wage was not about sense or logic. It was about power.

Once he settled himself in Jacobs' office, Merrick put on one of his most pyrotechnic displays of screaming. From time to time Schoenfeld would drift into Jacobs' office to see how the negotiations were proceeding. There were no negotiations, just screaming, capped by the traditional stomping out and slamming of the door.

Merrick had retreated to his office. He had left behind a lieutenant, one of his co-producers, who had said not a word, watching the screaming match in horror. After the slamming of the door Jacobs reached for the contract and signed it. Nothing, his beleaguered face registered, was worth this much screaming.

The field marshall returned to the Merrick office jubilant, thrusting the signed contract before Merrick, expecting to see a smile of triumph spread across his face. Merrick glanced at the contract and tore it up. "This is unfair to Bernie," he observed.

What seemed more unfair to Bernie was the emotional toll of the confrontation. Though Jacobs was well acquainted with Merrick's emotional performances, discounting even the *coup de theatre* of the thunderously slammed door, a few weeks later he suffered what was described as a heart attack. Some thought it stemmed from his encounter with Merrick. It was, in fact, an inflammation of the linings of the lungs, a condition that could be fatal but was not, technically speaking, a heart attack. It had been precipitated, Jacobs later learned, by dental surgery, not Merrick's performance. Merrick had made inquiries and learned the distinction, not because he was particularly solicitous of Jacobs' health, but because a general must have a clear view of the damage he has inflicted on the enemy.

Ultimately it was all academic. The chances of Williams' play reaching New York were slim. Merrick had decided to make them even slimmer. Merrick, whose $90,000 investment in the $360,000 show was Foundation money, proposed to his producing partners, Doris Cole Abraham and Robert Colby, that one way they could save money was by using winches—devices to move scenery—from his own company. His partners applauded this measure of economy.

When the play floundered in Boston, as he knew it would, Merrick claimed there was not enough money to go on. Colby demanded to see the books. Everyone had been convinced the two weeks they had played in Boston had been profitable, despite the reviews.

Merrick thrived on that kind of demand. It allowed him to strike a posture of defiance. He refused to allow anyone to see the books.

What's more, he didn't like the tone of his partners' demand. In spite, he withdrew his winches. Stranded in Boston, unable to raise money either to keep the show going or to build new winches, the other producers threw in the towel. Variety reported it would have cost $200,000 to recapitalize the show because of its complex sets. Both Williams and Sherin questioned where the original $360,000, of which only a quarter came from the David Merrick Arts Foundation, had gone, since "we made profits both weeks in Boston."

Anthony Quinn told a reporter, "Tennessee Williams, one of

the great talents of all time, has been treated like an assembly line butcher. . . . Blame it on too many producers. One misses the day when L.B. Mayer or Darryl Zanuck made a decision and took the responsibility. I talked to the producers and they said they weren't closing the show. Then they posted the notice. One producer [Colby] said his name was forged."

The Red Devil Battery Sign closed in Boston in June of 1975. When a *New York Times* reporter asked Merrick if the play was closing for good, he replied, "It is not closing for good; it's closing for bad." Interestingly, Merrick's first choice to direct *Red Devil* had been none other than Michael Bennett. Bennett had read the script and suggested possibilities for rewrites. He also had an idea for a unit set that might have saved some grief. The play uses a Mexican mariachi band. The Mexicans in this production were so authentic they spoke no English and constantly collided with the actual set, which was constantly in motion. Bennett's simpler set might have posed less of a threat.

In December that year it was produced in English in Vienna, where the cast included Keith Baxter and a young English actor named Pierce Brosnan. It was a success, as it was when it was transferred to London. All these years later, it has never been produced in New York. This production marked the end of Williams' relationship with the "sweet man in the Shumlin office."

Merrick inflicted one more blow against the Shuberts. Over the years, when one of his shows closed he would invite Ed Kook to give him an estimate of the value of the lighting equipment. Kook's estimates tended to be on the low side, making them an attractive investment. Merrick charged the purchase to the show's budget. With the huge volume of production he maintained during the Fifties and Sixties he had acquired an enormous amount of lighting equipment. It was originally stored for him by Century Lighting, which was taken over by Four Star Lighting in 1968. Francis DeVerna, of Four Star Lighting, agreed to continue storing lights for Merrick. He was also allowed to rent out the equipment to other productions as long as there was enough to supply Merrick's shows. Over the years it was almost impossible to distinguish between Merrick's equipment and that of either Century or Four Star.

In December of 1974, as he set his sights increasingly on Hollywood, he decided to sell the equipment to Four Star. Around the same time he began discussing with his master carpenter Ted Van Bemel the idea of having their own lighting company, which Merrick would establish with both some seed money and the equipment being held by Four Star.

Both Merrick and Four Star had been sluggish about coming to terms on exactly what equipment belonged to him and what its market value would be. On March 23, 1975 Merrick obtained a court order that would allow him to claim the equipment on July 3.

On July 15 Four Star began to hang lights for *A Chorus Line*, which was moving to the Shubert from the Public Theater. Merrick's lawyer, Ben Aslan, arrived at the theater with a writ of attachment and a deputy sheriff, claiming the lights being hung belonged to Merrick.

Whether or not they belonged to him, it was the worst possible breach of etiquette to try to disrupt the preparation of a show that was supposed to begin previews in ten days. That was exactly the point, a longtime associate who helped him execute the move suggested. He had in fact hired seven trucks, at $400 apiece, and stationed them outside seven theaters where "his" equipment might be in use. Merrick decided on *A Chorus Line* because it would do the most to reinforce his image as "evil."

Pete Feller, the largest supplier of computerized equipment on Broadway, watched the altercation between Aslan, the sheriff and DeVerna. He also saw, outside the theater, the unmistakable figure of Aslan's boss enjoying his handiwork.

DeVerna was up against a wall. There was the possibility that some of the equipment belonged to Merrick. There was no time to sort it out. With the Shuberts worried about the opening of their hit show, without benefit of counsel—his own lawyer was in court trying to counteract Merrick's writ of attachment—DeVerna, at the mercy of both Merrick and Aslan, agreed to pay Merrick $50,000 on the spot, $150,000 the next morning by certified check and the balance of 410,000 in weekly installments of $1,000 each.

DeVerna signed the agreement and paid the $200,000, then hired a Wall Street firm to sue Merrick. Five years later a judge found in DeVerna's favor. Martin Stecher, a justice of the New York Supreme Court, found that Merrick was guilty of "unpalatable . . . bits of chicanery." Yes, Stecher ruled, Merrick was entitled to have his lighting equipment back, but it was dishonest to have claimed that the equipment was made expressly for him. It was standard equipment, and there was enough in the Four Star warehouse in the Bronx to have met Merrick's demands.

Most damaging, the document Merrick filed March 23 had been altered. Where it once claimed that the equipment was located in the Bronx, it now stated that some of the equipment was also in the Shubert Theater. There was no way of knowing for certain on March 23 that *A Chorus Line* would be moving to the Shubert from the Public. Merrick received $1 in damages because some of the equipment was clearly his, but he was required to pay DeVerna the $200,000 he extracted July 15 and the interest between July 16, 1975 and June 3, 1980, when Judge Stecher made his decision.

The various trials over the lights had been endless. The courtroom transcripts consumed over 4,000 pages. At one point Judge Stecher had to reprimand Merrick, who, he felt, was "performing" on the stand and trying to manipulate the proceedings.

"I don't tell you how to produce shows," Judge Stecher admonished him. "You don't tell me how to run my courtroom."

When the judgment was rendered against him, Merrick insisted Aslan ought to pay. Aslan refused. Merrick sued Fitelson, Aslan and Lasky, the firm that had represented him for almost twenty-five years. In fact even while the suit, later dropped, was pending, Merrick thought they should continue to represent him and was miffed when Aslan refused to take his calls.

Why had he become more belligerent than ever? In part it was because he was producing far fewer shows. He could concentrate his destructive energies on a smaller range of targets. Some thought it related to a habit he had picked up in Hollywood—cocaine. At one point in the course of labor negotiations the head of the stagehands' union told Bernard Jacobs, "We are not taking any shit from that cokehead."

Jacobs was startled. "David is the most abstemious man I know," he countered. But more and more he began to realize that the allegation was probably true. If the stagehands were aware of his habit, it was because they were often his suppliers.

It was another way that Hollywood weakened Broadway's most renowned strongman.

CHAPTER THIRTY-FOUR

ON A WEDNESDAY AFTERNOON sometime in the spring of 1969, Alan Delynn's assistant, Elizabeth Kaye, who was manning the switchboard, received a call from the police, who asked to speak immediately to Mr. Merrick. She put the call through and was astonished to see, seconds later, Merrick and Schlissel running out of their offices toward the elevator. As they waited for the elevator Merrick waved and called out, "Take any messages."

Perhaps, she thought, there was a crisis at one of the theaters: an actor has fallen sick; one of the matinee ladies in the audience has had a heart attack. Before she had much time to think about it, policemen stepped out of the elevator Merrick and Schlissel had so precipitously entered only a minute before.

It was a bomb squad, somewhat surprised to find that the whole office had not been evacuated once the threat became known.

Merrick had made an executive decision, placing the organization's most valuable assets out of harm's way. It was one of the last times he made Schlissel seem valuable. Increasingly in the ensuing years Schlissel felt he was playing second fiddle to Delynn. In some ways it was understandable. Delynn could be very charming, a delightful traveling companion. Schlissel was all business.

Around Christmas of 1974, shortly after the closings of both *Mack and Mabel* and *Dreyfus in Rehearsal*, Schlissel quit.

It was an unemotional departure. Schlissel felt he had been used. He had been the hatchet man, the man who took the blame for a lot of Merrick's malevolence. But when Merrick had set his sights Westward, he had left Schlissel behind. Part of Schlissel's resentment may have been economic—New York theater was increasingly less lucrative, and the financial horizons in Hollywood seemed boundless.

It was, however, more than that. Schlissel had consecrated his life to the cause of David Merrick. He had profited by the relationship, but he needed to mean more to Merrick than just a henchman to do the dirty work. It was, after all, his day to day dedication that kept the organization running flawlessly; and which allowed Merrick to travel the world in search of new properties. That Merrick now favored Delynn, whose judgment had often been so catastrophic to the organization, cannot have sat well with Schlissel.

He left to form his own production company with Jay Kingwill, who had worked as a company manager in the Merrick office in the late Sixties. (Although Schlissel remained circumspect in speaking of his former boss, it seems telling that when he died, in the spring of 1981, his family specifically requested that Merrick *not* attend the memorial service.)

One immediate consequence of Schlissel's departure was the promotion of Helen Nickerson to the post of general manager. For Merrick it was less a way of rewarding her loyalty than one of saving money. By acting as both his secretary and his general manager, she saved him a salary.

It was also a way of insulting Schlissel: the work he had done could be taken over as extra duties by an already overburdened secretary. Merrick had gone even further, telling an associate that when he made the decision to replace Schlissel, "It was either Helen or Saul." Saul was the elevator operator in the St. James Building.

Merrick's limited production schedule might have prevented

problems from surfacing for some time. Instead one presented itself immediately. The last show to be produced in the spring of 1975 was Moliere's *The Misanthrope,* with Alec McCowen and Diana Rigg. When Nickerson went to Capezio to order shoes for the cast, she was told none would be made until the bills were paid.

Schlissel had not paid Capezio for the shoes they had supplied for *Mack and Mabel.* This, of course, was standard procedure for both Merrick and Schlissel. You didn't pay the bills. They threatened to sue. They did. You settled. When the Merrick office teemed with new shows, this was an equitable arrangement. Now that he was producing fewer and fewer shows Merrick could no longer dictate terms to his suppliers.

The Merrick office was in the humiliating position of actually having to pay for the *Mack and Mabel* shoes and, the greatest heresy of all, to pay in advance for *The Misanthrope.* This was not the way Merrick enjoyed doing business.

After *The Misanthrope,* he produced two more shows in 1975, both transfers. *Travesties,* Tom Stoppard's brilliant meditation on the proximity of Joyce, Lenin and Tristan Tzara during World War I in Zurich, had started its life in London. One of his co-producers, who had worked with him on *The Red Devil Battery Sign,* was astonished to hear him dare suggest that one way to save money would be for him to supply the winches. The idea was rejected immediately.

The other transfer was *Very Good Eddie,* a 1916 Jerome Kern musical that came from the Goodspeed Opera House, a restored jewel of a theater that specialized in vintage musicals. The revival also revived his association with Max Brown and Byron Goldman. For the first time in their thirty year relationship, he allowed them to share billing with him, very aberrant behavior for Merrick, though the production had been their idea.

At sixty-five, his strength was beginning to falter. His mood shifts, which he might have orchestrated in his younger days, had begun to tyrannize him. Merrick was losing control, yet another consequence, no doubt, of the coke habit he had picked up in Hollywood.

Etan had been able to persuade him to see a psychiatrist, not with any anticipation of formal therapy—she knew Merrick would have no compunctions about lying—but with the hope of some pharmaceutical relief for him.

In 1972 Merrick began a program of therapy called father-hood. He and Etan had had a daughter, named Marguerita. At first he was livid. "When she's twenty, I'll be an old man," he raged to an associate. "What will I be able to teach her?"

But, as he had with Cecilia Ann, he softened. Unlike Cecilia Ann, whose very existence had been a reproach, Marguerita, a beautiful, healthy child, was a sign that, late in life, he had been able to accept the conventional idea of being a father.

People who had known him for years were astonished to see him on the floor—in pinstripes to be sure—playing with his baby daughter, pretending that his elbow was a place for her to rest her little finger, talking to her in a high-pitched, silly voice.

The mellow Merrick was, of course, only transitory. In the summer of 1976 the relationship with Etan, ever tenuous, finally fell apart, and she sued to Americanize the Mexican divorce she had won seven years earlier.

The divorce complicated the major project he worked on in the fall of 1976, a project that he thought might help him reclaim his position on Broadway. He had toyed with making a musical of another Marcel Pagnol film, *The Baker's Wife*, twenty years earlier. *The Baker's Wife* is the story of a man learning to accept his own humiliation. The baker in question is an older man who marries a young woman. She leaves him for a younger man but soon returns. He loves her so much he takes her back, using an analogy with the family cat to express his anger. It is more important to have his wife again than give full range to his outrage.

Perhaps when he made the initial choice of *Fanny* rather than *Baker's Wife*, Merrick sensed that the latter is inherently an unsatisfying story, one that works in Pagnol's film only because of the great performance by Raimu, but the idea of doing another musical based on Pagnol was a symbolic way of starting anew, of recapturing the ground he had lost.

For years Pagnol, who had always considered the success of *Fanny* as a musical an unrepeatable oddity, had refused to grant anyone the rights to make a musical of *The Baker's Wife*. Zero Mostel had tried. So had others. Always Pagnol told them, "That's my baby—no, no, no."

But when Merrick approached him, the relationship the two men had enjoyed twenty years earlier softened him. By this time Pagnol was extremely ill. At their final meeting he was in bed, Merrick sitting solicitously by his side. There had always been a great respect between the two men and even a special affection.

Perhaps because he knew they would not likely be meeting again, Pagnol decided to tell Merrick something that might explain why he had acceded to Merrick's request many years earlier and why, after so many refusals, he would do so again.

"Are you Jewish?" he asked Merrick.

Never eager to admit it, Merrick was willing to concede the fact where he thought it might be to his advantage.

"So am I," Pagnol told him. His family had been Sephardic Jews, which is to say, descendants of the Jews who had been expelled from Spain in 1492 (as opposed to the Ashkenazi Jews like Merrick, whose forebears were Eastern European). It was implicit in the actual family name, Espanol, which is the French word for Spanish. He had shortened it to Pagnol.

When Merrick began to secure the rights to *The Baker's Wife* Neil Simon was going to write the book. But in the mid-Seventies, Simon was no longer interested. He had suggested the project to Joseph Stein, whose last musical with Merrick had been *Take Me Along*.

The composer of *Baker's Wife* would be a man in his mid-twenties, Stephen Schwartz. Schwartz had been brought to Merrick's attention in 1968 by his agent, Shirley Bernstein. She brought Schwartz, then barely twenty, to Merrick's office to play him some songs from what would be his college dissertation, a musical based on the life of a medieval French king.

Merrick was impressed with the young man's work and drew up a contract to produce the musical, assuming he could find a book-writer. Schwartz collaborated with someone recommended by the photographer Richard Avedon. In the meantime, another musical he had created, *Godspell*, became a huge success, with productions around the country and a 1972 film. Shirley Bernstein arranged for Schwartz to collaborate with her brother Leonard on his 1971 *Mass*.

Despite these impressive credits, after a while it became clear that the musical about the French monarch, who was seen as a prototypical hippie, was not working. Merrick released him from his contract, and Schwartz pursued the idea on his own. It was eventually produced by Stuart Ostrow and staged—spectacular-ly—by Bob Fosse under the title *Pippin*.

When the show opened in Washington it was obvious that it would be a big hit. "Well, you sure stole something from me," Merrick told Bernstein. She promised him he could have Schwartz's next work, which turned out to be *The Baker's Wife*.

Stein and Schwartz worked well together, and the score to *The Baker's Wife* remains Schwartz's most ambitious and most impressive effort.

Perhaps the first decision to doom *The Baker's Wife* was the choice of a star. Chaim Topol, the Israeli actor, had scored a triumph in the London production of *Fiddler on the Roof* and gone on to star in the film version. Topol, an abrasive offstage personality, was hardly a proper choice to play the shy, humble baker. To make matters worse, he insisted on a number where he could strip to the waist and dance on a table.

The tryout tour began at the huge Dorothy Chandler Pavilion in Los Angeles, where everyone first saw the set by Jo Mielziner, who had died before construction began. *Baker's Wife* had been envisioned as an intimate show, with a cast of a baker's dozen. Mielziner, however, had scaled it as grandly as he had *Mata Hari*. The set was gigantic, with two enormous turrets and a wall as high as the stage of the Chandler.

Merrick immediately sensed it would have to be reconstructed for the St. James in New York. "This is for an opera, and we have thirteen people," he intoned. "Fellas, it is only salvageable," he said as he left the theater.

Though the tryout tour was unusually long (seven weeks in Los Angeles, seven in San Francisco, then shorter stops in Boston and Washington), the creators rarely saw him. A steady stream of directors and choreographers would arrive in the various cities along the tour, but they invariably shared Merrick's view that the show was not worth attaching one's name to.

What surprised Shirley Bernstein was that Merrick did not post a closing notice. Sometimes he did so even when he had no intention of closing a show—simply to scare people into working harder. But with a show that even the creators came to feel was hopeless, it seemed extremely odd that he did not hoist the white flag.

True, the long road tour meant that there was money to be made. Topol was a draw, even if his performance did little to help the show. It wasn't until Washington, the last stop before new York, that he was finally replaced by Paul Sorvino.

Merrick was appalled at the length of some of the musical numbers. One, "Meadowlark," an unusually lyrical song that is now frequently performed, elicited from Merrick the observation that "nothing in life should last more than five minutes."

Merrick had other objections to the song he referred to contemptuously as "Dickiebird." The song, he and Nickerson felt, was really too sensitive for the character, a vulgar girl—a role assumed on the road by Patti LuPone. For Boston, Schwartz shortened it considerably. Nickerson, in her capacity as general manager, told Schwartz there was no point in abbreviating it. It only made sense at its original length. Rather than shorten it, why not just eliminate it. Schwartz would not abandon it.

When the show reached Washington, lo and behold, the music for "Meadowlark" had disappeared from the musicians' stands. Merrick had dispatched Nickerson to remove it.

"I can't do that," she said.

"I did it," he told her. "You can do it."

When this had happened a dozen years earlier with Anthony Newley, Merrick brandished the musical parts in front of the composer and threatened to burn them unless Newley complied with his wishes. This time he feigned innocence but reassured people, "We're in Washington, the home of the FBI. We'll find our little 'Meadowlark.'"

Paul Sorvino, who had replaced Topol, was giving a remarkable performance by the time the show was about to close in Washington. So was the young Patti LuPone. But it was clear that even with these huge gains the show was not working.

Finally Shirley Bernstein confronted Merrick—why was he insisting on bringing into a New York a show he knew would be an instant flop?

Bernstein, like other female agents, had a good rapport with Merrick. She had been warned that he would crush her, but she found his tactics amusing. When she was looking through the contracts Merrick deliberately placed little Marguerita on her lap as a distraction. Throughout the relationship she found his humor compensation for his abrasiveness. Throughout their wrangling she stood her ground, realizing that, like all bullies, he was at heart a coward who would not attack if she showed no fear.

The rapport between them may have accounted for the fact Merrick decided to level with her. The financing for *The Baker's Wife* had been put up entirely by Motown Records. He had not invested a penny of his own. An essential part of his contract with Motown was that he bring the show to a Broadway opening. He intended to fulfill his commitment. (By fulfilling his commitment, of course, he may also have been venging himself on Schwartz and Bernstein for having let *Pippin* get away from him.)

Ten days before the opening Bernstein flew to Detroit, where she knew a Motown executive. She persuaded him that whatever glamour he hoped to achieve for Motown by a Broadway opening night would be undone the following morning by the critics.

Both Stein and Schwartz had pleaded with Merrick to close the show on the road. It was the only sensible thing to do. With Motown's blessing, Merrick closed *The Baker's Wife* in Washington.

The divorce from Etan was final later that year. Etan's advice lasted longer than she did. Even after she left he continued to use the drugs that had been prescribed. They evened his moods but the results made him a different man.

Merrick was losing his legendary obsession for work. And when David Merrick loses his appetite for work, one need not add that he lost his taste for life as well. One morning he dragged himself into the office. Helen Nickerson was surprised that he had not buzzed her at all. She went in to find him sitting forlornly on the sofa.

He must have suffered apprehensions so severe that he was prepared to watch the most fundamental core of his personality disappear rather than face the demons that tormented him. And his failing health encouraged his latent reclusive tendencies.

The announcement of a David Merrick divorce, like the openings of his shows, received extensive press coverage. It was read with great excitement by a very sick woman living in London, Jeanne Gilbert Merrick. Jeanne had cancer, which was complicated by the fact that she had never treated her body very well.

She had had only sporadic contact with Merrick since their divorce a decade earlier. In 1973, she had tried to visit Cecilia Ann at a time other than that specified in the custody agreement; he had ordered her arrested for trespassing.

When *The Great Gatsby* opened to mixed reviews, in 1974, she was in London with her friend David Pelham, whom Merrick had once employed as a favor to Jeanne. (As a favor to Merrick, Pelham had introduced him to members of the Mandy Rice-Davies circle in London.) As a testimonial to *Gatsby*'s fate the two sent him a telegram reversing his own sentiments. "It's not enough that you should fail. Others must succeed."

Despite all his cruelty to her, she had never ceased to love him.

All during her final years of illness she kept wondering if she did this or that, he might come back to her. Did the divorce from Etan mean she might again become Mrs. David Merrick? In the next few years they met several times, formally, at the Ritz in London.

Shortly before she died, in 1980, she returned home to Lexington, Kentucky. Officially, she died of Hodgkin's disease, but, as her friend Judy Bryant put it, "she died of absolutely everything."

During the next four years Merrick produced nothing for the theater. In 1977 he completed a film of Dan Jenkins' novel *Semi-Tough*. Originally he had wanted Jenkins to adapt it as a musical, but then he decided it worked better as film.

Curiously, what attracted him to the novel was its subject, football. Though he had little interest in sports in general, the exception was football. In the mid-Seventies, in fact, he had even contemplated buying the Jets, convinced he could reverse their slump by applying his own brand of showmanship.

Eventually he made *Semi-Tough* as a film, starring Burt Reynolds. It was a box office hit, but even his new financial standing was not enough to encourage him to pursue a career in Hollywood. He made one more film, *Rough Cut*, which starred Burt Reynolds and David Niven. (The latter had to sue Merrick to receive $91,667 in salary payments that had been withheld.)

He still traveled and optioned shows. He optioned but later dropped a French farce called *La Cage Aux Folles*. Would the younger Merrick have dropped the option?

Then, in the fall of 1979, he heard some snippets of news about a former employee, Mark Bramble, toward whom he had taken a godfatherly position. Bramble was from a well-to-do Baltimore family whose friends included Tallulah Bankhead. Bankhead had sensed the young Bramble's passion for the theater. "You must learn the business of the theater," she told him. "And the only man who really understands it is David Merrick."

In the spring of 1970, when he was eighteen, Bramble was attending Emerson College, which had a flexible work-study program. He had written Merrick offering his services for free if Merrick would teach him about the theater. Over the years Merrick had numerous such young interns. From time to time he would tell Helen Nickerson, "I'm tired of them. Go out there and fire the free help."

There was always room on Merrick's payroll for first rate free labor. He found Bramble amusing. Bramble would blush every time Merrick spoke to him. Sometimes he would rush out of his office and order Bramble, "Blush!"

When it came time for Bramble to leave, he was touched by Merrick's kindly plea, "You can't leave. I've just learned your name." Nevertheless Merrick encouraged him to finish his degree.

In 1979, Bramble got an unexpected call from Merrick, in Los Angeles. "I understand you have acquired the rights to *42nd Street*," he said. "Would you consider me as a producer?"

Bramble was too stunned to respond.

"Can you wait until I get to New York?" Merrick asked him.

"When are you coming to New York?" Bramble replied.

"In two days."

They had lunch at the Plaza with Michael Stewart, who was one of Merrick's oldest employees and fitful friends. Even during the many periods in which the two were not officially speaking, Stewart would call and ask Nickerson, "How's the old queen?"

Bramble and Stewart had two projects, *42nd Street*, and a musical based on the life of P.T. Barnum. They thought Elliott Gould would make a good star for the latter. "If you could see your way to using Jim Dale, I'll produce it," Merrick told them.

Of the two projects the one that most interested him was the stage version of the Warner Bros. musical. His vision took shape immediately.

"David, it's a big show," Stewart told him. "Do you think we could have sixteen girls?"

"Absolutely not," Merrick said. "I won't do it with less than twenty-four. I would prefer thirty-six."

Ultimately Merrick did the groundwork for *Barnum* and brought Cy Coleman in to work with Bramble and Stewart on the score. He withdrew from the production but continued to give the team great avuncular assistance.

He spoke to Bramble on a daily basis to see how the show was progressing. He did not attend rehearsals, but understood the problems and strengths of the show entirely from having read the script. When the production was short of funds and not all the sets could be built, Merrick specified which ones he considered important.

The night before the show opened, when the producers were still in a quandary about whether it would succeed, he attended a preview. As he came up the aisle he informed Bramble, "This is all right. You will now be solvent."

He was right. More important, now Bramble and Stewart were free to work on *42nd Street.*

CHAPTER THIRTY-FIVE

I N THE SPRING OF 1980, shortly before he went to New York to supervise *42nd Street*, Merrick held a meeting in San Francisco with Francis Ford Coppola, who had written the screenplay for *The Great Gatsby*. At that point Coppola's colleague was Bernard Gersten, who had been a stage manager for Merrick on *Do Re Mi*.

Merrick was glad to see Gersten. He was always happy to see people from New York, especially people who had once worked for him. Gersten was surprised to see how ill at ease Merrick seemed in Coppola's office at Zoetrope Studios. Merrick never had a West Coast office, nor, for that matter, a proper home there. He based his activities at his Beverly Hills Hotel suite.

At the beginning of the meeting Merrick took a large white handkerchief out of his suit pocket. Throughout the meeting he held it in his hand and fidgeted with it.

It was a gesture that seemed out of character for the great producer. It betrayed a nervousness comparable to what he had shown in Ruth Gordon's dressing room when he first approached her about bringing *The Matchmaker* to New York.

The gesture—that of an indecisive, nervous man—surprised Gersten, who had had little contact with Merrick in almost twenty years—since, in fact, Merrick tried to fire him from *Do Re Mi* for showing too much consideration for the needs of the chorus.

Merrick's fidgeting with the handkerchief was the culmination of three years of inaction. He had spent most of the last three years in Los Angeles. He had devoted much time to planning his debut as a TV producer, with a ten-hour miniseries based on *Blood and Money*, Tommy Thompson's novel about a bizarre crime in Texas, which would be directed by Billy Friedkin.

For Merrick the difference between movies and television was the care that went into the filming. TV films were shot in a hurry. Movies were shot with more care—he saw *Blood and Money* as a way to bring movie-level quality to television. But ultimately he never got the production off the ground.

In November of 1979, after numerous rewrites, CBS sued Merrick to rescind its contract with him. The suit was settled in May of 1982 in favor of CBS, which won $916,667 from Merrick. He regained the rights to the property, but by then NBC had already aired *Murder in Texas*, a fictionalized account of the same case.

In a career astonishing for its prolificacy these three years, from 1977 to 1980, stand as the great desert. Between the release of *Semi-Tough* in 1977 and *Rough Cut* in 1980, he produced nothing for either stage or screen. Over the years there had been many projects that had not reached culmination. In some cases it was his fault. Robert Anderson and Richard Adler, for example, had written a musical version of *Roman Holiday*, in which they were toying with casting the very young Liza Minnelli. They were already casting when Merrick declared he no longer wanted to produce it. In some cases the projects foundered despite his good intentions. Adler and Bob Merrill wrote a musical version of Somerset Maugham's *Of Human Bondage*, which Merrick liked well enough to give them a check for $150,000. He also gave them Sam and Bella Spewack to write the book, and the project floundered. He optioned Mark Harris's novel *Bang the Drum Slowly* well before the film version, but never managed to produce it as a musical. Among the plays that never got produced was *Plymouth Rock*, by the *New Yorker* cartoonist and novelist Bill

Hamilton. Toward the end of 1968 he finally found a composer to tackle a project he had long cherished, a musical version of *National Velvet*. The composer was the great Frank Loesser, who had not had a Broadway show since *How to Succeed In Business Without Really Trying* at the beginning of the decade. Loesser began working with Jerome Weidman, who found it strange that, though Loesser would play themes for him, he wrote nothing down. Weidman had no idea that Loesser was riddled with cancer. He died before completing anything for the project.

In some cases he floated ideas without any real conviction. Shortly after *Fiddler on the Roof* opened he urged Sheldon Harnick to read Donald Barthelme's somewhat avant-garde novel *Snow White*. Harnick couldn't imagine why he saw it as a musical. When he asked Merrick about it, Merrick revealed he hadn't even read it.

But even these failures paled against the backdrop of his phenomenal success. During these years in Los Angeles, however, there were no successes, no ideas.

In 1978 Michael Stewart persuaded him to be interviewed by a young actress named Dona Vaughn, who had been in the original cast of *Company*, had been Ed Sherin's assistant on *The Red Devil Battery Sign* and who now had a radio show.

The one condition Merrick insisted on, Stewart stressed, was that she must not ask any questions about his personal life. "Manic depression" now seems too simple a term to describe complex mental patterns. But if for most of his life Merrick's behavior had a relentless energy suggestive of clinically "manic" behavior, then these three years seemed one of sustained depression.

When he spoke to Vaughn his voice was low keyed, very subdued. At first Vaughn had trouble making eye contact with him. He stared intently at the microphone instead of at her. She lowered her head to the level of the table and grinned up at him. He understood. Little by little he became more animated.

He claimed he had never tyrannized his staffs. According to him he had tried to win them over by "conversation." Once, he explained, rather than direct confrontation, when a show was in trouble in Philadelphia, he had written a letter in the guise of an audience member who had seen the show and had some suggestions. He had had a stage manager mail it from Baltimore. When it arrived the director showed it to him and asked him what he thought. Merrick thought the suggestions were valid.

"I have a reputation for being a meany," he told Vaughn. "As you can see, I'm a pussycat."

Now in the spring of 1980 he was back in New York, but he still had not regained his stride. Bernard Jacobs had heard that Merrick had negotiated a deal with the Nederlander Organization to put *42nd Street* in the Mark Hellinger theater. So he was surprised to receive a phone call on a Friday night that Helen Nickerson—who had handled all the preliminary decisions on *42nd Street* while her boss was still in California—had called. Merrick wanted to meet with Jacobs immediately. He arranged to meet Merrick at the bar of the Regency Hotel on Monday after-

David Merrick receiving an honory doctorate from his alma mater, St. Louis University

noon. Jacobs knew how fickle Merrick was when it came to theaters. In 1974 he had heard Merrick would book the Minskoff for *Mack and Mabel*. He knew Merrick was a weekend guest of his neighbors on Shelter Island, Jerome and Gladys Minskoff. On Saturday afternoon Merrick and Etan paid Jacobs an unexpected visit. In the midst of the social call Merrick said he wanted the Majestic for *Mack and Mabel* and they shook hands on the terms. The Merricks then returned to partake of the Minskoffs' hospitality.

At the Regency Merrick talked about everything except *42nd Street*. Jacobs left the meeting mystified. The following weekend he got a call from Robin Wagner, who had gotten a call from Merrick informing him to re-orient his designs for *42nd Street* for the Winter Garden rather than the Hellinger.

Jacobs' colleague Phil Smith, the treasurer of the Shubert Organization, received a call from Nickerson asking if the work had begun on the Winter Garden. Smith informed her that, to his knowledge, Merrick had not yet negotiated for the Winter Garden.

"Phil, I'll send him over," Nickerson said. "Tell Bernie to lock the door and don't let him out until he signs the contract."

From the moment he heard from Wagner, Jacobs knew it was definite that Merrick would request the Winter Garden. He drew up two contracts, one to his advantage, one to Merrick's. When Merrick arrived he presented the first of the contracts. Without any of the customary theatricality Merrick read it through and began to sign it. Jacobs, not wanting to take advantage of him, presented the one with terms he felt were fairer to Merrick.

The opening of *42nd Street* restored Merrick to himself. Needless to say, this was not necessarily a boon to everyone. A few weeks after the show opened he fired Helen Nickerson, who had been his secretary for seventeen years. Shortly after she arrived in 1963 he had told her, "Everybody leaves me."

"I won't leave you," she told him. "You'll have to throw me out." And that was exactly what he did. She had called him that morning about a matter regarding Cecilia Ann. Should she make reservations for a trip to Florida for her? "No," her boss barked and hung up. A minute later he called her back.

"Pack your bags. You're fired," he told her.

"What did I do?" she asked, dumbfounded.

He hung up. She tried to reach him. He wouldn't answer the phone. She began packing things from her desk into a shopping bag. She tried him one more time. What had she done, she wanted to know. "You've badmouthed me all over town," he told her.

He had not been an easy boss, and, though she had been scrupulously loyal in following his orders, of course there had been times when she had unburdened herself to others. She suspected who had reported back to Merrick. There was, however, nothing to be done. She left the office with her belongings and, dazed, took a bus uptown, incredulous that her years of service had ended so crudely.

Perhaps mindful that no good deed should go unpunished, Merrick felt compelled to torment Bernard Jacobs, who had handled the negotiations for the Winter Garden so graciously. In part it was that he enjoyed negotiating with Bernie Jacobs. He considered him a worthy adversary.

He pestered Jacobs daily, sometimes waiting for him when he arrived at his office in the morning. Jacobs sometimes called the office by cellular phone to see if Merrick was there. Jacobs decided to take a vacation in the Virgin Islands and Frank Weissberg agreed to handle Merrick. He would take Merrick's first call of the day himself. The second call would be handled by Weissberg's secretary, the third by a low level assistant. The frequency of calls diminished substantially.

One of Merrick's proposals was to charge $100 at the box office for house seats for *42nd Street*. (Top price in 1980 was $30.) When Jacobs refused to hear of it Merrick demanded the Shuberts redesign the Winter Garden to squeeze in more seats and maximize his profits. He presented a plan whereby, instead of seats of uniform size, there would be alternating seats 18" wide and 16" wide (the larger, of course, for men, the smaller for women).

Rather than yield to this plan, which Merrick promoted with his accustomed tenacity, Jacobs let him move *42nd Street* to the Majestic, which has a larger orchestra section. Merrick designated an unusually high number of prime seats "house seats" and attached a $15 surcharge, an unprecedented policy. His capacity to rile his fellow producers re-emerged, completely undiminished despite years of disuse. A radio commercial for *42nd Street* had a character named Alex boasting about his new musical, *22nd Street*, which had a cast of seven and two songs. (That spring Alex Cohen had produced *A Day in Hollywood/ A Night in the Ukraine*, which had the exact same resources.) The commercial ended with Alex's friend noting that David Merrick's musical *42nd Street* is considerably grander. A spokesman for Merrick, of course, denied that there was any intention to needle Cohen. Several years later, when *Cats* became a hot ticket, the commercial for *42nd Street* suggested it was a perfect antidote for people who were "allergic to Cats."

The new Merrick hit brought back all the megalomaniacal behavior of years past. This was apparent at the recording session for the cast album, which took place a few weeks after the opening on a Sunday morning at the RCA recording studios on West 44th Street. Strangely, he had not actually wanted to have a recording made. He sensed, correctly, that *42nd Street* was a dance show, a visual show, neither of which could be captured on an album.

Early in the session he complained that the sound of the tapping was not loud enough. Thomas Z. Shepard, the preeminent producer of Broadway cast albums, who was running the session, pointed out that if the taps were louder it would destroy the balance between them and the orchestra.

Merrick was not in the mood for expert technical advice. "By the time David got to the recording studio, I think he thought he wrote this show," Shepard later observed. "The guy who put it together had died. Merrick had ignored the composer, Harry Warren. He hadn't even invited him to the opening. He barely acknowledged the book writers and had fought with them over whether they would even get billing. He thought it was his show."

Until this argument Shepard had found Merrick unobtrusive. Merrick, in fact, had been extremely complimentary toward him, promising billing greater than he had ever had. That quickly changed. To counter Merrick's proposal that the taps be made louder Shepard suggested perhaps the album could begin with a rehearsal piano.

Merrick wasn't interested. He wanted the orchestra "dialed out."

Shepard refused.

"He didn't even make any threats," Shepard recalled. He simply announced over the loudspeaker, "OK, the session is over."

The cast, experienced in Merrick's whims, was nonetheless stunned. Shepard immediately told them, "Today you are being employed by RCA. You can't leave."

By chance the head of RCA, Bob Sumner, happened to be in the otherwise deserted building. Shepard knew his minutes were numbered. RCA would not welcome a showdown with Merrick. Shepard was right. RCA did not want to be bogged down in legal battles with David Merrick. He, after all, had contributed $100,000 to underwrite the album, minimizing the risk for RCA.

Shepard decided to confront Merrick: "Why do you go from nothing to looking as if you want to murder me?"

Merrick walked away. Shepard was relieved of his duties, which were assigned to his assistant, Jay David Sacks.

In May of 1981, the spring after *42nd Street* opened, Merrick produced what would be his last original play. As had always been the case, it was not a matter of his having read and admired a script. He saw it in production in Buffalo and transferred it to New York at the very end of the season, convinced it would win the Tony for Best Play that year. There was no doubt but that *42nd Street* would win Best Musical. To win both Tonys would be a delicious first for him.

The play, *I Won't Dance*, was by a talented playwright and

screenwriter, Oliver Hailley, who had never received his due in the theater. This play was not likely to bring him laurels. It was artificial and annoying. Even if it had been a better play than it was, Merrick's wager that it would beat Peter Shaffer's *Amadeus* for the Tony was a glaring miscalculation. Not only did it not win. It was not even nominated. It closed the night it opened.

For the Tony party that year, Merrick took the entire cast of *42nd Street* to the ball, footing the bill—$6,000—himself. *42nd Street* did win the Tony for Best Musical. There was really no competition. When Merrick came onstage to accept the award, he said, in a gruff, belligerent tone, "Imagine what this season would have been without *42nd Street*." He added nothing that might indicate he was joking. He left the stage as ungraciously as he had entered.

The previous summer, a few days after the show had opened, there had been a memorial service for Gower Champion in the Winter Garden Theater. If *42nd Street* itself brought to a close a great chapter in the American musical, the tribute to Gower inaugurated what would become a golden age of memorial services, some for venerable figures who had led full, productive lives, too many for younger men cut down in their prime.

At the service for Gower his first wife Marge recalled their courtship and their early career as a dancing duo. David Hartman, who had been in the original company of *Hello, Dolly!*, recalled Gower's modesty. In a pep talk Champion had told the cast, "The dance steps are not that great. The choreography's not either. Go out there and give it 108 percent or we're all finished."

After the others, Merrick advanced to the microphone. "I was just talking to Gower," he began genially. "He's quite pleased."

For a minute Merrick dropped the mask of the stern taskmaster, the bullying producer. He recalled an interviewer years ago asking who had done what on one of the Merrick-Champion musicals. In answer to every one of the interviewer's questions Merrick had said, "Gower Champion."

Finally the interviewer asked him, "Mr. Merrick, what did you do on this show?"

Merrick answered simply, "I picked Gower Champion."

Calling *42nd Street* Gower's "Lullaby of Broadway," Merrick shouted to an offstage technician, "Come on with the finale." He thanked the mourners for coming as, over the loudspeakers, the title song of *42nd Street* blared forth.

Merrick strode from the center of the stage to the side. The lights on the stage had grown dim except for a spot trained on the producer, who now leaned against the proscenium, beaming at the first puzzled, then appalled audience. His smile, people recalled, could only be described as diabolical. He had paid his respects to the man with whom his career had been so intimately linked. He had allowed the spotlight to fall on someone else (someone whose name, in a few days, he would remove from all the posters and advertising for *42nd Street*). He had been uncharacteristically humble and gracious.

But now it was back to business. The spotlight, as per his instructions, was back where it belonged.

He was like an actor recreating his favorite role, the one with which he is most identified in the public imagination. The part gave him the same pleasure, the same sense of power that it always had.

CHAPTER THIRTY-SIX

N LOS ANGELES, a few weeks later, there was another memorial for Gower. This time it was not in a theater, but in a setting that seemed very Los Angeles—the beach at Malibu. Everyone arrived in casual attire except, of course, for Merrick, who was wearing a black suit and black shoes. As he spoke he gestured toward the sky. He was not, however, speaking to Gower. He made it clear to the assembled that Gower was speaking to them through him. The cosmic connections that had begun while he waited for The Courier were becoming ever more mystic.

In the months after *42nd Street* opened, Merrick had removed Champion's name from the marquee. Gower's son Gregg fought to have it restored. In suppressing Champion's contribution, he was appropriating the work of the man with whom he fought the most and to whom perhaps he owed the most. Was he perhaps attempting to erase the debt?

During this time Merrick's most frequent companions were Wanda Richert and her roommate, who was also her understudy in *42nd Street,* Karen Prunczik.

Champion had hired Prunczik because she was an especially strong tap dancer. The first day of rehearsal Merrick went over to Champion: "That girl is pockmarked and she's ugly. I want her fired." Champion paid no attention. She was a strong dancer and

With Karen Prunczik.

he needed strong dancers. Shortly afterward, watching a dress rehearsal of one of the most lavish numbers in the show, "Dames," in which the girls wore elegantly designed gowns, Merrick told Champion, "She's too ugly to wear those clothes."

Champion, however, felt she was an asset to the show and eventually made her Richert's understudy. One night, when the show was enjoying its successful Broadway run, Richert was unable to go on. Prunczik thought she would have the break every young performer hopes for, the kind of break *42nd Street* was about. But Merrick cancelled the performance rather than let her go on.

It seemed characteristically perverse of him that, at the same time he was impeding Prunczik's Broadway career, he was seducing her.

In the year after *42nd Street* opened he saw a lot of Wanda Richert. She brought out the protective father in him. She had, after all, gotten virtually nothing when Gower Champion died— the stool from which he had conducted rehearsals of *42nd Street,* his sweatshirt, and a picture he had torn out of a book, on which he had written, "I love you." There had been money someone had given her from a safe, but Carla, who was, after all, his wife, had asked for it back and she had returned it.

After a while people began to notice that Merrick did not hang around backstage any more to wait for Richert. They didn't see him much at all. But they also began to notice that Prunczik was dressing better. She was no longer waiting for other "gypsies" to go out after the show. She would leave almost immediately after the curtain came down. At times Lee Roy Reams noticed her getting into a limousine he was pretty certain was Merrick's.

In July someone in the New York cast of *42nd Street* received a phone call from his mother, who lived in Hawaii. Guess whom she had just seen on the street—David Merrick and his new wife, Karen Prunczik!

They had been married July 1, 1982, in a courthouse in Alexandria, Virginia. Her parents, whom he had met on two separate occasions—even making the Victorian gesture of asking her father for permission to marry her—flew in from Pittsburgh.

Merrick had then whisked her away to Lima, Peru, where he had gone to judge the Miss Universe Contest. He told columnist Liz Smith that he originally thought he would join the disciples of the Rev. Sun Myung Moon, thousands of whom were married in a mass ceremony in Madison Square Garden, a bizarre event that had attracted enormous media attention. "We knew we would get lost in the crowd," the publicity-shy Merrick told Smith. "But when I learned that we had to wait a forty-day grace period before consummating the marriage, I said the hell with it."

The decision to marry Karen had been a sudden one.

He phoned Byron Goldman, with whom his relations had been strained for some time. He knew that one of Byron's passions was collecting rare stones. "I want you to find me a ruby," he told Goldman. Goldman was excited at the thought of shopping for so rich a stone—until he heard the price limit Merrick had set: $2,500. It would have to be a bargain basement ruby. As if that were not ridiculous enough, Merrick told Goldman he had to have it in two days, before the happy couple flew to Peru. Because his acquaintanceship among jewel merchants was so diverse, Byron was able to find a ring.

As another wedding gift Merrick arranged with a furrier in New Jersey to have a mink coat made for Prunczik. The furrier asked if he should stitch in a label with her monogrammed initials on it. "Don't bother," Merrick told him.

As had generally been the case with his marriages, Merrick's mood soured immediately. In Lima they went shopping. Merrick hired a limousine and he drove Karen to the better stores. She went in to shop and brought a salesclerk out to the limousine with the charge slip. Merrick, who remained in the car, signed it. At one point he got bored and locked her out of their hotel room.

Then had come the honeymoon in Hawaii. At the beginning of August the couple had returned home. Merrick threw a party to introduce his bride to the cast of *42nd Street,* most of whom she already knew. Whatever queasiness she felt at her treatment on their extended wedding trip, she showed nothing. Her mood was one of enthusiasm. "I'm very, very happy," she told a reporter.

A few months later she decided to become a working wife. Rather than cast her at home in the New York company, Merrick sent her to Chicago. By a curious coincidence she was going to replace an actress named Nancy Sinclair. It was Sinclair's precipitate departure during rehearsals for the original production of *42nd Street* that had created the opening Prunczik filled during the out-of-town tryout in Washington.

Through an uncharacteristic bit of inefficiency, Prunczik's name was not yet on the program when she opened in Chicago. She was hurt and angry. Marriage was changing her. She no longer accepted Merrick's callous treatment submissively. She made her displeasure known. Then, at the opening night party, to which she wore her wedding dress—a copy of the dress she wore in the "Shuffle Off to Buffalo" number in the show—she was angry to see her husband dancing with Nancy Sinclair.

Merrick claimed that Sinclair had asked him for the first dance. Prunczik didn't believe him. Her father, who had become unhappy with the way his son-in-law treated his daughter, doubted that Sinclair asked Merrick to dance. "Who do you believe, me or your father?" Merrick challenged her. "I always believe my father," she replied.

Merrick stormed out. He found the company manager and told him, "Fire her from the show and fire her as my wife."

When, later that night, she got back to their hotel she discovered that Merrick had flown back to New York —and stuck her with the bill.

Divorce proceedings were initiated immediately. Unlike the marriage to Etan, Merrick had not taken the precaution of getting an immediate, secret Mexican divorce. He had to do it in a more conventional way and hired the well known matrimonial attorney Raoul Lionel Felder, who, paradoxically, had represented Etan in her divorce from Merrick.

It might have been a quick, bloodless procedure except for one complication. His health deserted him.

Only a few years earlier, shortly after *42nd Street* opened, Merrick had made Mark Bramble, then only twenty-eight, the executor of his will. Bramble was flustered at the thought of dealing with what he assumed would be a complicated estate.

No, Merrick explained to him. It would all be very simple. There would be an allotment for Cecilia Ann. All the rest would go to Marguerita. The most important thing was that "not one cent" would go to Etan.

But, with the passage of time, he had softened toward her. Their relationship had become increasingly civil. They were to lunch the day before Valentine's Day, 1983, to talk about Marguerita. When he did not show up Etan became concerned. A huge snow storm had descended on the city that day, but she knew that natural obstacles would not deter him. She went to his apartment in the Galleria. The door was locked but she could see lights on inside.

She called Mort Mitosky. As a close friend of Merrick's, he was in a better position to authorize breaking down the door than a former wife. When they got inside they found Merrick on the floor of the bathroom. He had suffered a stroke.

Because of the snow storm it took almost three hours for an ambulance to arrive.

Doctors finally determined that his mental functioning was not seriously affected. The stroke had impaired his ability to walk. Most crucial, however, was that it had robbed him of the weapon he had wielded mercilessly for more than forty years— his tongue.

Without it, he was at the mercy of others, specifically his not-yet-divorced wife, Karen Prunczik. She flew back to New York, discharged him from the hospital and brought him back to the apartment they had shared.

At first she thought she could cope with him at home. Her father advised her that even if the divorce proceedings continued it would be advantageous if she could demonstrate that she had cared for him in a dutiful and loving manner. But she was not equipped to manage him day in and day out, even with round the clock nursing care. On March 7 she moved him to the Rusk Rehabilitation Center on First Avenue and 34th Street, where he would receive excellent medical care.

But for a man accustomed to absolute rule, to be subject to orders from nurses and orderlies was the height of humiliation. Not only was he deprived of normal rational communication. He was also deprived of his own normal means of expression, irrational but always effective—screaming. Merrick had held himself aloof throughout his life, but had always been in a position to strike out at will. His involuntary mute isolation must have made him want to scream more than ever.

A man of fewer resources and less daring might have been defeated in such circumstances. But the next day, when he had been left unattended, Merrick steered his wheelchair down a corridor and out of the hospital onto First Avenue into driving rain. With no umbrella, nothing to protect him except his savage determination, Merrick managed to navigate six blocks over to Second Avenue, where he took refuge in a Korean noodle factory.

The Koreans, not recognizing their eminent, rain-soaked visitor, had called the police. When the police arrived Merrick, unable to speak coherently, handed them a piece of paper with Mort Mitosky's phone number. He had no other identification.

"There's a guy, he has your number in his pocket," the officer told Mitosky, who had no idea what could have happened. Merrick, he knew, was secure at the Rusk Institute. Who could this be?

It was Joy Klein, Cecilia Ann's caretaker, later Mitosky's wife who became convinced that it must be Merrick. By the time Mitosky and Klein determined what must have happened the police had returned Merrick to the hospital. Prunczik had been notified about his escape and took him back to the apartment. She provided nurses, but she didn't think to get guards. Merrick was finally able to reach Mitosky, who managed to spirit him away from Prunczik's apartment.

Mitosky flew Merrick to Los Angeles, where he was checked into a hospital for tests. When they returned to New York Merrick was installed in Etan's townhouse on East 71st Street.

Both women, whom Merrick had dominated, controlled and rejected, now fought for the right to control him. The grand master of litigation and manipulation, Merrick had become a pawn in a legal battle between Etan and Karen.

Prunczik's lawyer, Lester Wallman, filed a writ of habeas corpus to force Merrick back into her care. Her claim that he had been kidnapped and was being held against his will by Mitosky was dismissed. Former State Attorney General Louis Lefkowitz, who had been active in investigating "ice" on Broadway, was now appointed Merrick's "guardian." He reported that Merrick was content under Etan's care and supervision.

Merrick's own attorney, Raoul Felder, instituted divorce proceedings against Prunczik, charging she had only married Merrick for his money. A damaging witness against her was her former roommate Wanda Richert, who thought Merrick had been "victimized" by Prunczik. (Richert's attitude, to be fair, was "a plague on both your houses." When she left *42nd Street* she had given Merrick a Bible in which she had underlined a phrase in the 73rd Psalm: "the prosperity of the wicked.")

Prunczik realized she needed bigger guns. She hired the celebrated "palimony" expert Marvin Mitchelson. Prunczik accused Merrick of paranoia. More damaging, she told the court her husband had a drug problem. Probably she was correct in both instances, but her posture of attacking him undercut her claim of only wanting the best for him during his illness.

Ultimately the hearing at which Merrick was granted the divorce set a record for speed. It began at 10:30 a.m. and was over by 12:20 p.m. A financial settlement had been made out of court. The fact that so many grievances had already been aired in the press apparently made the judge eager to settle the case rather than let it become a courtroom circus.

What normally takes a minimum of eight weeks took only a few hours. This was the way he liked to do business.

Merrick had been deemed by his doctors too sick to appear in court, but he apparently wasn't too sick to appear at the celebration immediately afterwards at a swanky Italian restaurant on East 62nd Street, Nanni Il Valletto.

As an honored customer, Merrick and his party were seated near the front of the restaurant. Shortly after they had toasted the judge's speedy decision, the door opened. It was Karen, her lawyer, and her father, who had also come to mark the end of her ordeal. Merrick did not even look up as she passed his table.

Though Merrick was happy enough to have escaped Prunczik's care, he was not entirely happy to be at the mercy of Mitosky. Weighing his limited options, he was beginning to wonder if it might not be advantageous to return to Etan. But Etan found that caring for her incapacitated, frustrated former husband was too demanding, at least on 71st Street. Instead she would minister to him personally in the altogether more salubrious surroundings of the South of France. She found a large, sumptuously furnished villa on the outskirts of Cannes, where she brought David, Marguerita, a staff of nurses and a speech therapist.

Michael Stewart had owned a summer place near Cannes for years. As often as he and Merrick had fought—it was part of doing business with Merrick—the two were remarkably close, and Stewart made a point of visiting him. Jerry Orbach and his wife, on vacation, also stopped to see him. Everyone who saw him instantly knew he was deeply unhappy. If there had been no other reason, the tremendous expense of the villa would have been sufficient.

Mark Bramble, who was passing through Cannes, phoned ahead to say he was coming. When he arrived he was told that Merrick was upstairs in his room and was seeing absolutely no one. Bramble, who would not be staying in Cannes long enough to make the trip again, insisted on seeing Merrick.

He was led to a luxuriously furnished bedroom, where Merrick appeared to be dozing under the careful eye of a nurse. Merrick groaned, and for the first time Bramble sensed how deeply ill his former employer was: "He looked like he was down for the count."

After the groan Merrick, virtually unintelligible, barked something at the nurse. She understood and left. With a gesture of his hand, Merrick beckoned Bramble to his side.

Bramble could see that any speech required superhuman effort, but he also recognized Merrick's determination. There could be no pleasantries. Every word mattered.

"When are you going?" he asked Bramble.

Puzzled, Bramble said he was leaving on Friday.

"I'm coming with you," Merrick said.

"Of course," Bramble laughed, assuming Merrick was joking. Then, also with effort, Merrick pulled down the covers of the bed. Under the blanket, in the sweltering heat of a Mediterranean June, Merrick was wearing his pinstripe three piece suit and a trenchcoat, as if, Bramble thought, he were due in court in a matter of minutes.

Bramble knew his former boss was not joking.

"I'm moving into your hotel," he said.

Bramble was confused. "Why are you leaving this beautiful place?" he asked.

"I hate it."

With Bramble's help and to the amazement of the company gathered downstairs, Merrick announced his departure.

Back in New York they went to the apartment of his former intern. Merrick headed straight to the bedroom. "I'll stay here," he announced. "You'll sleep up there," he gestured, pointing to a room Bramble had constructed in a skylight. Arrangements were made for Merrick to share the expenses of the apartment and to have daily nursing care.

Bramble's West 58th Street apartment became Merrick's headquarters as well. Bramble found himself playing inadvertent host to lawyers and, quite frequently, to Bernard Jacobs of the Shubert Organization. To his surprise, Bramble found himself enjoying his guest's company.

There were limits to the care Bramble could provide. He hired a nurse to look after Merrick and to accompany him to doctors' appointments. He was very struck by her assessment of the patient: "This man has channeled his self-destructive instincts into something positive—his work in the theater. It is rare that someone with that much destructive energy can find such a constructive outlet."

As a reward Merrick took Bramble along to the place he called his favorite in the world, Rio De Janeiro. Bramble was amazed to see that Merrick was as at home in Rio as he was in New York or London. He knew writers, journalists, musicians and intellectuals. Among them was the celebrated novelist Jorge Amado, whose book *Gabriela, Cinnamon and Cloves* he eventually hoped to turn into a musical.

By the time he returned to New York, he was strong enough to return to his own quarters in the Galleria on East 57th Street. Although his physical strength had been impaired and though only a few people could understand him, Merrick had no intention of retiring. All those years he had schemed to control others; now he planned to regain control of himself.

One way of ending Mitosky's conservatorship would be to replace him with Etan. The most efficient way to accomplish the shift of power would be to make Etan Aronson, for a second time, Etan Merrick. Etan agreed. The night before the wedding they both seemed nervous. She found it endearing that he looked at her softly and said, "You don't have to."

They were married in Greenwich, Connecticut, on the lawn of the courthouse. Among the celebrants were Michael Stewart, Mark Bramble, Helen Montagu, her daughter, the Merricks' daughter, Marguerita, and Bernie and Betty Jacobs.

Fortunately for both bride and groom, marriage did not require co-habitation. By mid-autumn Merrick had regained the use of his body and was living alone again. His mind, however, which had been extremely clearheaded during the divorce and remarriage, now began to scatter: the legacy, perhaps, of his poor, crazy mother. There had always been a screw loose. Now it got looser.

Over the years Merrick's bachelor apartment might have been

taken for that of a vagrant. Nothing was clean. There might be sheets on a mattress on the floor. There might not. If there were, they might not have been changed in months. Sleeping, after all, was not a matter to which he devoted much time or thought.

In the old days he could get by with four or five hours of sleep a night because his mind was feverish with ideas, overflowing with plans he had to put into practice. Now the mind was disturbed. He was seen wandering the streets of Manhattan muttering threats against Walt Prunczik, his former father-in-law. He would go to banks where he had safe-deposit boxes and stuff his pockets with money, hundreds of thousands of dollars.

Walt Prunczik filed court papers alleging that Merrick had been heard mumbling that he had put out a contract on him. A psychiatrist testified that Merrick did indeed harbor "homicidal impulses" against his former father-in-law. The psychiatrist suggested the reason Merrick had withdrawn these huge sums of money was in order to pay off the contract on Prunczik's life. (A more likely reason was to buy cocaine, which had been found scattered on the floor the day of his stroke.)

In December of 1983 Etan was appointed his conservator, along with Robert Wagner, the former mayor of New York. In February Mitosky was removed from the conservatorship. Mitosky received the sum of $350,000, or $35,000 a month, during the time he was charged with "conserving" and protecting Merrick's interests and assets. Even an immensely wealthy man could not afford such "conservation" for very long.

Even apart from Mitosky's fee, the conservatorship was getting very expensive. Knowing Merrick was not in total control, many people who claimed he owed them royalties or other fees were applying for redress and in some cases getting it.

In April of 1984, Merrick suffered a most curious and ignominious blow. Supreme Court Judge Arthur Blyn, who now decided matters relating to the Merrick estate, issued an order barring Merrick from investing $1.5 million in a projected London production of *42nd Street*. The court declared it considered theatrical investments "too speculative." Felder, who now represented Merrick on non-matrimonial matters, asked, "What is Merrick going to do, invest in supermarkets?"

To point up the absurdity of the order, Felder cited an article in Variety that very week, noting that Merrick, as the sole producer of the Broadway and touring productions of *42nd Street,* was earning $500,000 a week, "by far the greatest weekly profit total for any producer in U.S. stage history."

Merrick's fortune was estimated at between $20 million and $50 million. But just as there had been the public, witty Merrick, and the secret Merrick, there was also the public fortune and the private one.

The private one existed in safe deposit boxes all over New York, London and various places outside the jurisdiction of the U.S. government. Even Merrick probably had no real idea of its value.

Merrick had no intention of allowing Judge Blyn to assert any authority over his London production of *42nd Street.* With Bramble as his accomplice, Merrick spent several hours in a limousine driving around Manhattan dipping into the safe deposit boxes and stuffing cash into the pockets of his coat. Once in the limo, the huge sums were put into an unpretentious traveling bag. Although he had not used a wheelchair in many months, a wheelchair was waiting for him when he arrived at Heathrow Airport. The customs officials there did not even bother to search the invalid who was wheeled past them.

The money was distributed—in piles that astounded and intimidated the recipients—to the firms that built costumes and scenery. Work began in earnest on the London production of *42nd Street.* In late May, Judge Blyn reversed his decision on allowing Merrick to invest in his own show. By then it didn't matter. The show was already well on its way.

In an affidavit she filed to help Merrick regain control of his financial affairs, Helen Montagu, the English producer who would be his associate on *42nd Street,* observed that Merrick's mind operated differently in the theater from the way it did in personal matters. "It seems to me that David is only himself when he produces, because he can be quite mumbly at one stage, if it is just social. Then he comes into theater situations . . . and he is as clear as a bell."

It had always been true. The theater had always mobilized his energies and cleared his mind. It had always been the force that turned him from a soft, unprepossessing figure on the periphery to the powerful, mesmerizing tyrant who controlled others' lives. The theater gave him control of his own life.

For the next few years he actively supervised his productions of *42nd Street*. For the first time in his career, Merrick became an international producer. Instead of confining his operations to the U.S. and England, he produced *42nd Street* in Australia. There were plans for one in Tokyo.

In part this expanded vision stemmed from his acquaintance with a young British producer named Cameron Mackintosh. The two had first met in 1973, when Gillian Lynne directed the second musical Mackintosh produced, *The Card*, an adaptation of an Arnold Bennett novel about a man who knows everything about making money, but nothing about women. At Lynne's invitation, Merrick came to a final preview of *The Card*, whose score was by Tony Hatch and Jackie Trent, the English equivalent of Bachrach and David. "It's not perfect," Merrick said. "But I think it could be a big hit."

Seven years and numerous London hits later, Mackintosh happened to be in Washington, D.C. when *42nd Street* was trying out there. He went to see it. It was three hours long—half an hour would be trimmed before it reached New York. Whatever its problems, he thought, "You just smelled that Gower and Merrick were at the height of their powers again."

Mackintosh ran into Michael Stewart, declared his enthusiasm for the show and wondered if he might be associated with it if and when it came to London. Stewart suggested he speak to Merrick, who was staying at the Watergate Hotel. (Merrick had, in fact, requested a room next to Champion's.)

With some trepidation Mackintosh went to the Watergate and

phoned Merrick's room. Merrick himself answered. Mackintosh reminded him where they had met. "I've just seen the show," he said. "I think it's wonderful."

"Hold on a minute, and I'll come down," Merrick said.

Mackintosh felt the blood draining from his cheeks. But Merrick spent the next few hours discussing the business with him, never lecturing him, often, in fact, seeming genuinely curious about Mackintosh's own achievements.

Before they parted, Merrick invited Mackintosh to the opening of *42nd Street* in New York. The day of the opening, when Merrick might easily have been preoccupied with many other matters, he instructed Helen Nickerson to make an appointment with Mackintosh for the following afternoon.

Considering what happened that night, Mackintosh assumed the appointment would be cancelled. Not at all. Merrick showed the young Englishman around his office and discussed his advertising strategy for *42nd Street* with him. Mackintosh was flattered to feel how cordially Merrick treated him.

A few months later, in fact, Mackintosh raised the issue of being associated with *42nd Street* in London. "As far as I'm concerned, it must be your production," he told Merrick. "You are as much the star as Gower." Mackintosh was not even concerned with billing. He just wanted to be able to observe Merrick at work.

In the intervening months, Mackintosh produced a show in London called *Cats*, which made his offer to assist on *42nd Street* more interesting to Merrick, who wanted to co-produce *Cats* in New York.

When they began negotiating, however, Mackintosh found Merrick exasperating. "From seeing me as a surrogate heir, he now suddenly saw me as a threat," Mackintosh recalled. "I wanted to be associated with a man and a show I admired, but I kept *not* playing Cat and Mouse with him, and his demands became more and more convoluted." Mackintosh withdrew.

In 1985, a year after *42nd Street* opened in London, Mackintosh and Merrick lunched at the Savoy. By then both *Cats*

and *Les Misérables* were becoming enormous international hits, and Merrick was fascinated by how to finance shows in other countries without losing control.

"He treated me now like an equal," Mackintosh felt. "I had done a thing he hadn't dreamt of."

And thus, in 1987 Merrick went to Australia to open his first production Down Under.

There was still, of course, the original production in New York, for which he was constantly devising new promotional schemes. At one point he had a poster with a huge photograph of his own scowling face, finger pointed in the manner of Uncle Sam on World War II recruitment posters, "David Merrick Wants You . . . to see *42nd Street*." When *The Phantom of the Opera* displaced his show from the Majestic and he had to move across the street to the St. James he instituted a well-publicized policy of holding the curtain until 8:15 to attract stragglers who had been unable to secure cancellations for *Phantom* and still might be in the mood for a musical.

He seldom went to the theater. For a man so particular about his public image, it was humiliating to have to require an escort down the aisle, to speak and see a look of bewilderment on the face of his auditor. But in the spring of 1985 he made the effort. He went to see a revival of *Take Me Along*, the musical he had conceived in 1953 when he was still uncertain about what would happen to *Fanny* and which had provided him a glittering hit in 1959.

This revival had been produced at the Goodspeed Opera House. Like many Goodspeed revivals, *Take Me Along* had looked better in the jewelbox of a theater in East Haddam, Connecticut, than it did in the cavernous Martin Beck. Bob Merrill, who first saw the revival in Washington, had not wanted it produced in New York at all. He felt it was a weak spokesman for the show's virtues, but he was persuaded that his opposition to the transfer would be a huge letdown to the cast. Against his better judgment he consented to let it come to Broadway.

The night Merrick came to the theater, Merrill was in a

quandary. He knew the show in no way met Merrick's own high standards. Stomach churning, after the curtain came down, he made his way down the aisle to where Merrick was sitting. Merrick's face brightened. Merrill, who had not seen him since the stroke, found he could understand the slurred, consonant-less foreign tongue Merrick was speaking. It was the glib language of the theater, the reassuring words professionals tell each other in lieu of honesty. "It's a hit," Merrick said, a phrase that for so many years had mattered so much to him. The two men looked into each other's eyes. Both burst into tears. The show ran less than a week.

His ability to speak was still extremely limited. Sometimes he could make himself clear, but the nuance, the edge, the inimitable Merrick manner was not there. In the winter of 1986 he decided to transfer a production of Joe Orton's *Loot*, which had received excellent reviews at The Manhattan Theater Club, to Broadway.

Leo Cohen, his general manager, would sit with him in the Music Box Theater and ask him questions. "What is it, Mr. Merrick?" Merrick made a pantomime of a box in the air.

"Is it the portal, Mr. Merrick?" Merrick nodded. "Is it the color, Mr. Merrick?" "Is it too dark?" Merrick had developed a shorthand to deal with his co-producers, Charles Kopelman and Mark Simon, who had supervised the original production at Manhattan Theater Club. If he raised his hand high in the air, it meant Kopelman, who was tall; lower, it meant Simon, who was shorter.

Cohen, who had worked with him for several years, told a reporter for the *Times*, "He has to share more information than he did before. He's learned that he has to trust, which is interesting for a man who has not trusted before."

Cohen, aware that he had been more forthcoming than virtually anyone had while still in Merrick's employ, added, "That doesn't mean I couldn't be fired in half an hour."

At the opening night party for *Loot* at the Water Club,

Merrick sat at a large table near a window overlooking the East River and the unexciting industrial vistas of Queens. With him were Etan, Mitosky and Joy Klein, Kopelman and Simon and their wives. It was a large, noisy room. Merrick was by no means the center of attention, sitting with the handful of people with whom he felt comfortable.

At one point a photographer came toward the table and knelt to shoot the glum Merrick head-on. He stood in anger, pointed at her and shouted something unintelligible. She withdrew, more out of politeness, even embarrassment than intimidation.

He had accomplished his purpose. But the amount of effort it had required, the amount of frustration and, ultimately, weakness he had displayed in the simple gesture were all disturbing to anyone who had seen him during the many years he could have accomplished whatever he wanted with ominous quiet, using a few well chosen words.

Loot had a dispiritingly short Broadway run. There were no other projects on the horizon. Merrick became increasingly reclusive. His weakened physical condition made him reluctant to go out. When he did venture forth, Etan was with him, a gracious presence by his side. With old friends they might go to dinner parties.

Someone who had not seen him in many years was shocked by his appearance. The eyes, once so penetrating and withering, now seemed watery and wary. The smile, once so overbearing and infuriating, was now tentative. The face was lined. As if to compensate, Merrick had taken to wearing rouge, but he applied it crudely, as he had always done with his wig.

He was not forgotten. Lee Roy Reams, with whom he developed a friendship during the run of *42nd Street,* invited him to see his nightclub act at an East Side club called Freddy's. Etan thanked Reams for the invitation, said she and David would love to come, but she asked that their visit not be publicized. David did not look well and she knew he would not want to be made a public spectacle.

It was arranged that they would come to the club after seeing a performance of *42nd Street*. When they arrived at Freddy's Reams was at the door to greet them, to escort them back through the bar toward the room where he performed. The bar area was dimly lit, and the trio made their way slowly through a narrow passageway. Suddenly Reams was horrified to see Merrick dive to the floor. Had he suffered another stroke? Had he tripped? No. A few seconds later Merrick stood up beaming. Between his fingers he held a penny, the reward for his diligence and alertness.

His entrance may have seemed like that of a crazy person, but later in the evening Merrick reassuringly gave Reams evidence he was still a would-be despot. After the show Reams sat with the Merricks. Merrick took out his program, turned to the cast list and pointed to various names. He was able to grunt out his harsh assessments of their work: "No good—out!" "Too old—out!"

One summer day, Garson Kanin, who had married Marian Seldes several years after Ruth Gordon died in 1985, called to invite Merrick to lunch. He and Etan met the Kanins in an East Side restaurant with a garden. He was, as always, impeccably dressed. For most of the luncheon he was quiet, sitting politely, nodding at the conversation around him. Then it was clear he had something he wanted to say. Each of the others was at pains to try to guess what he might want to communicate, assuming it was something to add to what they had been discussing.

Then Etan realized all he wanted was lemonade. A waiter brought him a glass. He beamed, Kanin remembered, "like a child who has been given an ice cream cone."

On another occasion his humiliation could not be publicly seen but it was profound. In 1984 the national company of *42nd Street* played Washington, where the show had begun its life tentatively four years earlier. Now it was a huge Broadway hit, the latest in the panoply of David Merrick musicals, and it had been selected to open the refurbished National Theater.

The opening was attended by President and Mrs. Reagan. Etan

was struck by how much the event symbolized his accomplishment.

"Don't you feel glorious?" she asked her husband. "For a little boy from St. Louis?"

"I want to shoot my brains out," he told her.

CHAPTER THIRTY-SEVEN

I N THE FALL OF 1988 there was a benefit in honor of David
Merrick in the grand ballroom of the Waldorf-Astoria. The
conductor was Don Pippin, who had been on friendly terms
with Merrick since he had conducted *Irma La Douce* nearly thirty
years before. After the performance, Pippin found himself cross-
ing the empty stage looking out at the ballroom, which had
rapidly cleared of guests.

The lights had been turned on. What had been a magical
atmosphere earlier, where aging faces were lit flatteringly by can-
dles and muted lamps, was now bright and harsh. Looking out at
the room, now peopled largely by the waiters removing table dec-
orations and dirty plates, Pippin saw the guest of honor, accompanied by Etan. Merrick did not want to make an awkward exit
in front of people who had remembered him as a fearful strongman; so he waited patiently until he could leave in quiet.

Pippin looked out at David and Etan, smiled, and then moved
along the rim of the stage, assuming they did not want to be disturbed. He was surprised to see Merrick beckoning to him. He
walked down from the stage and went to his former boss's table.

He greeted the Merricks. Etan told him how grateful David
was that Pippin had conducted that evening. Pippin, still a polite
Southerner after three decades in New York, thanked Merrick for
giving such a powerful boost to his career in its earliest stages,

At a testimonial dinner at the Waldorf, with Carol Channing, Jerry Herman
and Etan.

making everything else possible.

Merrick smiled. And then Pippin noticed tears were coming down his cheeks.

"No one ever thanks him," Etan said.

Embarrassed, touched, Pippin thanked them both and withdrew.

Many years earlier, in the fall of 1963, at the beginning of that miraculous season in which he produced eight and a half shows, something similar had happened. A stagestruck youth had encountered Merrick in Shubert Alley. The youth, who had just seen *The Rehearsal* in its brief run, thanked Merrick.

Merrick looked at him suspiciously.

"What did you say?

"I said, thank you, Mr. Merrick," the youth replied, explaining the reason for his gratitude.

Merrick stared.

"No one ever thanks me for a fucking thing," he muttered as he walked away.

Although David and Etan maintained separate residences— after years of experience with each other it was the most sensible arrangement—during these painful years they remained close.

In 1987 Etan wanted to adopt two children, one Philippine, one American. David not only supported her decision, he was an active participant. Because Etan had never become an American citizen, it was necessary for David to petition the Department of Justice to classify the Philippine boy an "immediate relative" for whom he promised to provide care. It was the only way to circumvent the quotas. Merrick had to go down to the Federal Building in Lower Manhattan and do something he almost never did—stand in line, largely with Haitians and Puerto Ricans. Etan was moved by the gesture.

In May of 1988, his alma mater, St. Louis University, awarded him an honorary doctorate. Overcoming his longstanding aversion to his hometown, he went to accept it. Etan went with him. His mood was subdued and gracious.

With no show to produce, Merrick was indeed a man without a country, a displaced person. Helen Montagu had been right when she told the judge that Merrick came to life when he worked in the theater. He needed a project. He thought he had one. It was, in effect, a "remake" of *42nd Street*. It would be based on another early Thirties Warner Bros. movie musical, *Golddiggers*. Again, it would largely be a pretext for a series of lavish musical numbers. His lawyer was now William Goodstein. They had met when Goodstein was an associate of Raoul Felder's.

Considering that, in the summer and fall of 1989, the show was in its early phases, Goodstein was surprised at how often Merrick was in his office. Once Merrick had given up his own office in the St. James building, he used Goodstein's office as his own and even contributed some furniture and paintings to dress up the place. Goodstein knew Merrick had little to do. He was, in fact, in danger of seeming pathetic.

Occasionally Merrick could make himself understood. Fred Golden, who had spent so many years working on advertising for him, would come to visit Merrick and reminisce. Merrick, he found, could speak slowly and clearly. Then the phone might ring. If it pertained to business, Merrick would tense up and his speech would be slurred, vehement and incomprehensible. Michael Stewart visited him regularly and tried to teach him to speak again, but Stewart died of pneumonia in 1987.

The playfulness was still there. When he ran into Neil Hartley in London, he pointed to Hartley's hair. "Neil—gray, gray, gray," he said. Hartley's fondness for him forbade him from pointing at Merrick's "rug" and saying, "David—black, black, black."

The sense of humor was also there. When he met the son of Jerry and Marta Orbach at a party he asked, "*Carnival* or *Promises, Promises?*" knowing they had had a child during each early Merrick show Orbach had done.

For some men a placid existence might be tolerable if their minds were clear enough to remember past achievements. Nor was he likely to see the autumn years as a time to contemplate the hereafter. He had never been a man of a philosophical disposition.

He had never been able to cope with the idea of death either as a metaphysical or a practical reality. When the loved ones of colleagues died Helen Nickerson knew he could not be expected to write—or even affix his signature to—a letter of condolence. The simplest way to deal with it, she knew, was simply to send a wire, SHOCKED AND SADDENED. DAVID. Even the word LOVE before his name seemed risky.

For some men the end of a career might mean enjoying a luxurious lifestyle, the fruit of a lifetime of hard work—and no one ever denied that Merrick had put in a lifetime of hard work. But luxury had never meant much to Merrick. His apartments over the years were decorated by his wives. Decor—except for the one he created in the red office—did not matter to him. Nor did the pleasures of the table. For many years, when he lived alone at the Galleria, he could be seen ordering cold cuts across the street at the Dover Delicatessen to take home.

Nothing mattered to Merrick but his work. For a man who had created his existence on a daily basis, building a legend and making a profit by it, this enforced silence was disabling.

Not all of the time Merrick spent in Goodstein's office was devoted to trying to communicate his ideas for *Golddiggers*. Often Merrick seemed perfectly content to sit in the outer office trying to make conversation with the stone-faced woman Goodstein employed as a receptionist.

Natalie Lloyd, nee Natalie Ting Teresa, a short woman, with penetrating eyes, had a genial exterior and an iron sense of determination. She had the patience to listen to this strange, somber man trying to chat with her. She was smart enough to see that her patience might be generously rewarded.

Born in Hong Kong, Lloyd spoke fluent English. She gave her neighbor, the actress Carole Shelley, the impression of having had an excellent education. The fact that she was very reserved, Shelley felt, made it easy for others to attribute to her "Dragon Lady" stereotypes Shelley never saw.

Most evenings Merrick and Goodstein would go out to dinner together. One evening Goodstein was surprised to see Merrick gesticulating fervently in the direction of Lloyd. He wanted her to join them, and so she did.

The relationship was clearly getting much closer. When Lloyd failed to report to work one day and Merrick failed to make his daily visit, Goodstein, on a hunch, visited some of the banks where he knew Merrick had accounts. Merrick and Lloyd had preceded him, by barely twenty-four hours. By now they were across the globe in one of Merrick's suites at the Savoy.

When they came back to New York, Lloyd moved out of her spartanly furnished apartment in the Parc Vendome, on West 57th Street, for the grand apartment Merrick owned in the Galleria, down the street.

Once ensconced, Lloyd set about consolidating her own power base. Until Natalie moved into the Galleria, Etan often came to prepare his dinner. She often brought the children for him to play with before he went to bed. But after Natalie took charge of Merrick, the visits of the children—even Marguerita and Cecilia Ann—ceased. When the older children came to the Galleria, they were told their father did not want to see them. By the end of 1989 Merrick had instituted divorce proceedings against Etan.

Part of his hostility toward Etan may have been animated by Natalie. Part of it stemmed from general behavior that seemed increasingly erratic. Early in 1989 Etan filed papers to have him returned to a conservatorship.

In October of 1989, two very odd incidents occurred at Kennedy Airport. On October 27, Merrick, before boarding a British Airways flight to London with Natalie, told a ticket agent he was carrying a .38 caliber revolver and nineteen rounds of ammunition. The gun was not licensed, and he surrendered it voluntarily. He was not allowed to board.

Two days later, when they returned, he had no gun. But police insisted on searching him and discovered he was carrying $140,000—$95,000 in cash in a handbag, and $51,000 in cash and travelers' checks in his jacket pocket. Americans leaving the country are not allowed to take more than $10,000 without declaring it. Merrick had reported only $5,000. He was again forbidden to board. Around the same time Frank Langella, flying to London, found himself behind Merrick, who was in a wheelchair, waiting to board the first class section. At a certain point he simply stopped. A stewardess came toward him. Out of his pocket he withdrew an enormous pile of $100 bills. He peeled one off and gave it to her. "I want to be well taken care of," he said.

Earlier that year a significant chapter of his life had come to a close. In August of 1989, Leonore died. During the last months of her life she had extensive surgery for a brain tumor. The medical bills had been staggering. At Etan's insistence he paid them.

By the time Leonore died Natalie Lloyd was already his second in command. To her friends, Leonore referred to Lloyd as "Plum Blossom."

It had been a long time since Leonore had seen her former husband. Over the years she had been invited to his openings. At the intermission of *42nd Street,* clearly as a gesture to show he considered her important, he made a point of coming over to her to whisper that Gower had died that morning.

When she left the hospital after her brain surgery, the indomitable Leonore had made plans to sail to Europe, though she knew she did not have much time left. She imagined it might be possible to see David again, though, when nothing could be arranged, she realized how humiliating it would be for him to see her and be unable to communicate.

She had never remarried, never ceased to regard him with affection. Friends who knew her well were always surprised at how kindly she spoke of him, never expressing rancor, often recalling how long they had been in love before they were able to be married.

More amazing, he never spoke ill of her. Once, a writer, on being introduced to Merrick, said he knew one of his wives and that she was a wonderful woman. "If she's wonderful, it must be Leonore," Merrick said.

After those early years in which she stood by him waiting for him to get the break he needed, his career had always taken precedence over her. When she was asked when she had known that their marriage was over, she said it was the night *Fanny* opened. Merrick had once declared to a reporter that the opening was the night he truly became Merrick. Once that happened, there was apparently no longer room in his life for Leonore Beck, who had made David Merrick possible.

But all these years later he could finally make a grand gesture. In the years since their divorce he had been generous financially, increasing her annual subsidy to keep up with the cost of living. Only now was he able to go beyond writing a check to make the kind of generous emotional gesture that came much harder to him.

He sent Natalie to see her with a message: "You are the only woman I ever considered my wife."

It pleased her. She told friends about it. Shortly afterward she died. Alma McCardle, the executor of her estate, made arrangements for a luncheon to be held in her memory at her favorite restaurant, the Restaurant du Village in Chester, Connecticut. Over 200 friends came to celebrate a woman everyone agreed was the soul of generosity and warmth. Her good friend, the writer Sanford Dody, declared Leonore "the most un-dead dead person I know."

As part of the celebration, McCardle arranged for a young musician from New York to play music from the shows Leonore's ex-husband had produced. It turned out to be a more complicated request than she imagined. The 28-year-old keyboard player had never heard of David Merrick.

AT LAST, PEOPLE ARE HOLDING HANDS IN THE THEATRE AGAIN!

"IF THERE IS ANY SERIOUS DOUBT THAT DAVID MERRICK IS ONE OF THE GREATEST SHOWMEN IN BROADWAY HISTORY, IT CAN BE DISPELLED BY THE FACT THAT HIS FLOPS ARE AS FABLED AS HIS HITS."

—Frank Rich, New York Times
November 2, 1990

"THINGS ARE NOT AS O.K. AT DAVID MERRICK'S 'OH, KAY!' AS AT LEAST ONE CAST MEMBER WOULD LIKE."

—Alex Witchel, New York Times
November 2, 1990

TO FRANK
AND ALEX—
ALL MY LOVE,

David Merrick

CHAPTER THIRTY-EIGHT

E AST HADDAM, CONNECTICUT, is about a two hour drive from New York. A sleepy little town full of beautifully restored Victorian buildings, it is the home of the Goodspeed Opera House, which, since the mid-Sixties, has revived classics of the American musical theater. (In 1975 Merrick had transferred the Goodspeed's production of Jerome Kern's *Very Good Eddie* to Broadway.)

By the end of the two hour trip, most travelers are pleased to arrive in this 19th century American Brigadoon, but few of those who make the journey could have been as relieved to see the gingerbread towers of the Opera House, across the placid Connecticut River, as the occupants of David Merrick's rented Cadillac, who arrived there one weekend in July, 1990.

There were only four people in the car. Normally four people should have been very comfortable in a spacious Cadillac. There were also, however, two tub chairs, which meant there was only room for one person in the back seat. Three others had to squeeze into the front.

The tub chairs had come on board in Greenwich, where Merrick had a small apartment. He was moving the chairs to the city. Rather than stop in Greenwich on the way back, he had picked them up on the way to East Haddam. They shared the back seat with Merrick's general manager, Leo Cohen. In the front were Cohen's associate, Matt Farrell, who drove, and Merrick himself. Between them was Natalie Lloyd.

When *42nd Street* had closed, in January 1989, Merrick had mentioned he would open it again with an all-black cast, the formula that had renewed the life of *Hello, Dolly!* twenty years earlier. But, in pursuing his usual shenanigans during the course of that show's long run, he had lost the rights.

In 1986 he had abruptly stopped paying royalties to Mark Bramble, whose idea the show had been in the first place. Bramble's lawyer, Alvin Deutsch, notified Merrick that, according to the Dramatist's Guild contract he had signed, failure to pay royalties would result in the loss of his rights to the property.

An arbitration proceeding was arranged, which Merrick, as Deutsch expected, did not attend. Instead his lawyer, William Goodstein, arrived. In a tradition that had begun with Fitelson, Goodstein surpassed his employer in belligerence.

Nevertheless, the lawyers reached a settlement and Goodstein gave Bramble a check from Merrick. It bounced, having been drawn on a long closed account. (At another negotiating session Merrick sent a Chinese girlfriend of Natalie's, whose English was minimal.)

Ultimately, when Bramble was in Australia for the opening of *42nd Street*, he and his agent, Helen Harvey, came to terms with Merrick. Unlike many occasions, in which the aggrieved party settled for half rather than continue battling with Merrick, this time Bramble received full payment, partly in cash, partly in travelers' checks.

In the course of this protracted squabbling, however, Merrick lost the rights to *42nd Street*. Ultimately he never applied to Bramble for the rights. Had he done so, Bramble would have refused. "Ten years was enough," Bramble felt.

For a long time it looked like the musical that might bring Merrick back to life would be *Golddiggers*. Shortly before rehearsals were to begin in London in the spring of 1990, Merrick and Goodstein were driving through a park. Merrick asked the driver to stop. He got out, and sat on a bench. Goodstein sat beside him. As if he had been visited by an oracle, Merrick announced to Goodstein that he would not do *Golddiggers*. He paid off everyone in cash (Douglas Schmidt, the set designer, was horrified to be handed a paper bag with $30,000), and that was that.

But he wanted—he needed—to produce something, and he remained convinced that Broadway could use an all-black musical. He was thus very receptive when Michael Price, the artistic director of the Goodspeed, and Dan Siretta, Price's associate, who had conceived and choreographed an all-black version of George and Ira Gershwin's *Oh, Kay!*, wrote to him suggesting he transfer it to Broadway.

Price and Siretta were invited to Merrick's apartment in the Galleria. Lloyd welcomed them. Merrick, seated, did not rise, but he smiled benevolently. Lloyd spoke for him. "There are no producers like Mr. Merrick," she told them. "He *needs* to produce," she continued, stressing that doing the show would be good for him. Price and Siretta were delighted. *Oh, Kay!* would go into production in the fall of 1990.

And so, on this warm day in July, Merrick, Lloyd and their traveling companions had come to Goodspeed to see the summer production that Siretta had directed and choreographed, *Pal Joey*. The Rodgers and Hart musical had first opened the year Merrick and Leonore had come to New York, fifty years earlier.

The drive through Eastern Connecticut had been extremely uncomfortable. Perhaps because he had been so cramped in the car, perhaps because he had mis-timed taking a laxative, toward the end of the first act of *Pal Joey* an unmistakable odor filled the Goodspeed's tiny auditorium. Merrick had lost control of his bowels.

The entire audience was asked to leave during the intermission, so the seat could be cleaned and an attempt made to clear the air. Merrick went to the men's room, where he did what he could to clean himself, and then was taken downstairs to Price's private office. Price asked an assistant to bring a chair. After

Merrick left, rather than having it, the chair was eventually thrown away. To save embarrassment, the party might have gone back to the city immediately. But Natalie insisted on staying for the second act.

If the incident during the summer suggested Merrick was not in control of himself, once casting began his demeanor suggested otherwise.

His powers of speech had indeed been curtailed, but his face remained extremely expressive. Siretta, who would direct and choreograph the show, had the advantage of his experience with his father who had suffered a massive stroke. He learned that you study a stroke victim's face for emotional responses, which are enhanced to compensate for an inability to articulate.

Equally important, there might be a disparity between what Merrick's eyes would say before he began to speak and what he would then actually say. What he might say would be limited by his inability to articulate, but what he intended to say, registered in his eyes, was very articulate.

Siretta quickly saw that Merrick's most decisive gestures were nods. No was easy to understand. Yes was subtler. If Merrick tilted his head slightly and moved his eyes sideward, it meant Siretta might try whatever it was he had suggested. But if Merrick dipped his chin and looked directly at him, it meant he was to do something "and do it right now." If Merrick refused to answer a question it was in the form of an annoyed grunt.

"Being a master of moods is the privilege of a large primeval animal," Siretta decided. "Many times I had the feeling, working with him, that I was in a primeval forest full of ominousness. He had a silence that was deafening, a silence that was full of threats. Sometimes, looking at him, I saw an enormous darkness, a darkness that if you entered you might never find your way out of."

It had been fourteen years since Siretta had worked on *The Baker's Wife*, when Merrick had not been around much. This time he was always there. He sat at Siretta's side during the early casting. The tilt of the head in this instance, Siretta determined, meant, do what you want. The dip of the chin meant, get rid of her.

But, remarkably, if he really liked someone, he would say, "Good, wonderful, beautiful." Also remarkable, if lamentable, was his occasional ability to make himself understood when he had something negative to say. "What an awful actor," he might say even before the auditioner left the stage.

Worse, some of the auditioners heard him mutter, "Too black. Too black."

Sometimes Natalie would serve as his interpreter. He would make a few growls and she would expound on them. Occasionally he listened placidly to her exegesis. Other times, after she finished, he would say, "No, No, No. All wrong." At times there would be another coda: "She's a bitch."

The early casting took place in the studios of the Manhattan Theater Club, far West on 16th Street. While there, Merrick fell in love with a big plush English armchair. When he seated himself in it it took on the dimensions of a throne. He liked it so much he asked to borrow it, and the chair then accompanied him wherever he went.

Rehearsals began in a studio across from Cooper Union. Merrick enjoyed watching people struggle to take the large chair up and down stairs and through narrow doorways. When rehearsals eventually moved to the 46th Street Theater, now renamed the Richard Rodgers, the armchair would be placed in the aisle, where Merrick would preside.

Out of his general principle of contentiousness, Merrick decided to take back the furniture he had lent Goodstein. Rather than go about it in a civil way he selected Rosh Hashonah, the Jewish New Year, a day when Goodstein's office would be closed. Natalie still had a key. The pair arrived with movers, and Merrick instructed them which pieces of furniture and art were to be removed. Files relating to his cases were also taken.

Everything was put on a truck, which pulled up at the back of the Galleria, where there was a hydraulic elevator. Merrick seldom entered the prestigious building through the front, on 57th

Street, because there were a lot of steps. If he entered from 58th Street he could step right onto the elevator. On this occasion, as the back of the truck was opened, there was Merrick poised on his beloved chair. He was lifted onto the elevator with the purloined furniture, an image of authority both stern and comical.

After years of powerlessness, producing a Broadway musical restored Merrick to his former imperiousness. He had Natalie call Fred Golden to meet with him about advertising.

Golden had sympathy for Merrick in spite of the treatment he had received during the good years, not because of it. Yes, he had profited by the association, but he had earned every penny. At one point, in fact, at the height of his career, Merrick had summoned Golden to his office. He pointed out that because he threw so much business his way he was entitled to a break in fees.

Golden explained that he could not offer him a discount because Merrick took more of his time than any other client; not because of the volume of his business but because of the way he went about it. It was a service he was willing to provide, but he could not do it at less than the customary rate. Merrick informed Golden he would take his business elsewhere. After a brief tenure with another agency, Merrick returned to Golden's office and care. During the years Merrick was largely in Los Angeles he would frequently phone him at three in the morning New York time. When Golden complained, Merrick fired him.

But now, when the call came to work on advertising for *Oh, Kay!*, he felt he came to the Galleria as both a friend and a businessman.

Natalie didn't see it that way.

"I would like to see some proposals," she said.

Golden looked to Merrick, assuming he would object. He did not. Golden explained that he had been working with Merrick for almost forty years. Natalie reiterated her desire to see proposals. Golden shepherded his staff out. Another agency, LeDonne Wilner, handled the ads for *Oh, Kay!*

It is customary, on the first day of rehearsals of a Broadway musical, to invite the press for a photo opportunity. Merrick made the first day of rehearsals for *Oh, Kay!* memorable. One of the reporters in attendance was Leslie Bennetts, who had written a scathing portrait of him for *Vanity Fair* the year before

As he entered the rehearsal studio Merrick asked his press agent, Josh Ellis, "Where is she?"

"Who?" asked Ellis.

"Leslie Bennetts."

Ellis pointed her out. Instead of taking his seat before the assembled reporters and photographers, Merrick walked over to where Bennetts was sitting and stood glowering at her. "Out!" he bellowed.

She began explaining that she had requested and been given permission to attend the press conference. He cut her off. Twice more he screamed, "Out!"

She left.

When rehearsals began, Siretta quickly noted that Merrick, despite his inability to speak, was in charge of everything. "I had the feeling we were characters he created, and at the end of the day, when he was finished with us, he erased us."

Compared to *Baker's Wife*, which exuded a mist of gloom from early on, *Oh, Kay!* had a relatively peaceful rehearsal period. There were the usual finicky complaints about items on the set. There was the now customary delay in the opening, with two weeks of performances in an empty theater with an audience of two, Merrick on his borrowed throne and Natalie in attendance nearby.

Lloyd had, in effect, brought him back to life by encouraging him to return to the theater. But, as someone observed, she also "fed him his daily anger." As had been the case on *The Baker's Wife*, he was in the midst of a divorce with Etan, and Lloyd would remind him of it. "Etan—kill her," she might propose. "Get rid of the lawyer."

Oh, Kay! finally opened November 1, 1990. Merrick had insisted that the opening night party be at Sardi's. That fall, in fact, there was no Sardi's. For the first time in almost sixty years the restaurant that had been at the heart of the theater district was closed. A few years earlier Vincent Sardi, Jr., the son of the founder, had sold the restaurant, hoping to retire. His successors had made a financial mess of it and he reclaimed it. But he didn't expect to have the restaurant open in time for Merrick's party.

Merrick summoned Sardi and his banquet manager to Sofia, an unpretentious Italian restaurant across from the Richard Rodgers Theater, where he would camp out between rehearsals.

As it happened, Sardi felt a debt to Merrick. In 1980, as the theater district was coping with the increasingly unfavorable image New Yorkers had of it, there had been an opportunity to help make it safer. A piece of property became available on West 42nd Street, which might be used to house stables for the horses of the mounted police, which were perceived as a positive factor in making theatergoers feel safe. To purchase the property, $25,000 in cash was necessary within a matter of days.

Sardi, who had been apprised of the situation, could not himself provide the sum. It was shortly after the opening of *42nd Street*, and it occurred to Sardi that Merrick might be amenable. He phoned and spoke to a young man, who insisted on knowing why Sardi wanted to speak to Merrick. Sardi felt it was a delicate matter, not something that could be broached to an intermediary, however polite; but, as there seemed no alternative, he explained what he wanted. The next morning he received a check for $25,000 from Merrick.

Merrick had never mentioned the matter again, but Sardi had always felt grateful for the gesture. Now he felt he could repay it by getting the restaurant ready for the opening of *Oh, Kay!*

(At a later date there was an altercation with Merrick about how many would attend the party. He refused to pay for more than 300 people. But, Natalie reminded him, they had already sent the invitations out. There would be more than 500 people there. At first Merrick refused to budge. Natalie began to shout at him, "I'll stand. My friends and I won't sit down." He backed down.)

Oh, Kay! opened to largely favorable notices, infused in part with nostalgia for Merrick himself. The most negative was the one by Frank Rich in the *New York Times*. But the pan was, for Merrick, almost a godsend. It was a deliberately, personally insulting review, at one point declaring, " *Oh, Kay!* can be labeled a Merrick enterprise only because of the size of his billing and the ubiquitousness of a shade of red that has been standard issue in all his productions since *Hello, Dolly!* Romantically or not, I would like to believe that this legendary showman, notoriously the toughest of audiences, is seeing another kind of red as he surveys the pallid entertainment to which he has unaccountably lent his name."

It was the kind of remark for which Merrick had prepared himself. At most performances, he and Natalie sat on the aisle, house right, at the corner where people turned into the choice seats at the front of the orchestra section.

Here, they "received." Many alumni of Merrick productions dropped by to pay their respects. The animosity had softened. They were actually touched to see what had become of him. One night Carol Channing and Jerry Herman were in attendance. When Herman was introduced to Lloyd, she blurted out, "Jerry Herman! We thought you dead." But, realizing what she had said, she corrected the impression she made by revealing that when they woke up every morning they listened to *Hello, Dolly!* One night Peter Stone came to see the show and stopped by to say hello to his old antagonist, who was surprisingly voluble. "He said more to me tonight than in the days when he could talk," Stone told a friend.

The night that Frank Rich and his then girlfriend, later wife, Alex Witchel, attended, however, there was no time for socializing. Merrick, seated across the aisle and a few rows behind them, studied their behavior throughout the performance. There was, for his taste, too much giggling and cuddling.

He wrote a letter to Arthur Sulzberger, the publisher of the *Times* to register his disapproval: "Ms. Witchel whispered to Mr. Rich throughout the performance. At one point the whispering must have gotten loud because the woman sitting in front of them had to turn around to hush them . . . I violently object to Alex Witchel's unsuitable behavior at *Oh, Kay!* and will always wonder how her shockingly unprofessional behavior in the theatre influenced Frank Rich's judgment of my show . . . Mr. Rich's savage, unappropriately personal attack is so extreme, it forces me to ask what—or who—could have ignited him to such a virulent extreme?" Not so mysteriously, the letter, delivered to Sulzberger by hand on November 8, appeared on many newspaper fax machines the same day. There was no response from the *Times*.

At six in the evening on the previous Friday, the *Times* advertising department had received an ad for Monday morning's paper. Unlike the celebrated ad for *Subways are For Sleeping*, which had arrived at the last possible minute, this was submitted at the proper time. But, until Frank Rich bought an early edition of the paper Sunday night, nobody noticed the ad's contents.

The ad had a large heart. Above it the copy read, "At last, people are holding hands in the theater again!" Inside the heart were parallel quotes from Rich's review and Witchel's Friday column. Next to the heart was the message, "To Frank and Alex, All My Love," followed by David Merrick's wobbly signature.

When Rich saw the ad late Sunday night, he saw a deeper red than the shade he alluded to in his review. He called his editor, Paul Goldberger, and demanded the ad be yanked. In subsequent editions the space was filled by an earlier ad with favorable quotes from other critics.

Merrick had designed the ad himself, drawing it on a yellow legal pad at the agency. Jon Wilner, who supervised the *Oh, Kay!* ads, said he had difficulty understanding Merrick's speech—except when he said either "Frank Rich" or "Alex Witchel."

The ad had the same effect as the one Merrick had used twenty-nine years earlier with *Subways Are For Sleeping*. It yielded floods of ink about how the legendary producer had outwitted the all-powerful *Times*. Both news magazines wrote about it. So did *People*. So did newspapers across the country as well as the *International Herald-Tribune*. If there were any doubt about

Merrick's continuing power and celebrity, this disproved it.

There was, however, a difference. The trick ad for *Subways* was probably one reason that show ran longer than *I Can Get It For You Wholesale*, which had received better reviews. But in 1990 all the publicity did not produce a surge at the box office for *Oh, Kay!*

In 1961, Broadway musicals received the same national attention as major league baseball. In 1990, they were of interest only to a small number of readers, even in New York.

The realm in which Merrick sought to reassert his power was sadly diminished. Half the theaters on Broadway were dark. The longest running shows were British imports. They had redefined the musical. These shows tended to have almost no spoken dialogue, which meant the elimination of what was often the most difficult element to get right in a musical, the book. The scores tended to be heavy-handed, closer to rock than the traditional Broadway idiom. The attraction tended to be the subject matter and the visuals. The content was secondary. If Merrick had pioneered the "merchandising" of musicals, the British, notably Cameron Mackintosh, had brought it to new heights.

Compared to these grand spectacles, *Oh, Kay!* seemed quaint, though its virtuosic dancing reminded theatergoers of a level of talent seldom in evidence on Broadway any more. The show limped along until Christmas, when Merrick announced it would go on "winter vacation." The months of January and February are traditionally the toughest time to keep a show going. Tourist business is at its lightest. The locals had as yet shown little interest in *Oh, Kay!* It might be sensible to reopen the show in the spring, when New York is flooded with visitors. Announcing it would go on hiatus might be a graceful way to close it without having to admit defeat.

Natalie did not want to admit defeat. She had seen *Oh, Kay!* as a training program to help her begin her own career as a producer. Their relationship was full of antagonism—it was part of the way she nurtured him. Fighting was as essential to his well-being as his daily bread. As Helen Nickerson once observed, "He was incapable of a non-volatile relationship."

He was dependent on Natalie. And yet he resented that dependency. (Once he had suddenly shown up, unannounced, in the office of his general manager, Leo Cohen, grinning and declaring, "I escaped.") He knew he was indebted to her, and nothing enraged him more than being in someone's debt.

With Natalie he devised a way to "repay" the debt and teach her a lesson at the same time. He would let her supervise the spring production of *Oh, Kay!* He would agree with her every decision. It would be a disaster.

All through the early casting period, Merrick had carried a crumpled piece of paper in his pocket with the name Rae Dawn Chong on it. She was a movie actress. Natalie thought she should play the lead in *Oh, Kay!* Whether she could sing or dance was a question, but Natalie thought she would give the show star power. Attempts were made to locate her. She was shooting a film in Vancouver. Merrick was informed of this several times. He seemed unable to understand that meeting a prior commitment by filming a movie was a justifiable excuse for not appearing in a David Merrick musical.

When the show went on hiatus he renewed his efforts to secure her. By now the film was finished. She was available. For the sake of form she even came to New York to audition. The question as to whether she could sing or dance was now answered. She couldn't. Even her ability to act seemed dubious. None of this mattered. She would star in the revival of the previous fall's production of *Oh, Kay!*

Merrick also had an idea for a leading man, the comedian Flip Wilson. Unlike Rae Dawn Chong, Wilson was a genuine star. His agent thought he should be paid a star's salary. Although there was the usual dickering about the amount, an agreement was finally reached—until Wilson's agent insisted that this fee be paid even during rehearsals. At this point Merrick claimed never to have heard of Wilson, and Lloyd refused to sign the contract.

Oh, Kay! could not return to the Richard Rodgers, which had been booked for a new Neil Simon play, *Lost in Yonkers*. Merrick booked the Lunt-Fontanne, across the street.

Booked, but did not pay for. *Oh, Kay!* almost did not reopen because he had yet to pay the rent. At the very last minute Leo Cohen was dispatched with a brown paper bag full of cash—$150,000—so the show could open.

Ever the believer in grand gestures, Merrick, on opening night, had climbed a flight of stairs to congratulate his leading lady after the performance. Someone who saw him slowly forcing his way to the top imagined this might be the end of him. What a fitting end for a producer—in the dressing room of the leading lady he fought to hire. But no. Merrick managed to make his way up and back down again.

This time there would be no party at Sardi's. Several members of the cast had arranged to celebrate at Gents, a gay bar that catered to blacks on a frowzy stretch of 42nd Street. Merrick insisted on going. A limousine dropped him in front of the place. Merrick hobbled in and propped himself up at the bar. An associate brought him barbecue chicken wings. He seemed entirely out of place.

Whether or not he ever really imagined the idea of a winter break was viable, the box office made it clear this "innovation" had failed miserably. One night the take was $3,800. The next it was $1,500. The total was barely enough to pay the stagehands. *Oh, Kay!* closed abruptly before it began a second week of performances.

Among the astonishing events during Merrick's "comeback" was a television interview with CBS's "60 Minutes," which was doing a piece on Frank Rich. In the course of the interview Rich mentioned that, after his unenthusiastic review of *42nd Street*, Merrick attempted to take one of his celebrated minuscule ads at the bottom of the *Times* front page: "Producer looking for arsonist to burn down major metropolitan New York newspaper. Contact David Merrick."

Although several producers were willing to speak about Rich "off the record," few were willing to appear on camera. Emanuel Azenberg was one. Merrick was the other. Merrick had one stipulation. The remarks he would make would be read. He feared he might look ridiculous on national TV if he tried to speak.

Morley Safer came with the crew to film him. Merrick and Safer had known one another for many years. They began to chat. In talking about Rich, Merrick seemed to have regained his powers of speech almost completely. All his abilities at self-control had been restored by the sheer force of his hatred for Rich.

"Why can't we record this?" Safer asked. Perhaps not realizing how fluent he had become, Merrick barked a refusal. Safer complied.

The statement Merrick made was ferocious: "He loves to kill. He derives joy from the kill. He is power-hungry and lusts to destroy. Not a critic, a dictator—a savage dog."

Even in defeat, Merrick was defiant.

As usual, there were casualties in the production of *Oh, Kay!* One was the Goodspeed itself. It quickly became clear to Michael Price that Merrick would not give the Goodspeed any percentage of the profits of the production they had originated. Price wanted Siretta to make the dramatic gesture of withdrawing from the show just before dress rehearsals began. Siretta knew it would make no difference to Merrick. The second casualty was the friendship between Siretta and Price. By staying on, he alienated himself from Price, who had been his closest friend, and from the Goodspeed, which had been his artistic home. Loyalty to Merrick had its cost.

Another casualty was Warren Pincus, who had originally cast the show. Casting is the one job on a Broadway show not covered by a union. Merrick, who had praised him frequently during the casting process, now fired Pincus and refused to pay him his weekly salary. Pincus had no recourse but to sue.

When *Oh, Kay!* reopened in April, Pincus bought a ticket to the opening performance, and, at the intermission, went to the seats from which Merrick and Natalie held court. Politely, deferentially, Pincus acknowledged Merrick's preeminence at what he did and then called his actions "despicable." Merrick and his companion ignored him.

Almost a year later Pincus received a call from Natalie that a check was waiting for him at the concierge desk of the Galleria. When he went to pick it up, there was, of course, nothing for him. The concierge called up to Merrick's apartment. Natalie was apologetic. The accountant must have forgotten to deliver it. They had mailed it instead.

Pincus thought it was hopeless. Then a few days later when he returned to his walkup apartment there, under the door, was an envelope, slit open, with a check from Merrick, dated a year earlier.

This was the adult equivalent of a playground bully preventing a younger child from retrieving a ball. But that had been a game, a role that Merrick had played for many years.

Being a producer had given Merrick the constant opportunity to negotiate. And in negotiations he had been able to sense his power, his intelligence, his shrewdness. Had Descartes known Merrick, he might have reformulated his famous dictum as, "I negotiate, therefore I am."

Without a show, Merrick might have retreated into the painful silence in which he had so long endured. Happily there was another "production" already on the boards into which he could pour all his hostility, all his creative powers—the divorce from Etan.

Some, in fact, had seen *Oh, Kay!* itself as a ploy in the ongoing divorce. It was a way of spending large sums of money that might otherwise find themselves in Etan's hands.

Many years together had given them many points to contest. One was the adoption, in 1987, of the two children. As the divorce picked up steam, Merrick denied that he had been a willing partner in the adoption. A judge backed up his denial. Another judge reversed the first's decision. There were, of course, many financial decisions that could be questioned, ruled on, contested. The opportunities for negotiation were endless, though, by the spring of 1993, Merrick was losing his appeals more often than he was winning them, including the one about the adoption of the children.

Merrick and Natalie lived in London in one of his suites at the Savoy. He seldom went out. He kept odd hours, waking at midday, eating, returning to bed, waking in the early evening, then perhaps later at midnight, feasting at 1:00 a.m., rarely seeing those few friends he had ever made or maintained.

He still talked of producing a musical version of *Gabriela, Cinnamon and Cloves*. He and Natalie still fought. It was the one evidence of vitality in an otherwise vegetative existence. In Natalie he had found a stern adversary as well as someone willing to cater to his needs twenty-four hours a day.

There is a Strauss waltz called "Perpetual Motion," which consists of a limited number of measures of music repeated endlessly, until the conductor turns toward the audience and says, "Und so Weiter [and so forth]."

Was *Oh, Kay!* Merrick's last Broadway show? Will he ever divorce Etan? In Merrick's life there is no sense of neat endings. The stroke might have been a neat ending. It wasn't. For a lesser producer, *Oh, Kay!* might have been a graceful valedictory. It may not have been. For a man to whom domestic tranquility had seldom seemed desirable, the divorce from Etan might have seemed a useful end to petty squabbling. It isn't.

And so, probably the only sensible way to conclude this biography is to declare, "Und so Weiter."

And to wait for the next David Merrick extravaganza.

AFTERWORD

Dostoyevsky tells the tale of an odious peasant woman who arrives at the gates of heaven. The angels sift through her records and fail to find even one good deed that might gain her entrance. She is flung down to the fiery lake of hell. But just before she sinks irretrievably away, an angel discovers that she once gave an onion to a beggar. The angels lower the unraveled onion skin to hoist her into heaven.

It is, of course, the task of a biographer to find such onions in the life of his subject. He should be mindful, though, of two things. One is the demurral of Primo Levi, who was perhaps better acquainted with the peculiarities of moral algebra than Dostoyevsky, and who declared, rightly, that one onion is not enough.

Dostoyevsky himself seems to have known this. People tend to remember the onion but not what comes after. Some of the sinners on the lake of fire saw the peasant woman ascending to heaven and tried to latch onto her skirts. She kicked them off. When the angels saw this, they dropped the onion and its passenger.

What onions are there in David Merrick's life? Few, alas. One is that when the actor Henry Lascoe died during the out-of-town tryout of a Merrick musical, Merrick insisted that his widow receive Lascoe's salary for the next two years.

Once the box office informed him that an actor in one of his shows was passing bad checks. Merrick thought about it and said, "He's an actor. I'm the biggest producer on Broadway. He must need the money. Let him go."

In 1981 he heard that Stephen Sondheim was depressed by the negative reviews for *Merrily We Roll Along.* He had no reason to consider Sondheim a friend. Twenty years earlier he was supposed to have produced *A Funny Thing Happened on the Way to the Forum.* Originally, George Abbott was to be the director. But Sondheim wanted Jerome Robbins, who refused to work with Merrick. Merrick agreed to relinquish control of the musical on the condition that if Robbins withdrew he could return as producer. Robbins withdrew (returning later as a "doctor"), but Sondheim did not bring the show back to Merrick.

Nevertheless, when he heard Sondheim was in need of consolation after *Merrily,* Merrick took him to lunch to cheer him up.

When his loyal stagehand Willard Shaffar ran up $40,000 in hospital bills during a bout with cancer, Merrick paid them without even telling him about it.

He paid for some of Ted Van Bemel's children to go to college.

In the early Sixties a relative, Carol Felberbaum, came to New York hoping to be an actress and a writer. Perhaps because her father had helped him in his legal efforts on behalf of Leonore's estate, Merrick gave her all the money she needed to produce a revue at the Provincetown Playhouse, on the condition that his name not be associated with it.

In 1965, Eugene Wolsk, who had been a company manager for six years, left to produce his first show, *The Lion in Winter.* The office space he planned to rent would not be available for several months. He knew Merrick had unused space on another floor of the St. James Building and asked Schlissel if he could rent it temporarily. Schlissel reported back that Merrick said he could use it for free. Then Wolsk discovered how expensive it would be to set up a new phone line for a few months. Could he use the existing phone, keep track of the calls and pay Merrick? Schlissel reported back that Merrick said to use the phone with his compliments, a gracious going away present.

On two occasions he made contributions to Catholic University (apart from what they received from the Foundation). In 1962 he established a scholarship in the name of Walter Kerr, who had once taught there (and whose wife had been a student there). Kerr in that year won the $1,000 David Merrick Award to honor an outstanding drama critic. This award was not continued. In 1964, however, when the New York Drama Critics Circle named *Luther* as Best Play and *Hello, Dolly!* as Best Musical of the season, he gave Catholic University $1,000 in honor of retiring critic Jay Carmody. In 1956 he established an annual scholarship at Mace School for professional children to support a promising student.

Not many other onions have turned up.

Despite his shortcomings, Merrick's career remains an important chronicle of the American theater, for it is a remarkable instance of how one man's drive, his hunger for success and prestige enriched the lives of those who created theater and those who enjoyed it.

Moreover, it seems important, at this late date, simply to look back and see what was meant by the term "commercial theater," which, for many years, has been uttered almost exclusively in tones of deep opprobrium.

Even before Merrick's career had begun, voices had been raised decrying "the commercial theater." Merrick would in time become a lightning rod for such voices. But it should be remembered that the odious "commercial theater," all during the years it was being denounced, was mounting the work of Tennessee Williams, Arthur Miller and Eugene O'Neill, not to mention the musicals that, in their time, were regarded as nothing more than diversions for tired businessmen, but are now studied in university theater departments.

That much of the commercial theater's output was dross cannot be denied. Nevertheless, it seems useful to look back over the last thirty years, in which the focus of the American theater has been on the regional theater and the avant-garde.

It should be pointed out, by the way, that although they bill themselves as "not-for-profit," both rely heavily on corporate subsidies; we have apparently reverted to pre-Renaissance notions of finance—money that yields no interest or profit is evidently free of "commercial" taint.

Financial considerations aside, have the regional or cutting edge companies produced more vibrant, more substantial, more enduring works in the last thirty years than the commercial theater did, say, between 1933 and 1963? I do not think so. With some major exceptions, they have yielded merely a different, more pretentious sort of dross.

For that matter, it is useful to take a closer look at what the commercial theater was capable of producing. Remember that during the 1963-64 season, for example, Merrick produced an astonishing eight plays and musicals.

They included: a much-admired import of Jean Anouilh's *The Rehearsal*, starring Coral Browne; an equally lauded production of Bertolt Brecht's *The Resistible Rise of Arturo Ui*, directed by Tony Richardson, starring Christopher Plummer, and featuring a background score by Jule Styne; an import of John Osborne's *Luther*, with Albert Finney; an unsuccessful adaptation of Ken Kesey's novel *One Flew Over the Cuckoo's Nest*, starring Kirk Douglas; an equally unsuccessful revival of Tennessee Williams' *The Milk Train Doesn't Stop Here Any More*, starring Tallulah Bankhead and Tab Hunter; as well as several musicals—*110 in the Shade*, *Hello, Dolly!*, and *Foxy*. Merrick's office also laid the groundwork for *Funny Girl*, whose star his office had "discovered" a few years earlier.

What regional theater would not be proud to produce a season that included Anouilh, Brecht, Kesey, Osborne, Williams and, perhaps, *110 in the Shade*? (The Jones and Schmidt musical was recently revived by the New York City Opera, thus giving it a greater claim to intellectual respectability than, say, *Hello, Dolly!*)

What regional theater could afford to do such a season?

Is such productivity and variety possible outside the commercial theater—the commercial theater, that is, of yore? In England, one can answer affirmatively. Here, one cannot.

Moreover, it is worth noting that even if several of the above ventures were commercially unprofitable, they provided work for a large body of actors, writers and crew people.

As the playwright Albert Innaurato has observed, when America had a commercial theater, it was possible for writers and actors to make a living, often a substantial one, in the theater. They did not have to treat it as a hobby in which they could indulge only after they had paid their bills—and their agents'—with work in films or television.

By contrast, he points out, we now have a not-for-profit theater, in which no one can make a living except the administrators.

The methods of financing, of course, are not the only thing that has changed. Perhaps the most important thing to remember is that, for many years, there was no disparity between great theater and commercial theater. *A Streetcar Named Desire* was a Broadway hit in every sense of the word. So was *Long Day's Journey Into Night*. (The point can be carried even further—both Shakespeare and Moliere wrote for the commercial theater; even Brecht, ardent Marxist though he was, before he took up residence in East Germany, secured Austrian citizenship so that his Western royalties could be deposited in Swiss banks.)

That people were willing to pay Broadway prices—always considered hefty—to see demanding plays like *Streetcar* or *Long Day's Journey* makes it clear that it is not merely the finances or the modes of production of the theater that have changed. So has the audience.

Which is why it was probably naive of me to imagine that, even if I had found the paradigm of the perfect producer and even if the procedures he used were easy to document and imitate, we could ever return to the kind of theater this book describes. Humpty Dumpty cannot be put back together again.

Nor do the circumstances exist for the creation of a latter-day David Merrick. A man today who had aspirations like those Merrick had fifty years ago would go to Hollywood. There he would achieve the same prestige that Merrick won by presenting

Anouilh, Brecht, et. al., on Broadway merely by producing *Terminator VII.* Merrick, in fact, enhanced his prestige simply by presenting Anouilh and Brecht, whether or not they made money. (Neither did.) The prestige of the producer of *Terminator VII,* by contrast, depends exclusively on the grosses.

In a curious way, the commercial theater was less preoccupied with money than its not-for-profit successors, if for no other reason than that there always seemed to be plenty of it around. The profits of a *Hello, Dolly!* could subsidize the losses of an *Arturo Ui.* When money was not so problematic, other values could take precedence.

One of the fascinating things about Merrick's career was the great success he enjoyed with plays he produced through his foundation, which was established largely for tax advantages, but also to finance plays that did not seem "commercial." Invariably these ambitious, intellectually stimulating works—many of the plays of John Osborne, for example, or the epochal *Marat/Sade—*proved considerably more "commercial" than many whose "commercial" potential seemed unmistakable. The theater's chemistry is so powerful even money comes under its spell.

It may seem odd that someone who makes his living reviewing plays should have devoted so much effort to writing about a commercial producer. If a theater reviewer writes the life of a playwright or an actor, it requires no apology. He is using biography as another way to describe the art of the theater.

But the life of a producer? A man whose essential creative gift was an ability to instill in everyone working on a given project such incalculable fear that they did the best work of which they were capable?

"A life in the theater" has always been a phrase that exuded magic for me. I, too, have associated it largely with writers and actors, whose conjuring powers can create a more intense, a more vibrant world than the one that exists outside the stage door.

But Merrick's, for all its crassness, was also "a life in the theater." Even people whose resentment of him has abated little in the years since they worked for him confessed that one of his more endearing qualities was his constant effort to conceal what was clearly a deep love for the theater.

His life, in fact, suggests the conjuring powers of the theater itself, which can transform a man beyond his own abilities or even his imaginings. The theater's inimitable alchemy can take something as vulgar and crude as ambition and turn it into something magical.

To return to the "problem" of a critic writing about a commercial producer, let me say one more thing. Criticism, it has been observed, arises out of a debt of love. Some of the plays Merrick produced were among the first plays I saw, the plays that made me fall—hopelessly, I'm afraid—in love with the theater. Chronicling his career has been a way to understand my own obsession.

DAVID MERRICK:
A PRODUCTION HISTORY

THEATER

1942
The Willow and I
(Associate Producer; Donald Blackwell and Raymond Curtis, producers)
Author: John Patrick
With: Martha Scott, Cora Witherspoon and Gregory Peck
Opened: Dec. 10, 1942 at the Windsor
Closed: Jan. 2, 1943.
Performances: 28

1944
Bright Boy
(With Arthur Beckhard)
Author: John Boruff
With: Carleton Carpenter, Liam Dunn
Director: Arthur Beckhard
Opened: March 2, 1944 at the Playhouse
Closed: March 15, 1944
Performances: 16

1949
Clutterbuck
(With Irving Jacobs)
Author: Benn Levy
With: Ruth Ford, Arthur Margetson
Director: Norris Houghton
Opened: Dec. 3, 1949 at the Biltmore
Closed: June 10, 1950
Performances: 218

1954
Fanny
(With Joshua Logan)
Book: Joshua Logan and S.N. Behrman (Based on the *Fanny* trilogy of Marcel Pagnol)
Music and Lyrics: Harold Rome
With: Ezio Pinza, Walter Slezak, Florence Henderson
Director: Joshua Logan
Sets and Lighting: Jo Mielziner
Costumes: Alvin Colt
Orchestrations: Philip J. Lang
Musical Direction: Lehman Engel
Choreography: Helen Tamiris
Opened: Nov. 4, 1954 at the Majestic
Closed: Dec. 22, 1956
Performances: 888

1955-56
The Matchmaker
(With the Theatre Guild)
Author: Thornton Wilder (Based on his 1938 *The Merchant of Yonkers*)
With: Ruth Gordon, Loring Smith, Robert Morse
Director: Tyrone Guthrie
Sets and Costumes: Tanya Moiseiwitsch
Opened: Dec. 5, 1955 at the Royale
Closed: Feb. 2, 1957
Performances: 488

1957-58
Look Back In Anger
Author: John Osborne
With: Kenneth Haigh, Mary Ure, Alan Bates
Director: by Tony Richardson
Sets: Alan Tagg
Costumes: Howard Bay
Opened: at the Lyceum Oct. 1, 1957
Closed: Sept. 20, 1958
Opened: Nov. 1, 1958 at 41st St. Theater
Closed: Feb. 15, 1959
Performances: 408

Romanoff and Juliet
Author: Peter Ustinov
With: Ustinov, Jack Gilford, Henry Lascoe, Elizabeth Allen, Natalie Schafer
Director: George S. Kaufman
Sets: Denis Maldes
Costumes: Helene Pons
Opened: Oct. 8, 1957 at the Plymouth
Closed: Sept. 13, 1958
Performances: 389

Jamaica
Book: E.Y. Harburg and Fred Saidy
Music: Harold Arlen
Lyrics: E.Y. Harburg
With: Lena Horne, Ricardo Montalban, Adelaide Hall, Ossie Davis, Josephine Premice, Alvin Ailey
Director: Robert Lewis
Sets: Oliver Smith
Costumes: Miles White
Lighting: Jean Rosenthal
Choreographer: Jack Cole
Orchestrations: Philip J. Lang
Musical Director/Vocals: Lehman Engel
Dance Music/Additional Vocals: Peter Matz
Opened: Oct. 31, 1957 at the Imperial
Closed: April 11, 1959
Performances: 558

The Entertainer
Author: John Osborne
With: Laurence Olivier, Joan Plowright, Brenda de Banzie, Peter Donat
Director: Tony Richardson
Sets: Alan Tagg
Costumes: Clare Jeffrey
Lighting: Tharon Musser
Music: John Addison
Opened: Feb. 12, 1958 at the Royale
Closed: May 10, 1958
Performances: 97

1958-59
The World of Suzie Wong
(With Seven Arts Productions, Inc., and Mansfield Productions)
Author: Paul Osborn (Based on the Novel by Richard Mason)
With: France Nuyen, William Shattner
Director: Joshua Logan
Sets and Lighting: Jo Mielziner
Costumes: Dorothy Jeakins
Opened: Oct. 14, 1958 at the Broadhurst
Closed: Jan. 2, 1960
Performances: 512

Epitaph for George Dillon
(With Joshua Logan)
Author: John Osborne and Anthony Creighton
With: Robert Stephens, Frank Finlay, Eileen Herlie
Director: William Gaskill
Sets: Stephen Doncaster
Costumes: Helene Pons
Opened: Nov. 4, 1958 at the Golden
Closed: Nov. 22, 1958
Performances: 23

Maria Golovin
(With Byron Goldman and NBC)
Author: Gian Carlo Menotti
With: Patricia Neway, Ruth Kobart, Richard Cross, Franca Duval
Staged: Gian Carlo Menotti
Production Supervisor: Samuel Chotzinoff
Conductor: Herbert Grossman
Sets: Rouben Ter-Arutunian
Opened: Nov. 5, 1958 at the Martin Beck
Closed: Nov. 8, 1958
Performances: 5

La Plume de Ma Tante
(With Joseph Kipness)
Written, Devised and Directed: Robert Dhery
Choreographer: Colette Brosset
Music: Gerard Calvi
English Lyrics: Ross Parker
Musical Director: Gershon Kingsley
Staged: Alec Shanks

Opened: Nov. 11, 1958 at the Royale
Closed: Dec. 17, 1960
Performances: 835

Destry Rides Again (In Association with Max Brown)
Book: Leonard Gershe (Based on the Story by Max Brand)
Music and Lyrics: Harold Rome
With: Andy Griffith, Dolores Gray
Director and Choreographer: Michael Kidd
Sets: Oliver Smith
Costumes: Alvin Colt
Lighting: Jean Rosenthal
Musical Direction/Vocal Arrangements: Lehman Engel
Orchestrations: Philip J. Lang
Opened: April 23, 1959 at the Imperial
Closed: June 18, 1960
Performances: 472

Gypsy (With Leland Hayward)
Book: Arthur Laurents (Based on the Memoir by Gypsy Rose Lee)
Lyrics: Stephen Sondheim
Music: Jule Styne
With: Ethel Merman, Jack Klugman, Sandra Church, Mort Marshall,
Lane Bradbury, Peg Murray, Maria Karnilova, Faith Dane
Director and Choreographer: Jerome Robbins
Sets and Lighting: Jo Mielziner
Costumes: Raoul Pene DuBois
Orchestrations: Sid Ramin and Robert Ginzler
Musical Direction: Milton Rosenstock
Opened: May 21, 1959at the Broadway
Closed: March 25, 1961 at the Imperial
Performances: 702

1959-60
Take Me Along
Book: Joseph Stein (and Robert Russell) (Based on *Ah, Wilderness!* by
Eugene O'Neill)
Music and Lyrics: Bob Merrill
With: Jackie Gleason, Robert Morse, Walter Pidgeon, Una Merkel,
Eileen Herlie
Sets: Oliver Smith
Costumes: Miles White
Lighting: Jean Rosenthal

Choreographer: Onna White (With Herb Ross)
Orchestrations: Philip J. Lang
Musical Direction: Lehman Engel
Opened: Oct. 22, 1959 at the Shubert
Closed: Dec. 17, 1960
Performances: 448

Juniper and the Pagans
Author: John Patrick
With: David Wayne
Director: Robert Lewis
Sets: Oliver Smith
Lighting: Jean Rosenthal
Costumes: Noel Taylor
Opened: Dec. 8, 1959 in Philadelphia
Closed: Dec. 26, 1959

The Good Soup
Author: Felicien Marceau
Adapted and Directed: Garson Kanin
With: Ruth Gordon, Diane Cilento, Mildred Natwick, Sam Levene,
Jules Munshin, Ernest Truex
Sets and Costumes: Jacques Noel
Lighting: Albert Alloy
Opened: March 2, 1960 at the Plymouth
Closed: March 19, 1960
Performances: 21

1960-61
Vintage '60
(In association with Zev Bufman, George Skaff and Max Perkins)
Revue: Jack Wilson, Allan Jeffreys, Maxwell Grant, Sheldon Harnick,
Fred Ebb and others
With: Bert Convey, Michelle Lee
Director: Jonathan Lucas
Sets: Fred Voelpel
Opened: Sept. 12, 1960 at the Brooks Atkinson
Closed: Sept. 17, 1960
Performances: 8

Irma La Douce
(With Donald Albery in Association with H.M. Tennent, Ltd.)
Book and Lyrics: Alexandre Breffort
Music: Marguerite Monnot
English Book and Lyrics: Julian More, David Heneker and Monty Norman
With: Elizabeth Seal, Clive Revill, Elliott Gould, Robert S. Irving, Fred Gwynne, Keith Michell
Director: Peter Brook
Choreographer: Onna White
Sets and Costumes: Rolf Gerard
Orchestrations: Andre Popp
Vocal Arrangements: Bert Waller and Stanley Lebowsky
Additional Orchestrations: Robert Ginzler
Dance Music: John Kander
Musical Direction: Stanley Lebowsky
Opened: Sept. 29, 1960 at the Plymouth
Closed: Oct. 28, 1961
Performances: 527

A Taste of Honey
Author: Shelagh Delaney
With: Joan Plowright, Angela Lansbury and Billy Dee Williams
Director: George Devine and Tony Richardson
Set: Oliver Smith
Lighting: Jean Rosenthal
Opened: Oct. 4, 1960 at the Lyceum
Closed: March 18, 1961
Performances: 391

Becket
Author: Jean Anouilh
Translator: Lucienne Hill
With: Laurence Olivier, Anthony Quinn, Arthur Kennedy, Louis Zorich
Director: Peter Glenville
Sets: Oliver Smith
Costumes: Motley
Lighting: Jean Rosenthal
Music: Laurence Rosenthal
Opened: Oct 5, 1960 at the St. James
Closed: Dec. 17, 1960
Opened: Dec. 19, 1960 at the Royale

Closed: March 25, 1961
Opened: May 8, 1961 at the Hudson
Closed: May 27, 1961
Performances: 197

Do Re Mi
Book: Garson Kanin
Lyrics: Betty Comden and Adolph Green
Music: Jule Styne
With: Phil Silvers, Nancy Walker, Nancy Dussault
Director: Garson Kanin
Associate Director: William Hammerstein
Associate Producer: Jones Harris
Choreographer: Marc Beaux and Deedee Wood
Sets: Boris Aronson
Costumes: Irene Sharaff
Orchestrations: Luther Henderson
Musical Direction: Lehman Engel
Vocal Direction and Arrangements: Buster Davis
Dance Arrangements: David Baker
Opened: Dec. 26, 1960 at the St. James
Closed: Dec. 16, 1961
Opened: Dec. 25, 1961 at the 54th St.
Closed: Jan. 13, 1962
Performances: 400

Carnival
Book: Michael Stewart (Based on the Screenplay for *Lili,* by Helen Deutsch)
Music and Lyrics: Bob Merrill
With: Anna Maria Alberghetti, Jerry Orbach, Kaye Ballard
Director and Choreographer: Gower Champion
Sets and Lighting: Will Steven Armstrong
Costumes: Freddy Wittop
Orchestrations: Philip J. Lang
Dance Arrangements: Peter Howard
Associate Choreographer: Gene Bayliss
Creation and Supervision of Puppets: Tom Tichenor
Magic/Illusion: Roy Benson
Opened: April 13, 1961 at the Imperial
Moved: Dece. 21, 1962 to the Winter Garden
Closed: Jan. 5, 1963
Performances: 719

1961-62
Sunday in New York
Author: Norman Krasna
With: Robert Redford, Pat Stanley, Conrad Janis, Sondra Lee
Director: Garson Kanin
Sets and Lighting: David Hays
Costumes: Patricia Zipprodt
Opened: Nov. 29, 1961 at the Cort
Transferred Jan. 3, 1962: to the Golden
Closed: May 12, 1962
Performances: 189

Ross
Author: Terrence Rattigan
With: John Mills
Director: Glen:am Shaw
Sets and Costumes: Motley
Opened: Dec. 26, 1961 at the O'Neill
Moved: April 2, 1962 to the Hudson
Closed: May 12, 1962
Performances: 159

Subways Are For Sleeping
Book and Lyrics: Betty Comden and Adolph Green
(Based on Stories by Edmund Love)
Music: Jule Styne
With: Carol Lawrence, Phyllis Newman, Orson Bean
Director and Choreographer: Michael Kidd
Sets and Lighting: Will Steven Armstrong
Costumes: Freddy Wittop
Orchestrations: Philip J. Lang
Dance Arrangements: Peter Howard
Musical Direction: Oscar Kosarin
Opened: Dec. 1961 at the St. James
Closed: June 23, 1962
Performances: 205

I Can Get It For You Wholesale
Book: Jerome Weidman (Based on His Novel)
Music and Lyrics: Harold Rome
With: Elliott Gould, Lilian Roth, Sheree North, Barbra Streisand,
Marilyn Cooper, Harold Lang
Director: Arthur Laurents

Sets and Lighting: Will Steven Armstrong
Costumes: Theoni Aldredge
Choreographer: Herb Ross
Orchestrations: Sid Ramin
Musical Direction: Lehman Engel
Dance Arrangements: Peter Howard
Opened: March 22, 1962 at the Shubert
Moved: Oct. 1, 1962 to Broadway
Closed: Dec. 8, 1962
Performances: 300

1962-63
Stop the World — I Want to Get Off
(In Association With Bernard Delfont)
Book, Music and Lyrics: Leslie Bricusse and Anthony Newley
With: Anthony Newley, Anna Quayle
Director: Anthony Newley
Opened: Oct. 3, 1962 at the Shubert
Closed: Feb. 2, 1964
Performances: 556

Tchin-Tchin
Author: Sidney Michaels (Adapted from a play by Francois Billetdoux)
With: Margaret Leighton, Anthony Quinn, Charles Grodin
Director: Peter Glenville
Sets and Lighting: Will Steven Armstrong
Costumes: Theoni V. Aldredge
Opened: Oct. 25, 1962 at the Plymouth
Closed:
Performances: 222

Oliver! (With Donald Albery)
Book, Lyrics and Music: Lionel Bart (Based on *Oliver Twist* by Charles Dickens)
With: Georgia Brown, Clive Revill, Barry Humphries, Alice Playten
Director: Peter Coe
Designed: Sean Kenny
Musical Direction: Donald Pippin
Opened: Jan. 6, 1963 at the Imperial
Closed:
Performances: 774

Rattle of a Simple Man (With Michael Codron)
Author: Charles Dyer
With: Tammy Grimes, Edward Woodward, George Segal
Director: Donald McWhinnie
Opened: April 17, 1963 at the Booth
Closed: July 6, 1963
Performances: 110

1963-64
The Rehearsal
Author: Jean Anouilh
With: Coral Browne, Keith Michell
Director: Peter Coe
Sets: Jane Graham
Costumes: Tony Walton
Lighting: Will Steven Armstrong
Opened: Sept. 23, 1963 at the Royale
Closed: Dec. 28, 1963
Performances: 110

Luther
Author: John Osborne
With: Albert Finney
Director: Tony Richardson
Sets and Costumes: Joycelyn Herbert
Music: John Addison
Opened: Sept. 25, 1963 at the St. James
Moved: Jan. 13, 1964 to the Lunt-Fontanne
Closed: March 28, 1964
Performances: 212

110 in the Shade
Book: N. Richard Nash (Based on His Play, *The Rainmaker*)
Lyrics: Tom Jones
Music: Harvey Schmidt
With: Robert Horton, Inga Swenson, Stephen Douglass, Lesley Warren
Director: Joseph Anthony
Choreographer: Agnes DeMille
Sets: Oliver Smith
Costumes: Motley
Lighting: John Harvey
Orchestrations: Hershey Kay
Dance Music Arrangements: William Goldenberg

Vocal Arrangements: Robert de Cormier
Opened: Oct. 24, 1963 at the Broadhurst
Closed: Aug. 8, 1964
Performances: 330

The Resistible Rise of Arturo Ui
Author: Bertolt Brecht
Translator: George Tabori
With: Christopher Plummer, James Coco, Sandy Baron, Madeleine Sherwood
Director: Tony Richardson
Sets and Costumes: Rouben Ter-Arutunian
Music: Jule Styne
Opened: Nov. 11, 1963 at the Lunt Fontanne
Closed: Nov. 16, 1963
Performances: 7

One Flew Over the Cuckoo's Nest
(With Edward Lewis, In Association With Seven Arts and Eric Productions)
Author: Dale Wasserman (Based on the Novel: Ken Kesey)
With: Kirk Douglas
Director: Alex Segal
Sets and Lighting: Will Stephen Armstrong
Costumes: Noel Taylor
Music: Teiji Ito
Opened: Nov. 13, 1963 at the Cort
Closed: Jan. 25, 1964
Performances: 82

The Milk Train Doesn't Stop Here Any More
(Associate Producer, Neil Hartley)
Author: Tennessee Williams
With: Tallulah Bankhead, Tab Hunter, Marian Seldes, Ruth Ford
Director: Tony Richardson
Sets and Costumes: Rouben Ter-Arutunian
Lighting: Martin Aronstein
Music: Ned Rorem
Opened: Jan. 1, 1964 at the Brooks Atkinson
Closed: Jan. 4, 1964
Performances: 5

Hello, Dolly!
(With Champion-Five, Inc.)
Book: Michael Stewart (Based on *The Matchmaker* by Thornton Wilder)
Music and Lyrics: Jerry Herman
With: Carol Channing, David Burns, Eileen Brennan, Alice Playten, Charles Nelson Reilly, Sondra Lee, David Hartman
Sets: Oliver Smith
Costumes: Freddy Wittop
Lighting: Jean Rosenthal
Orchestrations: Philip J. Lang
Dance Arrangements: Peter Howard
Musical Direction: Shepard Coleman
Opened: Jan. 16, 1964 at the St. James
Closed: Dec. 27, 1970
Ginger Rogers Opens Aug. 9, 1965
Martha Raye Opens Feb. 17, 1966
Betty Grable Opens June 11, 1967
Pearl Bailey Opens Nov. 12, 1967
Phyllis Diller Opens Dec. 26, 1969
Ethel Merman March 26, 1970
Performances: 2,844

Foxy
Book: Ring Lardner, Jr. and Ian McClellan Hunter (Based on Ben Jonson's *Volpone*)
Lyrics: Johnny Mercer
Music: Robert Emmet Dolan
With: Bert Lahr, Larry Blyden, Gerald Hiken, David Rounds
Director: Robert Lewis
Sets: Robert Randolph
Choreographer: Jack Cole
Musical Direction: Donald Pippin
Orchestrations: Edward Sauter and Hal Schaefer
Opened: Feb. 6, 1964 at the Ziegfeld
Closed: April 18, 1964
Performances: 72

1964-65
Oh What a Lovely War (With Gerry Raffles)
Director: Joan Littlewood
With: Victor Spinetti, Murray Melvin, Reid Shelton
Sets: John Bury

Costumes: Una Collins
Lighting: Martin Aronstein
Opened: Sept. 30, 1964 at the Broadhurst
Closed: Jan. 16, 1965
Performances: 125

A Severed Head
(With Donald Albery)
Author: Iris Murdoch and J.B. Priestley
With: Joan Fontaine, Lee Grant, Robin Bailey
Sets Supervisor: Stewart Chaney
Lighting: Martin Aronstein
Opened: Oct. 28, 1964 at the Royale
Closed: Nov. 21, 1964
Performances: 29

I Was Dancing
Author: Edwin O'Connor
With: Burgess Meredith, Orson Bean, Pert Kelton, Barnard Hughes,
Eli Mintz, David Doyle
Director: Garson Kanin
Sets: Oliver Smith
Lighting: Martin Aronstein
Opened: Nov. 8, 1964 at the Lyceum
Closed: Nov. 21, 1964
Performances: 16

The Roar of the Greasepaint — The Smell of the Crowd
(With Bernard Delfont)
Book, Music and Lyrics: Leslie Bricusse and Anthony Newley
With: Anthony Newley, Cyril Ritchard, Gilbert Price
Director: Newley
Choreographer: Gillian Lynne
Associate Choreographer: Buff Shurr
Orchestrations: Philip J. Lang
Sets: Sean Kenny
Costumes: Freddy Wittop
Lighting: Martin Aronstein
Musical Direction: Herbert Grossman
Opened: May 16, 1965 at the Shubert
Closed: Dec. 4, 1965
Performances: 232

1965-66
Hot September
(In association with Leland Hayward)
Book: Paul Osborn (Based on *Picnic,* by William Inge)
Music: KennethJacobson
Lyrics: Rhoda Roberts
With: Lee Lawson, Sean Garrison, Eddie Bracken
Director: Joshua Logan
Sets: Oliver Smith
Costumes: Theoni V. Aldredge
Opened: Sept. 14, 1965 at the Shubert in Boston
Closed: Oct. 9, 1965

Pickwick
(With Bernard Delfont)
Book: Wolf Mankowitz
Music: Cyril Ornadel
Lyrics: Leslie Bricusse
Additional Material: Waterhouse & Hall, Sidney Michaels and Lan O'Kun
With: Harry Secombe, Charlotte Rae, Roy Castle
Director: Peter Coe
Choreographer: Gillian Lynne
Sets: Sean Kenny
Lighting: Jules Fisher
Opened: Oct. 4, 1965 at the 46th Street Theater
Closed: Nov. 20, 1965
Performances: 56

Inadmissible Evidence
(Presented by the David Merrick Arts Foundation)
Author: John Osborne
With: Nicol Williamson, Ted Van Gruythiesen, Jill Townsend
Director: Anthony Page
Sets: Joycelyn Herbert
Opened: Nov. 30, 1965 at the Belasco
Closed: Feb. 6, 1966
Opened: Feb. 8, 1966 at the Shubert
Closed: April 23, 1966
Performances: 167

Cactus Flower
Author; Pierre Barillet and Jean-Pierre Gredy
Adapted: Abe Burrows
With: Lauren Bacall, Barry Nelson, Burt Brinckerhoff, Brenda Vaccaro, Robert Moore
Director: Abe Burrows
Sets: Oliver SMith
Costumes: Theoni Aldredge
Lighting: Martin Aronstein
Opened: Dec. 8, 1965 at the Royale
Lloyd Bridges replaced Barry Nelson Oct. 23, 1967
Betsy Palmer Replaced Lauren Bacall Nov. 20, 1967
Closed: Nov. 23, 1968 at the Longacre

The Persecution and Assassination of Marat As Performed: the Inmates of the Asylum of Charenton Under the Direction of the Marquis DeSade
(Presented: the David Merrick Arts Foundation)
Author: Peter Weiss
English Version: Geoffrey Skelton
With: Ian Richardson, Glenda Jackson, Patrick Magee
Sets: Sally Jacobs
Costumes: Gunilla Palmstierna-Weiss
Music: Richard Peaslee
Opened: Dec. 27, 1965 at the Martin Beck
Closed: April 30, 1966
Performances: 145

Philadelphia, Here I Come!
(Presented by the David Merrick Arts Foundation, With Oscar Lewenstein and Michael White)
Author: Brian Friel
With: Donal Donnelly, Patrick Bedford
Director: Hilton Edwards
Set: Lloyd Burlingame
Opened: Feb. 15, 1966 at the Helen Hayes
Closed: Nov. 26, 1966 at the Plymouth

1966-67
The Loves of Cass McGuire
(Presented by the David Merrick Arts Foundation; Associate Producer, Samuel Liff)
Author: Brian Friel
With: Ruth Gordon, Don Scardino, Brenda Forbes

Director: Hilton Edwards
Set: Lloyd Burlingame
Costumes: Noel Taylor
Opened: Oct. 6,1966 at the Helen Hayes
Closed: Oct. 22, 1966
Performances: 20

We Have Always Lived in the Castle
(Associate Producer, Samuel Liff)
Author: Hugh Wheeler (Based on the Novel by Shirley Jackson)
With: Shirley Knight, Alan Webb
Director: Garson Kanin
Opened: Oct. 19, 1966 at the Barrymore
Closed: Oct. 26, 1966
Performances: 9

Don't Drink the Water
(In Association with Jack Rollins and Charles Joffe; Associate Producer, Samuel Liff)
Author: Woody Allen
With: Lou Jacobi, Anthony Roberts, Kay Medford, Donna Mills, Jonathan Bolt
Director: Stanley Prager
Sets and Lighting: Jo Mielziner
Costumes: Motley
Opened: Nov. 17, 1966 at the Morosco
Closed:
Opened: Jan. 22, 1968 at the Barrymore
Opened: March 25, 1968 at the Belasco
Closed: April 20, 1968

Breakfast at Tiffany's
(With Samuel Liff)
Book: Abe Burrows, later Edward Albee (Based on the Story by Truman Capote)
Music and Lyrics: Bob Merrill
With: Mary Tyler Moore, Richard Chamberlain
Director: Abe Burrows
Choreographer: Michael Kidd
Assistant Choreographer: Tony Mordente
Sets: Oliver Smith
Costumes: Freddy Wittop
Miss Moore's Wardrobe: Geoffrey Beene

Vocal Arrangements and Musical Direction: Stanley Lebowsky
Orchestrations: Ralph Burns
Dance Music Arranged: Marvin Laird
Previews Began: Dec. 5, 1966 at the Majestic
Closed in Previews: Dec. 7, 1966

I Do! I Do!
Book, Lyrics and Music: Tom Jones and Harvey Schmidt (Based on
The Fourposter by Jan deHartog)
With: Mary Martin and Robert Preston
Director and Choreographer: Gower Champion
Musical Direction: John Lesko
Opened: Dec. 5, 1966 at the 46th St.
Closed: June 17, 1968

The Astrakhan Coat
(Associate Producer, Samuel Liff)
Author: Pauline McCauley
With: Roddy McDowell, Brian Bedford, James Coco, Carole Shelley
Director: Donald McWhinnie
Sets: Lloyd Burlingame
Opened: Jan. 12, 1967 at the Helen Hayes
Closed: Jan. 28, 1967
Performances: 20

The Unemployed Saint
(Opened and Closed in Ft. Lauderdale)

1967-68
Keep It in the Family
(Associate Producer, Samuel Liff)
Author: Bill Naughton
Adapted: N. Richard Nash
With: Patrick Magee, Maureen O'Sullivan
Director: Allan Davis
Sets: Lloyd Burlingame
Costumes: Mary McKinley
Opened: Sept. 27 at the Plymouth
Closed: Sept. 30

Rosencrantz and Guildenstern Are Dead
(Presented by the David Merrick Arts Foundation in Association With Samuel Liff)
Author: Tom Stoppard
With: Brian Murray, John Wood, Paul Hecht
Director: Derek Goldby
Associate Director: Claude Chagrin
Sets and Costumes: Desmond Heeley
Lighting: Richard Pilbrow
Music: Marc Wilkinson
Conducted: Robert Mandell
Opened: Oct. 16, 1967 at the Alvin
Closed: Oct. 19, 1968 at the Eugene O'Neill

Mata Hari
Book: Jerome Coopersmith
Music: Edward Thomas
Lyrics: Martin Charnin
With: Marisa Mell, Pernell Roberts, Martha Schlamme, Blythe Danner
Director: Vincent Minnelli
Sets: Jo Mielziner
Costumes: Irene Sharaff
Lighting: Jean Rosenthal
Choreographer: Jack Cole
Conducted: Colin Romoff
Orchestrated: Robert Russell Bennett
Dance Arrangements: Roger Adams
Opened: Nov. 20, 1967 at the National, Washington, D.C.
Closed: Dec. 16, 1967

How Now, Dow Jones
(Associate Producer, Samuel Liff)
Book: Max Shulman
Music: Elmer Bernstein
Lyrics: Carolyn Leigh
With: Tony Roberts, Marilyn Mason, Brenda Vaccaro, Hiram Sherman
Director: Arthur Penn, later George Abbott
Choreographer: Gillian Lynne, later Michael Bennett
Sets: Oliver Smith
Costumes: Robert MacIntosh
Lighting: Martin Aronstein
Orchestrated: Philip J. Lang
Musical Direction and Dance Arrangements: Peter Howard

Opened: Dec. 2, 1967 at the Lunt-Fontanne
Closed: June 17, 1968 (during Actor's Equity strike)

The Unemployed Saint
With: Shelley Berman, Jackie Vernon, Dorothy Loudon, Joe Bova
Opened: at the Royal Poinciana Playhouse, Palm Beach, Florida
Closed: March, 1967

The Happy Time
Book: N. Richard Nash (Based on the Play by Samuel Taylor, From the Novels of Robert Fontaine
With: Robert Goulet, David Wayne, George S. Irving, Charles Durning
Music: John Kander
Lyrics: Fred Ebb
Director and Choreographer: Gower Champion
Associate Choreographer: Kevin Carlisle
Sets: Peter Wexler
Lighting: Jean Rosenthal
Costumes: Freddy Wittop
Film: Christopher Chapman and Barry O. Gordon
Orchestrations: Don Walker
Dance Music: Marvin Laird
Musical Direction: Oscar Kosarin
Opened: Jan. 18, 1968 at the Broadway
Closed: Sept. 28, 1968
Performances: 286

Is The Real You Really You?
Author: John Tobias
With: Dick Shaw, Louise Lasser, Dorothy Loudon
Director: Richard Altman
(Florida Circuit Only March 4- April 6, 1968)

The Seven Descents of Myrtle
(Associate Producer, Samuel Liff)
Author: Tennessee Williams
With: Estelle Parsons, Brian Bedford, Harry Guardino
Director: Jose Quintero
Sets and Lighting: Jo Mielziner
Costumes: Jane Greenwood
Opened: March 27, 1968 at the Barrymore
Closed: April 20, 1968
Performances: 29

1968-69
Rockefeller and the Red Indians
(With Arthur Lewis; Associate Producer, Samuel Liff)
Author: Ray Galton and Alan Simpson (Adapted From *Du Vent Dans les Branches de Sassafras* by Rene De Obaldia)
With: Frankie Howerd, Peter Bayliss
Directed: Bert Shevelove
Sets and Costumes: Hayden Griffin
Lighting: Lloyd Burlingame
Opened: Oct. 24, 1968 at the Barrymore
Closed: Oct. 26, 1968
Performances: 4

Promises, Promises
(Associate Producer, Samuel Liff)
Book: Neil Simon (Based on the Screenplay *The Apartment* by Billy Wilder and I.A.L. Diamond)
Music: Burt Bachrach
Lyrics: Hal David
With: Jerry Orbach, Jill O'Hara, Edward Winter, A.Larry Haines
Director: Robert Moore
Choreographer: Michael Bennett
Sets: Robin Wagner
Lighting: Martin Aronstein
Costumes: Donald Brooks
Orchestrations: Jonathan Tunick
Musical Direction and Dance Arrangements: Harold Wheeler
Opened: Dec. 1, 1968 at the Shubert
Closed: Jan. 1, 1972
Performances: 1,281

Forty Carats
(Associate Producer, Samuel Liff)
Author: Pierre Barillet and Jean-Pierre Gredy
With: Julie Harris, Glenda Farrell, Murray Hamilton, Polly Rowles, Michael Nouri
Adapted: Jay Presson Allen
Director: Abe Burrows
Sets: Will Steven Armstrong
Lighting: Martin Aronstein
Costumes: William McHone
Opened: Dec. 26, 1968 at the Morosco
Closed: Nov. 7, 1970
Performances: 780

Play It Again, Sam
(In Association with Jack Rollins and Charles Joffe; Associate Producer, Samuel Liff)
Author: Woody Allen
With: Woody Allen, Anthony Roberts, Diane Keaton
Directed: Joseph Hardy
Sets: William Ritman
Costumes: Ann Roth
Opened: Feb. 12, 1969 at the Broadhurst
Closed: March 1970
Performances: 454

Why I Went Crazy
Author: Charles Dizenzo
Director: Joshua Logan
With: Imogene Coca, Arnold Stang, Mort Marshall, Richard Castellano, and Armand Assante

1969-70
A Patriot For Me
(Presented by the David Merrick Arts Foundation; Associate Producer, Samuel Liff)
Author: John Osborne
With: Maximilian Schell, Dennis King, Salome Jens, Richard Jordan, Tom Lee Jones, Stefan Schnabel
Director: Peter Glenville
Sets: Oliver Smith
Costumes: Freddy Sittop
Lighting: Tom Skelton
Music: Laurence Rosenthal
Opened: Oct. 5, 1969 at the Imperial
Closed: Nov. 15, 1969
Performances: 49

The Penny Wars
(Presented by the David Merrick Arts Foundation; Associate Producer, Samuel Liff)
Author: Elliot Baker
With: George Voskovec, Kim Hunter, Kristoffer Tabori
Director: Barbara Harris
Sets: William Ritman
Lighting: Martin Aronstein
Costumes: Jane Greenwood

Opened: Oct. 15, 1969 at the Royale
Closed: Oct. 18, 1969
Performances: 5

Private Lives
Author: Noel Coward
With: Tammy Grimes, Brian Bedford
Director: Stephen Porter
Sets and Lighting: James Tilton
Costumes: Joe Eula
Opened: Dec. 4, 1969 at the Billy Rose
Closed: April 25, 1970
Opened: April 27, 1970at the Broadhurst
Closed: May 30, 1970

Play on Love
(London; co-producer)
Author: Francoise Dorin
With: Ruth Goetz, Bart Howard, Dorothy Tutin
Director: Patrick Cargill
Opened: Jan. 15, 1970

Child's Play
(Associate Producer, Samuel Liff)
Author: Robert Marasco
With: Pat Hingle, Fritz Weaver, Ken Howard, David Rounds
Director: Joseph Hardy
Sets and Lighting: Jo Mielziner
Costumes: Sarah Brook
Opened: Feb. 17, 1970 at the Royale
Closed: Dec. 12, 1970
Performances: 343

1970-71
Four on a Garden
(Asociate Producer, Samuel Liff)
Author: Bartillet and Gredy
Adapted and Directed: Abe Burrows
With: Carol Channing, Barry Nelson, later Sid Caesar
Set: Oliver Smith
Lighting: MArtin Aronstein
Costumes: William McHone
Opened: Jan. 30, 1971 at the Broadhurst

Closed: March 20, 1971
Performances: 57

A Midsummer Night's Dream (Presented by the David Merrick Arts Foundation, The Royal Shakespeare Company Production)
Author: William Shakespeare
With: Ben Kingsley, Alan Howard, Patrick Stewart, Frances De La Tour
Director: Peter Brook
Sets and Costumes: Sally Jacobs
Lighting: Lloyd Burlingame
Music: Richard Peaslee
Opened: Jan. 20, 1971 at the Billy Rose
Closed: March 13, 1971
Performances: 77
Opened: March 16-21 at the Brooklyn Academy of Music

The Philanthropist (With Byron Goldman, Michael Codron and the Royal Court Theater; Associate Producer, Samuel Liff)
Author: Christopher Hampton
With: Alec McCowen, Jane Asher, Victor Spinetti, Carolyn Lagerfelt, Penelope Wilton
Director: Robert Kidd
Sets: Jon Gunter
Lighting: Lloyd Burlingame
Costumes: Sarah Brook
Opened: March 15, 1971 at the Barrymore
Closed: May 15, 1971
Performances: 72

1971-72
There's One In Every Marriage
(In Association with Byron Goldman; The Stratford National Theater of Canada Production)
Author: Suzanne Grossman and Paxton Whitehead (From *Le Dindon* by Georges Feydeau)
With: Roberta Maxwell, Peter Donat, Jeanette Landis, Joseph Maher
Director: Jean Gascon
Sets and Costumes: Alan Barlow
Lighting: Gil Wechsler
Opened: Jan. 3, 1972 at the Royale
Closed: Jan. 15, 1972
Performances: 16

Vivat! Vivat! Regina!
(With Arthur Cantor; Associate Producer, Samuel Liff)
Author: Robert Bolt
With: Claire Bloom, Eileen Atkins, Alexander Scourby, Ian Richardson
Director: Peter Dews
Sets: Carl Toms
Opened: Jan. 20, 1972 at the Broadhurst
Closed: April 29, 1972
Performances: 116

Moonchildren
(With Byron Goldman and Max Brown)
Author: Michael Weller
With: Ed Hermann, Maureen Anderman, Cara Duff-McCormick,
Kevin Conway, Stephen Collins, Jill Eikenberry, James Woods, Robert
Prosky, Louis Zorich, Salem Ludwig
Director: Alan Schneider
Set: William Rittman
Lighting: Martin Aronstein
Costumes: Marjorie Slaiman
Opened: Feb. 21, 1972 at the Royale
Closed: March 4, 1972

Sugar
Book: Peter Stone (Based on the Screenplay *Some Like It Hot* by Billy
Wilder and I.A.L. Diamond)
Music: Jule Styne
Lyrics: Bob Merrill
With: Robert Morse, Tony Roberts, Cyril Ritchard, Pam Blair, Pamela
Sousa
Director and Choreographer: Gower Champion
Associate Choreographer: Bert Michaels
Sets: Jo Mielziner, later Robin Wagner
Lighting: Jo Mielziner, later Martin Aronstein
Costumes: Alvin Colt
Orchestrations: Philip J. Lang
Musical Direction: Elliot Lawrence
Dance Music Arranged: John Berkman
Opened: April 9, 1972 at the Majestic
Closed: June 23, 1973
Performances: 505

1973
Out Cry!
(Presented by the David Merrick Arts Foundation and Kennedy Center Productions, Inc.)
Author: Tennessee Williams
With: Michael York, Cara Duff-MacCormick
Director: Peter Glenville
Sets: Jo Mielziner
Costumes: Sandy Cole
Opened: March 1, 1973 at the Lyceum
Closed: March 10, 1973
Performances: 12
Turtlenecks
Author: Bruce Jay Friedman
With: Tony Curtis
Director: Jacques Levy
Opened: Aug. 6, 1973 at the Fisher in Detroit
Closed: Sept. 23, 1973 at the Forrest in Philadelphia

1974-75
Mack and Mabel
(In Association with Edwin H. Morris; Association Producer, Jack Schlissel)
Book: Michael Stewart
Music and Lyrics: Jerry Herman
With: Robert Preston, Bernadette Peters, Lisa Kirk
Director and Choreographer: Gower Champion
Sets: Robin Wagner
Costumes: Patricia Zipprodt
Opened: Oct. 6, 1974 at the Majestic
Closed: Nov. 30, 1974
Performances: 65

Dreyfus in Rehearsal
(Associate Producer, Jack Schlissel)
Author: Garson Kanin (Based on the Play by Jean-Claude Grumberg)
With: Ruth Gordon, Sam Levene, Tovah Feldshuh, Avery Schreiber, Anthony Holland
Sets: Boris Aronson
Costumes: Florence Klotz
Director: Garson Kanin
Opened: Oct. 17, 1974 at the Barrymore
Closed: Oct. 26, 1974
Performances: 12

The Misanthrope
(The National Theater of Great Britain)
Author: Moliere
Adapted: Tony Harrison
With: Alec McCowen, Diana Rigg
Director: John Dexter
Sets: Tanya Moisewitsch
Opened: March 12, 1975 at the St. James
Closed: May 2, 1975
Performances: 94

Red Devil Battery Sign
(With Doris Cole Abrahams and Robert Colby)
By Tennessee Williams
With Claire Bloom, Anthony Quinn, Stephen McHattie
Directed: Ed Sherin
Sets: Robin Wagner
Costumes: Ruth Wagner
Closed in Boston

1975-76
Travesties
(With Doris Cole Abrahams and Burry Fredrik, In association with S. Spencer Davids and Eddie Kulukundis. The Royal Shakespeare Company Production)
By: Tom Stoppard
With John Wood, Tim Curry
Directed: Peter Wood
Sets and Costumes: Carl Toms
Opened: Oct. 30, 1975 at the Barrymore
Closed: March 113, 1976
Performances: 155

Very Good Eddie
(In Association with Max Brown and Byron Goldman. The Goodspeed Opera House Production)
Book: Guy Bolton
Music: Jerome Kern
With: Charles Repole, Travis Hudson, Nicholas Wyman
Opened: Dec. 21, 1975 at the Booth
Closed: Sept. 6, 1976
Performances: 193

1980-81
42nd Street
Book: Michael Stewart and Mark Bramble
Lyrics: Al Dubin
Music: Harry Warren
With: Jerry Orbach, Tammy Grimes, Wanda Richert, Lee Roy Reams
Sets: Robin Wagner
Costumes: Theoni Aldredge
Orchestrations: Philip J. Lang
Opened: Aug. 25, 1980 at the Winter Garden
Closed: Jan. 15, 1989 at the St. James
Performances: 3,486

I Won't Dance
(Associate Producer, Neal Du Brock)
Author: Oliver Hailley
With: David Selby, Gail Strickland, Arlene Bolonka
Director: Tom O'Horgan
Sets: Bill Stabile
Costumes: Marty Pakledinaz
Opened and Closed: May 10, 1981 at the Helen Hayes

1986
Loot
By Joe Orton
(Presented by the David Merrick Arts Foundation, In association with Cahrles P. Kopelman and Mark Simon. The Manhattan Theater Club production)
With: Charles Keating, Zoe Wanamaker, Alec Baldwin, Zeljko Ivanek, Joseph Maher, Nick Ullett
Director: John Tillinger
Sets: John Lee Beatty
Costumes: Bill Walker
Opened: April 7, 1986 at the Music Box
Closed: June 28, 1986
Performances: 96

1988
Emerald City
(London, With Helen Montagu; The Sydney Theatre Company Production)
Author: David Williamson
Director: Richard Wherrett

Sets: Laurence Eastwood
Costumes: Terry Ryan
Opened: May 9 at the Lyric
Closed: June 25

1990
Oh, Kay!
(Executive Producer, Natalie Lloyd; Associate Producer, Leo K. Cohen)
Book: Guy Bolton and P.G. Wodehouse (Adapted by James Racheff)
Music: George Gershwin
Lyrics: Ira Gershwin
With: Gregg Burge, Kyme, Angela Teek, Stanley Wayne Mathis, Kevin Ramsey, Helmar Augustus Cooper, Brian Mitchell
Director and Choreographer: Dan Siretta
Sets: Kenneth Foy
Costumes: Theoni V. Aledredge
Opened: Nov. 2, 1990 at the Richard Rodgers
Closed: Jan. 5, 1991
Performances: 77

FILM

1972
Child's Play
Screenplay: Leon Prochnik (Based on the Play by Robert Marasco)
With: James Mason, Robert Preston, Beau Bridges, David Rounds, Kate Harrington
Director: Sidney Lumet
Released: Paramount Pictures

1974
The Great Gatsby
Screenplay: Francis Ford Coppola (Based on the novel by F. Scott Fitzgerald)
With: Robert Redford, Mia Farrow, Sam Waterston, Karen Black, Howard Da Silva, Edward Herrman, Lois Chiles
Director: Jack Clayton
Released: Paramount Pictures

1977
Semi-Tough
Screenplay: Walter Bernstein (Based on the Novel by Dan Jenkins)
With: Burt Reynolds, Kris Kristofferson, Jill Clayburgh, Bert Convy, Lotte Lenya, Carl Weathers, Brian Dennehy, Ron Silver
Director: Michael Ritchie
Released: United Artists

1980
Rough Cut
Screenplay: Francis Burns (Based on *Touch the Lion's Paw* by Derek Lambert)
With: Burt Reynolds, David Niven, Lesley-Anne Down, Patrick Magee, Joss Ackland
Director: Don Siegel
Released: Paramount Pictures

NOTES

Chapter One: Material in this chapter is based on contemporary newspaper accounts, interviews with Charles Blackwell, Mark Bramble, Tammy Grimes, Fred Nathan, Helen Nickerson, and Jerry Orbach as well as the tape recorded interviews with the late Cliff Jahr assembled for his Sunday Times piece, which he was kind enough to lend me. The Tyrone Guthrie quote comes from *A New Theatre* (McGraw-Hill, 1964).

Chapter Two: Merrick was fond of recounting his childhood to people, though accounts do not always jibe. This chapter is based on interviews with Rubin Lapin, Rabbi Eli Pilchik, Harvey Sabinson, Sylvia Thea and the *Time* cover article.

Chapter Three: The most useful source for early material on Merrick is Helen Dudar's five-part series for the New York Post in December, 1960. Other sources, apart from newspaper clippings over the years, were Rabbi Eli Pilchik and several friends of Leonore Merrick-Sanford Dody, Jacqueline Rice and Alma McCardle.

Chapter Four: This chapter is drawn from clippings on Merrick, Beckhard and Shumlin in the Performing Arts Division of the New York Public Library as well as Interviews with John Bloomgarden, Milton Rosenstock and friends of Leonore

Merrick-Bill Becker, Sanford Dody and Alma McCardle. Some of the material on Sardi's is from Robert Sylvester's *Notes of a Guilty Bystander* (Prentice-Hall, 1970).

Chapter Five: This chapter is drawn from interviews with Byron Goldman, Bill Herz, Reubin Lapin, Norris Houghton and Rabbi Eli Pilchick as well as contemporary newspaper accounts. Material on Tennessee Williams comes from *Tennessee Williams' Letters to Donald Windham*, 1940-1965, edited with comments by Donald Windham (Holt, Rinehart & Winston, 1976, 1977) and from Gilbert Maxwell's Tennessee Williams and Friends (World, 1965).

Chapter Six: The primary sources for this chapter are the recollections of Joshua and Nedda Loganm whom I interviewed in 19991. The letters between Merrick and Jo Mielziner and Rodgers and Hammerstein are in the Katherine Cornell room of the Performing Arts Division of the New York Public Library. There are also abundant clippings on the subject and a useful account in The Playmakers (Norton, 1970) by Arthur Cantor and Stuart Little.

Chapter Seven: This chapter is based on contemporary newspaper accounts as well as interviews with Byron Goldman, Neil Hartley, Norris Houghton, Garson Kanin, Alec McCowen and Robert Whitehead. Some of the material is drawn from Tyrone Guthrie's autobiography, *A Life in the Theater* (McGraw-Hill, 1959).

Chapter Eight: Material for this chapter was drawn from contemporary newspaper accounts and interviews with Emanuel Azenberg, Carol Channing, Fred Golden, Jay Kingwill, Bob Merrill, Ginger Montel, Robert Schear and Sylvia Schwartz.

Chapter Nine: This chapter is based on contemporary newspaper accounts and interviews with Charles Blackwell, Charles

Bowden, Madeline Gilford, Byron Goldman, Robert Lewis, Judd Mathison, Anne Kaufman Schneider and Joseph Stein.

Chapter Ten: The introductory anecdotal material is from Martin Balma and Milton Rosenstock. The rest is based on contemporary press accounts.

Chapter Eleven: This chapter is based on interviews with Leonard Gershe, Dolores Gray, Mort Mitosky, Harold Rome and contemporary press accounts.

Chapter Twelve: This chapter is based on interviews with June Havoc, Arthur Laurents, Milton Rosenstock, Stephen Sondheim and Jule Styne as well as Craig Zadan's *Sondheim and Co.* (Harper & Row, 1988).

Chapter Thirteen: The material in this chapter is drawn from interviews with Peter Glenville, Garson Kanin, Bob Merrill, Michael Shurtleff, Joseph Stein and Robert Whitehead. The anecdote about Merrill "firing" Glennville wa recounted to me in detail by Merrill. Glenville does not remember it at all and disputes its having taken place, but it seems a vintage Merrick story and so I have included it. The material on Binkie Beaumont is from Richard Huggett's biography.

Chapter Fourteen: This chapter is based on interviews with Judy Bryant, Alexander Cohen, Rebecca Morehouse, Michael Shurtleff and contemporary press accounts.

Chapter Fifteen: This chapter is based on interviews with Emanuel Azenberg, Kaye Ballard, Marge Champion, Garson Kanin, Bob Merrill, Helen Nickerson, Jerry Orbach, Harvey Sabinson, Willard Shaffar and Charles Willard as well as contemporary press accounts. Some of the material on *Do Re Mi* is drawn from the incredibly detailed nightly reports of its stage mamger, Bernard Gersten.

Chapter Sixteen: This chapter is based on interviews with Garson Kanin, Bob Merrill, Rebecca Morehouse, Arnold Newman, Helen Nickerson and Michael Shurtleff.

Chapter Seventeen: This chapter is based on interviews with Ken Geist, Fred Golden, Arthur Laurents, Harold and Florence Rome, Robert Shear, Michael Shurtleff, Jerome Weidman as well as contemporary press accounts. Phyllis Newman's experience with Merrick on Tony night is recounted in her book *Just In Time:Notes from My Life* (Simon and Schuster, 1988).

Chapter Eighteen: The material in this chapter is drawn from interviews with Judy Bryant, Alexander Cohen, Max Eisen, John Fiorillo, Neil Hartley, Tom Jones, Dorothy Loudon, Bob Merrill, Marta orbach, Rabbi Eli Pilchick, Don Pippin as well as contemporary newspaper accounts.

Chapter Nineteen: This chapter is based on interviews with Richard Coe, Jean Kerr, Lee Solters and the clippings on Merrick in the Performing Arts Division of the New York Public Library. Richard Stoddard, whose Performing Arts Book is an invaluable source of second hand books on the theater, found a copy of the "valentine" to Walter Kerr.

Chapter Twenty: This chapter is based on interviews with Marge Champion, Fred Golden, Elizabeth Kaye, Rebecca Morehouse, Helen Nickerson, Juliet Taylor, Carol Wright-Haber as well as clippings in the Performing Arts Division of the New York Public Library.

Chapter Twenty-One: This chapter is drawn from interviews with Peter Brook, Agnes DeMille, Neil Hartley, Tom Jones, David Powers, Harvey Schmidt, Sylvia Schwartz and Robert Whitehead.

Chapter Twenty-Two: This chapter is based on interviews with Donald Brooks, Carol Channing, Neil Hartley, Jerry Herman, Peter Howard, Lionel Larner, Bob Merrill, Helen Nickerson, Charles Strouse, Charles Willard, Freddy Wittop and contemporary press accounts.

Chapter Twenty-Three: This chapter is based largely on contemporary press reports of the "ice" scandal as well as interviews with Emanuel Azenberg, Max Eisen, Neil Hartley and Lee Solters.

Chapter Twenty-Four: This chapter is drawn from interviews with Lauren Bacall, Max Eisen, Robert Larkin, Bob Ullmann, Harvey Sabinson and Ulu Grosbard as well as contemporary press accounts.

Chapter Twenty-Five: This chapter is based on interviews with Stanley Kauffmann, Rebecca Morehouse, Marta Orbach, Bob Ullmann and contemporary press accounts.

Chapter Twenty-Six: This chapter is based on interviews with Lionel Larner, Bob Merrill, Carole Shelley, Oliver Smith and contemporary newspaper accounts. The quote from Albee about the "tyrant" is in Dennis Brown's *Shoptalk* (Newmarket Press, 1992).

Chapter Twenty-Seven: This chapter is based on contemporary newspaper accounts of the Black and White Ball. The Hirschfeld anecdote was recounted by Margo Feiden.

Chapter Twenty-Eight: This chapter is based on interviews with Martin Charnin, Fred Ebb, John Handy, John Kander, Roger Lawson, Biff Liff, Helen Nickerson, Willard Shaffar and Freddy Wittop. The material on Stan Freberg is from his book, *It Only Hurts When I Laugh* (Times Books, 1988).

Chapter Twenty-Nine: This chapter is based on interviews with

Keith Baxter, Judy Bryant, Alvin Cooperman, Hal David, Pete Feller, Garson Kanin, Leonard Gershe, Fred Golden, John Handy, Biff Liff, Helen Nickerson, Linda Otto, Gerald Schoenfeld, Irene Selznick, Willard Shaffar, Joel Thurm, Jonathan Tunick and Charles Willard, as well as contemporary newspaper accounts.

Chapter Thirty: This chapter is based on interviews with David Brown, Irving "Swifty" Lazar, Sidney Lumet, Helen Nickerson and Billy Wilder, as well as contemporary newspaper accounts.

Chapter Thirty-One: This chapter is based on interviews with Alexander Cohen, Helen Nickerson, Harvey Sabinson, Irene Selznick and Joel Thurm as well as contemporary newspaper accounts.

Chapter Thirty-Two: This chapter is based largely on contemporary newspaper accounts, particularly a long interview Merrick gave to Rex Reed shortly before *The Great Gatsby* opened.

Chapter Thirty-Three: This chapter is based on interviews with Doris Cole Abrahams, Arthur Cantor, Frank DaVerna, Pete Feller, Bernard P. Jacobs, Biff Liff, John Mazzola, Bob Merrill, Helen Nickerson, Willard Shaffar, The Honorable Martin Stecher, Peter Stone, Dona D. Vaughn, Robin Wagner, The Honorable Frank Weissberg, Michael Weller as well as contemporary newspaper accounts. I have based my account of the Four Star case on these interviews and the 12-page summation by Judge Stecher.

Chapter Thirty-Four: This chapter is based on interviews with Shirley Bernstein, Mark Bramble, Judy Bryant, Josh Ellis, Elizabeth Kaye, Rebecca Morehouse, Helen Nickerson, Stephen Schwartz and contemporary newspaper accounts.

Chapter Thirty-Five: This chapter is based on interviews with Richard Adler, Bernard Gersten, Sheldon Harnick, Helen Nickerson, Thomas Z. Shepard, Dona D. Vaughn, Robin Wagner, Jerome Weidman, contemporary newspaper accounts, and the recording of the Gower Champion memorial made by Cliff Jahr.

Chapter Thirty -Six: This chapter is based on interviews with Mark Bramble, Judy Davidson, Byron Goldman, Garson Kanin, Cameron Macintosh, Bob Merrill, Mort Mitosky Lee Roy Reams, Marian Seldes, Willard Shaffar and contemporary press accounts.

Chapter Thirty-Seven: This chapter is based on interviews with Sanford Dody, Neil Hartley, Alma McCardle, Etan Merrick, Marta Orbach, Don Pippin, Marian Seldes, Donald Smith and contemporary newspaper accounts.

Chapter Thirty-Eight: This chapter is based on interviews with Michael Alpert, Mark Bramble, Carol Channing, Alvin Deutch, Max Eisen, Fred Golden, Warren Pincus, Michael Price, Vincent Sardi Jr., Willard Shaffar, Dan Siretta, Peter Stone, Jon Wilner and contemporary press accounts.

Afterword: The "onions" were contributed by Marta Orbach, Willard Shaffar, Stephen Sonheim, Robin Wagner and Eugene Wolsk.

Production History: This chart is based on three sources-the invaluable Best Plays volumes for the last 40 years; Sylvia Schwartz's meticulously kept record of Merrick's productions; and the excellent production history in Barbara Lee Horne's *David Merrick: A Bio-Bibliography* (Greenwood Press, 1992).

★

THE SECRET OF THEATRICAL SPACE

The Memoirs of Josef Svoboda

Translated and edited by J.M. Burian

Josef Svoboda is arguably the world's foremost living stage designer, the heir of Appia, Craig and the Bauhaus. This is the epic account of his Olympian career. It is drama which no one could render so poetically, so explicitly, so audaciously as Josef Svoboda himself. Guiding the reader through the heroic proportions of his life and career, he begins with his childhood influences, proceeds through his training and early theatre exposure, and on to his multiple crowning achievements in the world's theatre capitals working with the theatre world's brightest lights. His book is less a systematic survey of his life and productions than the revelation of restless, creative spirit joyfully in the throes of new challenges. THE SECRET OF THEATRICAL SPACE is also a contemplative commentary on the evolution of twentieth century stage art.

cloth•ISBN 1-55783-137-8

APPLAUSE

UNFINISHED BUSINESS

A Memoir: 1902–1988

by John Houseman

For over half a century, John Houseman played a commanding role on the American cultural scene. The *dramatis personae* of Houseman's chronicle represents an awesome roster of arts in twentieth century America. When he isn't conspiring with Orson Welles, Virgil Thomson, Archibald McLeish or a dozen others to launch one of five major new theatre organizations, we find him in Hollywood with David O. Selznick, Alfred Hitchcock or Herman Mankiewicz producing one of his eighteen feature films.

In *Unfinished Business*, the 1500 pages of his earlier memoirs, *Run-Through, Front and Center* and *Final Dress* have been distilled into one astonishing volume, with fresh revelations throughout and a riveting new final chapter which brings the Houseman saga to a close.

paper•ISBN 1-55783-024-X

❦APPLAUSE❦

THE COLLECTED WORKS OF HAROLD CLURMAN

Six Decades of Commentary on Theatre, Dance, Music, Film, Arts, Letters and Politics

edited by Marjorie Loggia and Glenn Young

For six decades, Harold Clurman illuminated our artistic, social and political awareness in thousands of reviews, essays and lectures. In 1930 he began a series of lectures at Steinway Hall that would lead to the creation of the Group Theater. His work appeared indefatigably in Tomorrow, The New Republic, The London Observer, The New York Times, The Nation, Stagebill, Show, Theatre Arts and New York Magazine.

This chronological epic offers the most comprehensive view of American theatre seen through the eyes of our most extraordinary critic–the largest collection of criticism by a dramatic critic ever published in the English language.

cloth•ISBN 1-55783-132-7

❤APPLAUSE❤